W9-ARO-479

CONTEMPORARY PHILOSOPHY

CONTEMPORARY PHILOSOPHY

Phenomenological and Existential Currents

By

REV. REYNOLD BORZAGA

THE BRUCE PUBLISHING COMPANY

MILWAUKEE

NIHIL OBSTAT:
JOHN E. TWOMEY, S.T.L., PH.D.
Censor librorum

IMPRIMATUR:
✠WILLIAM E. COUSINS
Archbishop of Milwaukee
March 15, 1966

Library of Congress Catalog Card Number: 66–22583
© 1966 THE BRUCE PUBLISHING COMPANY
MADE IN THE UNITED STATES OF AMERICA

To Mario Larcher, M.D.
WITH GRATITUDE AND FRIENDSHIP

Acknowledgments

The author and publishers of CONTEMPORARY PHILOSOPHY: PHENO-MENOLOGICAL AND EXISTENTIAL CURRENTS are grateful to the following to reprint copyrighted material:

A. & C. Black, Ltd., for excerpts from Gabriel Marcel's *Being and Having;*

Geoffrey Bles, Ltd., for excerpts from Nicolai Berdyaev's *Freedom and the Spirit* and *The Divine and the Human;*

Farrar, Straus & Giroux, Inc., for excerpts from Karl Jaspers' *Reason and Existence;*

Harper & Row, Publishers, for excerpts from Nicolai Berdyaev's *The Destiny of Man* and Martin Heidegger's *Being and Time;*

The Philosophical Library, for excerpts from Gabriel Marcel's *The Philosophy of Existence;*

Frederick A. Praeger, Inc., for excerpts from G. Janouch's *Conversations with Kafka, Notes and Reminiscences;*

Henry Regnery Co., from excerpts from Karl Jaspers' *Philosophy and the World* and Martin Heidegger's *Existence and Being;*

Routledge & Kegan Paul, Ltd., for excerpts from Karl Jaspers' *Man in the Modern Age;*

The University of Chicago Press, for excerpts from Karl Jaspers' *General Psychopathology* and *The Future of Mankind;*

Yale University Press, for excerpts from Martin Heidegger's *Introduction to Metaphysics* and Karl Jaspers' *The Origin and Goal of History.*

Preface

This volume has been written primarily for students who have some familiarity with realism and theism, particularly Thomistic realism and theism.

Several happy years of teaching experience at Manhattan College, New York, have convinced the author that the interest of college students for philosophical and theological problems is fast growing, particularly among those students who, while aiming to a profession of technical-scientific nature, feel the need for more knowledge about human and religious problems. With this goal in mind, emphasis has been given in this book to the problem of God in contemporary philosophy and to the agreements and disagreements between empirical sciences and philosophical thinking.

This volume discusses historicism, the phenomenological and existential aspects of contemporary philosophy; a second volume will deal with logical positivism, pragmatism, idealism, realism, and neoscholasticism. A critical appraisal is also made, from a Thomistic standpoint. But it must be kept in mind that it was done with the purpose of finding new insights and enrichment in contemporary philosophers for the basic perennial ideas of Christian realism.

My main debt in preparing this book is to Frank Cadin, Ph.D., my former student of philosophy, whose help and advice cannot be stressed enough. I must also express sincere gratitude to Brother Joseph Wiesenfarth, F.S.C., Ph.D., of the English Department of Manhattan College for reviewing the manuscript, and to Mrs. David Voelzke for typing and presenting it in this present edition.

Fr. Reynold Borzaga

Manhattan College
Feast of the Immaculate Conception, 1965

Contents

Acknowledgments vii

Preface ix

Introduction xv

I. Søren Kierkegaard, Karl Marx, and Friedrich Nietzsche 1

    Introduction   1

    1. Søren Kierkegaard   5
        I. *The Problem: Possibility as a Category*
        II. *The Aesthetic and Ethical Spheres*
        III. *The Sphere of Faith*
        IV. *Man and God in Kierkegaard*

    2. Karl Marx   20
        I. *The Formative Years*
        II. *Marx's Original Contribution to Philosophy*
        III. *Communism*

    3. Nietzsche   36
        I. *The Birth of Tragedy*
        II. *Zarathustra*
        III. *The Overman*

II. The Problem of Historicism 48

    Introduction   48
    1. The Kierkegaardian and Nietzschean Renaissance   49
    2. Dilthey's Historicism   53
    3. Windelband, Rickert, and the "School of Values"   58
    4. Historicism and Weber   59
    5. Spengler's Philosophy of History   61
    6. Ortega y Gasset, Benda, Huizinga   63

III. Karl Jaspers 69
Introduction   69
1. The Need for a Worldview   78
2. The Problem of Transcendence   83
3. *Dasein*, Consciousness, Existence   84
4. Freedom   90
5. Jaspers' View of Metaphysics   93
6. Man, Technology, and Society   96
7. The Encompassing   98
8. Logic and Truth   101
9. Guilt   107

IV. The Phenomenology of Edmund Husserl . . 114
Introduction   114
1. Franz Brentano, Bernhard Bolzano, Karl Stumpf   115
2. The Phenomenology of Husserl   121
   I. *Formulating the Problem*
   II. *Subjectivism or Subjectivity?*
   III. *Husserl's Followers*

V. Martin Heidegger 139
Introduction   139
1. Heidegger's Development to *Sein und Zeit*   140
   I. *From Aristotle to Husserl*
   II. *Martin Heidegger and Nicolai Hartmann*
   III. *The Background of* Sein und Zeit
   IV. *Heidegger's Political Activity*
2. *Sein und Zeit*   151
   I. *The Problem*
   II. *The Meaning of* Dasein
   III. *The "Worldishness" of* Dasein
   IV. *The Existentiality of* Dasein
   V. *The Temporality of* Dasein
3. Realism and Martin Heidegger   168
4. Martin Heidegger after *Sein und Zeit*   174
   I. *Einführung in die Metaphysik* (*Introduction to Metaphysics*)
   II. *Language and Metaphysics*
   III. *Die Überwindung der Metaphysik*
   IV. *Gelassenheit* (*Serenity*)

VI. The Philosophy of Jean-Paul Sartre . . . 203
Introduction   203
1. A Vocation to the World of Aesthetics   203

2. Sartre and Phenomenology   208
3. The Theory of the Imagination   211
4. Being and Nothingness   216
5. Le Diable et Le Bon Dieu (The Devil and the Good Lord)   225
6. Sartre and Communism   226
  I. *Communism: Appealing yet Disturbing*
  II. *Critique of Dialectical Reason*

VII. Christian Existentialism in Russia and France   .   235
Introduction   235
1. Existential Themes in Russia   237
  I. *Fyodor Dostoevski*
  II. *Vladimir Soloviev*
  III. *Leo Shestov*
  IV. *Nicolai Berdyaev*
2. Existential Themes in French Philosophy: Gabriel Marcel   248

VIII. Existentialism and Literature   262
1. Franz Kafka   263
2. Rainer Maria Rilke and Michael Unamuno   267
3. Albert Camus   271

Index   285

Introduction

The following work is a study of the phenomenological and existential currents in contemporary philosophy. Contemporary philosophy, by the very meaning of the terms used, may seem to limit our inquiry to those philosophers who have lived or are living in the twentieth century. But, in a broader sense, all intellectual movements, even those of the distant past, which are a source of the forces prevailing today and which have created the present striving for an enlargement of the dimensions of human knowledge, must be considered as belonging to contemporary philosophy. For instance, Thomas Aquinas and Duns Scotus have clearly influenced Husserl and Heidegger. Immanuel Kant's philosophical successes and failures are a necessary background for an understanding of almost all contemporary philosophers. Søren Kierkegaard and Karl Marx, though chronologically of the nineteenth century, are present as teachers of first magnitude in our century.

Contemporary philosophy is therefore a term whose meaning is quite flexible. It is a militant philosophy engaged in the battle of winning new meanings for and new solutions to the perennial problem of existence, specifically, the problem of human existence. To avoid misunderstandings, it must be said that contemporary philosophy does not claim absolute solutions to any problem. But if searching more than finding is the essence of philosophy, contemporary philosophy can be said to have reached the highest philosophical level.

Almost all previous philosophies have based their inquiries on one fundamental element universally accepted, that is, the analysis of "reality," that reality seen either as subjective or objective. Disagreements among previous philosophers have centered around the interpretation of the word *reality*. All have agreed that reality must be analyzed, but few have agreed as to what reality is.

Contemporary philosophy often seems to doubt the very existence of this philosophical problem. In many instances philosophy today has reached a crisis beyond which any other crisis is impossible. It is no longer a question of a choice between idealism and realism or between skepticism and dogmatism. It is no longer possible to ask which philosophy describes reality. The question now is: Is philosophy needed at all? Rebellion, therefore, is a relevant aspect of contemporary philosophy — an authentic rebellion against the past, considered as rich in "prefabricated solutions, closed, vicious, and repetitious circles, enormously useless verbiage." The plea of the contemporary philosopher is simple: Do not give us perfect formulas for understanding reality. Let us live our lives. Let us try to find the solution to living by living.

The student of philosophy easily understands the limitations imposed on this work. To attempt with some pretention to apply the laws of historical criticism to contemporary philosophy would be intellectually irrelevant and morally deceitful. Because we are all actors on the contemporary scene, we cannot presume to make a final judgment of contemporary philosophy; nevertheless, we must make every effort to understand and evaluate it as best we can.

❖   ❖   ❖

A few words must be said here to set the historical background of contemporary philosophy. We have already mentioned the rebellious attitude prevalent in our times. Now a rebellion cannot be reduced totally to logical reasons; the irrational and the imponderable are always present, often preponderantly. But it can be said, without the presumption of stating a comprehensive final diagnosis, that there are two essential factors preparing the way for contemporary philosophers: first, the interpretation of the philosophy of Kant by the philosophers of the first half of the nineteenth century and, second, the subsequent appearance of scientific positivism.

Immanuel Kant, in his messianic desire to lay the foundations of a new philosophy, began his criticism as an introduction to philosophy and never quite reached the first chapter of real philosophy. That Kant's philosophy, therefore, is an introduction to philosophy and its paradoxical nature is apparent if one observes that his introduction proved philosophy to be impossible as a science, i.e., as a body of demonstrated truths. The followers of Kant, therefore, found themselves in double jeopardy. He left them with a mandate for progress and with a simultaneously well-developed and carefully explained system of ideas proving that progress, as it had formerly been viewed, was impossible. An amused commentator of the past century, with a liking for a baroque flavoring of expression, compared Kant's successors[1] to surgeons hastily called to the bedside of a critically ill patient. Quickly ushered to the operating room, they found themselves faced with a most unusual problem: "Was the patient *really* on the operating table?" The patient, whom Kant had left in such critical condition, was the main object of

---

[1] Henry Jacobi (1737–1819), Leonard Reinhold (1758–1823), Salomon Maimon (1753–1800), and James Sigismond Beck (1761–1840).

the traditional philosophy, "the thing in itself." Therefore, the question of the philosopher-surgeons is a most serious one even to the ordinary man, for it asks whether such things as house, father, or honesty exist or whether they are mere illusions.

Contemporary philosophy is acutely aware of Kant's position, which presents us with an unstable and delicate balance between a universe organized under physical laws, rigorously deterministic, and deprived of freedom, and the activity of the mind, free and absolutely unconditioned by experience and conditioning it. It must be said that contemporary philosophy respects Kant's sincerity, which was so different from the pride of the romantic philosophers — of Hegel, above all.

Preceded by less domineering philosophers, Fichte and Schelling, Georg Friedrich Wilhelm Hegel determined that the enemy to be overcome was the "thing in itself." After all, everybody agreed that philosophy as a scientific knowledge could not leave any dead end unexplored. Hegel did not have any respect for Kant's schematism. Yet he borrowed from the solitary philosopher of Königsberg the very principle — "the synthesis of the a priori" — that forced Kant to accept in humility the failure of the mind to understand the whole of reality. Hegel applied this principle of the Kantian dialectic to the universe and, as a final result, announced that "the thing in itself" had become a crystal-clear center of rationality. Therefore, logic became metaphysics, and metaphysics history. The Kantian dilemma was resolved; the mind had divinized itself; the Absolute was Logic, History, Theology. God becomes, develops, identifies Himself with History, which is consciousness, or, better, self-consciousness. Ultimately Hegel eliminated from the field of metaphysics any consideration of existences, in order to concentrate on intelligibility, on the essence of things.

Under these circumstances it may seem strange that Hegel should proclaim himself the pontiff of an open philosophy and affirm, moreover, that his was the only open philosophy and that it admitted no possibility of being superseded. Kant did not exhaust the task of philosophy and consequently kept alive the possibility of progress. In the end, the absolutism of Hegel triggered the greatest rebellion in the history of human philosophical venture. Kierkegaard rebelled and became the hero of the finite man, of the individual. Marx rebelled to protect the meaning of material values and accomplished his task with such a vehemence of desperation that he reached conclusions diametrically opposite Hegel's — conclusions that were at once antagonistic to Hegel's and as wrong as Hegel's.

In this introduction we cannot forget another movement which followed romanticism and dominated the second half of the past century, that is, scientific positivism.[2] The disagreement between positivism and idealistic romanticism stems from positivism's inconclusive efforts to explain and justify religion, morality, and art. But it is also acknowledged that positivism is, in its own way, the continuation of idealism, because positivism is, by the intention and desire of its founders, a romantic exaltation of science. Science, for positivists like August Comte, Jeremy Bentham and John Stuart Mill, absorbs religion and morality and art. Therefore the great design of Hegel is continued by the positivists. Hegel proclaimed the absolute as spirit; the positivists declared that science is the absolute.

Contemporary philosophy, suspicious of the enthusiastic solutions offered by the romantic philosophers, renews the intensity of its suspicion when it confronts positivistic dogmas. It will be seen that all contemporary philosophers can be grouped into movements reacting against, or integrating the philosophy of positivism.

The principles considered axiomatic by the positivists can be reduced to the following two. First, facts, as they appear in nature, are the only existing reality. Science is the only possible knowledge of facts. Second, scientific laws, absolute and unchangeable, are the only possible relations among these facts of nature.

But this scientism of the positivists could neither solve nor eliminate the problem of human existence, nor could it reduce human existence to a merely scientific problem. Like Hegelian transcendentalism, scientific positivism attempted to reduce "reality" to a problem stated and solved by the human mind, conceived as infinite in its power. The mystery of existence is watered down to an absolute principle of rationality or to the rigidity of physical laws. Hegel and the positivists lost the meaning of metaphysics, which is knowledge of the existent and an unfailing search for a more meaningful understanding of its mystery. From this point of view, contemporary philosophy shows a violent shift to a position of defense for the individual and his metaphysical values. We must be specific on this essential issue.

Metaphysics possesses a peculiarity which is its own and which no other science shares. Once something is said in metaphysics, we realize that much remains to be said and that man will never come to the final solution because a final solution would mean the end of man himself.

Philosophy is searching with progressive finding. The emphasis is on the "searching," not on the "finding." Many contemporary philosophers are distressed by this fact. Marcel prefers to talk about mysteries to

[2] In a subsequent volume we will examine some present-day philosophies which are in the positivistic tradition, among them logical positivism and linguistic analysis.

be lived rather than problems to be solved. Camus feels the necessity of living so that the absurdity of life might offer a faint hope of rationality. Husserl pretends to disregard the existent, to dissolve it into the meaning of the essence. The American pragmatists seek to disregard the metaphysical problem as a tautological waste; their philosophy is an interesting and honest example of how man cannot forget himself. Kierkegaard preferred to speak of a "leap" from deceitful reason to the tranquillity of religious faith. Sartre, in his orgiastic pursuit of destruction, would not be himself without the human values he tries to destroy and which give him perennial support for his writings against them. Something of this kind can be said of each twentieth-century philosopher.

This work is meant to study contemporary philosophy precisely from a metaphysical point of view. It is our basic conviction that metaphysics is possible and necessary for any philosophical endeavor. Furthermore, metaphysics cannot be confined to an intuitive act of knowledge, neither can it be the object of a blind act of faith. Both faith and intuition can be arbitrary when applied to philosophy, with disastrous consequences for the individual ruminating its problems. Reason is capable of metaphysical research. Reason understands its own limitations and therefore sees metaphysics as *an open* venture to which all human beings and particularly great philosophical minds have made valuable contributions. Yet reason knows how to reach some fundamental truths which are the cornerstones of metaphysical research.

It seems essential to enumerate some of these truths, which evidence cannot deny, that constitute the perspective from which this books aims to view contemporary philosophy. Although these truths will not be discussed with any thoroughness here, they need to be recalled, for on them the logic and consequence of this study depend.

Metaphysics is defined as the knowledge of being insofar as it is being. This definition includes all existing and possible beings, for instance, the material and the immaterial, the logical and the real. Hartmann[3] has noted that when we speak of being as such (*sic et simpliciter*) we anticipate and sidestep the polemics of realism and idealism, because thinking itself must be something, must be in its own way "being." Heidegger agrees on this basic idea about metaphysics. He says[4] that we always have an initial understanding of being, vague and tenuous as it might be. He also contends that this notion of being

---

[3] N. Hartmann, *Zur Grundlegung der Ontologie* (Berlin, 1921), p. 40.

[4] M. Heidegger, *Sein und Zeit* (Halle, 1927), p. 5. [Eng. tr. by John Macquarrie and Edward Robinson, *Being and Time* (New York: Harper & Row, 1962), p. 24.]

is presupposed and implicit in our knowledge of anything.[5] Now it is difficult to think that Heidegger, well acquainted with medieval thought as he is, did not paraphrase in the above references a famous paragraph of Thomas Aquinas, who wrote: "That which *first of all* the intellect understands as absolutely evident is being, which necessarily is implicit in the knowledge of every thing. Because *being* is implicit in every thing (in other words, because every thing is being), it is necessary that all the other ideas be conceived by molding them to the idea of being, because they themselves are in being. Therefore it is mandatory that all concepts in our mind converge somehow into the concept of being and that they express something that was already contained in the idea of being."[6]

Those who deny the usefulness of metaphysics offer some common objections. They say: If there are such things as spirit and matter, what does metaphysics find in common between them? One answer is that a spiritual being *is* and a material being *is*. Therefore, there is something in common. The task of the metaphysician will be to establish the degree of that unity between matter and the immaterial world.

A second objection: Why metaphysics at all? Do not the natural, inductive sciences exhaust the knowledge that man needs today? This is precisely the problem: Is it clear and scientific to announce that the experimental world of inductive sciences is the only existing reality? An answer to this problem cannot be given if we take for granted that the material universe is the only existing reality without considering *being in its totality*, or, which is the same, without considering being as such, the object of metaphysics.

Besides, each inductive science takes for granted the notions of time, space, matter, energy, motion. Philosophy explains them. Therefore philosophy is presupposed by empirical sciences. Furthermore, these natural sciences use the laws of logic without proving their value, and this value could not exist without a corresponding ontology. Therefore empirical sciences demand the existence of metaphysics.

One question must naturally be in the minds of those who are not familiar with these topics. Should they come to the conclusion that metaphysics deals with *one being*, comprehensive of all material and immaterial entities, or should they think that each material and immaterial being participates in a different way in the meaning and the value of existence? The question deals with one of the most basic decisions to be made by a philosopher. Is monism a true philosophy or

---

[5] *Vom Wesen des Grundes* (Halle, 1929), p. 6.

[6] St. Thomas Aquinas, *De Veritate*, q. 1, art. 1.

should pluralism of substances be accepted at the beginning or the end of metaphysical research?

Individual freedom, the dignity of the human person, the ability to decide goals in life and to be personally responsible — all these are sufficient reasons for our rejecting all forms of immanentism and for defending the individuality of our own persons. From personal experience we know that we began to think and to speak about "things," taken one by one. If each one of them is not one, each must be a union of many. But we could not talk about "things" unless we began with one thing that was not reducible to others. Therefore, if thinking is valid, individual things must exist.

Once we are successful in formulating problems of this kind, metaphysical meditation becomes necessary in our daily life. We are forced to recognize that each day we deal with a plurality of beings and that the mind aims toward a unity of this plurality. It becomes clear that each being *is* itself, one and identical with itself, and that though a being may change, it changes only because it is itself. Each being necessarily precedes its own actions.

The fact that each being is itself is therefore an important one, and it allows us to speak of each being as true and ontologically good. Knowingly or unknowingly each human being comes to terms with metaphysical problems and solutions.

Another topic cannot be neglected if we are to understand the impact exercised on us by contemporary philosophy. This is the interdependence of beings and their interrelatedness. Contemporary philosophy has inherited a heavy burden of ideas from David Hume and Immanuel Kant concerning the principle of causality, which of necessity reflect on the interrelationships between beings.

A cause is that which is capable of contributing to the total or to the partial existence of something else. This proposition cannot be denied without falling into contradiction; therefore it is analytic, a priori, universally valid.[7] This validity is challenged by many in modern and contemporary philosophies. To see why, we need only consider the impact of Hume and Kant.

David Hume led the attack against the principle of causality. Causality, he said, is a complex idea, that is, a result of the sum of many ideas. Causality aims to make us accept the existence of objects which are not present to our perception. We do not use sound logic, he said,

---

[7] Some contemporary philosophers in the Thomist tradition maintain that the causal proposition, while universally and necessarily true, is nonetheless not a principle but a conclusion. Cf. Joseph Owens, "The Causal Proposition" in *The Modern Schoolman* (1956).

when we think that everything that has had a beginning must have a cause. *That which begins* and *that which is caused* are two ideas which are autonomous, independent; the first does not need the second to be understood. Therefore causality is not an analytic principle. The only way of proving it is through experience. But experience is always contingent, never necessary. Therefore the principle of causality is not valid; our use of it stems from a mental habit.

Hume misunderstood the meaning of analytic knowledge. He thought that analytic sentences (he called them "relations of ideas") are such that the predicate merely repeats the subject ($A = A$). In other words, according to Hume, analytic propositions are useless tautologies because they do not result from experience. Yet Hume acknowledged that pure mathematics results from analytic propositions, and it is not a useless tautology. This consideration is sufficient to prove him wrong. But there are other points to be made. Hume failed to see the difference between the level of physics and the level of metaphysics. He announced the principle that all concepts are copies of impressions obtained through experience. This principle is not self-evident, yet Hume did not think it necessary to demonstrate it. The tragedy of modern philosophy is that Hume's criticism of the principle of causality has been accepted as an absolute truth by the great philosophers who followed him. Everybody knows that Immanuel Kant spoke with gratitude of Hume who "woke him up from his 'dogmatic slumber.'"

The great philosopher of Königsberg agreed with Hume's criticism on all the aspects of the principle of causality except one. Kant did not like to speak of the principle of causality as a habit of the mind. Kant explained causality as one of the twelve categories, that is to say, as a product of the transcendental creativity of the mind. "Though in the things as they are in themselves it is quite impossible to understand the reasons which make us think that A requires B if we want to avoid contradiction, we must recognize that A and B as phenomena must be tied somehow on the level of experience and they cannot be separated without contradicting their connection which makes the experience possible. Of this experience they are the objects and in it *only* they are known."[8] Therefore causality is not for Kant a law of the thing in itself; it merely establishes a connection among the objects of experience. We are not concerned with the transcendental idealism which Kant saw as the reason for the existence in our minds of the law of causality. Our interest lies in another aspect of the problem. If Kant, subservient to the philosophy of Hume, holds that the principle of causality is limited to experience, its absoluteness and universality cease to exist. No posi-

_____

[8] Kant, *Critique of Practical Reason*, p. 52.

tive contribution to the solution of the problem is added. When Kant contends that the laws of physics are simultaneously synthetic (from experience) and analytic (*a priori* or above experience), we agree that experience brings new applications and therefore new knowledge, but deny that experience gives to our knowledge the absolute universality which is a prerequisite of science.

Heisenberg has shown that, independently of the accidental errors due to the imperfections of our instruments, an observation cannot allow us to determine precisely the situation or the movements of a corpuscle (electron). The greater the precision of one of the coordinates of the electron, the smaller the precision with which we know the other coordinate establishing the velocity of the electron and vice versa. In the same way we can increase the precision of our measurements of the instant in which a corpuscle crosses a given point of space, but to do this we cannot simultaneously measure precisely the *energy* of the same corpuscle.[9]

Hence a dilemma: either the cause-effect relation must be denied as a law of physics (and Kant himself refused to accept this conclusion) or the principle must have another origin independent of experience. We submit that the principle of cause and effect is solely analytic, above and before experience, and that Hume and Kant misunderstood the meaning of analytic knowledge.

In each analytic principle ($A=A$) the negation of the predicate leads by necessity to the negation of the subject. In other words, it is not possible to state the validity of the subject, removing from it the predicate, without a contradiction. The sum of the internal angles of a triangle always equals 180 degrees; this is an analytic principle. Kant objected that analytic principles are tautologies. We cannot agree with him. To use the precision of the old scholastics, in each analytic statement there is material identity between the subject and the predicate, but not a formal identity. This amounts to saying that what I perceive when I think of a triangle is the same as to say that the sum of the internal angles of a triangle equals 180 degrees. But the concept of "triangle" is different from "having the internal angles equaling 180 degrees." Because this is true, mathematics as a pure science is possible and, what is more important, metaphysics is possible. Knowledge begins with experience, and here we agree with Kant, but in each experimental datum the mind sees a "nexus" between subject and predicate, and this nexus, this link is *a priori*, independent of experience. Moreover, this objective nexus makes metaphysics possible. In

---

[9] L. De Broglie, "Déterminisme and causalité dans la physique contemporaine," in *Revue de Métaphysique et de Morale* (1929), p. 438.

brief, Kant conceived knowledge as the synthesis of an empirical datum with an empty mental category ready to organize it into a mental concept. Therefore Kant declared metaphysics impossible insofar as the physical datum must be contained in each act of knowing.

We conceive human knowledge as an abstraction from the empirical data of those elements which are transcendentally true, analytical in their nature. Thinking of them constitutes that branch of knowledge which is called metaphysics. The classical example is the notion of contingency. If I think of the "meaning" of contingency, I come to recognize the logical conclusion that each contingent being demands the existence of a perfect being causing and explaining all contingencies.

If, on the other hand, I confine my knowledge of a contingent to what experience offers to me, then I will never be able to understand the notion of contingency as such. The empiricist is right when he says that all knowledge comes from experience. The empiricist is wrong when he explains the *universality* of human knowledge as a generalization of individual experiences. For John Stuart Mill, for instance, the internal angles of all triangles are equal to 180 degrees, because it has been universally seen as a fact always true. For us, truth is registered in the mind, whose task is to abstract the universally true values from the empirical aspects of reality.

This whole discussion would be impossible if I deny my own individual existence as a person. The idea of an impersonal mind is contradictory. A person is a living, knowing, and loving *ego*, whom one cannot, without doing himself an injustice, treat as a thing. The question arises: Are there other persons besides human persons? "It is true that we naturally model our distinct concept of a person on the ever-present reality that we are. But a more careful reflection reveals, beneath this anthropomorphic image which usually conceals them, certain features that do not necessarily imply the mode of human existence and which surpass human limitations."[10] If the principle of causality is applied, with the whole impact of its universal value which has been previously discussed, human reason cannot be denied the *possibility* of reaching a perfect being who possesses in an eminent way the ontic perfection of being a person. This must be so if human persons, inadequate to explain their own existence, must logically be considered as effects of a cause which cannot be inferior to them. Therefore we are in agreement with Maritain when he says that "the whole anthropomorphic burden that weighs the word *'person'* down, refers uniquely to that in us which connects personality with individuality

---

[10] L. De Grandmaison, *Le Dogme Chrétien*, p. 297.

and thus with material conditions."[11] However, we must hasten to add that once the existence of God is reached by human reason "all that man can say is said about God. The divine essence, whose existence man proves, is not penetrated by his intellect, and we know that of himself he will never reach it. Denys (the Pseudo-Areopagite) is right in saying that the God toward whom our reason strives is still, so to speak, an unknown God. "For we know well that He is, and what He is not. But what He is, remains for us entirely unknown."[12]

These are the basic truths which we hold. They are not a profession of faith. On the contrary, they constitute the result of a long meditation, which is a necessity of life for anyone who happens to love philosophy.

These truths, solidly possessed as a priceless intellectual patrimony, are the reason for a deep respect for all philosophers, regardless of their conclusions, often totally unacceptable. For philosophy is a sublime occupation and binds all concerned persons in a common bond of intellectual humility in face of the mystery of existence. This humility has never been more evident than in contemporary philosophers. Their sweat and toil are rich with new insights that enrich, with energy, vigor and youth, the perennial truths of Christian realism.

---

[11] J. Maritain, *The Degrees of Knowledge* (New York: Charles Scribner's Sons, 1959), p. 462.

[12] E. Gilson, *The Spirit of Medieval Philosophy* (New York: Sheed and Ward, 1939), p. 258.

CONTEMPORARY PHILOSOPHY

chapter I

Søren Kierkegaard, Karl Marx, and Friedrich Nietzsche

INTRODUCTION

In this chapter we shall present the main philosophical themes developed by Kierkegaard, Marx, and Nietzsche. Chronologically, of course, they do not belong to what is commonly termed "contemporary philosophy," but it is impossible to discuss any contemporary problem without referring to their influence on current thought and to their role in mediating the thought of previous philosophers to writers of this century.

Although Søren Kierkegaard (1813–1855) and Karl Marx (1818–1883) were contemporaries and lived close to each other, they never met. Neither had they the opportunity for an intellectual confrontation with each other's philosophy. Kierkegaard knew and refuted Feuerbach, and with firmness and clarity of mind criticized the utopian communism of Fourier and Proudhon, but he did not write one word on the scientific dialectical communism of Karl Marx.

With this in mind, the student of the history of philosophy cannot fail to note a strange parallelism in their lives which seems to assure a meaning greater than a purely coincidental chronology provides.

The year 1841 was important for both Marx and Kierkegaard, for in it Marx published his thesis on *Democritus and Epicurus,* the founding fathers of materialism, and Kierkegaard published his *Concept of Irony* — both vigorous statements of individual independent thinking outside the generally accepted Hegelian atmosphere.

1

Two years later, both Marx and Kierkegaard declared open war on Hegel. Kierkegaard denounced the assumptions of Hegel in the two monumental volumes, *Either-Or* (*Enten-Eller*); Marx wrote *Critique of Hegel's Philosophy of Law* (*Kritik der Hegelschen Rechtsphilosophie*). In 1844 Kierkegaard, in the *Concept of Dread*, accused Hegel of sacrificing the existence of the individual; Marx reversed the dialectic of Hegelian philosophy in his *Philosophical Economical Manuscript*. In 1845 Kierkegaard wrote the *Acts of Love*, his masterpiece on the religious nature of man, while Marx published his *Theses on Feuerbach*, the most fundamental catechism on irreligious man ever conceived by the human mind. In 1846 Marx published the *German Ideology* (*Deutsche Ideologie*), whereas Kierkegaard organized his ideas in his *Concluding Unscientific Postscript*, which introduces the reader to the meaning of the act of faith. In the following year, 1847, Engels and Marx made the transition from ideas to action with *The Communist Manifesto*. Kierkegaard was involved in a revolution of another type: he meant to be "the spy and the poet of a vigorous reawakening" of the love of a Christ forgotten or misinterpreted by European society.

The problem for Marx and Kierkegaard is the same: man needs to be saved from the theorizing of philosophers. Man is not a puppet, passively accepting the manipulations and deformations of philosophers more interested in their syntheses than in solving or helping to solve the problem of human existence. For both Marx and Kierkegaard man is a concrete individual: a king because he has freedom, a potential beggar because in exercising his freedom he can lose it.

Therefore Marx and Kierkegaard considered the Aristotelian and Hegelian dialectic, for different reasons, *abstract, formal,* and *inconclusive*. For it they substituted a *real, factual dialectic* against the established order of things. For Marx the established order was the bourgeoisie exploiting the workers; for Kierkegaard the exploitation came from the official church, the "Establishment," as he called it. For both of them the overcoming of the static order of society was meant to be "a leap": the act of faith in Christ for Kierkegaard, the violent revolution for Marx.

But once we have stressed the similarity of *methods*, we cannot go further. Seldom in history have men been expected to accept, simultaneously, two philosophers with a set of doctrines always diametrically opposed and often mutually contradictory. Marx fought for one specific purpose: the fulfillment of the social and biological needs of human beings. To Kierkegaard this was a complete waste. The truth is (and Kierkegaard spent his whole life in its defense) that the spirit is man's inalienable wealth, the spirit which cannot be reduced to matter and which was redeemed by Jesus Christ. Marx wrote to Weydemayer, on May 5, 1852, "I have done these three things, which are new and which nobody else dreamed of doing: I have demonstrated (a) that the existence of social classes is the result of specific phases of economic production; (b) that the proletariat will be the final winner by a law of historical necessity; (c) that the proletariat will destroy all social classes."

Kierkegaard looked with fear on the conglomeration of many persons, on vociferous crowds which, as history showed, had proved to be the easy tools of demagogues and agitators. A crowd, Kierkegaard reminds us, sent Socrates to his death; another crowd spat upon Jesus, shouting, "Crucify Him!" Kierkegaard defended man, the individual, the *res sacra* of St. Augustine. For Marx, violence was the determining force of the old society and the secret of success for the new socialistic triumph. Kierkegaard worked to promote a renewal of the spirit of Christ among men. Love of God and love of man were for him the secret of success. The history of mankind is not, for Kierkegaard, a progressive dialectical sequence whereby the past is rejected; it is not a restless uneasiness with the present, a groundless hope for the future. Those were the Hegelian lucubrations of sedentary professors out of touch with reality. Marx was in agreement with the Hegelians on this point. The problem was different for Kierkegaard. Man had to go back to the authentic Christ. The salvation of man is to be found by reestablishing that "contemporary contact" with Christ, whom centuries of "Christian" history have alienated from men through the bureaucracy of "official religion."

Both Marx and Kierkegaard preached the equality of man, Marx reducing it to the economic sharing of material goods, whereas Kierkegaard based it on the fact that all men are equally "God's children." For the latter, true equality among men is found only in the religious act of faith. "Each man, absolutely each man, is capable of conceiving the loftiest thoughts: otherwise Christianity would be meaningless. It is frightening to me to see how foolishly philosophers differentiate between genius, talent, etc. . . . as compared to religiosity. I had one lonely consolation in my life, i.e., the knowledge that there is something capable of consoling man *absolutely*. This something is God."[1]

Men are equal because each one of them is a person. This doctrine is basic for Christian philosophy. Therefore each person is the source *preceding* society and making it possible. Kierkegaard's philosophy aims at the defense of the individuality of the person. Marx aimed at the same goal: the defense of the individual. But Marx's key principle was

[1] S. Kierkegaard, *Journals* (Copenhagen, 1920), 1850, X2 A.

dialectical materialism. For him, therefore, the human person is a result of materialism, a *posterius,* resulting as a natural event from the absolute dialectic of matter. There is no doubt that the progressive dissolution of Marxism as a philosophy — so evident in our days among the professional followers of Marx — finds its explanation in this basic principle accepted as a dogma by Marx from Hegelian theories.

Kierkegaard began from the historical man and made the transition to metaphysics. One might question the way he did it (from despair to faith), but he reached the metaphysical value of man. Marx, though violently attacking Hegel's historicism, never succeeded in extricating himself from it. He tried to save the individual but failed because he never reached the individual as he is — only what historically appears of him.

Nietzsche came later: he was born in 1844, the year of Marx's important *Manuscript.* Nietzsche is known as the fury who swept Europe with words of discontent and scorn for tradition, civilization, religion. In common with Kierkegaard and Marx, he had one concern: the individual.

More specifically, he shared with Marx the conviction that history makes man instead of man making history. Therefore, in his own exalted way, he did not abandon the Hegelian conception of reality, though he claimed he did. With Kierkegaard he conceived human living *existentially,* heroically. He shared with him a profound distrust for human institutions, particularly for the organized churches. Kierkegaard's target was the Lutheran National Church. Nietzsche hit hard against Christianity as such.

From this perspective, Nietzsche considered himself the instrument of a revenge long waited for in Germany. In the sixteenth century, Luther caused an unhealthy split in man, between his intelligence and his will, his desire for good and his inability to perform it: man became paradoxically his own accuser. The Christian Churches, Protestant and Catholic, mutually suspicious, strongly organized within their own juridical walls, were expected to heal that abnormal division. But they did not succeed.[2] Organized religions had become, Nietzsche thought, in the history of Germany, monumental tombstones to a dead God. And Germany lived through centuries of stagnation, conscious of the condemnation pronounced by Luther upon the destiny and possibilities of man.

---

[2] This opinion is not inevitably true. But it is true that in the past few years, under a common spirit of Ecumenism, the Protestants and Catholics of Germany and of many other countries have become more aware of the presence of God among them and of the gigantic work of sharing the gifts of the Holy Spirit, a work that God expects them to do.

Finally, Kant did not make things better. At the end of his honest trying, the same split, almost schizophrenic, appeared wider and more alarming. After Kant, men understood that reason had no answer for the problem. The romantics, Schopenhauer and Wagner, tried different ways, but the final prophet, the high priest of the overman was Friedrich W. Nietzsche, the gravedigger of the old God of the Christians.

*   *   *

Indeed it is mandatory that we become acquainted with these three philosophers since their tragic existence and thought are all too visibly our heritage.

1. SØREN KIERKEGAARD

"I have been concealing in my flesh an incurable wound . . . that wound explains the impossibility of association with other people. So I came to the conclusion that the task given to me was extraordinary."

So spoke Søren Kierkegaard in the last moments of his life to his friend Emil Borsen. These words represent quite adequately this strange paradoxical philosopher and theologian, a prototype of the Nordic European soul, who lay in his grave almost completely unknown for thirty years and who was discovered in Germany during the great turmoil of World War I.

We know that Søren Kierkegaard was born in Copenhagen on May 5, 1813, when his father was fifty-six and his mother forty-five years old. Luck plus business acumen gave his father sudden wealth. At forty years of age he had retired, financially secure, proud of a large family. Søren was the seventh and the last of his children. Born with a hunched back and uneven legs, Søren also inherited a more complex legacy from his father — a fervent imagination, a dexterity in dialectic, and a brooding Christian melancholy. The elder Kierkegaard was evidently a victim of all the complexes which imprison people who reach success suddenly. Like many other *nouveau riche*, he regarded his fellowmen and even almighty God as jealous of his newly gotten wealth.

From this strange father originated what Søren called "a great earthquake." He was about twenty-two years of age when a sudden intuition took complete possession of his life. He remembered his father, surrounded by his children, telling them that once, when he was a poor, underfed shepherd boy in Jutland, he raised his fist in rebellious blasphemy against God. Søren, his mind obsessed by the magnitude of his parent's sin, saw, because of his father's cursing, the avenging hand of God. He felt that the whole family would suffer for this sin. He writes in his *Journals:* "then a suspicion dawned on me that the old age of my father was not a blessing, but a curse from God . . . that our family was destined to ruin. Then I felt the silence of death grow around me, and my father appeared to me as a cursed man condemned to survive all of us; he was a huge cross casting his shadow on the grave of all of us."[3]

In this atmosphere this facinating and puzzling personality begins to take shape. Kierkegaard used to call himself *Janus bifrons* because "The terror of sin is always united with the pleasure in this terror. Sin is simultaneously loved and feared, hated and enjoyed";[4] sin is the essential category of man. This explains the unhappiness which he suffered and loved. He lived with a burden of secret guilts, oppressed by his own melancholy, crushed by the consciousness of sin.

Any attempt by him at reconciliation with life ended in failure. Although he experienced the joy of love with a girl named Regine Olsen, achieving at the beginning of his romance unbelievable success by winning her from a previous suitor, his joy was short-lived. Bitter delusions followed. The engagement was unbearable. Regine was gay, joyful, in love with life. He was withdrawn, sad, "an eternity too old" for her. A grotesque sequence of ideas ran through his mind. He was eager at the same time both to keep her and lose her. He thought of making her his concubine, of marrying her without revealing the secret of his life, of running away from her. Finally, the experience ended. Regine's love was sacrificed. But sacrifice and self-denial breed exceptional Christians. Therefore, his infidelity to her, his "sin" was the cause of his closer union with Christ. Again we witness another case of his twisted interpretation of Lutheran thought: sin brought to him melancholy, boredom, despair, a sense of separation from all other human beings, a "complete" sickness of body and soul: *felix culpa,* for suffering generates happiness, overcomes finitude, and reaches infinity. Indeed he was *filius senectutis,* a child of old age, who never passed through young manhood. He was old before his birth. "Nine months in my mother's womb were sufficient to make me an old man."

Never before had the insufficiency of the human person been considered as the central positive element giving dignity and nobility to human existence. Another significant event in the life of Søren Kierkegaard added new dimensions to his insight. He became the target of a scandal-mongering paper, *The Corsair.* Each Danish household waited for the paper with curiosity. Each issue brought forth new insults

[3] *Journals,* (1837) II A 662. Some of these have been translated by Alexander Dru in *The Journals of Søren Kierkegaard* (Oxford University Press, 1938).
[4] *Ibid.*

relating to "the great philosopher with uneven pant legs." For a moment Kierkegaard thought of retirement. But the public and prolonged abuse was more than personal. It appeared to Kierkegaard "a menace originating from the Hegelian contempt for the individual." A defense was imperative and *The Corsair* soon disappeared under his attacks.

The next challenge — one long delayed — came to Kierkegaard from the official Protestant Church of Denmark. His last *Journals* are a vivid account of the growing crisis. The year 1843 marks the beginning with the *Edifying Discourses*. His theme leaves no room for compromise: God is no respecter of persons, nor is He a respecter of "Establishments" (a word full of unwritten meaning by which Kierkegaard designates the official Church of Denmark).

The second "earthquake" of Kierkegaard's spiritual life came in 1848. His experience at this time was similar to the famous "night" of Pascal. God, he came to see, was not to be comprehended by complacent syllogisms or described in bland and empty terms derived from earthly experience. God is reached only through suffering, dedication, absolute abnegation. The "Establishment" has betrayed God; it has chosen the way of the world; it has created "Christendom" in the place of Christianity. Christendom for Kierkegaard is a collection of selfish individuals linked only by external institutions which themselves are basically selfish. Christianity, on the other hand, is living faith.

Kierkegaard did not spare his energies. He challenged Martensen, the primate of the Danish Church, to a public debate and he turned out pamphlets at the feverish speed of a man short of time.

Finally he fell in the breach. His lifelong friend Emil Borsen is the witness to his last words. Asked whether his hope rested on his confidence in the redeeming grace of Christ, he answered: "Yes, of course, what else?" In this state of mind, Kierkegaard died on November 11, 1855.

I. The Problem: Possibility as a Category

An orderly exposition of Kierkegaard's philosophy presents great difficulty. Kierkegaard was an enemy of "the system" as all existentialists have been and probably will be. His thought is inextricably bound up with his autobiography in which his main philosophical theories are expounded.

If we keep in mind that philosophy for Kierkegaard is search for *a meaning that man can give to himself, for his birth, his life, and ultimately for death,* we can say that there is one problem which runs constantly through the works of Søren Kierkegaard: *Is it possible* for man to answer the questions posed by his own existence?

Possibility here is taken in its Aristotelian sense. It means the capacity for existence which is the absolute logical condition preceding actual existence. But this meaning is also associated with the Kantian interpretation in which possibility is the only category which should give the individual the joy of thinking; it provides the individual with the satisfaction of organizing the universe of phenomena. Kant recognized this as a real possibility, a key to the partial success achievable by man. "The honest Kant" does not conceal the limits of these human capabilities, but these very limitations testify to the *positive* aspects of man. Kierkegaard discovers the *negative* aspects of these human possibilities, and he is both frightened and overjoyed by the ruinous conclusion. The only possibility is the *possibility of nothingness*. His life testifies to his thesis: his deformed body, the anxieties of his family, his broken engagement, his writings derided by his compatriots, his religious conscience in perpetual conflict with the official clergy of his country. All these are instances of possibilities whose results for him were dreadfully impossible and contradictory.

The final pages of *The Concept of Dread* underline this theme in masterful words: Existence, with its alternatives, paralyzes, petrifies, and dissolves the individual. His own existence is a "series of futile efforts in experimentation filled with mysteries." "I am nothing. This conviction offers to me and to my genius one pleasure. I know that I must keep my existence at the 'point zero' in between cold and warm, wisdom and madness, something and nothing. I am a pure 'perhaps.' "[5]

Possibility, the category of hope, conceived as the norm and the testimony of achievement, becomes for Kierkegaard the cornerstone for his failure.

In his works Kierkegaard attempts to conceal from the public his identity as author. Different interpretations are given to his constant desire for concealment under pseudonyms. It has been said that "Kierkegaard never steps forward *in persona propria*"[6] to claim any of the opinions as his own because Kierkegaard in the first phase of his philosophy is only searching for a logical possibility and is paralyzed by the nothingness of his findings. The pseudonyms are thus perhaps intended to prevent recognition from falling on a man who has so much to say and so little to defend.

Our work, in an effort to capture the most outstanding thoughts resulting from Kierkegaard's long meditation, will be centered on the category of possibility analyzed in the three spheres of existence: the first two are the aesthetic and the ethical; they represent the vain

---

[5] *Werke* IV, p. 246, trans. ours.

[6] James Collins, *The Mind of Kierkegaard* (Chicago: Henry Regnery, 1964), p. 57.

effort of philosophy. The third sphere, that of existence, transcends philosophy, which he had found inadequate, and makes religious faith the answer to the human search.

II. *The Aesthetic and Ethical Spheres*

Kierkegaard's aesthetic philosopher, as he presents himself in the *Dissertation on Irony*, the *Diary of a Seducer*, and *In vino veritas*, etc., does not appear as the vulgar victim of human passions, but as the elegant hedonist, obedient to the whim of the moment — what we might call the "playboy." He knows how to forge the correct atmosphere for his own refined pleasures. The future does not bother him, he uses the past as a tool of expression with which he creates the joy of an immediate delight. The atmosphere of his work is romantic. Here poetry is the secret to success. The aesthetic phase is dramatized for Kierkegaard in the personal, spiritual adventures of three figures famous in the history of Western literature for the fascination which they created in the minds of the simple and the great. These three figures were Don Giovanni, Faust, and Ahasuerus.

Mozart's Don Giovanni, the hero of sensual immediacy, lives for the joy of the instant, the instant before logical reflection destroys it. Kierkegaard sees the goal at this temporary stage in the refusal of Don Giovanni to recognize what it means to be a "self." Self-commitment would destroy this ideal. Don Giovanni makes contact with the existent material world. His life vibrates with the pleasure of the sensuous experience connecting the subject with the object, in direct defiance of the means which Hegel had set forth to unite subject and object. We must recognize here the presence of a romantic soul, dreaming a world of ideal innocence existing between the guilt of a life of lust and the responsibility of a life of the spirit.

Goethe's Faust continues the development of this aesthetic experience which, in the character of Don Giovanni, did not reach a final solution. Sensual immediacy, always thirsty for renewed emotions, eventually induces doubt and despair. Faust is the hero of doubt and despair. "Anyone who reflects upon the futility of trying to satisfy the human spirit in the sheer flow of immediate feeling and pleasure is liable to become skeptical about every supposed certainty, resting place and moments of joy."[7]

The Faustian doubt does not reject sensual immediacy; therefore, it is not meant to be a logical doubt, either real or methodical. This doubt is an expression of demonic activity. The word *daimon* has

---

[7] *Ibid.* (1853), X^5 A146

Platonic origins. Kierkegaard conceives it as a hidden force focusing the intentions and the achievements of a person on one all-absorbing idea. The surrounding world, with its conventional standards, is forgotten. The demonic person creates his own destiny. Faust's intense search reveals the inner substance of this situation of doubt. Search, however, is not coexistent with complete despair. There is, of course, a positive aspect, though too feeble and too fluent, in Faust's life, and it goes into the preparation of the final stage. Aesthetic existence, with its profound common ground of instability, kills *the possibility* of happiness which requires secure continuity. The mind cannot long remain at this level. The erotic exaltations of Don Giovanni and the demonic doubts of Faust lay the ground for the third and last hero: the wandering Jew Ahasuerus, who is the hero of despair, because his soul does not harbor hope in God or in man. He rolls, like a free ball, from one situation into another. Ahasuerus seems to live by the message handed down by Greek wisdom: life is a monotonous repetition of the same standards of hope, pretended achievements, indifference, and failure. The Greeks reacted to this insight drastically, by abstention from desire and with stoic indifference, which became the emblem of their crusade. Ahasuerus reacts by despairing. It is hopeless to prepare for an exploration of all the secrets of existence, but even if it were not hopeless, man lacks the strength to be an explorer.

It is of interest now, if we want to understand Kierkegaard, to notice that the proper reaction to this kind of aesthetic despair, so often spoken and so well explained in accordance with the rubrics of the romantic mind, is not bleak skepticism or any of the forms of distressing gnosticism. The proper reaction and the one Kierkegaard gives is the gentle use of *irony*.[8]

Irony awakens the aesthete from his pleasing torpor. Irony makes him aware of the grotesque side of his love affair with life. Irony detaches man from the universe in which he is subconsciously submerged. Irony strikes at the heart of one of the fundamental dimensions of man. It calls him back to the facts of life and it frees him from the voluptuous sirens of the world of aesthetics while introducing him to higher values, where responsibility and morality offer true dignity to human nature. In this context irony fosters courage, a courage which enables the individual to make a choice. The act of choice gives dignity to man, to be more precise, it is the act of choosing which gives dignity to man, because freedom is discovered by man in that moment of suspension which precedes the actual choice. That moment confirms a "decision towards a future which is rich with a new existence; for a life that is

---

[8] Cf. *The Concept of Irony*, passim.

nothing, through the act of choosing, comes to have meaning and true being."[9]

Ethics is born from this act of choice. Ethics, unlike aesthetics, persuades man to be faithful to himself. Whoever chooses himself rejects all extraneous elements as intruding and unwanted evils, and this rejection also entails repentance. It is clear, therefore, that ethical freedom is impossible without an act of self-accusation which severs the individual from all the factors in his life which had been accepted but which did not belong to him.

This insight has profound implications. If morality is stability, the isolated individual man, given over to the luxury of a sensual extraordinary existence, is not a man of morality. The ethical man is ordinary, and, therefore, married. Paradoxically, Kierkegaard, a bachelor and unsuccessful in his love life, considers marriage the cornerstone of the ethical life. Marriage, he felt, is within the reach of all human beings; whereas aesthetic love demands exceptional persons, the moral life does not. Ordinary life finds its strength in will power while the extraordinary life of the aesthete finds both its fulfillment and its weakness in human passions.

These are the general principles of morality which, after Kierkegaard has reached them, left him vexed with many problems. The dilemma will be quite clear to all those who know the history of philosophy: does Kierkegaard accept as the essence of morality the Kantian doctrine of the categorical imperative which postulates duty before love, which destroys teleology and ignores theology? Is morality *possible* without religious faith and love? Is morality duty alone? Again Kierkegaard looks to the category of possibility in search of an answer. Kierkegaard, in *The Concept of Dread*,[10] explicates the answer he has found. Without God moral effort is doomed to failure. Ethics without God is a nominalistic exercise in abstract terminology. Ethics demands a recognition of the *historical dimensions of man,* his original sin, the redeeming death of Christ, the drama of the intelligence which understands and of the will that rebels against the intelligence's understanding, and the obscure presence of passions, often so powerful, always so unpredictable. These are the elements which "pure" ethics pretends to ignore, but which pretended ignorance does not destroy. In effect, this answer reveals to Kierkegaard that the category of possibility in which he placed so much hope is now reduced to impossibility. The gap between aesthetics and ethics not only remained wide open, but "pure" ethics itself creates an abyss which must and can be filled only by the

---

[9] Louis Lavelle, *Le moi et son destin,* p. 83.
[10] *The Concept of Dread, passim.*

presence of God. Kiergegaard's famous work, *Fear and Trembling,* dramatizes this new realization with numerous observations on the life of patriarch Abraham.

Abraham, in a solemn moment of his life, is called by God to suspend all ethical rules in obedience to the divine order which demands the sacrifice of his son Isaac. In that eventful moment, the tragic choice had to be made, either ethics or God. That is to say, either reason or faith. Could human reason attempt a daring assault on God in the vain effort of establishing an autonomous morality? The answer is given by the intrepid Abraham. He brandished his sword in the supreme act of obedience to God. He was ready to kill his son. The Bible adds a most proper comment: "He had faith against all reasonable hopes and he became the father of many nations."

Reason is the enemy of faith. Reason would have suggested to Abraham resistance, flight, or some consultation with his closest relatives — Sarah, Eleazar, or even Isaac himself, in order to argue God out of His purpose. All these benign, humanly prudent ideas appear to Kierkegaard as partial concessions to the Kantian postulate that ethics is molded by universal human agreement; but to apply the same principle to faith amounts to the destruction of faith.

III. *The Sphere of Faith*

Dread and Despair. Without anticipating our discussion on the nature of existentialism, it is evident that Kierkegaard is a "new philosopher, or, according to the traditional term, Kierkegaard is not a philosopher at all. Yet he must be classed among the philosophers of the contemporary period because his problems are at the heart of most contemporary philosophical discussions. In place of the traditional epistemology and ontology, Kierkegaard substitutes a new orientation of the human person with his desires, hopes, and fears. We have seen that aesthetics and ethics did not, for Kierkegaard, give answers. Now it is time to examine the other sphere of human existence: faith.

Religious faith, Kierkegaard felt, does give answers. But what can we say about faith except that we do not understand it?

The soul does not plunge into the stream of faith without a crisis which constitutes the most dramatic moment of Kierkegaard's meditation. Faith, for Kierkegaard, is thus the offspring produced by a frightful gestation period of dread and despair.

The Concept of Dread, written in 1845, examines the *human situation* of instability and the doubt which humans must accept in dealing with the universe. *Sickness Unto Death,* written in 1850, is a masterpiece of theological phenomenology of sin and analyzes the responsibilities which a man has to himself.

Both works, fundamental to the understanding of Kierkegaard, presuppose an awareness of the long struggle of this lonely philosopher against the absolutistic ideas of Hegel which were universally accepted by the schools of his time.

Kierkegaard is not a specialist in Hegelian philosophy. He studied Hegel as the founder of an intellectual movement that had almost completely conquered European society. From the early years of his philosophical career Kierkegaard carried the understanding that Hegel's purpose was to divinize man, to make him absolute, and therefore to kill the truly human individual. Kierkegaard found Schleiermacher's answers to Hegel to be poor expressions of a camouflaged immanentism, too timid for the defense of God's freedom and man's finiteness and too conscious of the universal enthusiasm for Hegelian immanentism. The more confidence Kierkegaard acquires with the written word, the more pungent and often sarcastic his criticisms of Hegel appear. And yet in one respect Kierkegaard is more Hegelian than Hegel himself: Kierkegaard considers the system of Hegelian panlogism the most advanced, indeed the final word, in Occidental thought from Thales to his day. He said once, not without evident irony, that the Hegelian dialectical process of thesis, antithesis, and synthesis is a process of rumination of all reality consummated by the beast with the three stomachs: philosophy is finished because the rumination is terminated.

Hegel does not understand Christian existence (that is Kierkegaard's main argument) because he claims an identification of a logical system (which is possible as Aristotle has demonstrated) with a metaphysical dialectic (which is impossible because metaphysics requires individual existents). This dynamic identification is the basic unjustified *postulate* of Hegelianism which Kierkegaard rejects with disdain. Once he quipped that no one should criticize Hegel who is not equipped with sound common sense, a share of humor, and a dose of Greek ataraxy.[11]

This epic fight will end only with Kierkegaard's death. *The Concept of Dread* and *The Sickness Unto Death* are most solemn answers to Hegel because more than criticism, which is not completely forgotten, they expose positively and often poignantly what the philosopher of Stuttgart failed to understand about human dignity.

The theme of the *Concept of Dread* is centered on the biblical narrative of the fall. Dread came into man's consciousness in progressive stages:

---

[11] *Postscript*, p. 34, note. Cf. Collins, *op. cit.*, p. 120.

a) The state of Adam, prior to the original sin, was a state of innocence. Innocence is ignorance of good and evil. Innocence therefore is the cause of dread, because it is suspension, tense expectation of the unknown: a situation of moral nothingness. Adam was innocent; therefore, he was subject to dread. The paradox causes the pure anxiety of *pure possibility*. "Here you do not find knowledge of good and evil, but the whole knowledge is projected into the monstrous nothing of ignorance."[12]

b) From innocence to sin. The mind will never understand this mystery. Kierkegaard calls it a *"saltus qualitativus"* — a leaping of *qualitative* nature. Innocence and sin are two different levels of existence which one cannot expect to explain: they must simply be accepted. This stands in opposition to the purely *quantitative* Hegelian doctrine which explains evil dialectically as a moment of good. Adam is forbidden to eat the fruit of knowledge of good and evil: in that moment Adam knows that he is *free*. *Pure possibility* becomes *possibility of something*. Of what? Adam does not know as yet. God was so categorical and so laconic. But then came the terrible announcement: "If you will eat of the forbidden fruit, you will die."

c) Dread is projected into the future. Dread is related to what does not yet exist but might exist in the future. The future is always in company with death. Now Adam *really* knows, and knowledge is the cause of perdition, because knowledge gives to Adam the possibility of sin. The nature of dread is therefore anxiety caused by an unknown possibility. Kierkegaard wrote pages full of drama in the final chapters of *The Concept of Dread*. The most frightening words pronounced by Christ were not "My God, my God, why hast thou forsaken me?" but the others uttered to Judas: "What thou dost, *do quickly*." The first sentence is a torturing awareness of what is actually happening. The second is an unbearable suspension caused by what might happen. Here the human Christ fulfills all the requisites of His humanity. Dread is the wealth of life. Lack of dread humiliates human living to the biological level of a vegetative organism.

IV. *Man and God in Kierkegaard*

The discussion among philosophers on Søren Kierkegaard proceeds peacefully enough as long as it deals with the topics which we analyzed: the impotency of reason, the trauma of the soul that seeks and does not find a meaning to life.

But when the *real* Kierkegaard is taken into consideration — we mean

---

[12] *Concept of Dread*, p. 53.

the passionate believer in God and the man who demands "a leap" from "dirty reason" to "radiant faith," then the consensus among the students of this great man is far from unanimous. The venerable J. De Tonquedec's unbelievable statement is an outstanding example. He said that Kierkegaard dared to attempt "the panegyric of the absurd, understood in the most brutal meaning."[13]

Agreement with Tonquedec on this matter is utterly impossible. Kierkegaard reaches a clarity of ideas when he discusses faith and God which is not evident in other writings about other subjects. You almost feel the exultant satisfaction of the man who prefers to build with God than to destroy with blind and ephemeral confidence in reason.

We like to follow, step by step, his *itinerarium mentis in Deum:*

a) Dread is the inheritance of man when he lives outside or without faith. Dread does not represent the essential elements of human nature; it is a condition originated by his fall. Kierkegaard says: "The thought that God might be responsible for a temptation man must endure cannot be too horrifying. It depends on that way we understand this thought. The unbeliever and the man who is a victim of melancholy think that God enjoys seeing man's perdition. The believer thinks that God wants to give man the chance to be a winner. . . . To climb from the abyss of dread to the joy of faith is hard challenge: it requires the actual reversal of a man's situation; he must be filled with hope and faith when something happens which before was the cause of dread and despair. This hope and faith are signs that he was chosen to possess the light of faith. To hold to the thought that God is love, this is the first abstract form of faith, the time will come when he will experience concretely his relation to God."[14]

The two dimensions of man are clear: dread for the fugitive from God, faith for the Christian seeking God.

b) Human freedom is absurd until the presence of God gives meaning to it. The Greek philosophers were instrumental, though unconsciously so, in preparing the background for •the success of the Christian message. The opposite is true in the present time: an abyss has been built between man and God. To reach God, a leap is necessary, a generous, daring jump into the arms of God. Worldly affairs breed involvement for the spirit, involvement causes loss of freedom. I am myself only in the presence of God. Here existentialism becomes pure metaphysics. Kierkegaard speaks of a theological intentionality which alone gives freedom and salvation to man.

---

[13] P. J. De Tonquedec, *L'existence après Karl Jaspers* (Paris: Gallimard, 1945), p. 136.

[14] *Journals*, 1850, X² A433 (*Samlede Vaerker*, 2nd ed., Copenhagen, 1920).

Seldom in modern times were more profound words written than the following: "The problem of divine Omnipotence and the existence of evil does not present great difficulty. Here is my solution: to help someone to be free is one of the most challenging of human goals. But freedom requires omnipotence. This might seem strange because omnipotence seems to limit freedom. Yet omnipotence rightly conceived allows the individual to keep his own independence, precisely because omnipotence does not suffer for the presence of others. This is the reason which prevents a man from making another man free. The powerful man is always preconditioned and limited by his power. . . . Omnipotence alone preserves its own self while giving itself to others. This relation between the Omnipotent Being and a finite being secures the independence of the finite being receiving its existence from the infinite Being. Finite power imposes dependence and limitation of freedom, God's omnipotence is identical to God's liberality. . . . This consideration is the key of another mystery: the divine omnipotence was successful in producing the most astonishing of all things, the universe, and the most fragile of all things, human nature *independent* of divine omnipotence. God omnipotent could have handled the world with a very heavy hand; in fact, he deals with the universe with the softness of a maternal touch. Those who lump together divine omnipotence with the brutal exercise of constriction and despotism have shallow minds subservient to materialistic and mundane deception. It is much better to think with Socrates that power is an art and it makes people free. But this relation is not possible between man and man; it is a prerogative of the Omnipotent God. Therefore if man could be absolutely autonomous of God, God would not have the power to help him. I am free because I received my freedom from God to whom I owe everything. If each created thing did not depend on God, he would not have had the power to make me free nor would we be free if he lost anything creating me."[15]

This quotation is remarkable for several reasons. Kierkegaard reveals here the depth of his metaphysical understanding of the existent. God is an infinite person, transcendent, immaterial. This God of Kierkegaard is reached by the impetus of faith. But once reached God unfolds His qualities: infinity, immateriality, omnipotence. The reader is taken back to St. Thomas Aquinas and the Scholastics. Both speak an existential language which is based on common ground that matter cannot be considered an autonomous existing being but only a principle of being, limited and incapable of existence by itself.

c) God is for Kierkegaard a powerful magnet. Creatures must go

---

[15] *Ibid.*, 1846, VIIA 181. Dru, #616, p. 180.

back to God. This return is conditioned by different degrees of perfection inherent in each being. Man is, of course, the most privileged of all. But man is often engaged in hunting transient ephemeral goals. Aesthetic man lives a life of immediacy, without a vision of the Absolute. But the ethical form of life demands a religious conscience. Religion without morality is a mockery. The Protestant revolution — Kierkegaard repeats in his *Journals* — consummated this mockery when the Reformers of the 16th century rejected (on the pretext of the corruption of the Roman Curia) the objective norm of morality at the same time that they continued to accept God and to implore His friendship with emotional and sincere devotion. The thought that Kierkegaard had a Roman Catholic conscience while living in a Protestant society has occurred to many critics.

The first moment of man's return to God requires an awareness of His existence. Kierkegaard sees a growing conspiracy against the existence of God. God has been assailed by modern culture; He is no longer a person with whom we communicate and from whom we expect protection. God has become an atmosphere produced by man himself through the divinization of his own conscience. Kierkegaard contemplates with horror the shambles produced by Hegelianism. History, philosophy, the official Protestant Church tend to humanize God, to reduce the absolute to the relative: they meant to introduce God into the universe and they made the universe god.

Kierkegaard wrote: "A man might live ten or twenty or thirty years of his life and suddenly this man deserves God's punishment. It must be horrifying that God should lose his patience with a man. Because God is a loving father and the first form of love is that he disposes things in such a way that one acquires consciousness of his divine existence. Living without the awareness of God is a wandering type of existence filled with foolishness. This is the wrath of God: to allow a man to wander like an animal, without hearing the divine calling."[16]

Kierkegaard abhors vague exhortations: man's return to God has an historical meaning. It means that we are sinners, that we need a Redeemer and that "we decide to imitate him." Man before Christ was trapped by philosophies which gave him reasonable convictions that human freedom was a benign disguise of fatalism and that the gods of Athens and Rome were a popular travesty of rigid immanentism. With Christ, man reaches the personal God in a way both dramatic and rewarding. Man accepts a confrontation between his own person and the person of God. Both God and man are free individuals, they exchange ideas, they come to agreements or to disagreements. Man

[16] *Ibid.*, 1848, X^1 A75.

reached the highest paroxysm of deceit and perfidy when the second Person of God was killed by human persons.

d) The imitation of Christ. "Watch your step," Kierkegaard admonishes, "when you enter the house of God. Even if you come from the most horrifying situation in which a human being can find himself, when you seek refuge from the outside horror in the house of God, you will discover something even more horrifying. Here in the house of God the center of universal concern is a danger that the world does not know. In comparison with this danger all the dangers of the world are a plaything for children. This danger is sin. Here in the house of God horror occupies everybody's mind. This horror is so huge that all misfortunes of this world are in comparison vain trivialities: this horror is that mankind has killed God."[17] Christ is for Kierkegaard the first religious discovery, and from Christ, through a profound introspection, man reaches the concept of God, of sin and justice. "Take a child before his innocence has vanished, give him an album of photos of well known leaders, for instance Alexander, Napoleon and mingle in with these the picture of Jesus Crucified. As soon as the child sees it, the question will come 'Who is he?' Your answer will be: 'He was the most amiable of all human beings.' And the child will interrupt you with surprise: 'Who killed him and why?' If we mature people could maintain something of our childhood!"[18]

And Kierkegaard lived his doctrine. He says: "If you ask me: How do you succeed in keeping silence and peace of mind among the thousand of persons who laugh at you, provoke you with calumnies and gossip? . . . Here is my answer: 'First of all when I speak, there is a high Person listening to me: God in heaven. . . . Secondly, since I was a child, I was told with solemn words that the *crowd* spat upon Jesus. Those who were passing by . . . spat upon him and cursed him. . . . He was the Truth. Hence my great veneration since the early days of my intellectual life, for Socrates whom the *crowd* condemned to death."[19]

Kierkegaard rejects this idea of impossible reconciliation between the individual person and the crowd in most of his works. The crowd is mediocre because it prevents the individual soul from imitating Christ.

e) A profound effort to imitate Christ is for Kierkegaard the source of scruple. Let us try to understand this original doctrine of Kierkegaard.

Scruple is the Christian form of fear. We desire to pattern our life on Christ's life, yet we fear the possibility of a wrong decision. Scruple is the result of this confrontation between our finitude and the divine

---

[17] "Christian Conversations," in *Journals*, p. 205.
[18] *Journals*, 1848, IX A395.
[19] *Ibid.*, 1849, X A272.

infinity. "Luther says that scruples come from the devil. That is wrong. Scruples originate from the divine presence which often is too unbearable to our soul. We dare to come in personal contact with God, with Christ: that is more than sufficient to 'lose our minds.' "[20] Kierkegaard has kind words for Job's wife, who was unwilling to accept God's severe decisions: "Humanly speaking, Job's wife was right. To suffer as Job suffered and to think that God is love, is a formidable task! Despair is much easier. The thought that God is love often makes suffering unbearable. Again humanly speaking a person that bears the load of great pains could be justified by saying: 'Everything would be less painful if the thought of God would not accompany me.' It is frightening to be like a sparrow when you feel able to understand the meaning of our suffering. You must accept the fact that suffering is a flight from God who calls himself love. But you must persevere. If you do not abandon God, at the end you will find yourself in happy agreement with him. God wants to be believed in. He is infinite and therefore he is entitled to demand an infinite price for the faith he gave us in him. The higher the price, the higher the beatitude of believing. A lover uses the same language: the more difficult it was to win his beloved one, the greater is his joy."[21]

f) The last step of this itinerary of the soul toward God is a complete surrender, a total commitment to his majesty. "I must admit that a partial commitment to God is impossible. It is impossible to say to him: 'I want your friendship just to some extent. I do not care about being "a spectacle to the world" as a religious person should be because his relationship to you has made him a stranger to the world. On the contrary, I want to belong to the world and yet I do not want to give up a little sentiment for you.'

"God is absolute and our commitment to him must be absolute, as we do not commit ourselves to anyone."[22]

The *Journals* are filled with these ideas which place Kierkegaard very close to the greatest mystics of the Christian experience. An honest evaluation of his works allows one conclusion: Kierkegaard accepts a transcendent God, the divinity of Jesus Christ, the immortality of the soul. It is a difficult task, contrary to the evidence given by his writings, to condemn Kierkegaard and number him among those who deny metaphysics or among those who accept exclusively the existential fact of the finite and reject the infinite.

This documentated analysis of the religious thought of Kierkegaard,

---

[20] *Ibid.*, p. 22.
[21] *Ibid.*, p. 478.
[22] *Ibid.*, 1850, X² A644.

we think, must be properly completed with a famous and sublime page written by him in 1846, when, from the columns of the *Corsair*, a storm of mockery and public derision gathered around his person. "Heavenly Father, so immense is Your kingdom! You govern the immensity of heaven and the laws of the universe were made by You. The human beings that You protect are as numerous as the grains of sand in the ocean. Yet You listen to each one of them in a different paternal way, and You do not have any preference. You do not listen only to those who are sheltered by the loving hearts of their friends and relatives, no, the most miserable man, the most abandoned, the loneliest in the crowds is the center of Your attention. If solitude torments him, if the crowd ignores him, You know where he is hiding, in the desert in the crowd. If he is buried in the deepest darkness of anxiety and fear, burdened by horrible thoughts, forgotten by men, forgotten by the very language they speak . . . You do not forget him. You understand his language, You know how to find his hiding place, with swift celerity like lightning or thunder. If You drag your feet, You are not lazy but prudent. You are our Father and therefore You know how to choose the best moment and the securest place.

"Lord our God! to You cries the soul tortured by tribulations, to You cries the soul overtaken by joy. Your gifts are good and perfect and it is so heartwarming to thank You when life is filled with joy. But it is more wonderful to thank You when life becomes difficult, when our heart is heavy with sorrow, when the soul is surrounded by darkness, when our reason becomes confused with ambiguous ideas and our memory is overrun by oblivion. . . . For he who is thankful to God in such difficult circumstances is bound to love God and therefore he is entitled to tell him: O Lord in Your omnipotence You know everything, You know that I love You."[23]

2. KARL MARX

Karl Marx was born on May 5, 1818, in Trier, a prosperous little town in the Mosel valley, famous for its wine and numerous landmarks of Roman history. His blood, his inclinations, his Talmudic concern for analytic precision belonged to a Jewish family proud of many generations of rabbis. But his father neglected the Jewish faith, victim as he was of the more earthly ideas of the Enlightenment. In August, 1824, he went so far as to bring his seven children, Karl was the second of them, to the Evangelical church for baptism. Perhaps considerations of

---

[23] *Ibid.* (1846, VII A), p. 132.

practical nature, economical and social advantages, were the source of this negated identity.

Karl must have been a handsome boy: a full face, illuminated by piercing dark rabbinical eyes, a gently aquiline Jewish nose, and a generous crown of curly hair: the nickname of "The Moor," which his father had given him, was more than justified.

Two characteristics, strikingly different, puzzle the student interested in the life of Karl Marx: his mind was absorbed by abstract theories; persons and things were obedient tools of abstract thought. Yet his life proved to be an untiring succession of very close relations with a few friends who seemed to appear at the right moment to urge this extraordinary man to the fulfillment of his historical destiny.

Dr. Koeppen, professor at the University of Berlin, where the young Karl was a student from 1836 to 1841, was one of them. Those were difficult days for Karl: his father had died, he felt the loneliness of the big city and he gave himself up to the Bohemian life of the coffee-house intellectuals: "Professors' Club" they called themselves, or "Young Hegelians," as they are better known by the historians. In 1841 Dr. Koeppen convinced that lonely student from Trier to write and defend his doctoral dissertation on Democritus and Epicurus, the founding fathers of materialism. The Young Hegelians were seething with hatred for the Christian God, the stumbling block to the ascendency and fulfillment of Hegel's panlogism. For them God could not exist: David Frederick Strauss had tried to prove that the Gospels lack any historical authenticity, and Ludwig Feuerbach exposed to public derision the person of Jesus Christ: humans could not hope for any future until they cease to be "the lackeys of His Heavenly Majesty." Karl Marx shared these ideas with enthusiasm; he was in need of a fitting environment in which to defend them. Moses Hess, a modest intellectual author of a book about a new philosophy called "socialism" or "communism," offered this occasion. The moment they met, Moses Hess knew he had discovered a genius. Marx was introduced to the editors of the *Rheinish Gazette* of Cologne with words that cannot hide the zeal of this unusual missionary of a new gospel. Hess wrote to the editors of the *Gazette* that "Dr. Marx is still a young man, twenty-four at the most. He combines the deepest philosophical earnestness with a biting wit. Imagine Rousseau, Voltaire, Holbach, Lessing, Heine, and Hegel all fused in one person — and I mean fused, not lumped together — and you have Dr. Marx."[24] But the *Rheinish Gazette* was a nest of subversive atheism: the Prussian government could not be tolerant. Marx loved his freedom more than his country; therefore, he chose exile. First he lived in

[24] Marx-Engels, *Gesamte Ausgabe,* Erste Abteilung, Band 1, Halfband 2, p. 260.

Switzerland and then in Paris, through the good services of another "providential friend," Arnold Ruge, with whom he published the *German-French Yearbook* in which the theories of inevitability, revolution, proletarianism appeared.

Again the publication was denounced by the Prussian government and financially strangled. Marx was without money, in a foreign city, completely stranded, with a wife, Jenny von Westphalen, who gave him unceasing faithful understanding and a long line of children. He contributed articles to *Forward,* a paper of the German exiles in Paris, and he met for the second time "the friend" of his life, Friedrich Engels, with whom he authored *The Holy Family,* a controversial work rich with biting answers to the Hegelianism of Bruno Bauer.

In 1845 an attempt was made on the life of the King of Prussia. The *Forward* of Paris published articles expressing disappointment that the attempt was unsuccessful. A few days after, Marx was deported. The wandering Jew of Trier landed in Brussels with his family and his friend Engels, and a very unusual human being was this Friedrich Engels. Rich son of a businessman from Barmen, he was sent to head a branch of his father's business in Manchester, England. There he lived a double life: the impeccable businessman during the day; the scrupulous socialist after work, when he found pleasure spending long hours with his Irish wife, Mary Burns, roaming the slums of Manchester. Now in Brussels Engels was literally overcome by the strong personality of Marx: he stuttered and blushed in his presence. Engels was born to be a follower; his mind wanted to accept and to be protected. "I am meant to play a second fiddle," he said of himself. And Marx was meant to lead, to order, and to command. They grew together into a single person, with one abiding dream, which, in the spring of 1845, when Marx freed himself from the philosophy of Feuerbach, seemed to take logical wording: the ineluctability of dialectic in the economic philosophy of history.

The political situation in Europe was rapidly changing and Marx knew that the times were ripe for action after so much discussion. He overcame his distaste for crowds, the *profanum vulgus,* and he founded the "Communist Party," the first with this name, with seventeen members, among them Engels and Hess. The *Communist Manifesto,* published in January, 1848, was their catechism. It was supposed to be brief, concise, easy to grasp: an historical adaptation of factors that made each economical system obsolete and decadent when pressed by and compared with the system immediately following. The whole construction was tailored to introduce the main thesis: the bourgeoisie, i.e., the capitalists must make room for the proletariat. Slogans, the weapon of all demagogues of all times, buttress the shaking structure of the *Manifesto:*

some of these slogans had been made famous by other agitators; for example, Marat used to repeat with annoying frequency that "the proletarians had nothing to lose but their chains" and that "the workers have no country." A German student had launched four months before the battle cry: "Workingmen of all countries, unite."[25]

Louis Philippe of France, Metternich of Austria, and Wilhelm IV of Prussia learned with horrifying terror the power of the shouting mobs. On January 23, 1848, the Parisians were gathered in the Place de la Bastille; their aim, revolution. It failed; Archbishop Affre was killed in the effort to establish peace; but Marx was jubilant: his ideas were working.

Exhausted by the unceasing work, betrayed by friends, haunted by the police, he sought refuge in London, haven of all conspirators. One among the many companions remained faithful, Engels. Another companion never abandoned Karl Marx and in London more than ever continued to impose its bothersome presence upon him and his family: a squalid poverty, or, to be precise, a downright beggary. Reading the correspondence of Marx to Engels from the fall of 1850, when he began his London exile, is a memorable in instructive experience. He became ill, suffering from a liver ailment. He was untidy; it was rare for him to wash; he drank to excess. His family grew, some of the children died: little Franziska when she was one; Edgar, the life and soul of his father, when he was nine. Few pennies came from a few articles written by Engels for the *New York Tribune* and published under Marx's name. In June, 1858, he published *The Critique of Political Economy,* incomplete and a real delusion for his friends. It was to become the first part of another future work, *Capital.*

Finally came other disappointments: Bakunin, a Russian socialist, and Dr. Ferdinand Lassale seemed to dream of a German Communism autonomous and in conflict with Marx's ideas. Lassale became the target of the violent sarcasms of Marx. Engels received letters from Marx describing Lassale as the little Jew, the little kike, Baron Izzy. When Lassale died, Marx wrote that it was "hard to believe that such a noisy, restless, pushing fellow is as dead as a doornail."[26]

In 1864 *The Working Men's International Association* made its first appearance; one of the first official doings of the Association was to send a message of congratulation to Lincoln.

On September 2, 1867, the first volume of *Capital* appeared. Arrangements were made that anyone who could write at all should write

---

[25] Karl Marx and Friedrich Engels, *Selected Correspondence — 1846–1895* (New York: International Publishers), p. 43.

[26] *Letters,* September 7, 1864.

laudatory comments. Engels pretended to attack the book from a bourgeois point of view. And when his friends were slow to help in selling *Capital* and the reviews were difficult to obtain, Marx became his own reviewer: he wrote articles for the press, some filled with hyperbole and praise; others, with vitriolic and sarcastic comments.

History finally came to aid Marx's cause. Bismarck's soldiers in the spring of 1871 were bivouacking in the streets of Paris. The peace treaty with Prussia was the most humiliating of all events in the centuries of French history. Paris rose in revolt. The Commune governed the city. Riotous revolutions followed: the Archbishop of Paris, Darboy, gave his life in the effort to bring peace to his people. The members of the *International* gave enthusiastic support; Marx, "the overlord of the International," became famous overnight.

He closed his eyes in death on March 14, 1883, when he could not yet imagine the influence his troubled life and rebellious thought would have upon history.

I. *The Formative Years*

From the days of his early philosophical experience at the University of Berlin (1836) to the publication of his *Theses on Feuerbach* in 1845, the year that signs the beginning of his original thinking, Marx searched relentlessly for an answer to one problem: What is the meaning of man? It might be useful to remember here again that philosophy is often a mysterious business. It builds now what tomorrow it will destroy; the Greeks loved to talk of Penelope, undoing at night what she had spun the previous day. The mystery in philosophy, fascinating and disturbing, finds its origin in human nature, in our case in the person of Karl Marx. Aristotle and Thomas Aquinas thought that objective evidence, expressed by the principle of contradiction, was the logical beginning of all thinking. Hegel denied the same principle of contradiction and enthroned contradiction as the principle of logic and ontology. Marx rebelled against Hegel and established the individual as the cornerstone of his philosophy.

Engels testified that Marx's *philosophical method was Hegelian,* but *his point of departure was Aristotelian.*[27] Without trying to straitjacket Marx's mind into pretailored categories, with the clear understanding that Aristotle's philosophy led to diametrically different developments, it can be said that the study of the early years of Marx bears witness to Engels' testimony. The basic question for Marx in those days was:

[27] Engels, *Ludwig Feuerbach und der Ausgang der klassischen Philosophie,* Duncker ed. p. 28.

Is the spirit before nature? That is, does thinking originate from the existent or does the existent originate from thinking?

Hegel proclaimed that the Absolute is Spirit, self-becoming, and that philosophy is the thinking view of things, the rationalization of the existent. In Hegel's system "reason" was identified with "reality" because "reality" was identical to "reason." Strange as it might seem to us, Hegel in those days was considered the mouthpiece of God, because, in his words, his philosophy was "an exposition of God as He is in His eternal essence before the creation of the world and man."[28]

Marx never agreed to these premises. His personal psychological make-up, as was common to all the young Hegelians, was impregnated with an inborn hatred for all types of divinities, transcendent and immanent, revealed or deistic. An adequate explanation for this state of mind will probably continue to be an unanswered question. But we cannot be wrong if we keep in mind that Marx thought of Hegel more as a theologian than as a philosopher. "*The Phenomenology* [of Hegel]," Marx writes in the *Holy Family*, "ends by putting in place of all human existences absolute knowledge."[29] This is a gratuitous assumption, "the method of advancing from the abstract to the concrete . . . is by no means the process which itself generates the concrete."[30]

The concrete individual is there before philosophy begins, because philosophy is just a description, as it is found by science and experience, of the concrete and the individual. History is for Hegel the triumphal march of the Spirit; therefore, it is the autobiography of God. For Marx history is not a cause, it is an effect of a cause called man, real and individual. With Engels, we agree that Marx's starting point was Aristotelian.

In this game of Marx's undoing what Hegel had done, religion is the main culprit because it gives to all the Hegelian dreams a substance which is called god. Therefore, the individual will always be a slave as long as religion continues to muddle human relations.

The common goal of the "left wing" Hegelianism or the young Hegelians was the extermination of God. Marx was among the most active members; he admired his associates, but he was progressively disenchanted by them as soon as he discovered in them a residue of religious transcendence. Thus we witness a process of elimination: Strauss, Bauer, Ruge, Stirner are milestones in the molding of the young Marx. Each contributed to his ideal of man as individual, and each was

---

[28] *Nachlass,* p. 304.

[29] *Ibid.*

[30] Marx, *A Contribution to the Critique of Political Economy* (English tr., 1904), p. 293.

rejected as a compromiser in the struggle of man's independence from God.

David Friedrich Strauss tried to destroy the authenticity of the Gospels. He reduced them to the mythopoieic activity of the early Christian community: a myth which, according to Strauss, was justified by the human desire for immortality. Marx agreed with Strauss on this point, but when the conversation between them centered on the source of human knowledge and cultural activity, Marx grew restless because he could not explain how human thinking and social relations could originate and be explained from matter.

Particularly social relations! From the outset of his intellectual life Marx felt that something new had to be said about social relations. His mind struggled for years before he reached the solution of the problem in 1845, with the help and the cooperation of Engels.

Two other Young Hegelians, Bruno Bauer and Arnold Ruge, focused the problem with greater precision. Bruno Bauer defended the thesis that Jesus Christ never existed in history. If man's goal is honesty, he must be an atheist. But Bauer could not denounce Hegel's transcendental idealism. Marx in cooperation with Engels wrote the *Holy Family*, a book which is an aggressive challenge to the philosophy of Bauer. What prevents intelligent people — the team Marx-Engels insists in the *Holy Family* — from understanding that a speculative idealism, anxious to defend "self-consciousness" and eager to forget real human beings, is a montonous repetition of the error of the evangelists, "who taught that the spirit is life and the body is of no account."[31] Bauer tried to answer Marx's criticism by proclaiming his philosophy as a "true atheism." And Marx retorted with evident pleasure: atheism is a new form of religion. "The place of the Holy Ghost is taken by the infinite self-consciousness" but the error is always there, vague retrogressive theories when the world needs new dynamic actions.

Marx's cry in the desert was finally noticed by another Young Hegelian, Arnold Ruge. He thought that philosophy could not continue the discussion on transcendental values. Human society presents the real philosophical problem: the Hegelian thesis and antithesis became for Ruge a confrontation between "what society is" and "what society should be" regarding human relations. Marx was exultant: a great step was taken toward the vindication of the individual. Ruge's mind was far away from revolutionary ideas. He dreamed of reforms within the frame of a liberal democracy; therefore, the Marxian contention that the existence of the State and the existence of slavery were inseparable was

---

[31] *Holy Family*, introduction.

condemned heresy for Ruge; yet he destroyed Hegel's idolatry of the Absolute and Marx was thankful for that.

It might have occurred that Marx, in these formative years of his intellectual life, was more a listener than a leader: he studied, criticized, rejected, or accepted with reservation, but he did not have a system to defend. This period of listening continued with three other names: Max Stirner and Moses Hess are among the partial contributors of the intellectual patrimony of the young Marx, but they were not able to avoid the indictment to which their friends, mentioned above, succumbed. The third one, Ludwig Feuerbach, at last met all the requirements demanded by the rigidity of Marx's aspirations.

To proceed in order, Stirner was convinced that the traditional ethics, the pillar of the Christian Hegelian structure, had to be overthrown. God, Church, State are for Stirner formidable tools in the hands of the rich to exploit the poor. The ethical code must be revised; the Christian overstructures must be erased from society; above all, the Christian virtues of charity, resignation, purity are expressions of self-defeat and failure. Stirner's morality, built on the ruins of the Christian ethics, is based on Hobbes's *homo homini lupus* ("man is a wolf to his fellowman"). Morality is the exercise or, better, imposition of a right. Therefore action begets freedom; the immoral man is the man who indulges in idle contemplation. The hero is the superactive man: his power conquers and subjugates. He builds his Ego.

Marx grew suspicious of this Ego (with a capital letter). Did it conceal the usual German mania for a structure imposed on the individual at the expense of the individual? This suspicion caused one of the most violent clashes of personalities between Marx and Stirner. And Marx as usual was lavish in sarcasm for this philosopher who talked about the individual with the same tender phraseology which the medieval monks used to sweeten the minds of their Christians. Again Stirner is condemned on one count: sterile repetition of Christian ideas caused by mental insufficiency in understanding the rights of the individual in a modern society.

Moses Hess, the "communist rabbi," as he was nicknamed by his friends, was a Jew who renounced his faith, married a woman of easy morality "to atone his sins." He was the founder of "The True Socialism," a club of restless intellectuals without an organized philosophy. These dreamers thought themselves capable of giving existence to a new utopian society without conflicts between man and man, between class and class. The whole problem was reduced with candor to the competition of two forces: egoism and love. Egoism reproduces slavery, feudalism, exploitation. The source of egoism is private ownership which attributes to one human being an arbitrary power over others. Real human love is therefore impossible without the destruction of private property. Economic reform is the answer to social tribulations. Man needs love because his nature was made to love. Marx considers this interpretation of human nature utopian. The hard fact is that human nature is never the same for Marx; it is always conditioned to change by different conditions of different societies. Hunger, slavery, exploitation change human nature: revolution is closer to human nature than any form of love. Marx considered Hess a theoretician who forgets that socialism is not "a doctrine but a Movement. It starts not from principles but from facts."[32] Worst of all, Hess in his interest for theoretical definitions became a victim of disguised reactionaries who, in the words of Marx, "waved the beggar's wallet in their hand as a flag in order to get the people behind them. But as often as this took place, the people caught sight of the old feudal coat of arms upon their behinds and dispersed with loud and scornful laughter."[33]

During these years of fervent polemics and academic arguing, Karl Marx grew progressively closer and finally accepted without reservation the philosophy of Ludwig Feuerbach. This process of intellectual identification with Feuerbach began in 1841 and ended with the writing of the succinct but very important Theses on Feuerbach in 1845. It must be said that Marx in those years accepted Feuerbach with enthusiasm; he wrote in the Holy Family: "Who has unveiled the mystery of the [Hegelian] system? Feuerbach. Who has destroyed the dialectic of the Idea, this war among the gods known only to the philosophers? Feuerbach. Who has defended not 'the idea of man' (as if man could have other meanings besides that of being man) but man himself while old philosophies dreamed of abstract ideology, i.e., the Hegelian philosophy? Feuerbach, only Feuerbach."[34]

Feuerbach called himself the apostle of "real humanism," because his philosophy turned the Hegelian system upside down. "Philosophy's task is not to recognize the infinite as finite, but to recognize the finite as nonfinite, as infinite." Hegel was essentially a theologian because his interest is the infinite. Feuerbach, in his main work The Essence of Christianity, contends that theology is in its nature anthropology. What is the genesis of all religious experiences? Feuerbach answers: "Religion is the dream of the human mind. But our dreams do not force us to live our dream-existence in a vacuum or in heaven, but we always dream of earthly environment. In our dreams we see real things idealized

[32] Gesamtausgabe, I, 6, p. 294.
[33] Ibid., p. 546.
[34] The Essence of Christianity, Introduction.

by unconscious imagination and caprice instead of seeing them in the simple daylight as they actually are. Hence if religion is a dream I do nothing more to religion that to open its eyes. I change the object from what it is in the imagination to what it is in reality."[35]

Christian religion is the classical example siezed upon by Feuerbach. For the Christian God is love because love is the supreme human aspiration. Christ, human and divine, is for Feuerbach a superb projection of our human longing for eternity. Mercy and justice, forgiveness and power: all these are human ideals hypostatized in the personal God of the Christians. God is the anthropological projection of what we want to be and we are not. "Religion is consciousness of infinity, therefore, it is not the consciousness that man has of his limitations but of the infinity of his being."[36]

Homo homini deus! "Man is god to himself." Feuerbach is against all previous forms of materialism because they cannot explain human thought; he is against rationalism which does not explain human love and human emotions; he is against atheism because it denies the divinity of man; he is against theism because it gives existence to a nonexisting God. Feuerbach is the theologian of the divinity of man. With these considerations in mind we understand why he liked to call his philosophy "humanism."

II. *Marx's Original Contribution to Philosophy*

Karl Marx was not a philosopher. His ideas belong more to economy, to sociology, and to the arena of practical politics. Yet he came from a Germany that was filled with Hegelian ideas, he studied philosophy, and the background of his social theories was of solid philosophical origin. Our interest here is limited to the philosophical aspect of Marx's thinking.

The philosophy of Feuerbach brought Karl Marx to his own independent philosophy. Feuerbach was a metaphysician. He spoke of man from a contemplative and theoretical point of view. He ignored the practical and active value of human nature, which, according to Marx, finds realization in the social, economic relations of men. Feuerbach was the philosopher of an old materialism, contemplative and theoretical. Marx wants to be the founder of a new materialism, historical and practical. The last thesis, the eleventh, of the important work *Theses on Feuerbach* states: "Philosophers have only interpreted the world differently: the point is, however, to change it." This eleventh thesis

---

[35] *Ibid.*, ch. 1.
[36] *Ibid.*

announces better than any other statement the philosophy of Marx.

The transformation of man is possible only if the old essence of man, with his interior spiritual values (the main concern of the traditional philosophy), is forgotten. In his place a new man is taken into consideration, a man who acquires dignity and value *from his social relations with his fellowmen.* This point must be clear: man's reality *is* his social, economic existence. In other words, the main factor of this new man is to be found in his relations of work with his co-workers. This human fellowship, based solidly on the economic structure of society, is the only source of morality and human welfare.[37] The final result is that man does not determine his own social status, but man's social status determines his nature and the conscience.[38]

These ideas, of course, are far reaching: the Christian concept of man as a substance is denied and condemned. The human person, fulcrum of such rich philosophical insights for centuries, is reduced to extrinsic relations with other men. Marx claims that Hegelianism itself is a confused economic interpretation of history, and that he brought clarity and order to it. He refuses the old materialism of D'Holbach and La Mettrie: for them man was a composite of matter; for Marx man is the source of dialectical materialism.

We come now to the second and, philosophically speaking, the least generative and original idea of Marx's philosophy: the application of the Hegelian concept of dialectic to his new conception of man. Dialectic is as old as mankind. A dialectical situation exists wherever a relation of opposition exists from which an interaction between the opposite terms produces something qualitatively new. Aristotle confined dialectic to the realm of thought. He says that "to know is to become other as other," a most magnificent and profound analysis of human thinking. Hegel extended the dialectical process to the whole of reality. He used the triadic phases (thesis, antithesis, and synthesis), but the triadic phases are not essential to dialectic. Marx is not interested in the Hegelian dialectic which is metaphysical, unlimited, embracing the whole active totality. The Marxian totality is limited to society. His goal is to identify this historical datum which is human society (historical materialism) with the dynamics of dialectic (dialectical materialism). It is of importance to know that the first formulation of this original doctrine is found in the *Philosophical Economical Manuscript,* written by Marx in 1844, one year before the *Theses on Feuerbach.*[39]

---

[37] Marx, *Critique of Political Economy,* passim.

[38] *Ibid.,* passim.

[39] The original title is: *"Ökonomisch-philosophische Manuskripte aus dem Jahre 1844,"* published in *Historisch-Kritische Gesamtausgabe,* erste Abteilung, Vol. III, pp. 33–172.

In this work, which has recently focused the interest of many critics, Marx delineates with confident agility the errors of Hegel's dialectic and the unsatisfactory conclusions of Feuerbach's humanism. Marx rejects both of them and suggests that *both Hegel and Feuerbach taken together* offered him some necessary elements for his dialectical materialism. Marx agrees with Hegel that human nature is *"naturwesen,"* i.e., nature in action, projected toward its needs and aspirations to be fulfilled by achieving social economical goals.

Do not ask Marx for a proof of his statement. Too many after him questioned as wholly unjustifiable this identification of human nature (historical materialism) with outside economic changes of society (dialectical materialism). Too many protested this strange marriage of the material reality, which moves and operates according to the rules and regulations of the spirit, with the fundamental tenet of Hegel.

This doctrine is axiomatic for Marx and therefore all explanations are useless and unnecessary. Without this axiom Marxism does not exist as a doctrine. This is so true that the old Marx, forty years afterward in January, 1863, when he was almost completely oblivious of theoretical thinking and absorbed in the struggle of political and social turmoils, wrote in the appendix of the second edition of *Das Kapital*: "My dialectic is wholly opposite to the Hegelian dialectic. Hegel thinks that the 'Idea' is the force governing the universe, which is just the phenomenal aspect of the Idea. I am convinced of the opposite. Thinking is just a reflexion of what is real, a reflexion operated by and depending upon the brains of each human being. But although Hegel misrepresents the meaning of dialectic and obscures it with mystical meaning, *it must be said that he was the first to expound the rules of dialectic.* In Hegel's writings dialectic walks on its head, upside down. We must put it again on its feet and we will immediately recognize its face."[40]

To turn Hegel's dialectic upside down was Marx's goal. He does it with the help of Feuerbach. Man, as he was conceived by Feuerbach, takes the place of Hegel's Idea. But this man is not, as in Feuerbach, static and unrelated to the laws of dialectic. Marx's man is *menschliches Naturwesen*, i.e., a human nature in the process of manifestation and development. Marx says, "The human objects are not just simple realities existing in nature, neither are they just human thinking. Both these elements are present, but not *adequately*. They *must become*, they must be historical, they must be dynamic factors of their own mutual activity." Marx repeats that the real man is not the man of today but the man of tomorrow; history does not belong to *now*, but to *after*:

---

[40] *Das Kapital* (second ed., 1863), appendix.

"The nature of history is to overcome itself."[41] Marx transferred to man the creativity which Hegel had transferred from the Christian God to the transcendental Spirit. This creativity for Marx is production, basically production of material goods manifesting themselves in many ways: family, religion, state legislation. "The whole so-called world-history is nothing else than the production of man through human labor, nothing else than the becoming of the nature of man."[42]

We should pause for a while and look back to Marx's ideas. He began, like Aristotle, to talk of the individual. He thought that Hegel's panlogism had been unfair to the individual man. But then in his sharp analysis of Feuerbach's humanism, his impatience *to change* the world pushed him to identify man, a substantial unity, a *being,* with his social relation, which is an accidental *becoming* of man. In other words, Marx accepted Hegelian historicism against which he preached his whole life and applied it to the meaning of man, emptying him of his metaphysical structure. Once that was done, he continued to speak of man without knowing that man was not there any longer because he had destroyed him. We quoted his words from the *Holy Family*: "The Phenomenology [of Hegel] ends by putting in place of all human existences absolute knowledge." Now, paraphrasing, we are entitled to say of Marx: his philosophy ends by putting in place of the substance of man, man's own relation with other men, or, which is the same, by applying the laws of Hegelian becoming to the very nature of the individual.

This is the tragedy of Marx's philosophy; unlike Kierkegaard, who began with the historical man to discover his metaphysical values, Marx began with history and ended by forcing human nature to be a historical factor.

III. *Communism*

If the human person means essentially a relation of work and production in the family of mankind, it follows that the human person is totally dependent on *the structure* of this family of men. History is there to prove for Marx the existence of a tragic injustice, because history reveals that the produced objective world (capital) is hostile to man the producer. This *alienation,* as Marx calls it, this unbelievable hostility between the results of the worker's labor and the worker himself, is the crime perpetuated through the centuries against the worker, who is the only source of wealth. Money personifies this alienation, labor

---

[41] Marx-Engels, *Gesamtausgabe* (Frankfurt, 1927), p. 162.
[42] *Ibid.*

stolen from the worker. Money is the new greedy divine power that makes man a stranger and a slave to himself. Feuerbach had revealed that the Christian God was a deceitful, externalized projection of self-worshiping man. Marx now says that in the same fashion the activity of the worker is not his self-activity. It belongs to another; it is the loss of himself; it is alienated. Money has taken, according to Marx, the same despotic role that the idea of God had usurped during the Middle Ages. Look, Marx cries out to the worker, look at the splendid cathedrals of the Gothic and Romanesque times. Those superb conceptions of magnificent architecture, longing toward an infinite God hidden above the clouds, are shameful witnesses of generations of workers forced to slave inhumanly in a world of degradation and indigence. In the same way, when you see the policies in which aristocracy rots under the burden of money piled up by the laborer's sweat, you must remember the worker who earned that money and from whom that money was stolen. There is no other historical explanation for the horrible phenomenon of capitalism. Capital is not possible without a theft at its beginning. Money makes money because a theft is added to other thefts. Proudhon was right: if you own something, you have stolen it.

To right all these wrongs, a communist world revolution is inevitable. "For transcending a real private property, a real communist movement is required. History will bring this, and the movement, which we have already grasped in thought as a self-transcending one, will work its way in reality through a very long and hard process."[43]

The theme of irresistible movement of the historical process is borrowed from *The Phenomenology* of Hegel, and it becomes the backbone of Marx's communism. Marx does not speak, as did Hegel, of transcendental becoming of the absolute Idea. We know that Marx had little respect for these theoretical elaborations. But he does speak of man in his phases of self-externalization, alienation, and transcendence of alienation. History is, therefore, for Marx, the battlefield on which man is laboriously finding himself.

Man first of all externalizes himself. Man works, the products of his work are expropriated from him by the capitalist. The exploiter grows richer, more powerful, and more demanding. Progressively the chains of human bondage and misery are tied around the neck of the worker with an increasing abundance of laws and punishments. Slavery is against the nature of man. It breeds shame and rebellion. It is natural, therefore, that alienation originates consciousness, and consciousness brings about

[43] Karl Marx, *Historisch-Kristische Gesamtausgabe,* erste Abteilung, Vol. III, p. 134.

for man the need for revindicating his freedom or, as Marx calls it, reappropriating his freedom. The hostile capitalist is the obstacle. Reappropriation must, therefore, be violent by nature. It must be a revolution. The right to revolt is given to the worker by his own work, stolen and exploited. He must fight for the defense of his own rights: he is entitled to have back the product of his own labor.

Though alienation is a concept completely Marxian and opposite to Hegel, insofar as it implies a regression, it seems clear that Marx's ideas are Hegelian. Hegel's design of the transcendental spirit appropriating the universe by the laws of thinking was a disguised rendition of the proletarian act of the world appropriation. Hegel's difficulty in respecting the autonomous individuality of the free human person was reflected in the Marxian paradox of attempting to save the dignity of man by reducing him to a natural aspect of an evolving economy. It is of great interest to notice that Marx stated categorically[44] that national economy, as it exists now in Russia, is a gimmick hiding the slave status of alienation of the worker because it neglects the immediate relationship between the worker and the production.

The conquest of alienation is equal to the realization of true communism. But this conquest is never accomplished. It consists in an unending process of self-change, setting the scene for a subsequent self-change. The struggle against greed and capitalism is, therefore, infinite in duration as it is susceptible of greater perfection in depth.

Marx's main concern was *man*, the individual man. He understood man phenomenologically and historically more than metaphysically, on account of his Hegelian presuppositions, but it must be emphasized that Marx meant to understand man.

With this premise in mind, the reader will agree that great injustice is done to Marx by many commentators and writers of manuals, who reduce his thought to an abstract and often unclear parallelism between Marx's "dialectical and historical materialism." This confusion arose with the massive propaganda of the twentieth-century communists for whom the real Marx is the man who authored the works written after 1844, while the previous Marx up to and including the manuscript of 1844 was just an amateur philosopher of no practical value.

Is there a gap in the development of Marx thought? And, if there is this gap, could we establish a continuity of thinking between the two phases or do we have to recognize an abrupt interruption and turnabout of Marx' mind?

"There is an apparent gulf between the philosophical communism

---

[44] K. Marx, *Ökonomisch-philosophische Manuskripte,* p. 84, published in Marx-Engels: *Gesamtausgabe,* erste Abteilung, Berlin, 1932.

of Marx' manuscripts of 1844 or original Marxism as I have called it, and 'scientific socialism' as Marx and Engels expounded it in the *Communist Manifesto* of 1848 and other later writings."[45]

The first Marxism, as we expounded it in the previous pages, is the Marxism that aims to understand man. The second Marxism is depersonalized; it concerns itself with society, with the dictatorship of the proletariat; it becomes a discussion of economics. This explains the enthusiasm of all the communists for it and their eagerness to discuss the original Marx as a student of theoretical philosophy.

The key to the answer lies in the fact that the second Marx is meaningless without Hegelian dialectic, which, as we saw, runs through the first Marx too. Therefore, the two phases are not in opposition but are rather two moments of the same continuity of thought. The famous preface of the 1863 edition of *Das Kapital*, already quoted on these pages, reads in part: "In Hegel's writings dialectic walks on its head, upside down. We must put is again on its feet and we will immediately recognize its face."

"The transition to the seemingly 'dehumanized' mature Marxism actually occurred at that point of the manuscript of 1844 where Marx decided, uncertainly but irrevocably, that man's self-alienation could and should be grasped as a social relation 'of man to man.' Only man himself can be this alien power over man, he said, but this relation of man to himself takes practical shape as a relation between the alienated worker and another man outside him, i.e., the Capitalist. In this way the inner conflict of alienated man with himself became, in Marx's mind, a social conflict between 'labor' and 'capital,' and the alienated species-self became the class-divided society. *Self-alienation was projected as a social phenomenon, and Marx's psychological original system turned into his apparently sociological mature one.*"[46]

Sociological questions are usually treated after sufficient data are gathered from society; they are, in other words, empirical questions demanding an inductive solution. This was not the case for Marx. He did not discuss the laws of Hegelian historicism; he accepted them and applied them to history, with a hybrid copulation of Hegel's dialectic with his new one, "turned upside down and standing on its feet."

After the manuscript of 1844, Marx and Engels were busy developing their new conception of history and making it work with the masses. *The German Ideology*, 1845-1846, compiled by both, aimed to prove

---

[45] Robert Tucker, *Philosophy and Myth in Karl Marx* (Cambridge University Press, 1961), p. 165. Tucker discusses this problem with clarity and effectiveness. Cf. Chapter XI: "Two Marxisms or One?"

[46] R. Tucker, *op. cit.*, p. 175. Emphasis ours.

that human history does not start from heaven to descend on earth (Hegel), but it starts from earth to carry man up high as the King of the heavens.

They became progressively involved in economics and political activity. It is not our present interest to follow them further along their way. For an understanding of the tremendous influence of Marx's philosophy in our twentieth century, the student of philosophy needs to remember his main concern for the individual, whom he failed to understand as a metaphysical substance, reducing him to his phenomenological social aspects, and his dogmatic axiom that human history must obey the Hegelian laws of dialectic.

3. NIETZSCHE

Friedrich Wilhelm Nietzsche was born October 15, 1844, in Röcken, a lonely town between Prussia and Saxony. His father Karl loved the solitude of Röcken. He was a Lutheran pastor and an enthusiastic musician. The soul of the boy, still too young to reason, was filled every evening with melodies from the organ of the little church where his father used to spend long hours in religious and artistic dedication.

But too soon tragedy disturbed the peace of the family. The father fell, injuring his head, and died in 1849 after one year of insanity. The young Freidrich remained under the severe discipline of the mother and the influence of his sister Elizabeth, a gifted girl with an unusual sense of spirituality. He thought of becoming a minister like his father "to live close to God." Poetry, music, drama were the occupations of Friedrich in his first years of grammar school. When he was thirteen, he thought he understood that God was responsible for the evils of the world. At fourteen he won a scholarship in the famous school of Pforta, where he gained solid grounding in Greek and Latin literature. His intellectual interest broadened with his avidity for learning almost everything: astronomy, botany, ballistic physics, military strategy, among other studies, occupied the mind of the young student. At seventeen, Nietzsche, reader of Byron, Hölderlin, and Schiller, experienced the bitterness of Byron's Manfred. We read from his notes of those days the following: "What is humanity? We hardly know it: perhaps an instant of the eternal becoming, or a capricious product of God who knows the springs moving this enormous watch?"

In 1862 Nietzsche was a student at the University of Bonn. It seemed to be a parenthesis of gaiety and self-oblivion. Philosophical discussions, parties with a stress on beer-drinking competitions, choirs, and, of course, a duel (mandatory for every self-respecting student) were among his occupations. He even became engaged in a student association which he aimed to reform according to his ideas. But he was ousted for incompatibility of character. He entered the University of Leipzig in 1865, where his teacher was Frederich Ritschl, his mentor and advisor for classical philosophy. In Leipzig the first in a series of earthquakes came for Neitzsche: he read Schopenhauer's *The World as Will and Presentation.* For Neitzsche the book was a thunderbolt: perhaps Schopenhauer was right, perhaps we are attempting the impossible against the gigantic irrationality of being. For fourteen days Nietzsche could sleep only for short intervals between two and four o'clock in the morning. Ritschl cared for him with paternal concern and obtained a full professorship for him in the department of classical philology at the Swiss University of Basel in 1869. Nietzsche's friendship with Wagner, the master of infinite pathos, calmed the Schopenhauerian invitation to tragedy and despair. Richard and Cosima Wagner became his closest friends; their villa in Triebschen, on the lake of the Four Swiss Cantons, was his second home. This is the Wagnerian moment of Nietzsche.

During the winter of 1870, Nietzsche presented his ideas in two lectures on Greek tragedy. He had been in the German army that brought France the humiliation that Bismarck dreamed of. Finally on December 31, 1871, *The Birth of Tragedy from the Spirit of Music* was published. Wagner welcomed it with words too enthusiastic to be believed. Everyone else, including Ritschl and Burckhardt, ignored the book. And Nietzsche felt this silence with the furious emotional turmoil of a mother whose child is neglected. He became sick, suffering insomnia, nightmares, and long periods of depression. But his work was there, a new attempt at rebellion — a defense of the individual against Hegel, against the German and European society, and against the world. He was therefore in line with Marx and Kierkegaard as far as the common goal of all is concerned, but his means were altogether different. Nietzsche's means for individual freedom is art, tragic art, and Dionysius is his god.

I. *The Birth of Tragedy*

The Greek tragedy was born from the conflict of two ideals, represented by Apollo and Dionysus. Apollo was the deity of perfect harmony, of sublime synthesis; he was the dream of classic perfection in the plastic arts. There is wisdom in Apollo and peace, too, found in the ecstasy of the aesthetic contemplation. Maia's veil protects the artist, as Schopenhauer sees him, from the restlessness of unattainable goals. Dionysus was at the opposite extreme. His dancers are shaken by the rhythm of an infuriating and spasmodic music. The climax is convulsive identification of man with nature. Dionysus (or Bacchus) is the god of intoxication. His carriage is submerged in an ocean of flowers; thousands of panthers and lions, caught in a momentous instant of the universal rhythm, dance in unison. Millions of slaves are awakened by the miracle of the ecstasy. Man dances: he moves his body with a joy never experienced before. He has reached his freedom. He knows that he is good. Art and music have performed the miracle. History becomes a pure work of art.

Apollo and Dionysus are the thesis and antithesis of a new synthesis. The epic and plastic artist strives to create beautiful images. For him melody generates poetry, and poetry is an attempt to imitate music. The poet, through allegories and images, tends to a sublime expression of himself. His tension is a work of the will, understood in a Schopenhauerian way, to reach freedom. But absolute freedom, which is denied to Apollo, is possible only to Dionysus. The chorus of the Greek tragedy reveals the profound nature of art: it does not represent literature in the mode of Apollo, but rather the destruction of the individual and his identification with the original mystery of existence. The chorus is the voice of the crowd recalled by the Dionysiac demon: it creates vision; it shares the suffering of nature and gives a wisdom that springs from the artistic perception of existence as a coherent *unity;* it reacts against the dispersion of values brought about by reason.

Indeed, according to Nietzsche, we discover a strange similarity between Socratism, which sapped the strength of ancient Greece, and the corrosive force of Bismarck in Germany. Euripides, scornful of Dionysus, was abandoned by Apollo whom he worshiped. Thus Euripides found himself holding in his hands the slaughtered myth of tragedy, and he was forced against his own inspiration to indulge in the tedious and cold processes of reasoning. Socrates took the place of Dionysus. Action was halted by the man of Logos, who believed in reason. The same sad phenomenon, Nietzsche continued, was present in his times. Europe was infected by a phenomenon of decadence resulting in material prosperity and technological progress. Hence a false feeling of optimism invaded the minds of everybody from Kant to Goethe. Society became static, with a lost sense of unity and a forgotten sense of the dignity of the individual.

In this first phase of his intellectual pilgrimage, Nietzsche came to one conclusion: man must go back to the tragic meaning of life. He must understand with Schopenhauer (who at the time was his source of

inspiration) that music is the language of will power, a force of generation. Myth is the offspring of music and with myth the individual becomes nature and nature is life. Life, understood as a painful process
of generation, is suffering in which man finds his tragic joy in creation.
He finds himself.

Such was the first breathless phase of Nietzsche's intellectual activity.

Back to Basel after the war, still weak in body, Nietzsche plunged
into an intense work of meditation, under the inspiration of Montaigne,
who took the place of Schopenhauer. *The Untimely Considerations* was
published in 1874, a work which aimed to illustrate the *Birth of Tragedy*.
The Dionysiac furor has subsided. Cutting irony and dialectical subtlety
were now in order. The spirit of Montaigne is dominant.

David Strauss was the target of the first consideration. Strauss, the
author of *Von alten und neuen Glauben,* was the typical "culture
philistine." Without faith, without passion, and without originality,
Strauss embodied the perfect ideal of the useless intellectual, well
established with his complacent vision of history, unchallenged and
unaware that history is tragedy and drama rather than science and
understanding.

History for Nietzsche is a challenge for excellence, for aristocracy of
the spirit, which is always dissatisfied with present achievements and
always aiming for higher goals. History is not looking *back* into the past,
but looking *forward* to the future. An *unhistorical* element dominates
history. Therefore, one must forget the past so that something new will
be achieved, something which will be *superhistorical* and represent
progress.

We have the feeling here of a repetition of Hegelian terms and ideas.
And indeed the general atmosphere in which Nietzsche operates is
romantic and Hegelian. But the intentions and the final goals are
thoroughly new. History is useless if it does not produce the individual
"genius"; it must not interest itself in "the betterment of the majority,
who, taken as individuals, are the most worthless types." The individual
genius who *creates* his own morality and does not depend on higher
beings owns history. The shadow of the overman begins to take shape.
This genius has one destiny: to become himself. His freedom is absolute, all laws are beneath and obedient to him. He is the artist around
whom other human beings, like ants, continue their work of mediocrity,
unconscious of the meaning of life and history. Schopenhauer is an
example of a genius — Schopenhauer, not as he lived in reality, but as
he is presented in the third *Untimely Consideration.* This Schopenhauer,
artist, philosopher, poet, and hero, is surrounded by philistines eager
to reach grandiose schemes through rationalization. He stands among

them as the prophet of irrationality. He creates his own conscience, his own ethics, and his own history. He represents everything which Nietzsche worked for.

The most laudatory of these *Considerations* is the last one called "Richard Wagner in Beyreuth." Wagner is the new Siegfried, who is now inspired with the ardor of Dionysus.

But Nietzsche was pretending. His exaggerated enthusiasm for Wagner concealed clear reservations. Nietzsche had come to know that Wagner was half Jew, a hardly acceptable qualification for his conception of the German Siegfried. Perhaps Nietzsche resented Wagner's patronage of him with its overtones of paternalism and protection. Finally in 1876, during the Wagnerian celebrations in Beyreuth, Nietzsche's rebellion against Wagner came into the open. Wagner appeared to Nietzsche as a lamb disguised as a wolf. Wagner's romantic inspiration revealed weakness and decadence. His *Parsifal* was an exaltation of Christianity, of fleshless love, of mankind redeemed by "a fool dying on the Cross."

In *The Case Against Wagner,* written in 1888, we read the famous words: "Richard Wagner is a decrepit and desperate romantic, collapsed suddenly before the Holy Cross. . . . And yet I was one of the most corrupt Wagnerians. . . . I am the child of this age, just like Wagner, that is to say a decadent. But I am conscious of it, I defended myself against it."[47]

His confession "I was a decadent" cannot be neglected. Nietzsche, sick in body and feverish in mind, fought against the cruel reality of his life with all his energies. He was born to be a romantic and he hated romanticism. He longed for love and understanding and he was blocked, psychologically, from talking to any woman. He needed protection and he hated God. And he became a classical case for psychoanalysis in all schools of psychiatry. But it cannot be denied that mankind will never be the same, because of this man, torn between Dionysus and Apollo. His experience revealed how thoroughly problematic and existential the nature of man is.

II. *Zarathustra*

Nietzsche, we saw, ignores and denies all human limitations. Therefore he is romantic in his intent to divinize human existence and make it infinite. Yet Nietzsche rejected the philosophical romanticism of Schopenhauer and the artistic romanticism of Wagner. They aimed to reach peace and mediocrity. Their romanticism was impoverished and feeble. Dionysius' romanticism is limitless, he finds happiness in the

---

[47] Nietzsche, *The Case Against Wagner*, p. 46.

luxury of destructions and wars; he creates life and fertility where hitherto death and sterility dominated. But huge obstacles were in the way of this divinization of man. First of all, the Christian God. Nietzsche set out to kill God. This fantastic endeavor is found in the important work *Thus Spake Zarathustra.* But it is prepared, progressively, by an epic and lyrical triad: *Human-all-too-human* (1876), *The Dawn* (1881), and *Joyful Wisdom* (1882).

The theme of *Human-all-too-human* develops a refined cynicism toward all forms of human civilization. All have missed the meaning of the actual and real to run in circles after imaginary values. It is the first hint of the famous doctrine of the *circularity of human thinking* which Nietzsche will later develop as a central theme. Metaphysics, he says, was an offspring of blind belief, but for centuries man considered it the solid backbone of his existence. Religion is a wishful projection of human hopes; the Christian religion, especially, is a diabolic, man-made structure that exploits people. Religion must disappear with its hell and its fears if the "Paradise" of nature is to triumph.

The pace of Nietzsche's life was frenetic, and in 1879 he broke down physically and mentally; death seemed imminent. He arranged for his funeral, telling his sister that only his friends should be allowed to stand about his coffin — no priest, no prayer. He wanted to be buried as an "honest pagan." But he recovered and accepted life with renewed enthusiasm. Even a woman entered his world, a sophisticated and disdainful woman by the name of Lou Salomé, who rejected Nietzsche, without knowing of the ardor and turmoil of his love for her. He became a traveler: Venice, Sorrento, Sils-Maria in the Upper Engadine, Sicily, Nice, Turin were visited.

The two works, *The Dawn* and *Joyful Wisdom,* reflect the confidence of the convalescent Nietzsche; they are more positive, almost philosophical in discussing themes filled with impetuous disdain for the traditional Christian civilization of Europe. One section of the 575 aphorisms which comprise *The Dawn* analyzed with anatomical exactitude the origin of morality. For Nietzsche morality is obedience to tradition, and tradition is based on authority that dares to inflict punishments and dares to declare a clear-cut distinction between good and evil. But who gave authority to tradition? Nietzsche cries out that morality is for fools and that human nature is beyond morality, which is an instrument of power and slavery. All the Christian values are derided: purity, charity, obedience; and so too are their acolytes: philosophers, priests, and saints. All of them are in bad faith because the origin of their authority is identical with futility.

Joyful Wisdom insists on the theme that the present need not measure up to criteria of the past; on the contrary, it must tend toward the future. The essence of man is the necessity for conquest; therefore, man is a dynamic problematic: the old categories of good and evil, honesty and dishonesty do not really count; they are merely the means to an end. The end is conquest: a man must be continuously a conqueror. Thus cruelty against the old and the dying is not evil; poetry and logic are tools of necessity, which itself is beyond logic; life itself is necessity; and life is always living and changing; it is not illogical, but only unrelated to logic. In *Joyful Wisdom* Hegelian principles were quite evidently carried by this self-professed anti-Hegelian to their most radical conclusion.

Both *The Dawn* and *Joyful Wisdom* were forerunners of Nietzsche's major work, *Thus Spake Zarathustra*.[48]

Nietzsche, vacationing in the Upper Engadine, while taking a walk around Silvaplane Lake, "six thousand feet high, but much higher in regard of all human things," understood intuitively the fundamental conception of his work and, we can say, of his whole philosophical thinking. We mean to speak of the eternal return of history, of the circularity of history. It is an instantaneous awareness that man, the real man, is identical with history; therefore, nothing exists that is superior to him. We know that Kierkegaard too spoke of this "instantaneous awareness," but the Danish theologian understood that this most precious moment is the instant in which man discovers from despair his metaphysical value as an existent spiritual individual, limited and longing for the helping hand of a personal God.

For Nietzsche the opposite is true: man is history, the forger of his morality and destiny. Nietzsche does not discover his own individual existence, he does not make the transition from history to metaphysics, he does not speak the language of realism, but of Hegelian historicism.

The prototype human specimen has a famous name: Zarathustra. Aged thirty, he abandoned his town, the little house by the lake, to ascend the mountain, in spiritual retreat. After ten years of meditation, he experienced the intuitive joy of his identity with history, a real awareness of the cosmic meaning of his existence. Now he must face the world and

---

[48] *Thus Spake Zarathustra* was written by Nietzsche at different times and in various places "when the demon of inspiration" invaded him. The first part was the result of ten days of spiritual conflict and tension when Nietzsche was in Rapallo in January of 1883; the last pages were added in Venice in February of the same year, perhaps as a last bitter reaction to Wagner, who died in the same city on February 13, 1883. The second part was written at Sils-Maria, Engadine, in July, 1883. During the winter of 1884, in Nice, Nietzsche wrote the third part. At Menton, February, 1885, the fourth part was finished. Nietzsche could not find a publisher for his work. Naumann of Leipzig published it in 1892 when Nietzsche was completely taken by insanity.

preach his new gospel to the populous cities. On his way, he meets an old hermit who speaks to him of God and mercy. Zarathustra is shocked: Is it possible that the old man does not know that God is dead? His success is more encouraging when he stands in the large square, surrounded by the crowds, and announces the new era of the last man. "Let us have the last man," they were shouting with laughter and mockery. He was pleading with them in dithyrambic cadence: "My brethren, remain true to the earth, and do not believe those who speak of super-earthly hopes. . . . They are poisoners. . . . Once blasphemy against God was the greatest blasphemy, but God died. . . . To blaspheme the earth is now the dreadfulest sin."[49]

And then he tried to convince them with symbols (the camel, the lion, the child), with derisive remarks about the virtuous life, with irony for the Christian's "love your neighbors" — an ill-concealed form of "love your own self."

Zarathustra goes from failure to failure: his very disciples are reluctant believers. Superior men, those who are images of the ideas of Zarathustra, do not need him because they feel superior to him.

Finally, after a moment of anxiety, he goes back to the mountain, where he again realizes the ineluctability of his mission. He goes back to the crowds to teach them that man is the bridge between present and future. The old values must give way. The spiritual brethren of Zarathustra will suffer in all countries because the act of creation is always an act of sacrifice. But overman is in the making and his making constitutes his existence.

Image follows image and symbol follows symbol in a style that is always close to hallucination and often incomprehensible. *Zarathustra* became the gospel of Nietzsche; his later books were commentaries, often more lucid and logical, of the faith of the new prophet. In *Beyond Good and Evil* (1885–1886) and in *Genealogy of Morals* (1887), the spirit of Zarathustra confronts the great minds of Western civilization.

Plato is the first target. He is found guilty of creating the "good in itself," the blind belief of all metaphysics. Spinoza and Kant are the "clowns" who spoke of absolute values. They failed to see life as it is: instinct, will, energy, and especially the will for power. But the abomination came with Christ, who preached sacrifice, which is an insult and mutilation of one's self.

Of course, once God is denied, the whole structure of absolute morality is overturned. For Nietzsche moral phenomena do not exist; there are only moral interpretations of phenomena. The basic Hegelian idea of sheer becoming does not allow absolute norms of morality. Morality

---

[49] *Thus Spake Zarathustra*, Prologue, 3.

is totally dependent on psychological interpretations of the different historical situations in which man acts.

History speaks of two prominent periods of morality: the *Herren-moral* (morality of the masters) was the Roman *virtus* (courage); the strong man seeks a challenging good. *Virtus* makes possible man's *ascent* of the mountain of military conquest and domination; it brings honor and makes man a spiritual aristocrat. Then came the *Heerden-moral* (the morality of obedience and consent). The Jews, a people born to be oppressed, were assigned by destiny to be the banner-bearers of this morality of abjection. Nietzsche could not stand the sound of their lamentations from one captivity to the next. Jesus is their spokesman: He preached penance, denial, obedience. He blessed those who mourn and suffer. His morality — Nietzsche exclaimed in anger — is "a monster of negations": it teaches assent to the opprobrium of slavery and submission to the master.

The pressure of the herd might sometimes provoke fear in the heart of the despot, who then yields his power. Modern democracy and the socialization of civil institutions are instances of this. But both are decadent Christian evolutions. Strangely enough, Nietzsche respected the person of Jesus, whom he considered, with Arius, an exceptional human being. But he saw in the Jewish Paul of Tarsus the mastermind who adulterated the meaning of Christ's life.

What Nietzsche did not see, because of his Hegelian frame of mind, is that Jesus Christ announced His good news with the evident philosophical presupposition that an impersonal mind is impossible. Jesus spoke to persons and He claimed to be a person. Nietzsche postulated what James Collins incisively called a "fieristic monism,"[50] a unity self-enclosed and becoming in which persons cannot maintain their individual unity. Again, the Aristotle-Hegel confrontation comes out in the open: does being originate from becoming or does becoming originate from being? If man is not in possession of his immortal individuality because he shares the monistic individuality of the self-becoming unity of the universe, we understand Nietzsche's obstacles in accepting the redeeming power of suffering, the sanctifying acceptance of physical death. Also we understand the other suggestions that the *Genealogy of Morals* propounds: for instance, that *cruelty* is a necessary foundation of human civilization; that *remorse* of conscience and *sin* are degenerations of warrior's instincts; that *asceticism* (always identified by Nietzsche with priestly celibacy) is a sign of dangerous morbidity. But what nobody will understand of Nietzsche is his un-

---

[50] James Collins, *History of Modern European Philosophy* (Milwaukee: The Bruce Publishing Co., 1954), p. 786.

warranted, wholly unjustified and instinctive denial that God *is* God and man *is* man.

III. *The Overman*

After the *Genealogy of Morals,* a new phase ensued, polemic and para-doxical, in which Nietzsche proclaimed himself the *legislator* of the new code of morality for the overman. His sister, Elizabeth Förster Nietzsche, collected all the fragments developing the "will to power." She published them with a foreword in the edition of 1891 with precious information about the intentions of her brother. He aimed to create his *opus maius* but insanity struck suddenly, January 9, 1889. The fragments were written, aphoristically, with a feverish perseverance, from the summer of 1887 to 1888. Composed at the same span of time, and written as distractions in moments of relaxation, were the *Twilight of the Idols* and *The Case Against Wagner.*

After the completion of the *Twilight of the Idols,* Nietzsche reduced the gigantic dimensions of his planned *Will to Power* to four topics: the *Anti-Christ,* a criticism of Christianity; *The Free Spirit,* a criticism of traditional philosophy; *The Immoralist,* a criticism in which morality is considered nefarious ignorance; *Dionysus,* the eternal return of civilization.

The fragments remaining, though bearing the fatal signs of the incumbent insanity in their cryptic and often mysterious meaning, give us the chance to glimpse the final description of the superman.

The superman, or literally overman, is bound to act beyond good and evil. Therefore we are confronted here with the question of a new definition of the nature of life. Nietzsche gives the answer: "life is the will to power." The Nietzschean "will to power" is a vital progressive affirmation of itself. Vitalism in its different forms (Bergson, Spencer, Dilthey, Croce) will share this trait of unmistakable Hegelian origin. But Nietzsche's "will to power" is different from other vitalistic interpretations. On one side, it presupposes the absolute becoming of the universe, absolutely amoral and indifferent, beyond good and evil, or, as Nietzsche called it, thoroughly *innocent.* On the other side, insofar as it is becoming, the universe tends to extend its power toward the infinity of space and time. The result is a striving of each atom against each atom, of each unit of energy against each unit of energy. Therefore, *man is will to power to become overman.* If this meaning of the "will to power" is understood, the specific techniques for its attainment on the social level must flow from a "realistic" consideration of the history of man. Domination is the goal. History, on the contrary, is a sad testimony that the mediocre, the "herd man," imposes his authority on the "will-power man." Thus society is plagued by the eternal pathological sickness of decadence. The world is filled with weak persons. Richard Wagner and Victor Hugo are among them.

Just a shade superior to the weak are the immense gray majority of the indifferent mediocre. They do a good job in securing the perpetuity of the species. Each of them is qualified by Nietzsche as "a specialized idiot," prone to some technical skill, well fed, economically and spiritually saturated: a product of the industrialized society.

These are the dynamics of society: the weak and the mediocre are the raw material upon which the superman exercises his will to power. Decadence and regression are the springboard for the overman from which he begins his prophetic flight beyond good and evil.

Nietzsche evidently runs toward the ineffable in his titanic effort to reduce a superhuman value to human terms. Some of the words which appear frequently in his fragments on the superhuman being are: strength of willpower, autonomy, *Meilenstainmensch* (progressively widening the distances from other men), passionate, almost irrational, warrior born to command. Lichtenberg, a respectable critic of Nietzsche's ideas, calls the overman "the hero of altruism." The idea is adequate, but unfortunately "altruism" remains meaningless if you do not accept an "alter" on whose behalf your actions are posited.

It is more adequate to use Nietzsche's own words and synthesize the life of the overman as dominated by *amor fati:* an absolute dedication to the fatal necessity of his destiny, which does not deny the opposition between good and evil because it transcends it.

A final observation is necessary. Could it be that the overman, legislator of his own existence, falls within the category of pure subjective individualism? Nietzsche denied this danger. The *amor fati* ties his hero to the endless cycle of things as they are. The overman seals his destiny when he suddenly understands, through the intuition of his identity with the essence of all things, the eternity of his missions. Perhaps, Nietzsche suggested, if you listen to Bizet's *Carmen* and you are transformed and identified with the triumphant harmonies of his music, you might sense the meaning of the will to power and the destiny of the overman.

We have expounded a few aspects of the literary and philosophical soul of Nietzsche. And we cannot claim that we have understood him. Perhaps the recognition that he cannot be understood is essential to his understanding. In fact, the two main themes, the will to power of Zarathustra and the "circularity of history," cannot be fused. They lay down the premises of the permanent contradiction of Nietzsche's doctrine. Nietzsche knew of this contradiction, and he wanted it to be the background of his philosophy. For Nietzsche, who thought of man as the hero of the future, taught that the future of man will be equal to his past. You must notice Nietzsche's satisfaction (which places him with Kierkegaard) in challenging the authority of Hegel's idea of the necessary progress in history. Yet his approach to man was historical and Hegelian. Nietzsche accepted the fact that some metaphysical situations present an insoluble contradiction. He always spoke of "situations" seen as personal perspectives. His interest was not the problem of "being," but the attitude of man standing before being. Truth is *human* and in process, yet *too human* because always conditioned to the temporal categories of man.

The same contradictory situation is found in Nietzsche's conception of God. Nietzsche was born with an innate distaste for Christ; he did not understand His sacramental message. Yet his thought is a continuous dialectical confrontation with Christ, whom he respected as a man and without whom his writings would almost be without value. The anti-Christian dialectic of his atheism demanded the existence of Christian ideas as *true* values to fight against. Nietzsche himself stressed this fact, and he insisted on distinguishing between Christ and the theological formulation of Christ's doctrine in St. Paul's writings and in both the schools of theology and the organized churches.

In a word, Nietzsche worked spasmodically to emphasize the living contradiction of human existence. His overman is meant to be beyond human understanding. His thought — if philosophy is an honest search for an organized systematic doctrine — does not have value. In other times it would have been dismissed with sympathetic hilarity. But at the beginning of this century, when irrationality was preparing a prominent role for itself, Nietzsche became important, as we will see in the following chapters.

chapter II

The Problem of Historicism

INTRODUCTION

At the end of the nineteenth century, Nietzsche's proclamation that the world was once more infinite was simultaneously an act of faith in his romantic desires and a strong rejection of the scientific pretenses of positivism.

This infinity of the world assumed many aspects and brought into the philosopher's vocabulary a new term, "vitalism." From every corner, philosophers spoke of life (*vita*) as a supreme reality and a supreme value. Croce, for instance, explained life in idealistic terms; James spoke of life in a pragmatic way; Bergson identified life with intuition; and Husserl based his phenomenology on the interpretation of life.

This chapter, written as an introduction to the important philosophy of Karl Jaspers, discusses the historical interpretation of the meaning of life.

To avoid confusion, we must state from the outset that all philosophical movements at the beginning of our century originated, predominantly if not exclusively, as a vigorous protest against positivism. Positivism could not be condemned completely: the accuracy of research and the perfectibility of experimentation remained a precious inheritance from positivism in every field of empirical knowledge. But other positivistic goals, first of all, the application of the mechanical laws of physics to human values, were evidently wrong. History, for instance, suffered unbelievable distortions when forced to obey mechanical laws.

Positivistic historians concentrated on the careful and diligent analysis of facts, scientifically related in a mathematical sequence of cause and effect. If the historical sources were not scientifically precise, traditional philosophy and theology were of no help either. The psychological appraisal of an historical document was held in suspicion too. The historical fact was reduced to a mechanical phenomenon. The free will of man was either the result of concurrent forces of the environment or of his physiological makeup. It is well known that the magnificent variation of colors in the paintings of the Flemish and Venetian schools was attributed to the different degrees of dampness in the Low Countries and on the shores washed by the beautiful Adriatic Sea. Another typical example of this rigid positivistic rule is offered by the cool acceptance that Marx received in the official circles of German positivism. Marx, we know, considered art, literature, and religion as historical super-structures of economy. His economic dialectic contained a shade of human free will. Therefore, according to the positivists, Marxism was one of the last residues of the Hegelian dream and was invalid because of its flagrant disobedience to the rules of mechanics.

Great historians lived during this "intellectual age of terror" ruled by positivism. Their names are famous: Mommsen, Niebuhr, Burckhardt. But they were isles of free thinking in a sea of conformism. They were outstanding exceptions who continued the glorious traditions of romantic historicism. Burckhardt, for instance, faced the historical problem with an open mind, which was at the same time *humanistic* (because he understood the history of the past as *magistra vitae* for the formation of the present man) and *romantic* (because he conceived his contemporary civilization as a result of the previous one and a preparation for the following).

This was, as far as history was concerned, the general picture at the beginning of our century. It was a situation, we must admit, of checkmate, darkened with clouds revealing the presence of dangerous storms in the air.

1. THE KIERKEGAARDIAN AND NIETZSCHEAN RENAISSANCE

The storm broke, ironically enough, in Germany, the land of intellectual confrontations on the meaning of history. Hegel's historicism had, at the beginning of this century, better fortunes in almost all European countries than in Germany. The Germans, faithful to their traditional ambitions, could not look back to search a solution of the present from the past. Besides, their Teutonic extremism had made them prisoners of the new scientific spirit; looking back to either the Kantian or the romantic formulae was inconceivable.

Equally gone was the sort of patriotism that brought them marching to the Elysée of Paris in 1870: in those days national unification and Bismarck's exploitation of patriotic enthusiasm were successful pretenses for an exalted concept of the destiny of Germany. After 1870 confusion was predominant in Germany: the sudden attack on religion, carried on in the name of science during the era of *Kulturkampf,* added to the widespread discontent. A vacuum was created in the souls of the masses, a vacuum which bore the disquieting signs of a national crisis because general industrial progress and economic welfare were coupled with the lack of values, of faith and of national goals. History teaches that those are ominous signs forewarning the disintegration of civil values.

In this atmosphere of indecision and suspense, Søren Kierkegaard and Friedrich Nietzsche gained universal attention. It is difficult to explain this phenomenon adequately. Perhaps the explanation lies in the fact that both Nietzsche and Kierkegaard foresaw and suffered in their lives the agonizing crisis of Western civilization. They lived their lives as a paradox, and they hoped for a renascence from the paradox. This was undoubtedly one reason for the sudden blossoming of their ideas, published voluminously and avidly read by a large public. Both appeared to the minds of the Germans as heroes unbent by the luring seduction of easy myths, restlessly rebellious against the idea of middle-of-the-road, "happy medium" solutions, ready to go down to the bottom of the bourgeois evil hidden beyond a hypocritical faith in the achievements of reason and science. Above all, we dare to say that the fascination exercised by Kierkegaard and Nietzsche was due to their reluctance to "hook up" their philosophies with previous systems. Their famous paradoxes (for Kierkegaard, faith sprang from despair; for Nietzsche, destruction of all values was the only real value) happened to interpret the general feelings of revulsion against the hypocrisy of the nineteenth century. They were a powerful stimulus to the national conscience without bridling it with preconceived codes of thinking.

It is most interesting to notice that Kierkegaard and Nietzsche, hailed on different occasions with such epithets as prophets, poets, geniuses, or madmen, were always considered together as if they represented two aspects of the same thought.

Karl Jaspers, from the very beginning of his intellectual life, stressed the complementarity of their philosophies.[1] Indeed, common factors working through the progressive development of Kierkegaard and Nietzsche's philosophies are numerous. For instance, Jaspers liked to

---

[1] Cf. particularly the first of five lectures given by Jaspers at Gromingen (Holland) in the spring of 1935: *Vernunft und Existenz* (Gromingen: Wolters, 1935), translated by W. Earle, *Reason and the Existent,* (New York: Noonday Press, 1955), pp. 10–50.

describe them both as philosophers of solitude, ready to sacrifice all their existence in a fight against the mediocrity of their countrymen. Both Kierkegaard and Nietzsche confronted reason with the severest of all trials, the trial of existence. They saw man as a possibility more than a reality; they stressed the mystery of being more than its rationality.

Jaspers went further: this parallelism saw no obstacle in the fact that Kierkegaard conceived despair as a dialectical *moment* necessary to reach faith in God, while Nietzsche spoke of atheism as *the category* for man's freedom. For Jaspers, the Kierkegaardian moment of despair and rebellion against the platitudes of an "ordinary" living filled with torments because empty of God, and Nietzsche's fanatic proclamation that "God is dead" were two different aspects of the same state of mind.

We can hardly agree with Jasper's analysis. Nietzsche always remained a stranger to Kierkegaard's concept of despair (and consequently of his act of faith) because he always believed that man took the place of the "dead God." Jaspers understood an essential aspect of Nietzsche and Kierkegaard when he pointed out that they both stressed the value of an instantaneous awareness that woke them to the mystery of their existence. In that moment, man, in an instant of supreme reflection that is thoroughly atemporal and ineffable, becomes existent to himself.

But Kierkegaard conceived this instantaneous awareness as an awareness of deficiency of being, as a distance and a longing for the completeness of being, that is to say, for God. As a consequence, Kierkegaard tells himself, "I know now that I exist, but I exist as a *possibility*, I feel deep in my consciousness that the existent that I am has meaning only if I relate it to the existence of God."

On the opposite side, Nietzsche thought that the "instantaneous consciousness" gives man plenitude of being because the duration of time is lived by the consciousness which identifies itself with the continuity of life understood transcendentally. Nietzsche says: "The instant I reach consciousness of the meaning of my existence, I reach eternity. Then things flow in front of me in their circular perenity with the authentic nakedness of their being, finally stripped from the mendacious appearances that reason superimposed upon them."

In other words, Nietzsche spoke the Hegelian language with Hegelian concepts which he detested sincerely but from which he could not free himself. Kierkegaard, on the other hand, could not be satisfied with history alone. Therefore, *from history he made the transition to metaphysics.* He postulated the existence of a personal God, he proclaimed that not only are human manifestations limited, but man himself is contingent, longing for what is not contingent.

Nietzsche's key idea in his Dionysiac research was the presupposition that history held the answer to the whole meaning of life. Therefore, he fought with the energy of an infuriated giant against what he labeled the superstructures of true history, attacking them one by one: the rationalism of Socrates, Christ's ethics of resignation, the hypocrisy of the nineteenth-century philosophies. They were all, in his estimation, false incrustations, laid upon the true man as layers of sand blown by the wind upon the living traveler in the desert, prostrated by fatigue, waiting anxiously for his rescuers.

He, Nietzsche, meant to rescue man. And his tragedy consisted in his blindness to the truth that criticism does not perform the miracle of reaching the *authentic man* if man's metaphysical values are ignored. Thus, at the end, Nietzsche, short of breath, aware of his failure and too proud to accept it, began to envision a "future" man who will be just himself and will master history. Nietzsche called him the "overman," that is to say, the real product of historical progress.

How staggering the disaster can be if history takes the place of metaphysics!

There is no need for long enumerations of Nietzsche's contradictions. He was fond of the doctrine of the "circularity of history." How could his overman be reconciled with the eternal return of historical courses, which deny the progress of history and which defend a monstrous identity of human living periodically repeating itself?

Even more contradictory was the interpretation of Nietzsche's philosophy during his last ten years of insanity, when he could not defend himself, and after his death. He was regarded as an acolyte of vitalism, when he was actually concerned with the individual man. He was proclaimed a prophet of nihilism, with an evident confusion between his doctrine and his intentions. Historicism, of course, saw in Nietzsche a champion of the values of history, and existentialism, particularly the existentialism of Heidegger and Jaspers, used Nietzsche as a powerful antidote against the religious enthusiasm of Kierkegaard. Above all, Nietzsche's theories of the overman were meditated on by Adolf Hitler. He found the Germany of the 1920's, humiliated by the treaties of Versailles, an eager ground for vengeful Nietzschean ideas. The same theories were also assimilated by a less fanatic but equally dangerous man, Benito Mussolini. He did not understand that the Latin mind of the Italians could not adapt itself to the "heroic furors" of Nietzsche. Blindly, Mussolini tried to make overmen out of his countrymen, and he failed because he tried the impossible.

2. DILTHEY'S HISTORICISM

If a man should be given the contemplation of the turmoil of ideas at the beginning of the century, he would conclude that all the problems reduce to one: the meaning of man in history.

This was not the same theoretical problem which the Scholastics discussed when they inquired into the nature of man, nor was it the same problem which occupied the minds of philosophers in the Renaissance. Now, after the exaggerations of the positivists and the restless experiences of Kierkegaard and Nietzsche, man was identified with his history, with the social environment in which he lived. Dilthey and Weber are irrelevant if we do not see them in this context. Actually they cannot be ignored since they are the forerunners, almost the prophets, of the tragedy which struck Europe in 1914.

Wilhelm Dilthey's (1833–1911) thought is known as historicism. His aim was twofold: (a) a solid reaction to the "absolute" interpretation of history by the positivistic and Hegelian philosophers; (b) an attempt to organize the moral and political sciences in a new organism of thought which he used to designate with a term that he made famous: *Weltanschauung*: "vision of the world."

Dilthey started off in perfect agreement with Kant, the "honest man" from Königsberg, responsible for the honest statement that "human reason was not capable of understanding the *totality of being*." Kant had rejected the impossible claims of Hegel and the positivists even before they lived. Hence Kant had succeeded in saving the nature and the methods of inductive sciences.

Dilthey, following Kant, agreed that "All knowledge is knowledge of experience; but the original unity of all experience and its resulting validity are conditioned by the factors which mould the consciousness within which it arises, i.e., by the whole of our nature. This standpoint, which consistently realizes the impossibility of going behind these conditions of seeing as it were without an eye or directing the gaze of knowledge behind the eye itself, I call the epistemological standpoint; modern knowledge can recognize no other."[2]

Dilthey regretted that Kant did not grasp the real meaning of his own findings. He saved natural sciences with his *Critique of Pure Reason*, but he was unable to give us "A Critique of the Historical Reason," with categories and values applicable to man. Dilthey says, "I was led, by my concern as historian and psychologist for the whole

---

[2] H. A. Hodges, *Wilhelm Dilthey, Selection, An Introduction* (London: 1944), p. 112.

man, to make this whole man, in the full diversity of his powers, his willing, thinking, being, the foundation for explaining even knowledge and its concepts (such as those of the external world, time, substance, cause) however much it may seem that knowledge weaves these concepts only from the material of perception, imagination and thought."[3]

The central point of Dilthey's philosophy is therefore to be found in the conviction that all categories originate from life and from the historical situation. He reasoned in the following way:

A basic distinction must be made between the natural sciences and the science dealing with man. Nature is made up of *facts*. Man is responsible for *events*. The atomism of the positivists tried to reduce the unity of human consciousness to a psychology of association, thus confusing natural *facts* with human *events*. They spoke of *sociology* instead of *history*. Human events are lived by man in his consciousness, where the fragmentary variety of a situation is organized toward a finality. For this reason, Dilthey considered time, and therefore history, the necessary category of human consciousness.

History is not possible if man is not there to live values, to make them meaningful. Indeed, it is wrong, Dilthey insists, to think that the external objects determine our knowledge. The historical event is not just known but *lived* by our consciousness. This identification of history with our vital experience is called by Dilthey *Erlebnis* (vital experience).

The *Erlebnis* constitutes the human style of sharing reality, it is a vital commitment of man to reality by interpreting events, giving them finality and creating history. Therefore, a coldly detached knowing, without interest, is not human. The *Erlebnis* or vital experience would not be itself without expression. This expression is a necessary process of becoming objective, visible, and comprehensible to others. "Only his actions, his formulated expressions of life and the effects of these on others, teach man about himself. Thus, he comes to know himself only by the circuitous route of understanding."[4]

Man understands himself by understanding others. Therefore the vital experience (*Erlebnis*) is always interpersonal and *therefore objective*. "From this world of objective mind the self receives sustenance from earliest childhood. It is the medium in which the understanding of other people and their expression takes place. For everything in which the mind has objectified itself contains something held in common by the I and Thou. Every square planted with trees, every room in which seats are arranged, is intelligible to us from our infancy because human

---

[3] *Ibid.*

[4] W. Dilthey, *Patterns and Meaning in History, Thoughts on History and Society* (New York: Harper Torchbooks, 1962), p. 72.

planning, arranging, and valuing, common to us all, have assigned its place to every square and every object in the room."[5]

Erlebnis therefore is not the result of intellectual knowledge alone; the intellect merely explains (*erklären*). A living experience results from a comprehension (*verstehen*), which is knowledge obtained by the concurrence of all rational and emotional forces of man. This truly human and profound comprehension is caught in its meaning if you analyze what happens when two persons meet and establish a relationship of friendship. When you begin an exchange of ideas and interest yourself in another person, you are influenced by the visible and objective expressions of this person. Thus you are *vitally involved* (*Erlebnis*), you live and imagine and re-create those expressions which are dear to you. Dilthey, before Jaspers, is the philosopher of communication among human beings.

The same phenomenon should be true if you try to understand human and historical sciences. Your objective is not the individualization of causal links with the scientific precision that Descartes expected from philosophy. Perhaps we should say that scientific precision is not to be disregarded as a means to the end. The analogies of behavior, the formation of individuals should be obtained scientifically. But once all this is achieved, we must proceed beyond and make the transition from reason to life. For instance "it is vain to wish to make the hero or the genius comprehensible in terms of miscellaneous circumstances. The most proper approach to him is the most subjective. For in him lies the lived experience of his effects upon ourselves, in the enduring conditions to which our life is subjected because of him."[6] Thus the circle comes to a close: we begin with life and we return to life through the understanding of the meanings expressed by life. And life has only one meaning: "Life does not mean other than itself."[7]

The themes which Jaspers' existentialism will carry to their final conclusions are those of Dilthey: the identification of man with his life, the immediateness of human experience, the disregard for abstract considerations, and, above all, the need for communication. Indeed, nobody denies that Dilthey's historical view of man is pregnant with original developments and suggestive perspectives.

But it is legitimate to think that Dilthey owes us an explanation of the meaning of philosophy, which seems to disappear and be totally absorbed by life.

Philosophy, Dilthey explains, corresponds to a natural desire to

---

[5] *Ibid.*, p. 120.
[6] Dilthey, *Selection*, p. 129.
[7] Dilthey, *Patterns and Meaning of History*, p. 107.

systematize the whole of reality. But it remains an unfulfilled desire. The philosopher in effect contributes to the understanding of *one dimension* of the world, therefore, to a *Weltanschauung*. When "a powerful philosophical personality" expresses himself about reality, we are all richer for possessing new ideas about *a new dimension* of being. But one dimension is never absolute and philosophy therefore will always deal with particular aspects of reality. "The last word of the historical conception of the universe is that human knowledge is always relative."

These statements leave our minds wandering. If everything is relative, this doctrine about an "absolute" relativity of everything will also be relative and therefore philosophically relative.

Another aspect of Dilthey's thoughts is related to his tenacious decision to explain every angle of reality from life. The act of thinking itself comes from life.

Parenthetically, this claim that human consciousness is identical with life reveals presuppositions diametrically contradictory to Kant's presuppositions which Dilthey had accepted at the beginning. Kant said: experience is not possible without unity of experience; this unity depends on the consciousness which is prior to any experimental knowledge. Now Dilthey says: "In the vein of the knowing subject constructed by Locke, Hume, and Kant, runs no real blood, but the diluted fluid of reason in the sense of mere Thought-activity."[8]

But besides the Kantian aspect, can Dilthey defend his position when he says that knowledge comes from life? When I speak with a person, do I understand the conversation because I am alive or because, besides being alive, I have the ability to understand? It is impossible to demonstrate that consciousness is generated from life, although it is true that once I have consciousness I understand that my life comes chronologically before my knowledge.

The same type of questions must be pressed on Dilthey in regard to his doctrine on motivations and finality. The individual man lives for his goals, but the universal *Erlebnis* is without freedom and without motivation. Freedom is possible only for the individual who reflects and believes in his ideals.

Dilthey accepted in this context the Schopenhauerean doctrine that man deceives himself and that the universe is without explanation. But Dilthey did not think that these premises were deadly weapons against every doctrine, including his own, about the meaning of history.[9]

---

[8] Dilthey, *Selections*, p. 114.

[9] George Simmel developed Dilthey's ideas, particularly in reference to the philosophy accepted as a partial view of the universe. Philosophy for Simmel is always an expression of a point of view. It does not reflect the objective aspect

His intentions were not relativistic; together with his pupil George Simmel and many others he believed in the power of man through history, but he could not recognize in man any metaphysical value. Dilthey's dread of metaphysics was shared by all philosophers at the beginning of the century, and it had one explanation: the only well known metaphysical system was Hegel's. It defended a logical succession of the forms of the spirit in history. It postulated an immanent God, whose nature was creative by necessity. It sacrificed individual freedom and the profound meaning of the plurality of beings to a transcendental unity, massive and Parmenidean, though dynamic and becoming. In a word, Hegel misappropriated some of the greatest truths of the Christian philosophy to arrange them in a fashion which was arbitrary and unilateral. Dilthey might not have agreed with our reasons for rejecting Hegel, but without doubt he rejected him as the main obstacle to the freedom of man and to new scientific research.

* * *

The historicism of Dilthey, with all its fluctuations and uncertainties, had enormous influence at the turn of the century. It moved the historical sciences to qualify their methods. Sociology, the history of economy, and historiography will never be treated again as one human phenomenon. Of course, Comte and Durkheim in France and Spencer in England contributed to that. Schmoller raised the problem of methodical differentiation, and Troeltsch did not disdain to investigate the materialism of Marx as a way to the study of economics rather than a philosophy of life. For the purpose of this study, we must note that Heidegger knew and followed Dilthey before Husserl's phenomenology won him over. Jaspers and Buber were in close relation with Dilthey. His historicism will condition their existentialism. Both philosophers shared the same concern for the individual, the same persuasion that man's original meaning is different from pure rationality. Buber in particular developed a theme taken from his teacher Dilthey (who borrowed it from Feuerbach) that made him famous: he emphasized "communication" as *essential* to the comprehension of truth: hence the centrality of the I-Thou rapport. Buber was inspired to transfer this

of reality, but only "typifies" human experience in a given set of circumstances. Thus we speak of the philosophy of Plato, or of Spinoza, or of St. Augustine, because we like to emphasize the personal view of these great men in reference to the similarity of view which we ourselves like to defend. Metaphysics is therefore a partial truth aspiring to an impossible totality. This totality is *life*, which cannot be reduced to the intellectual schemes of the metaphysicians. The only thing you can do with life is *live it*. The merit of philosophical thinking consists in the need which we all have of aiming, consciously, toward the totality of life.

colloquy (under the influence of the prophets of the Old Testament and not without the help of Kierkegaard) from the level of man-to-man to the level of man-to-God. Martin Heidegger dedicated a complete chapter of his *Sein und Zeit* to Dilthey's historicism. Jaspers, above all, we will see, is the philosopher of "communication"; his whole thought is a development of themes which belong to Dilthey.

3. WINDELBAND, RICKERT, AND THE "SCHOOL OF VALUES"

Another reaction to Dilthey's historicism is known as the "school of values," under the leadership of Wilhelm Windelband (1848–1915) and Henry Rickert (1863–1936). For Windelband, Immanuel Kant had solved one of the most perplexing mysteries that shrouded man's search for knowledge. Kant has insisted on the division between *judgments of reality* (they deal with the scientific relations between phenomena) and *judgments of value* (concerning beauty, morality, and, in general, spiritual values). Now Windelband, with a sudden switch of meaning that undoubtedly would have displeased Kant, said those *values* are necessary, but do not exist ontologically. Their meaning consists not in "what something is," but in "what something ought to be" and as yet is not. Related to the real existence, these values are a possibility; they are norms of perfection always before us as challenges and goals.

Value makes life worth living, it gives an ideal to life, it makes life possible. The eternal is not what exists eternally (a concept which Windelband called impossible), but what has an eternal worth. When I examine my conscience and I see the enormous difference between my existence and what "I ought to be," then I know that I am guilty. Guilt therefore is the consciousness of the norm within me and of my infidelity to it.

This theme will be taken up and made central by all existentialists; now we need only stress Windelband's parallelism between one's conscience and his values with the abyss existing between the physical cosmos and the world of values. The cosmos is finite, limited, and blind; the organic harmony of the spirit, of ethics and of aesthetics is open to the infinity of freedom. In this context, history is a natural science; it refers to the past and tries to guess the future according to the rigid rules of the past. If the future is impregnated with values, the possibility of a history vitalized by the universal harmony of what "ought to be" cannot be excluded. Human hope is always in what man is not and might become.

The reader might wonder what prevented Windelband from establishing God as the source of all values, as all positive religions do. The answer has Kantian overtones. God is unknowable by the human mind. And then, Windelband argues, even if God were knowable, how can you make him responsible for the evils of the world? "This is the profound mystery of life, and no one will be able to raise the veil and to discover the truth."

＊　　　＊　　　＊

Henry Rickert taught for a long period of time at Heidelberg where he met Karl Jaspers, without establishing a warm friendship with him. For Rickert the task of philosophy was to find a plausible foundation for the "values" which his teacher, Windelband, had postulated but not explained. "Values" cannot be transformed into real existents and yet they cannot be left in the realm of pure possibilities. Rickert turned to Kant for a solution. With Kant he agreed that knowledge is not having ideas (as for Thomas Aquinas, through a process of abstraction), but combining categories with empirical data through a process of synthesis. Therefore each act of knowledge is a judgment and as such it implies a "value" contributed by the spirit, permanent and necessary to the material existent, always fluctuating and contingent. But once this ambiguous structure of psychophysical nature is obtained, uniting the content with the form, the existent and the "ought to exist," Rickert faced the Herculean task that once confronted Kant, who tried to justify the mental existence of the twelve categories. "Values" are inexplicable if they do not represent a universal quality of existence. If, therefore, the philosophy of values is not founded on the metaphysics of being, values cannot be anything more than an exigency of the mind.

Rickert, whose honest attempt was the rational explanation of moral values, reached once more the conclusion that man is a mysterious being split between physical qualities, visible and existing, and spiritual qualities, invisible and nonexisting and yet categorically necessary.

4. HISTORICISM AND WEBER

Before the disaster of World War I, another German, Max Weber, made a supreme effort to bring harmony to the problem of man.

Weber aimed to continue the research on the meaning of history which Dilthey had initiated, but without running against the insurmountable obstacles which blocked Dilthey's work. In particular, Weber understood that history cannot take the place of philosophy, if it does not want to be self-destructive. Therefore by nature historical research must be modest in its ambitions and goals.

Weber did not hesitate to accept the positivistic methods of Comte and Spencer. Marx himself came in handy for Weber just as he was ready to reverse his method and explain that the impact of spiritual manifestations at a given time influences the economy of the same period.

Such a broad attitude allowed Weber to accomplish a great amount of work on economic, social, and religious history. It is well known that one of his theses dealt with the relations existing between Calvinism and the formation of the capitalistic mentality of Europe.

These are his basic ideas: we must be aware of the limitations of the meaning of scientific research and therefore of historical research. Historical research requires a well-defined ground: we must single out the event which we aim to explain. We have to advance hypotheses, which our research will verify or prove groundless. Historio-social sciences have as their object the understanding of human phenomena *individually*, by applying the principle of cause and effect. Therefore, Dilthey's *Erlebnis* and Windelband's values are disregarded by Weber as impossible but beautiful dreams that surpass the modest intelligence of man. This is not meant to remove a "value" from human actions (a value for the fulfillment of which human actions are posited), but history cannot concern itself about the meaning of those values if it does not want to become philosophy; history cares only about the relations of human actions.

This modesty of horizons in a man of unusually vast learning was the cause of results often paradoxical. For instance, Weber remained convinced that religions should be explained by the social classes in which they originate. Such a simplified phenomenological criterion allowed him to think that Christianity was a doctrine which emanated from apprentice workers who used to migrate from province to province looking for jobs.

From an opposite perspective, his resigned acceptance of a modest horizon of human investigation prepared the existential mind of Karl Jaspers, whose philosophy is a continuation of Weber's thought.

Some observations are in order to maintain the balance of our study. Weber's work defined the limits of historiography by denying its identification with philosophy. He proved that solid scientific research does not have to discuss the philosophical presuppositions without which the historian cannot be himself. But the ambiguity of the whole mentality of historicism remained. We agree that the historian's job is not to investigate philosophical presuppositions, but he cannot begin his work if true philosophical foundations are not taken for granted.

In the case of Weber, a discussion of the social, economical, and political behavior of man does not substitute for, but rather presupposes, the validity of formal logic. This does not mean that, in a specific case, I will consider logical any human behavior (as Hegel claimed), but that I will succeed in determining a human behavior as logical or illogical if I remain faithful to the principles of formal logic.

The principles explaining particular sciences cannot be all hypothetical. In the case of historiography, hypotheses must be advanced by a human nature which requires consciousness, freedom — in a word, man situated in history and capable of formulating the problem of history. Without the foundation of a conception of man and of history, historiography is evidently impossible.

World War I broke out from the relatively minor accident of Sarajevo. But the causes of the war were present for a long time. Dilthey's and Weber's meditations, unsuccessful as they were, assumed an enormous importance insofar as they offered a philosophical analysis of the causes of the great conflagration. Man appeared to them as a mysterious being, one who contradicted history, the masterpiece of his own mind. The same man organized from 1914–1918 the bloodiest slaughter of history. The question of the irrationality of man continued to be examined after Dilthey and Weber.

5. SPENGLER'S PHILOSOPHY OF HISTORY

Oswald Spengler (1880–1936) published the first volume of his apocalyptic book, *The Decline of the West*, during the War. The second volume was published in 1922. This work enjoyed, we think without deserving it, great success in every country of the world and consequently influenced the philosophical thinking immediately previous to existentialism.

Oswald Spengler was born in a little Prussian town, Blankenburg, in 1880, and he lived the peaceful life of a university professor in Munich, flattered by the veneration of thousands of students who listened to his lectures and resigned themselves to think of him as an extraordinary genius.

Spengler's main idea is connected with the doctrine of "historical courses." For Spengler each civilization is a closed organism. Within it all possibilities develop, come to maturation, and finally yield to a progressive senescence and die. The individuals belonging to one given civilization use the same categories of thinking, the same forms of expression, the same ideals of progress, of happiness and truth. These individuals, and they alone, really understand the civilization they belong to. Their followers speak about it, sometimes are puzzled by it, or perhaps might take advantage from it. But they never understand it completely. Everybody knows, Spengler says, that the modern state organizes its civil laws according to the pattern of the Roman jurisdiction. But only the Romans knew the efficiency of their laws in their times.

We will see that Spengler's historical relativism has much in common with Dilthey's conception of history. What we must stress now (and it seems almost unbelievable in Spengler, who so convincingly professed the value of history as relative to each civilization) is his assertion that from *his relativism* he thought it possible to establish an *absolute* norm comprehensive of the totality, present and future, of *all human history*. Spengler often sounded like a prophet. "I see a multitude of powerful civilizations begotten from the womb of the same maternal origin, to which they remain rigorously connected during their development. Each of these civilizations imprints an individual character in the history of man. They are the form, mankind is the matter. Each of them has its own ideas, feelings, passions, its own life, its own hoping and aiming, and finally, its own death. . . ."[10]

But notice, Spengler adds, "These civilizations, living organisms of a superior order, grow obedient to a magnificent absence of finality, just as the flowers of the fields."[11] And though without finality in the wholeness of history, they belong to the living nature of Goethe, not to the dead nature of Newton. Spengler explained that natural sciences study the development of nature after reducing it to pure mechanism (Newton). History, on the contrary, concerns itself with the profound nature of human development, vital and organic (Goethe). Thus he aimed to establish a *morphology of world's history*, by excluding finality from the historical process and ultimately by accepting the rigid mechanism of positivistic historiography. Romanticism and positivism, in their common goal of destruction of individual freedom, are essential ingredients in the understanding of the grandiose plan of history. But should history concern itself with the freedom of the individual? This question remains unanswered in the pages of Spengler. He preferred to project his mind into the future, since he thought that his new method of historiography allowed the historian "to determine times and civilizations yet to come, in their structures and span of existence, in their rhythms and orientations."

It is sad to notice that this reading into the future suggested to Spengler the imminent ruin of the West. But it is a logical conclusion if we accept the premises offered by Spengler, who stated that:

a) Civilizations are born and develop according to laws dictated by *spontaneity* in agreement with the "morphology of history."

---

[10] Spengler, *Decline of the West* (Munich, 1920), Vol. 1, p. 29.
[11] *Ibid.*, p. 81.

b) Reason is a post-factum aspect of history. Reason's task is to frame logically and crystallize the results obtained by history with the purpose of using them for the benefit of the masses. Once this goal is achieved, civilization is near to its end, because it has fulfilled its duties.

Spengler did not like the masses, because he was not interested in the individual, without whom the masses are not possible. His attention to the general laws of history prevented him from respecting the metaphysical value of the individual. This strange perspective brought him so far as to describe in nostalgic terms times of untold suffering for men. For instance, he described as ideal "the feudalistic structure of the state." For this aristocrat of pre-French revolutionary convictions, civilization began its fatal decline when the city took the place of the countryside, when liberalism opened the road to socialism. Unbelievably, Spengler complained about the masses learning how to read and to write, about the pretenses of "subjects" to cast a political ballot, about the hopes of a peasant for a free profession, far away from the fields and the plow and the stable. Democracy for him was the epitome of all evils. One may ask: Was he a romantic dreamer of the old times when the Prussian "Junkers" could not be challenged in their privileges?

In 1933 he faced Hitler's era with a new book, *Decisive Years.* His aristocratic soul could not rejoice. Yet he saw in the new events a confirmation of his theories and he wrote, not without adulation for the new tyrant, that one civilization was ended. "Now the process of civilization begins again. A healthy exultation of the warriors begins, a new confidence in one's own strength which reveals the resilient instinct of the race, a race ready to live in a fashion that will not suffer the burden of finical books about the wisdom of the past."

❊   ❊   ❊

6. ORTEGA Y GASSET, BENDA, HUIZINGA

Concern for the meaning and the destiny of man after World War I was not a monopoly of German philosophers; it was a universal European phenomenon.

To illustrate this aspect of the problem of history, we will add a few lines about the intellectual activity of José Ortega y Gasset of Spain, Julien Benda of France, and Johan Huizinga of Holland.

José Ortega y Gasset (1883–1955) belonged to the "Lebensphilosophie," to the vitalism of Nietzsche and Dilthey in Germany and of Bergson in France. He studied in Germany with Simmel, and he was not saying anything original when he announced that idealism and realism were unilateral interpretations of reality. Things do not exist independently of myself, therefore idealism is right when it claims that reality is in relation with the subject, but the subject himself would not exist without the existence of the object; therefore, realism is necessary too. The basic factor of reality consists therefore in the rapport between me and the things which are around me and this rapport is life, action, free choice of one of the infinite possibilities which are before me. Therefore, vitalistically, not being but doing is the foundation of reality. Substances do not exist; they become, or better, their existing in their becoming.

"To be free," proclaimed Ortega y Gasset, "means to lack a constitutive identity, to be independent from existing as one being, to be able to become another and to be unable to be the same." This quotation, if soberly understood, means absolutely nothing and taken literally would have prevented its author from writing it. Freedom does not exist without someone being free; the freedom of not-being is just not-being. Ortega y Gasset, the philosopher of freedom, once he denied the individual as the center to which freedom must refer, was forced to speak of freedom as vital spontaneity, as a drive toward expansion toward the unforeseeable and the unknown.

The same ambiguity is predominant in his political works (*España invertebrada*, 1922, and *La rebelion de las masas*, 1930). History, structured according to human generations, develops through two phases: the first is the age of ascension to power, which is expression of youth, of war and conquest. There is enthusiasm for life in this historical moment, for a community life striving toward a goal of progress and passion. The second is the phase of disintegration, of selfish egotism; the soldier is replaced by the lawyer, the hero by the businessman, risk by prudence. Then each member of the society rebels against the leader, in an outburst of hatred, ignorance, and envy. Do not ask the ascending hero of the first phase to be subservient to norms of morality. In his essay, *Mirabeau the Politician*, Ortega defended the thesis that the politician needs a variety of qualifications that, taken one by one, appear to be monstrous. Sulla and Caesar and Mirabeau were persons of exception: their passions, their pride, and their lust were exceptional. Their freedom was boundless.

When the age of the hero declines, the horrifying process of disintegration begins: for Spain, Ortega believed, it began after Philip II; for the other European nations in the nineteenth century. The liberal institutions created the industrial revolution: together they provoked the beginning of what is called now the phenomenon of "population explosion." The State declared its hopelessness in coping with the masses and thus we live hours of confusion and fear. The psychology of the masses is contained in one word: selfishness. They are ungrateful for the wisdom of history, they obey what is enforced by the law and despise what conscience demands, they hold all the ingredients for the birth of totalitarianism, either Fascist or Marxist, they expect everything from the State. Reading the brilliant prose of Ortega y Gasset turned loose against the masses is an unusual and perplexing experience. Who are these masses to be talked down to as if they were herds of animals? Why should they accept obedience when education and knowledge is not offered to them? Ortega thought that their prerogative was ingratitude and egotism.

How does he explain his utterly inhuman contempt for the individual who did not have the opportunity to assert himself either through learning or power or drive? Ortega y Gasset obeyed blindly the axioms of historicism: he spoke of progress, neglecting to recognize that man has the secret for progress. Nor do we mean to limit the potential for progress to an elite, to the heroes, the leaders, the politicians. No, man as such, with his metaphysical values, with his freedom to be right and to be wrong, has this potential. Ortega y Gasset did not understand that the dignity of man does not come primarily from his environment or from his education, because education and environment are not causes but effects of the primordial fact that man is man.

Again we repeat the question that is valid for all forms of historicism: Is reason, this vital reason of the historicists, itself or something else? If it is something else then the problem ceases to exist because historicism, as a product of reason, would not exist. If reason is itself as a manifestation of an individual, then metaphysics is a necessary condition for history. There is a difference between historicity (the truth that is discovered through history) and historicism (truth produced by history), and Ortega y Gasset, and before him Dilthey, did not understand this difference.[12]

Julien Benda (1867–1936) lived in France the life of an intellectual

---

[12] One year after the publication of *Rebellion of the Masses,* a coup d'etat deposed, in Spain, the dictator Primo de Rivera. Ortega y Gasset became the hope of his countrymen: to the celebrated essayist was offered a seat in the Cortes, Spain's parliament. He hesitated and then refused: perhaps the fear of the masses played an important role in that decision. And he began to travel: during the civil war of Spain he lived in exile, in France, in England, in Argentina and Portugal. In 1950, he returned to the fatherland to cure his intolerable homesickness. Francisco Franco did not object. In 1955, when his end was near, the state police distributed to the press of the land this information: "In case Ortega y Gasset should die, the news will be given on two columns and with sobriety of detail. One picture allowed and a few articles which will emphasize his merits together with his political and religious blunders."

hermit, antagonistic and pessimistic, in perennial disagreement with the spirit of his time, little loved and admired, wrapped up in the thought of a mission to accomplish, the redemption of the honor of intellectuals. He was led by the conviction that the *mal du siècle,* the evil of the times, was irrationalism, an unhealthy systematic destruction of reason in favor of the prevailing demands of passion, instinct, and feelings. The trouble was that he went to the opposite extreme. "I think," he wrote at the beginning of the century when France was in the process of a national reawakening provoked by the Dreyfus Affair, "I think that mankind is made up of two kinds of people whose functions are antithetic and from whose combination civilization comes. The first are responsible for the existence of institutions aiming to destroy morality; the second preach morality in spite of the institutions. The first are the founders of empires, the second are the intellectuals [he calls them clerics]. If the first group were to exist without the second, mankind would progress in an environment of barbarian living; if the second group were to exist alone, we would have morality without progress." This unfair statement, unacceptable both philosophically and historically, is understandable only if you place it as an extreme reaction to the situation in France before World War I. Cartesian traditions, so dear to the French, were dead: their place was taken by a rampant universal infatuation with irrationalism. It was, after all, an alarming phenomenon: France in particular and Europe in general swung from one extreme to the other: from the geometrical precision of positivism to the Dionysiac exaltation of Nietzsche and to the ineffable *élan vital* of Bergson.

Benda broke his silence and went to the attack in 1912 with a fiery little treatise: *Bergsonism or a Philosophy of Mobility.* The problem was evident: how could Bergson reach any result by denying reason and essence and by installing immediate vitality, instinct, and mobility? "Love, therefore, believe, feel and live; be saints, heros, poets: live in intimate communion with things, instantly, totally: they are all fusions and confusions which are denied to us. Moreover, *be* action, *be* life: we grant that to you. Only one thing we deny you: when you claim *to formulate* the shadow of *an idea,* then we cannot allow you to try."

The attack continued in 1918, with *Belphégor,* an implacable criticism of the aesthetics of the French society. It might well be Benda's best work for sharpness of argumentation and logical irony. He called the Bergsonian bent for immediate identification of man with the work of art a "womanlike aesthetics," blended with sweetness without substance, with emotions without true knowledge.

The man of knowledge, according to Benda, is interested in the world of essences, understood according to Plato, a world of objective beauty and order. The philosopher looks to the world of women, love, and human vicissitude with the detached eye of an aristocrat who disdains to walk through the ghettos of the poor.

A few words must be said about another work of Benda's *The Treason of the Clerics*, 1927. "Clerics" for Benda are all those active in the pursuit of joy through knowledge, arts, philosophy. They aim at the possession of an extratemporal good; they repeat with Christ, though with an intellectual not a religious meaning, His words: "My kingdom is not of this world." Lay people are at the opposite end; they hope to dominate this earth, they are the business people, traders, money lenders, stock market brokers.

In our days a tragic treason occurred: the clerics, whose business is to convert the blind who are submerged by material concerns, were unbelievably converted by them to adore the material, the economical, the perishable. Famous names are indicated by Benda: Valéry, Gide, Péguy, Rolland among others, not to mention the blackest traitors, the philosophers: Bergson, first of a long list to which belong Fichte, Hegel, Marx.

These are his main themes. Benda was a man who accepted the task of pronouncing universal judgments upon other men. He enjoyed the pleasure of destruction and did not realize that he came very close to emulating one of his most deprecated enemies, Nietzsche. When, at the end of his life, he began to construct on the shambles left by his fury, he finally realized how painful it was. He left a few suggestions echoing his belief in the perfection of the absolute, but he could not fill the gap between what is human and what he thought was divine. His philosophy, for whatever it is worth, is a drastic dualism.

And indeed Julien Benda does not deserve great attention for his thought, but it was imperative for us to know him because more incisively than any others he brought out in the open the antinomies of historicism and its futile efforts to understand man without acknowledging human values.

*   *   *

In concluding this panoramic view of Europe, we cannot forget Johan Huizinga (1872–1945). He brought the discussion of the meaning of history the sound, positive approach of his land, Holland, and the tenacious quality of his people, forged by the long victorious resistance against the invading pretenses of the ocean. It seemed to Huizinga that man, too, must resist the invasion of strange labels attached to history for the purpose of explaining it and resulting only in misinterpreting its meaning. Huizinga developed his ideas on this topic in 1935, when he wrote an essay on the *Uncertainties of the Present and a Diagnosis of the Evils of Our Times*. He was listened to because his famous works[13] of the previous years had made him an international celebrity.

History does not suffer labels like "Romanticism, Renaissance, Historicism." History is just itself. Huizinga supported this thematic idea with his own achievements. Gifted with a personal style that enjoyed the pleasure of analyzing psychological situations, aspirations, and fears, he presented man with his rationalities and irrationalities, with his virtues and his sins, with his follies and wisdoms.

---

[13] Huizinga wrote *The Waning of the Middle Ages* in 1919, *Erasmus* in 1925, and *The Crises of Civilization* in 1934. Equally famous are his essays on *Grotius* and his *History of the United States*.

chapter III

Karl Jaspers

INTRODUCTION

The historicism of Dilthey and Weber prepared the way for the important philosophy of Karl Jaspers. They offered him the opportunity of reevaluating Kant's thought from a perspective which had nothing in common with that of the Marburg Neo-Kantians.

Once Kant was rediscovered, he played an important role, together with Nietzsche and Weber, in curtailing Kierkegaard's influence in the formation of Jaspers' mind, particularly in connection with the problem of man's need for a religious faith.

The development of Jaspers' thought is entwined with his life, which he made public in 1956 in his philosophical Autobiography.[1] From this work it appears possible to gather telling conclusions. For instance, Jaspers seemed to be afflicted by an obsessive rebellion against what he called the "spirit of the system." Yet his insistent lecturing on new terms and new concepts, his medical precision and search for anatomical diagrams of ideas that lead toward a systematic philosophy, and his thirst for perennial values were all new testimonials to the fact that man needs metaphysics.

"I was indeed unprepared, by my own standards, when I took over the chair of philosophy at Heidelberg on April 1, 1922. Now I set out to study philosophy afresh, and more thoroughly."[2] In that same year

---

[1] Karl Jaspers, *Philosophische Autobiographie*, published in the collection *Philosophen des 20 Jahrhunderts*, ed. Paul A. Schlipp (Stuttgart: Kohlhammer Verlag, 1956). Later in 1958, the same *Philosophische Autobiographie* was published by Karl Jaspers in *Philosophie und Welt, Reden und Aufsätze* (München: R. Piper and Co. Verlag), pp. 275–402. An English translation, prepared by E. B. Ashton, was published by H. Regnery, Chicago, in 1963, under the title *Philosophy and the World*.

[2] *Philosophy and the World*, p. 228.

two other universities (Griefswald and Kiel) offered a full professorship
to Jaspers, a medical doctor who never in his life had studied philosophy
in a formal way.

His conversion from medicine to philosophy was not provoked by any
traumatic experiences. From his youth, Jaspers grew with the consciousness that he had a serious hidden illness which, according to all
the physicians consulted, could have ended his life at any moment. He
was eighteen years old when he was finally given a definite diagnosis.
He did not seek a prognosis from the medical profession. He reached
it himself after careful consultations of the treatises written by Virchow:
he would have lived, on the best of the hypotheses, to thirty years
of age.

It wasn't easy for the young Jaspers to be brave all the time. He
would run into the woods when he had to give way to tears. "The point
was not to let concern about my illness into the sum and substance of
life. My task was to treat it properly almost without noticing it, and to
keep working as if it did not exist."[3] His program was clear: he had to
work lest he remember his condition, yet he had to refrain from
excessive strain lest he succumb. Young Jaspers' friends were solitude,
introspection, and sadness; other German youths were seized by an
exaggerated worship of outdoor exercise. "It is amazing how much love
of health will develop in a basically stationary state of illness. The
remnant of health in it grows so much more conscious, gives so much
more happiness, that it may be almost healthier than normal life."[4]

In this situation Karl found love in his family, which lived clanishly,
almost purposely disdainful of the outside world. His father held an
important job as a public officer of Oldenburg county, on the shores
of the North Sea, where Karl was born in 1883. For Karl nothing could
represent a higher goal of living than his father's career. It had all
the ingredients of success by middle class standards. Life was peaceful
and orderly, filled with satisfaction for everyday achievements, for
temperate pleasures, for hunting and literature. God Himself was kept
within the limits of a well-paced moderation. Karl's father preferred
to talk, deistically, of a religion of humanity instead of a personal God.
Jaspers wrote, almost apologetically: "If Kierkegaard, asked why he
believed, replied, 'Because my father told me,' my father had told me
differently."[5]

Although Jaspers remained puzzled by Christ, he questioned his
father about the propriety of going to church, since he did not believe

---

[3] *Ibid.*, p. 198.
[4] *Ibid.*, p. 199.
[5] *Ibid.*, p. 290.

in God. The old Jaspers must have been embarrassed. But his German love for discipline rescued him: "We can live with others only if we go by rules. One set of rules comes from religion. To destroy it would mean the eruption of incalculable evil."[6] Karl's parents tried desperately to lead their children to a respect for the perennial values of truth, integrity and civil obedience, although they were afraid to question themselves about the genesis of those values. In their family they tried to fill all possible vacuums with their presence and their love. So they excluded God too, because of the complexity He created for the human mind with His invisible presence and unreachable nature. They were convinced, in obedience to shallow illuministic principles, that truth must be visible and touchable.

Later Jaspers wrote: "Truth is what unites us." He identified truth with the warmth of his family, of faces so dear to him because they expressed love and security for his insecure existence. "Something is wrong with the world of men and with myself — this was my basic feeling. And yet, how splendid was that other world: nature, art, poetry and science! Above all else, there remained a basic confidence in life inspired by my beloved parents, safe in their care."[7]

*   *   *

"Truth is what unites us." This is the *leitmotiv* of Jaspers' life. But truth has a peculiar nature: it becomes meaningless if it is not alive: it will be either fecund or sterile. Jaspers accepted this challenge. He knew that he had to make "new contacts," to establish new communications, to seek out spiritual exchanges with human beings outside the sanctuary of his family.

The German Gymnasium, a sort of American high school with pretenses of more critical formation of the student in the field of humanities, was a bitter disappointment for the young Jaspers. He had looked for an arena of free expression, but he found himself curbed by regimented fraternities and pigeonholed because of his father's income and position.

But the university was different. There Jaspers could finally breathe the air of freedom. "Ever since my student days, the University has been the institution to which I felt I belonged," he wrote in his autobiography.[8] His confidence in the formation of the future leaders by the institutions of higher learning was so great that twice he called the

---

[6] *Ibid.*, p. 287.
[7] *Ibid.*, p. 196.
[8] *Ibid.*, p. 244.

attention of his fellow citizens to the social and political importance of the University.[9]

Jaspers took up law but his interest was with every manifestation of human values which he called "individual experiences of greatness." Poetry, theater, graphology were among his subjects. What else could he have done in an environment where Nietzsche had killed the idea of God?

Perhaps under the spell of universal veneration for Nietzsche, who had died in 1900, Jaspers spent his vacations after 1902 in the mountains of Engadine, so dear to Nietzsche. He came back with a clear purpose for his life. He would abandon law and study medicine, because he needed a greater closeness to reality, to man in his own individuality, in his sickness. He wanted to know the extent and limitations of the influence of the natural sciences on man. Therefore, more than the anatomical aspect of medicine, he aimed to know the mysterious connection between the somatic and the psychic: "My main purpose in choosing medicine was to become acquainted with reality. All my efforts aimed at reality."[10] He studied medicine in Munich, Berlin, and Göttingen. But his fascination was for what lay beyond medicine and yet was presupposed by it.

---

[9] In 1923 he wrote *The Idea of the University*, which he re-issued in 1946 after the ruinous consequences of the Second World War. Western civilization, Jaspers thinks, is in danger, and the proportions of this danger can be assessed if we examine the situation of our universities. They have changed their lofty purposes and established a series of required courses for qualified technicians. We would say, using terms so common on our campuses, that the digital revolution took the place of creative thinking. The university fails, according to Jaspers, in its main reason for existence if it doesn't perpetuate the spiritual tradition of western civilization, freedom of thought and freedom of discussion. The university cannot be subservient to scientific research, but it must coordinate all empirical efforts toward the creation of the universal brotherhood of men. Democracy is the goal of man and the university must find the rules which preserve freedom for the individual and not allow the naïvite of the illiterate masses, easy prey of vicious indoctrination, to dictate rules and govern society with their shouting in the streets. In particular: (a) fraternities must be free associations where the ingenuity of each member finds free expression. When military discipline, uniforms, and a cult for physical achievements become preponderant in a fraternity, the whole concept of a university is in danger; (b) the university's first concern must be with the standard of teaching and learning, with the inalienable prerogative of the student in choosing his courses, with the stress of learning as a process of understanding rather than of memorizing; (c) university teachers must be active members of the community. They tend to separate themselves in an ivory tower, wrapped up in their own ideas, often irrelevant to the future life of the student.

Jaspers was not guided by religious faith; and the gap between his thinking and, for example, Cardinal Newman's on the idea of the university is enormous. But his concern for the organization of higher institutions of learning reveals the wholesomeness of his mind and his profound respect for the individual.

[10] *Philosophy and the World*, p. 197.

This anxious desire for greater horizons was stimulated by Ernst Mayer, whom Jaspers met in the anatomy class at the University of Tübingen in the summer of 1907. Mayer was an exceptional man. He belonged to an old Jewish family of Berlin and he had the gift, magnificent yet frightening, of becoming involved and identified with the problems and persons he encountered. Jaspers wrote that "Mental illness ran in his [Mayer's] family and cast a shadow of depression over his youth, but his spirit insulated and penetrated the spector. It was as though a wound in the roots of his constitution had made him the wonderful human being he was."[11]

They became close friends and spent hours discussing Fechner and Wundt, Schopenhauer and Kant, Spinoza and Giordano Bruno. Mayer was a living testimonial to the main conviction of Jaspers that "truth unites us." They frequently reflected on the nature of human dialogue. They agreed on the fact that each human opinion, when it is held in good faith, is sacred and eventually leads to the manifestation of a truth. Later we will discuss the Jasperian meaning of truth, which he defined more as *a love of charity for men* than as an *ontological distinction* of being from nonbeing.

Unfortunately, the young Jaspers was not exposed, as was Heidegger, to research that indicated the possibility of metaphysics. Jaspers oscillated between the acceptance of an existential truth valid only for each historical moment and an ontological existentialism patterned according to the principles of Weber.

What must be mentioned now is Jaspers' honesty in facing the problem of truth: a most remarkable honesty if we consider the general resignation, prevalent in those times, to inferior standards of philosophical discussion and social and political stagnation.

The summer of 1907 is important for another reason: Jaspers met Mayer's sister, Gertrud. In 1910 they became husband and wife, Gentile and Jewish for better and for worse. His books will be hers too: "The one great turn in my life was the union in which my wife and I were joined."[12] This marriage won Jaspers over to philosophy in general and to existential philosophy in particular.

His sickness had given him the awareness of himself; the necessity of conquering his illness convinced him to work with systematic moderation, to forget himself. His work in the field of medicine convinced him that it was possible to face his life and attempt to reach a clear vision of the psychological and physiological factors determining his own being, hidden and mysterious as it was. Finally, after he entered

[11] *Ibid.*, p. 238.
[12] *Ibid.*, p. 198.

the Mayer family, he learned, with surprise and joy, about the possibility of a larger dialogue, philosophical in significance, concerned with human nature. Gertrud Mayer, with love and prudence, invited him to a communion with the joys and sufferings and hopes of man as such. His sickness and his victory over it were not just a personal case. His life mirrored the human condition: filled with hopes, afflicted by sickness, but not condemned to remain permanently sick.

Gertrud was speaking out of personal experience: as a nurse in a clinic for various nervous conditions she came in contact with all kinds of human suffering. In fact she was getting ready to begin her formal philosophical education at the university level when she entered the home of Jaspers. "In her I saw the reality of a soul that would not bring concealment. . . . My own affirmation of life — naive despite everything — met a spirit which henceforth forbade any premature tranquillity."[13] Gertrud, let us not forget, was Jewish in the most complete meaning of this word and therefore she brought to her husband a living religious faith and a longing for home after the human exile. Jaspers felt the impact with acute sensitivity. His philosophy, we will see, is religious in inspiration. Yet he was puzzled and caught in the middle without sufficient reason for a definite choice. He had read and understood, as far as an intelligent adolescent could understand, Spinoza. The great Jew of Amsterdam appeared to be either a mystic, convinced that ethics and religion are the poles of human existence, or a sordid atheist, conquered by the rigid laws of physical determinism and immanentism.

Now Jaspers' wife, with tact and prudence and yet with Pascalian faith, was speaking to him of the God of Abraham and Jacob. Jaspers listened with reverence, but he refused to make a personal commitment. His position was clear: existence requires transcendence but this transcendence, philosophically, must be nameless. The books of Bishop Martensen (the man made known by his controversy with Kierkegaard) gave Jaspers some knowledge of Christianity. Kierkegaard's religious enthusiasms were watered down in Jaspers' mind by the vitriolic attacks of Nietzsche's atheism. Of the two, Jaspers felt that atheism was a philosophy without hope, a house without windows.

In a word, Jaspers remained an outsider to all positive religions, which he revered as daring human attempts to give a name to transcendence, which for him was essentially nameless. If he had a preference, it was for the wisdom of the Prophets of the Old Testament rather than for the good news announced by Christ. But Jaspers could never accept the possibility that human existence could be given light and mean-

---

[13] *Ibid.*, pp. 201–220.

ing through faith, by a supreme wisdom, different and higher but not contradictory to human wisdom.

❂ ❂ ❂

In 1908, Jaspers, after passing the state medical examination, began the six months of internship in the Psychiatric Hospital of Heidelberg. He concluded this internship with a doctoral disseration on *Nostalgia and Crime*,[14] winning thereby his M.D.

In those days the field of psychopathology was even more confused than it is at present. When Nissl, director of the clinic, asked Jaspers where he wanted to start his research, the answer came immediately: "From the library." Indeed a new theoretical approach was felt as something surely needed by the doctors in daily contact with their patients. Their confusion could be stated as a dilemma: either insanity was a physiological phenomenon (according to the principle of Griesinger: all mental illnesses are due to lesions of the brain) or insanity was a psychosomatic phenomenon (Scule's principle: mental illness is a personality illness). To make the situation more confused, Freud in the same years was expounding his own theory, thoroughly unilateral and enriched by a sizable amount of imaginary factors.

Jaspers looked anxiously for some light on the matter, ready to explore all possible avenues. After his work in the clinic, he was seen in many philosophical seminars on Kant, Descartes, and Aristotle.

His colleagues at the clinic nicknamed him "the philosopher." At one of the meetings of the department of psychiatry, in the heat of the discussion, Jaspers exclaimed, with strong conviction: "Psychiatrists must learn to think." Ranke, the brain histologist, jokingly answered: "Jaspers ought to be whipped." On another occasion Jaspers was late at the clinic and Nissl needled him: "Herr Jaspers, how pale you look! You are doing too much philosophy: the red corpuscles can't take that."[15] In this atmosphere of cameraderie, resulting as usual from loyal friendship tinged with a healthy subconscious feeling of jealousy and competition, an idea suddenly sprang up among the members of the department of Psychiatry at Heidelberg University: Jaspers, the doctor-philosopher, should author a treatise on "General Psychopathology." He accepted the challenge. The book, published in 1913, went through many editions[16] and it is still consulted today.

For the purpose of understanding the genesis of Jaspers' philosophy,

<hr>

[14] K. Jaspers, *Heinveh und Verbrechen* (*Nostalgia and Crime*), (Leipzig, 1909).
[15] *Ibid.*, pp. 214–215.
[16] K. Jaspers, *Allgemeine Psychopathologie* (Heidelberg und Berlin: Springer Verlag, 1913). English translation by Horig Hamilton, *General Psychopathology* (The University of Chicago Press, 1963).

the following ideas taken from his "Psychopathology" are of importance. Psychopathology is a more specific term to designate psychology, as Wundt had conceived it. If psychology is studied from the angle of theoretical and methodological problems, the discussion is philosophical; if psychology is studied empirically and clinically, we do psychopathological work. Both aspects deal with man and "in every individual event, *soma* and *psyche* form an inseparable unity."[17]

But the concept of *psyche* is filled with transcendence; we are included in it and hence are unable to define it. "We conceive the *psyche* as an unending effort of comprehension, an effort which can never be concluded wholly, though we are always advancing through the many methods of research. We have no basic concept in terms of which we could define man nor any theory that would wholly cover his actually objective existence."[18]

Jaspers described *psyche* as "being in one's own world" in a twofold way: the "inside" of the individual consciousness and the "outside" of the environment. This dual aspect of the *psyche* appears clear if man is compared with animals. "The animal is bound to a natural fate which automatically fulfills itself in accordance with natural laws. Man is likewise bound, but in addition he has a destiny, the fulfillment of which lies in his own hands."[19] Consider the differences between sickness in an an animal and in a man. The animal does indeed suffer but "the concept of human illness introduces a completely new dimension. Here the incompleteness and vulnerability of human beings and their freedom and infinite possibilities are themselves a cause of illness. In contrast with animals, man lacks an inborn, perfected power of adaptation."[20] Man can say "no" to a situation, he can rebel, pretend to ignore it, but he often experiences traumatic moments[21] (suffering, guilt, sin), which bring him back with violence to himself. Man, in a word, living the consciousness of his own limitations, must experience his existence.

The conclusion is evident: if man can exercise his freedom, the reduction of emotional abnormality to physiological factors (and therefore to a natural science) is inadequate and unscientific. Consciousness, with its power to choose, express and signify, has the final word.

Jaspers used Husserl's *epoché* (the methodical device which allows him to sidestep insoluble problems) in order to focus his attention on the elements present to the mind. But Jaspers does not, as did Husserl, carry

---

[17] K. Jaspers, *General Psychopathology*, p. 3.
[18] *Ibid.*, p. 6.
[19] *Ibid.*, p. 7.
[20] *Ibid.*
[21] This doctrine is called by Jaspers "Grenz-situation" or frontier situation, and it will be incorporated as a moment of his existentialism.

phenomenological reduction to the final identification of the phenomenon with the essence. The essence of the *psyche* is transcendent or beyond description: "We have no psychic master-plan, but we shall simply discuss a number of horizons within which the psychic realities present themselves."[22] The refusal to reduce the phenomenon to the essence, which is one of the premises of Jaspers' existentialism, was expressed even more forcefully in the preface to the second edition of the *Allgemeine Psychopathologie*: "In the midst of all the psychopathological talk we have to learn to know what we know and do not know, to know how and in what sense and within what limits we know something, by what means that knowledge was gained and on what it was founded."

Husserl therefore offered a method to Jaspers, but not a philosophy. The philosophy, or rather the philosophical atmosphere in which Jaspers breathed the air he was longing for, stemmed from Dilthey and Weber. From them Jaspers derived an aversion to any form of a systematic philosophy of man. As Jaspers saw it, the problem was not to discover an ultimate principle which could explain all psychic phenomena, but to describe an "understanding psychology," just as Weber had published a work on an "understanding sociology." The emphasis is on "understanding," that is to say, casting a little light on some aspects, though "the whole" was darkness. We cannot sufficiently stress this vein of historicism in the philosophy of Jaspers: he made all possible efforts to illuminate the limitations of philosophical inquiry, which is susceptible of change and improvement and which progresses through research and studies. Yet he does not hesitate to repeat with even greater insistence that man cannot be himself without transcendence, that he has consciousness and is able to reach other beings intentionally, that he was not born just to be led but reacts differently to different situations; in a word, that he is capable of initiative and freedom.[23]

---

[22] *General Psychopathology*, p. 6.

[23] Is not all this metaphysical discussion? We think it is, because it is reflection on the essence. In our times the metaphysical meaning of essence has been obscured because it has been overlaid with rationalistic principles stemming from Cartesian mechanism to transcendental idealism, which understood the essence as *a total and exhaustive determination of a being*. This prejudice has prevented the classical doctrine of essence from playing its important role in the philosophical developments of our century. Classically and traditionally, *essence limits itself to that characteristic of each being which allows it to remain itself* through all the changes which cannot reduce it to another being. This essential quality makes different beings possible. Without it individuals could not exist because they would not differ one from the other and they could not be named because they would not present anything for the mind to understand.

From Plato and Aristotle to Aquinas and to our times, classical ontology has always stressed the limitations and difficulties which are echoed by Jaspers. In particular: (a) We hold that each being is understood through its essence. But

Jaspers found a way out in the philosophy of Kierkegaard. Kierkegaard's good news was that the discovery of human possibilities and impossibilities does not result from a "search for essences," but from a strong assertion of the individual existent who reaches the consciousness of himself through dread and anxiety. Jaspers clung to Kierkegaard, but in doing so he postponed rather than solved the problem before him. In fact, Kierkegaard investigated *the way through which* man reaches understanding more than the truthfulness of understanding. Kierkegaard found a strong faith in his God, who guaranteed the truth which reason could not reach. But Jaspers was not able to accept God.

The publication of *General Psychopathology* brought Jaspers to public notice. Alzhiemer was ready to accept him at the University of Munich, Kraepelin at Breslaw. But Jaspers could not leave the clinic of Heidelberg. "Perhaps," he suggested to Nissl, "I can lecture on psychology in the philosophical faculty. We will found a colony there and later on I can come back to the hospital."[24] Windelband liked the idea, and Jaspers was hired as an assistant professor of psychology. When Nissl left for Munich, Jaspers was chosen to direct the clinic. It was a decisive moment. "I asked for a few days to think it over," he wrote. But he refused — philosophy was his vocation.

*   *   *

1. *The Need for a Worldview*

The uniqueness of Jaspers' intellectual itinerary consists in the way he happened to become a leading philosopher of our century. As we saw, he began with psychiatry as a particular field of medical knowl-

---

that does not mean that the essence is easy to determine. We know that the essence must be there, but often we do not succeed in reaching it. And when we do succeed, our knowledge is frequently partial and faulty. (b) It is fundamental, if we are to avoid the rationalistic pitfalls so filled with unacceptable conclusions, to understand that the knowledge of an essence does not suppose all the characteristics of a being, but only those which are essential and without which the being in question ceases to be itself. For instance, the essence of man requires an organic body, consciousness and freedom: these aspects do not exhaust the whole man but they qualify him as man. (c) The doctrine of essence does not deny that there are changes in a being nor does it deny diverse manifestations. On the contrary, these manifestations cannot exist if they do not belong to something. Man's freedom requires that man be essentially himself; man opens up to new possibilities to try the limits of his own possibilities.

Jaspers does not agree with these elementary observations, simple as they are. He saw the necessity of our essential approach, yet he denied the essence out of sheer fear of being bridled by a rigid doctrine of immutable essences.

[24] K. Jaspers, *Philosophy and the World*, p. 215.

edge, discovered its close relationship to psychology, and came to the realization that psychology was groundless without philosophy. But this realization did not come easy. After 1914 Jaspers taught a variety of courses in psychology: the psychology of perception and memory, and social, religious, and moral psychology. His center of attention was the human individual, particularly extraordinary human individuals. For instance, he wrote psychological analyses of Strindberg and Van Gogh,[25] and he investigated the mental sickness of Nietzsche.[26] Yet psychology was not enough. "What determined the future course of my thinking was the good conscience with which the name of psychology allowed me — based on Aristotle's dictum: 'the soul is all, as it were' — to delve into all that can be known. For there is nothing, in the wider sense, that has no psychological aspects."[27]

Jaspers' quotation of Aristotle's famous sentence, "the soul is all things," is a significant admission of the inadequacies of the purely psychological approach to man. Aristotle made a distinction, which Jaspers was not ready to accept, between psychology and logic. The latter allows the mind to attempt achieving a knowledge of absolute values, that is to say, the essences of things, while the former analyzes only one aspect of man. We have seen that Rickert was aware of the fact that the scientific nature of logic demands a metaphysical support.

Jaspers met Rickert in 1916: for twenty years they worked at the University of Heidelberg in profound ideological disagreement. Jaspers wrote: "Rickert claimed universal and cogent validity for scientific philosophy. I doubted it."[28] After all, laboratory research was responsible for a large number of successful scientific discoveries that had application to human life, which profited from them. Philosophy on the contrary was sterile in its results. Therefore Jaspers rebelled against the possibility of philosophy conceived as a science; at most, Jaspers was prepared to accept philosophy as "a meaningful way of thinking."

Yet all the works of Jaspers are in flagrant contradiction to the idea that philosophy is just a useful exercise of the mind. Philosophy is not a practical science; it does not aim at empirical findings: did not Aristotle call philosophy "first science," that is, contemplation or theoresis? Philosophy is not a technology, but it is a magnificent drive that human beings possess to search for the truth, as Jaspers knew from his whole life. Technology and politics and all the manifestations of human life presuppose philosophy but cannot be identified with it. Rickert himself,

---

[25] K. Jaspers, *Strindbergh und Van Gogh* (München: Piper, 1922).

[26] K. Jaspers, *Nietzsche, Einführung in das Verständis seines Philosophierens* (Berlin: de Gruyter, 1936).

[27] K. Jaspers, *Philosophy and the World*, pp. 218–219.

[28] *Ibid.*, p. 223.

though convinced of the scientific nature of philosophical thinking, missed the meaning of philosophy as "first science or metaphysics" and ruminated on particular aspects of being as ethics, esthetics, and politics. Croce in Italy and Scheler and Husserl in Germany adopted the same partial approach. Thus the academic life at Heidelberg was not without excitement for Jaspers[29] and the situation worsened after the death of Weber. Jaspers then authored *The Psychology of World Views*,[30] which is essential for understanding his future development.

The Psychology of World Views, rich with resonances from Kierkegaard and from Weber, was the result of long conversations with his wife during the First World War when Jaspers felt acutely embarrassed that he was physically unfit for military service. It was not meant to be a philosophical work representing Jaspers' convictions. It was meant to present different views of the world, different ideologies. The individual must make his own choice among them.

What is a *Weltanschauung, a view of the world?* We know the meaning from Dilthey: it is the way the world presents itself to the individual man, a world that is pregnant with meaning, reminiscence, values and structures different for different persons. This view evidently presupposes a viewer; in this sense it is not outside but inside each one of us. We belong so strongly to *our* view that for us it is no longer just a view, it becomes *truth, our* truth. The deeper and stronger this view becomes, the more it shrinks and grows restless when faced by other points of view: a tension is created between the individual convictions and the world that seems to rebel against a singular approach. In this way we explain great personalities, saints, heroes, leaders. They share one identical prerogative — *they are fighters* against the dissipating forces of the world always ready to accept dull mediocrity and gray anonymity. Their convictions are impossible without a driving force, "a vital enthusiasm," as Jaspers calls it.

"Contrary to life in the quiet of traditional customs, in which the

---

[29] Jaspers' disagreement with Rickert was punctuated by both strong accusations and a delightful sense of humor. Jaspers thought that Rickert underestimated Weber's historicism, as it appears from a note he wrote to him: "If you think that you and your philosophy will be still known in the future, that is only because a footnote to Max Weber's work will mention you as one to whom Weber gave thanks for a few logical insights." Rickert answered: "Fashioning a philosophy out of Max Weber may be your privilege, but to call him a philosopher is nonsense" (Cf. Jaspers, *Philosophy and the World*, p. 228). On another occasion, Jaspers paid a visit to the ailing Rickert, who was reading one of Jaspers' publications on Nietzsche. "I thank you," Rickert said, "I think it is an excellent book, Herr Jaspers; it is, if you do not mind me saying so — a scientific book" (*Ibid.*, p. 228).

[30] K. Jaspers, *Psychologie der Weltanschauungen* (Heidelberg und Berlin: Springer). Some passages are translated into English in *The World of Existentialism* edited by M. Friedman (New York: Random House, 1964).

antinomies of the world are not perceived, contrary to life in inner aloofness which, in spite of all superficial activity, remains in limited and relative spheres, the enthusiastic attitude is everywhere deeply agitated and at the same time strengthened, tested and invigorated by love and hate, by union the strife, by unconditional devotion. Contrary to a life either without solid substance or a life in which this substance is never affected, *the enthusiastic attitude* awakens man to life, a life of totality and authenticity."[31]

Notice the existential language used by Jaspers: he speaks of "authenticity" as a dilemma: either we are conscious or unconscious of ourselves. It is not, therefore, a question of knowing many subjects or of having a vast erudition. The problem is knowing ourselves, having the courage to discover the roots and motivations of our individual view of the world. No wonder Jaspers inquired with fanatic curiosity into the lives of troubled people like Kierkegaard, Nietzsche, Van Gogh and Strindberg. Actually, each man, by probing himself with merciless scrutiny, discovers the radical ineptness of his own desire for an absolute understanding of the universe. He feels his own limitations. He finds himself *ex-istent:* living a life which is longing to integrate the mysteries of a surrounding world, which is outside and yet looked to as an integral part of human consciousness.

Sometimes disaster strikes: death, suffering, despair disrupt our view of the world. Jaspers called these *Grenz-situationen* — "frontier-situations" — and he wrote with sadness that "At the limit [at the frontier], experience seems to find everywhere absolute chance, death and guilt. In the conditions underlying the origin of values, nothing to man's eyes is guaranteed and necessary; but the ultimate chance — and from this empirical point of view all objective existence of values — is followed by total destruction."[32] These limit-situations beget dread. Dread begets a monstrous and meaningless view of the world. The final result is *existential consciousness.*

Empirical sciences and philosophy, Jaspers suggested, do try to order life. But do they succeed? Jaspers does not think so. Sciences are particular, fractionary. They are useful, but they are not universal. Philosophy claims to be universal, but its universality is futile when you think of all the antinomies and contradictions that the Kantian *Critique* brought into the open. And after Kant, Hegelianism and positivism were equally unsuccessful in their search for universality. They reduced reality to one of its aspects. The positivist contradicts positivism, which does not explain his free choice and the quest for greater knowledge.

[31] *Psychologie der Weltanschauungen,* p. 119.
[32] *Ibid.,* p. 130.

Idealism has more capacity for integrating all contradictory obstacles. But contradiction itself cannot be integrated: something will always remain looming beyond what has been already understood. According to Jaspers, philosophy too is always partial: if everything is reduced to objectivity, we have objects without consciousness. If everything is consciousness, we forget that consciousness ceases to exist if it is not consciousness of an object.

Man indeed was made to suffer in despair and anxiety. So far Jaspers' reasoning. But it is difficult to accept suffering. Why should we try to reduce being either to subject or to object? Metaphysical investigation tends to think of being as being, and only in a second phase can being be structured in its different aspects. The traditional objection against metaphysics accuses human thinking of coloring the existence of being with shades that come from the mind and which do not respect the reality of being as it is. The answer is clear: either thought is thinkable, capable of representing intentionally an existing thing, or it is just a technical instrument distorting reality. In the first case, the possibility of thinking being as being (man as man, my house as my house) might be difficult, often imperiled by unforgiveable errors, conditioned by proper education, but undeniable. In the second case, if thought is an instrument falsifying its content, human existence and human living are meaningless: scientific, artistic, and factual knowledges are deceitful.

Jaspers was unable to understand the meaning of metaphysics because he accepted without question the Renaissance prejudice which held that thought is an instrument, a technical instrument bound to deteriorate and malfunction as all technical instruments do. With this fallacy dogmatically placed as the foundation of his structure, Jaspers was forced to agree to a relativistic view of the world. But as happens to many contemporaries, he could not be coherent and at the same time hold an absolute form of skeptical relativism. He rebelled against his own premises to announce that out of the universal fragmentation of the world, one value, the individual existent, is beyond any doubt existing. The existent, therefore, postulated as absolute and unchallengeable, is rescued from the ruins of a partial and relative view of the world. The perspective is reversed: from the contingency of the world springs the existence of the necessary individual.

The Psychology of Worldviews was evidently a work inspired by historicism. Kierkegaard (who already had criticized in *Either-Or* the life-ideas of Don Giovanni and Ahasuerus) suggested to Jaspers the possibility of criticizing *Weltanschauungen* and justifying *existential consciousness*. But Jaspers stopped there and refused to recognize with

Kierkegaard that the insufficiency of existential consciousness demanded, as a postulate, an absolute divine Being, a source of all existences. The extraordinary result of *Psychology of Worldviews* is contained in these few words written by Jaspers himself: "Unconsciously, this book led me to philosophy."

2. *The Problem of Transcendence*

Karl Jaspers, the medical doctor, the psychopathologist, the psychologist, now recognizes that the horizon is much larger, that psychology is just a particular science, useful and successful if kept within the limits of experimentation. But the whole man, responsible for his free choices, is the object of another investigation of an unmistakeable philosophical nature. He sealed his final dedication to philosophy in 1921, when he accepted, against the advice of Rickert, a full professorship in philosophy at the University of Heidelberg.

From 1921 to 1931 Jaspers wrote almost nothing. His time was taken up by his students, whom he cared for with intense and personal attention. His lectures were the result of long meditations, particularly on the meaning and limits of *transcendence* and also on the great leaders of the Neoplatonic tradition from Plotinus to Bruno, Spinoza, and Schelling. These men had been concerned, as he was, by the same problem of transcendence: Plotinus called it "extasis," Bruno, "heroic furors," Spinoza and Schelling, "intellectual intuition." Jaspers refused and still refuses to the present day to give a name to transcendence, which he considers beyond definition.

An insight into Jasper's "transcendence" might perhaps be offered by an attempt to combine the meaning which classical philosophy gave to the term and Husserl's understanding of it. Classically, the transcendent is opposed to the immanent. It is God, to whom the created universe is referred without identifying itself with Him. We know that Husserl used the term "transcendent" not with a metaphysical but with a logical meaning, referring to consciousness which, directed toward the mental object and not exhausted by it, proceeds to capture new meanings of the essence.

Both these meanings of transcendence are present in Jaspers. On the one side, he calls transcendence the going beyond what we actually know in the effort to explore the unknown; on the other, he holds that transcendence is *what reveals itself* to the unending human inquiry, with the implication that being must be infinite and that we do justice to it more by stressing what we do not know about it than what we know. The affinity of this doctrine with the "negative theology" of the Christian philosophers, who borrowed it from Neoplatonic sources, is evident. This affinity explains why Jaspers' philosophy is basically religious. The presence of Kierkegaard, the continuous use of Christian terms (for instance, "grace," "faith," "salvation") are so insistent in Jaspers that we are not surprised at the reaction of his students. One of them, a Catholic priest, exchanged a few words with Jaspers after one of his lectures, and Jaspers did not conceal his satisfaction in reporting them in his *Philosophical Autobiography*. "At the end of the 1927–1928 semester, in which I lectured on metaphysics, a Catholic priest came to thank me as one of my listeners and to express his agreements. 'I have only one objection,' he said, 'that in our opinion most of what you were teaching is theology.' I was quite put out by these words."[33]

Jaspers, a man of absolute intellectual honesty, felt the need to face the religious problem. He recognized religions as a prominent expression of transcendence; he spoke about all religious confessions with respect, but he refused to be a member of any of them. Rather than choose one positive faith, he preferred to make philosophy his faith. And he did not acknowledge that by doing so he excluded as wrong all positive faiths. We can go further and say that by accepting philosophy as his own faith he tried desperately to free his philosophy from its aspect of particularity, to place it on the pedestal of universality. Jaspers, so convinced that philosophy was not a science, was obsessed by the omnicomprehensive tendencies of the human mind. When he finally affirmed the *existent*, the obsession for infinity did not disappear, it just shifted from the infinity of ontological being to the infinity of the meaning of the free human act. Kierkegaard was there telling him that the human freedom finds explanation only in God, source of all freedom. But Jaspers could not listen and he continued to carry the burden of a heavy question: Is there any explanation for the freedom of the individual act?

Jaspers did not know, but he was ready to spend his life trying to find out.

3. Dasein, *Consciousness, Existence*

The great silence was finally broken by the publication of Jaspers' major work, *Philosophy*,[34] in three volumes, in December, 1931. It was a labor of love, resulting from years of meditation. Jaspers used to carry a notebook; every experience and every observation were carefully confided to his little book. He tells us in his autobiography: "I feel that

[33] K. Jaspers, *Philosophy and the World,* p. 217.
[34] *Philosophie,* Drei Bande (Heildelberg und Berlin: Springer, 1932).

if we do not dream a while each day, the star that may guide all work and everyday life will cease to shine for us."[35] His wife completed the job at home. She transcribed all his notes, with personal comments. The same topics were discussed with her brother Ernest Mayer, who made frequent trips from Berlin, where he was practicing medicine, to Heidelberg to help and encourage his brother-in-law in his challenging enterprise. Jaspers wrote of him: "His influence extended all the way to the chapter arrangements, to matters of substance and style."[36]

The *Philosophie* resulted in a sort of a "Summa" of Existentialism.[37] Jaspers himself defined the purpose of his book in a small volume, *Man in the Modern Age*, published at the same time,[38] "Existence-philosophy is the way of thought by means of which man seeks to become himself; it makes use of expert knowledge while at the same time going beyond it. This way of thought does not cognise objects, but elucidates and makes actual the being of the thinker. Brought into a state of suspense by having transcended the cognitions of the world (as the adoption of a philosophical attitude towards the world) that fixate being, it [i.e., Existence-philosophy] appeals to its own freedom (as the elucidation of existence) and gains space for its own unconditioned activity through conjuring up Transcendence (as metaphysics)."

The three volumes of *Philosophie* deal with the different modes of this Transcendence (understood as a condition that makes possible for man each particular view rather than as the overcoming of a given particular view of the universe) and they bear these titles: Volume I: *Philosophische Weltorientierung* (Philosophical View of the World); Volume II: *Existenzerhellung* (Illumination of the Existent); Volume III: *Metaphysik* (Metaphysical Interpretation of the Existent).

Volume I is a presentation of the questions and the terms, with a stringent analysis of the answers offered by contemporary civilization. "When I state questions of this nature: what is being? why is it there? why is it that something exists? who am I? what do I aim for basically (*eigentlich*)?, I know that with these questions I do not get to the heart of the problem. I formulate them from a given situation, my

---

[35] *Philosophy and the World*, p. 233.

[36] *Ibid.*, p. 240.

[37] Four years before, in 1927, Martin Heidegger had published another "Summa" of Existentialism: *Sein und Zeit*. Jaspers noted in a footnote of his *Philosophy*, Vol. 1, p. 66: "M. Heidegger wrote essential things on the existence of the world, as well as on history and empirical existence."

[38] K. Jaspers, *Die Geistige Situation der Zeit* (Berlin: de Gruyter, 1931). An English translation in London, 1933, was revised in 1951 by Routledge and Kegan Paul, under the title *Man In the Modern Age*. Anchor Books, New York, published it in 1957. Our quotation is from this last edition, p. 175.

own situation that depends on my particular and personal past."[39]

Let us pretend for a moment that I forget myself. Could I answer the questions given above? I would be running against insurmountable obstacles and into dead-ends: being cannot present itself in its generic and universal aspects; on the contrary, being is always determined by particular and individual qualifications. "If I think of a being, it is always a singular being, not being as such."[40]

This quotation — Jaspers must forgive our intrusion — in many ways sums up the principle of classical metaphysics. No being is vague and unessential in itself. But we differ from Jaspers in understanding his own words. We think that all beings are concretely determined and particular because they all agree in *being* what they are. Therefore, the mind cannot be refused the possibility of investigating this common ground of existence, shared in each case in the most diverse ways. Jaspers prefers to neglect this common aspect to focus his attention on the multiplicity of the elements determining and limiting beings. He reasons that if human thought always presents particular beings, it is because of its inborn inability to embrace the whole existence. Again, we must ask: Who, except an Hegelian Romanticist or a monistic Spinozist, wants to unify the whole existence? Jaspers, who takes the extreme idealistic ambition as axiomatic, finds himself the victim of the opposite extreme existential delusion, and he is forced to work out his thinking on the presupposition that man is allowed only to analyze the limiting elements of each individual situation. These situations, reduced to their limits, are redolent with unanswered questions. To answer them is the task of existential philosophy.

First of all, this strange limited being presents itself as *Dasein*. This German word, which Hegel had already used, is now in the vocabulary of philosophers of all countries. Literally, it means: *to be here, to be in one specific situation, in contact with a specific surrounding. Dasein* therefore designates an empirical situation in which man finds himself without knowing why and certainly without asking to be there. The emphasis is in freeing man of the responsibility for finding himself where he is: he did not choose his situation, he is *already* there. And he knows it. *Dasein* therefore is consciousness (*Bewusstsein*) of the situation, awareness of the surrounding existences. But this consciousness is not capable of being the object of its own thinking. Man knows that he cannot think of himself as an object. When I say: "I am myself, I was born in that town, on that day, I exercise this profession, I have these likings and dislikings," I know well that I will never be able to

---

[39] *Philosophie*, Vol. 1, p. 1.
[40] *Ibid.*, p. 19.

reduce myself to my thought. There is something else of myself, something else that exists beyond (*ex*), I am an *existent*. "Existence [Existing] cannot be an object and it cannot be reduced to its origins from which its ideas and actions are explained logically; *existence is what refers to itself and what simultaneously refers to something else beyond itself*.[41] Thus we have the three aspects: *Dasein*, consciousness, and existence: one including the other and all together postulating transcendence, insofar as it is essential for man to be in the continuous process of overcoming himself.

In addition to this temporal dimension of man and simultaneous with it, Jaspers saw another special dimension. *Dasein* is being in the world without being of the world. *Dasein* is a continuous effort to understand and overcome the world. Man engages in a struggle to clarify the enigmatic meaning of material beings and fights to shed some light on the complex variety of other men, who conceal themselves under their features and actions. They are objects for my consciousness, more difficult objects and more mysterious than the material world. "If there were only a contrast between being and non-being, between true and false, between good and evil, we would have only a one-directional movement in the *Dasein*. But the multiplicity of existences creates a pathetic situation. Existence is not only contracted with the absence of existence, but with other existences, which present a variety of profound and difficult meanings."[42]

The spectacle offered by the natural sciences, in this struggle of the *Dasein* to conquer the world, is for Jaspers exceptionally instructive. They all start from axioms which are beyond explanation; their aim is the same: to reach a synthesis. They even tried, particularly with the excesses of positivism, the utopian transformation of the universe into a technical formula, but did not realize the inherent contradiction of their effort: if *Dasein*, man, becomes an instrument, whose instrument will he be? There would be an instrument without anyone using it. Jaspers finally asserted: "Sciences aim to determine and crystallize everything and do not realize that what is stable is nothing, while what is becoming is the manifestation of being."[43]

Jasper's criticism of science is extended also to all "essential" or systematic traditional philosophies. According to him, they claim a final

---

[41] *Ibid.*, p. 15.

[42] *Philosophie*, Vol. 2, p. 437.

[43] *Philosophie*, Vol. 1, p. 253. Notice that Jaspers uses the expression: "manifestation of being" instead of "being manifesting itself." If becoming is the manifestation of being, becoming is an aspect of something which does not reduce itself to this aspect. Jaspers' logic is based on a presupposition that he refuses to accept but which is the self-evident result of a metaphysics of being.

understanding of being; they have both the questions and the answers.[44] But do they? The antinomies: rational-irrational, form-content, existence-wholeness, cannot be overcome. These philosophies are checkmated; consequently they cry for help either from religious faith or from philosophical faith.

Particularly obnoxious for Jaspers is religious faith: it is a total surrender: "The sermon of the mount ruins everybody."[45] It is the destruction of all beings in favor of a transcendent being. Philosophical faith is healthier; it approaches *Dasein* with an invitation to accept the challenge of transcending itself.

The second volume of *Philosophie* faces the task of analyzing the position of *Dasein* in its struggle to accept its own need for transcendence. Jaspers used the suggestive title of *Existenzerhellung*, "the illumination of existence."

It is axiomatic for Jaspers that nothing in man can be known with objective evidence, not even that man is himself. Therefore, the minimum requirement for a sound metaphysical beginning in this difficult venture of investigating man's complexities is denied by Jaspers, namely, the possibility of objectively certain self-knowledge. Hence his assertions fall logically in his content: man cannot be known as an object, he is unknowable to himself, the act of self-knowledge is incomprehensible. In this unstable situation, man slides from one impression to another, from one experience to the next, knowing that somehow they all belong to him and yet he is always tortured, as Tantalus and Sisyphus were, by an innate failure to understand himself.

Jaspers suggests that when I say "I am," I say it with two different meanings: the one, empirical, designates my being as *this* man, with this profession, in these circumstances. The other, transempirical and existential, stresses my destiny as superior to any temporary situation, my capacity to reach beyond my little world, my ability to make decisions or to refuse to make them.

The illumination of existence accepts these antinomies as they are, without pretending hypocritically to minimize or abolish them. This sincere profession of our own limitations is *the foundation of existential communication:* "Communication is possible only when we deny our-

---

[44] It is difficult to think of a philosophy in the history of Western thought that claims to know all the answers. Perhaps monistic philosophies, in particular Spinoza's monism, could be considered mathematically terminated. Without doubt, moderate realism that defends the knowledge of the existence of the essences cannot be accused of knowing all the answers. The field of inquiry for a metaphysics is open and mysterious and as infinite as being itself so as to make man curious and interested in all philosophical experiences.

[45] K. Jaspers, *Philosophie*, Vol. 1, p. 307.

selves the dubious privilege of becoming impersonal objects, of being the regimented objects of a State or a Church; objective metaphysics, objective morality, and ontologies are therefore against existential communication."[46]

Our way of thinking does not exclude but rather demands the possibility of an "ontological knowledge" to which every human being aims and which is the foundation of a moral order that is possible because of our innate faithfulness to truth, wherever it manifests itself.

Ultimately philosophical investigation is possible only if everyone concerned is aware of an "intellectual humility" binding all true philosophers to search for the truth. But "intellectual humility" is not possible when the philosopher begins his journey with the preconceived prejudice that truth is impossible. Then his prejudice becomes, dogmatically and irrationally, *his* truth, and his inquiry is not in proper focus and leads to conclusions that can only be self-centered and arbitrary. But communication, even in ideal conditions, is not easy among men. The greatest obstacle to communication is the inborn inadequacy of human nature to communicate. The root of this inadequacy is existence itself, which is singular and individual. Every time we make contact with another person, we accept risks and possible failures. This game between the possibility and impossibility of risks and successes constitutes the essence of man. Man is at the mercy of history, man is history (*Geschichlickheit*).[47] The historicity of man consists in the fate

---

[46] *Philosophie*, Vol. 2, p. 166. The question must be put to Jaspers: "Is there communication if different languages are spoken or if we know in advance that there is *nothing* in common among ourselves to communicate?" I am writing these lines now because I know that there is a truth which I want to discover and communicate to you. And I know that the truth, once obtained, does not suffer contradictions. Therefore, if a disagreement will exist between me and you, it will be necessary to establish which one of us is right. Suppose that I am wrong. That does not mean that I do not exist. My existence belongs to an objective metaphysics that Jaspers considers an obstacle to existential communication, and we do not agree with him.

[47] As a concrete historical event of existence, communication is always bound to a particular situation: "If I want to be fair to all the persons I meet, I am forced to be superficial, and if I pursue an imaginary possibility of universal communication, I renounce the possibility of being an historical being who is unique in his limitations" (*Philosophie*, Vol. 2, p. 60).

Jaspers seems to be the victim, here (contrary to the whole sequence of his philosophy) of pragmatic considerations. It is true that each individual is capable of few effective communications. Friendship, for instance, is the result of a labor of love; for none of us can be extended to a multitude of persons. But this does not mean that our own human limitations establish and justify the nature of communication. Communication is open to all beings. The limited group of friends represents the need of man to be social; if it represents only the desire of man to be social with those few friends, the friends become a clan of bigots. Note the importance of these principles in the struggle for the destruction of racial bias and

that he is open to others because he is constitutionally open to himself. He connects himself with the past and projects himself into the future by making decisions in the present.

In Jaspers, as in Heidegger, an understanding of the different meanings of *historisch* and *geschichtlich* is essential. One English word translates both: historical, although we might say that *historisch* is the "historical" whereas *geschichtlich* is the "historic." *Historisch* is the past, closed, done with, the object of chronology. The present and the future too could be shifted into this inhuman, deterministic light, particularly as they are seen as mechanical results of circumstances. Man rebels against such a possibility and his rebellion is the birth of *existential consciousness*. I look back to my past, "but I do not abandon myself to it, somehow I ought to wake it up to the reality of my present and of my future, which depend on my past."[48] Thus my temporal dimension is not *historisch*, it becomes *geschichtlich*: "I find unity in my life: my past originated my present and both of them are the promise of my future. . . . What I remember is present to me as an opportunity to live it again. Thus my present becomes, by virtue of this abundance of memories, an eternal present."[49] Man is therefore well rooted in time, he accepts time, thus he overcomes it and he decides his eternal goals in it. Man established his own eternity by this daring unification of the past and the future sealed in this instant of his present decision. The affinity of this doctrine with Nietzsche's eternal circularity of time is clear: for both eternity is reached in each existential decision which man makes in the instant of the present.[50]

4. *Freedom*

An important facet of this embrace of time and eternity is the consequent fusion of freedom and necessity. Rationalism has failed to overcome the antinomy, freedom-necessity, because it conceives them both as two mechanical entities. Everybody knows that Descartes was trapped, by his own clear and distinct ideas, into an unpleasant,

of nationalism. In the Christian context, thinking and desiring the good of all human beings does not remain on the level of pure aspiration; it takes knowledge of human limitations for granted and, therefore, through prayer, identifies itself with the sacrifice of the divine person of Christ.

48 *Philosophie*, Vol. 1, p. 269. See also Vol. 2, pp. 56–61 and p. 162.

49 *Ibid.*, Vol. 2, p. 126.

50 Heidegger is more faithful to Kierkegaard and to the Christian tradition. He stresses the importance of the future rather than the present, though the future itself is saddened by the reality of death. Another question Jaspers left unsolved: if eternity is reached in the present, what is the task of transcendence in his philosophy?

irrational dualism between spirit and matter. Jaspers offered a remedy to the Cartesian scheme: according to him, only a practical decision overcomes the necessity-freedom antinomy.[51] In fact we encounter the rigidity of physical necessity every time we exercise our freedom. We accept without question our own physical conditions of time, society, and work. Therefore, we freely adapt ourselves to the necessity under which our own freedom exists. This is the first duty we have as human beings. Freedom therefore comes from our inalienable consciousness that we are able to make decisions. Nothing is more obnoxious and false for Jaspers than to think of freedom as homage to truth or as a conclusion resulting from an objective view of the world. To be free freedom must be absolute, without condition, springing from inside man, as Minerva did from the head of Jupiter. Freedom comes only from the inside, when the *Dasein* discovers himself as existent and free. Therefore, democracy is the eventful conclusion of a process which each individual starts within himself, outside and against any abstract precept on the essence of man.

Freedom is also above knowledge and morality. It is above knowledge because if I knew my situation and had no angel of darkness within me, I would not be in need of making any decision. "I must will, because I do not know; my not-knowing is the cause of my will and my obligations."[52] Because I do not know, before my decision, I am ignorant of the meaning of good and evil. "As long as my action is in progress I am tied up to the situation which I am in. If I think of what kind of a person I would be outside this given concrete situation, I indulge in abstract, useless thinking. Therefore I become conscious of a situation only after I have committed myself to it."[53] Freedom is of an absolute

---

[51] This might be true; but when I recognize the truth of this doctrine, I do not decide, I simply reflect. Therefore the antinomy is overcome at the level of thought, which it does not articulate according to rationalistic schemes.

[52] *Philosophie*, Vol. 2, p. 191. It is obvious that in order to choose I cannot know everything, since my free choice aims to the future which I do not know. But this is not the complete picture: before my choice, I do not know everything, but I do know something, for instance, that I have a future, that I am myself. Limitation is of the nature of man, but limitation limits *something* (man) which is *more essential* than his own limit.

[53] *Ibid.*, p. 308. This Jasperian existential decision, previous and superior to thought and morality, is the origin of man as *Dasein*. Hence the tragic conclusions which Jaspers cannot avoid. Is this decision inclined to charity or to violence? We find ourselves stranded by the whim of a blind voluntarism. Notice the basic differences existing between realism, idealism, and existentialism in this context. Realism says: man accepts the guiding hand of reality which he essentially understands. Idealism says: the existent reality depends on the thought of man. Therefore, idealistically, there is a preeminence of thinking to being. The existentialism of Jaspers (and Sartre) goes further: existence is free decision. But what is a free decision that does not know and does not see — a decision without alternatives?

origin: from the raw material which I find in myself I constitute myself free.[54]

Jaspers is forced by his own logic to talk of a blind will, indeed almost of a satanic will, of autodeterminism. It is not without meaning that he brought up the literary example of Shakespeare's *Richard III*.

Now that man is defined as absolute self-decision Jaspers must face the consequences. First man is not free from guilt. He is absolute freedom and he lives a relative, contingent life, walled in by his situation, like an eagle in a cage. Second, guilt makes man aware that he lives in sin.[55] The terminology is evidently Christian; the doctrine, so pessimistic and hopeless, invites the recollection of the German mysticism of the fifteenth century and the Lutheran contempt for human nature. But the words "sin" and "guilt" are not used by Jaspers with Christian connotations. Their meaning is philosophical, springing from the traumatic experience of man absolute in his freedom and yet imprisoned in his existential situation. His freedom clamors for transcendence, his existential situation prevents the fulfillment of his transcendence.

This is man, as Jaspers sees him: a man checkmated, offspring of a philosophy that does not know how to proceed and fulfill its duty.

The confusion is due to the fact that Jaspers alternates philosophical reflection with psychological intuitions. It is, for instance, a suggestive intuition to say that sin was born from freedom, but it is philosophically unacceptable to assert that the consciousness of our limitations is the cause of our guilt and sin; it is philosophically true that man longs for infinity, but it is difficult to see why man should claim an infinity, which is only God's prerogative, in order to reach God.

Without doubt, Jaspers the psychologist often has the upper hand on Jaspers the philosopher. In fact his originality consists in his masterly ability to describe extreme radical human experiences, his ability to reach the very bottom of our lives. These experiences demand a philosophical or a religious answer.

Take, for instance, the philosophical meaning that Jaspers found in the *Grenz-situationen*.[56] Man often lives uncomfortably in a painful situation; he considers himself hopelessly trapped; outside circumstances seem to condition his actions and his life. But when he is about to give up, when suffering, shame, violence, and death are about to intone their paean of victory, man finds in himself the most profound value of his existence: his own freedom. Then the process is reversed: the situa-

---

[54] *Ibid.*, pp. 46–49.
[55] *Ibid.*, p. 196 ff.
[56] *Ibid.*, pp. 201–336.

tional circumstances do not lead any longer, but they are led. Man's freedom is no longer determined by the accidentals of the environment; no event, as frightening as it might be, has a conquering power. When the world shuts man off, he finds himself by shutting off the world. "Determination, which appeared before as a restriction, opens up an impenetrable depth in which the existence is revealed."[57] Nothing can vex me: "Death changes its meaning with my own changing of my meaning."[58] Once I know that I live an existence of unconditioned freedom, I feel my eternity, and death is powerless in its attempt to stop my thoughts, which are a constant witness to my transcendence. "Everything in the world is indifferent and, at the same time, everything can be of decisive importance."[59] It depends on the perspective from which the world is seen. If I see the world as a refuge for a life of indolent rest, then I am in bad faith. Money, prestige, social stature could be powerful instruments to foster *my alienation* from my destiny of transcendence. Their results are selfishness, hatred and boredom. True consciousness is love, faith, imagination. It is boundless, because freedom is boundless, and it reaches infinity and eternity.

Jaspers has been called a mystic without God, a traveler without a place to go, and a deeply Christian man without the religion of Christ. We subscribe to these definitions: for him, life is never a final possession but always a perilous conquest; existence is never a subjective viewpoint but always a striving toward transcendence; man must communicate, for no man is an island entire of itself, but each is a piece of the continent, a part of the mainland. Christ said: "Love each other" because you all are God's children. Jaspers says: "You must communicate with others, in whom you will find the simultaneous manifestation of transcendence in a magnificent variety of fashions. Truth is in being one for the other" (*Zueinandersein*).

5. *Jaspers' View of Metaphysics*

The third volume of Jaspers' *Philosophie* has a surprising title: *Metaphysik*. The surprise somehow dies out if you read the introduction. Jaspers explained that the word "Metaphysics" does not imply a rational recognition of the fundamental characteristics of being which experience cannot grasp, but is only a point of reference which is not wholly irrelevant to traditional metaphysics. Furthermore, the individual existent

[57] *Ibid.*, pp. 213–214.
[58] *Ibid.*, p. 229.
[59] *Ibid.*, p. 209.

(man, the *Dasein*) finds it only methodically useful in understanding himself.[60]

To be sure, Jaspers accepted the Kantian conclusions about "traditional metaphysics." Therefore reality in its transcendent connotation is ineffable, beyond definition and beyond any logical categories. Yet this reality must exist. Its enigmatic nature consists in the fact that its only knowable aspect is revealed by history and through history, whereas it cannot in itself be merely historical. Therefore, do not try to grasp the meaning of being — Jaspers admonished — because if you try, "the only result possible to your thought consists in the evidence that something must exist which is unthinkable."[61]

With this honest confession of failure, Jaspers thought that rationalism was finally defeated and existentialism was the new philosophy of man.

But was rationalism defeated? It is well known that rationalism refused to accept a distinction between the existence and the essence of being, with the conclusion that when the essence is impervious to the human mind, the existence too must be denied. Jaspers held the same position, particularly in reference to the supreme being. Another rationalistic axiom established the mind as the final tribunal proclaiming verdicts which cannot be appealed to a higher court. Therefore Christian revelation as a source of knowledge for man is impossible, as all positive religions must be. Jaspers pedantically accepted this conclusion. It is safe to say therefore that Jaspers retained, notwithstanding his protestations to the contrary, a profound rationalistic set of intentions.

In these conditions, *Dasein* — man as individual and existent — remains subject, in an emotional rhythm of challenge, to the Absolute of disillusion and dread or of confidence and presumption. It is a situation fluctuating between two extremes which Jaspers described, with romantic overtones, as the law of daylight and the passion for night (*das Gesetz*

---

[60] *Ibid.*, Vol. 3, pp. 3–10.

[61] *Ibid.*, p. 38. Any philosopher with a clear understanding of the nature of metaphysics takes issue with this statement. Jaspers claims that "something must exist which is unthinkable"; but if I reach the evidence of something existing beyond human experimental knowledge, I cannot call it unthinkable. On the contrary, my thinking it is so successful that I am able to discover its fundamental quality: existence, and thus I contribute to an act of knowing metaphysical qualities of being. The importance of this point cannot be overstressed. Consider, for instance, this second quotation which describes with clarity the unclear position of Jaspers. "Though transcendence is really only for the individual existent, he must behave in the presence of it as if it were a being completely independent in its existence." The statement is self-contradicting and, though it is not the human task to institute a process to human intentions, you gather the impression from Jaspers' work that he likes this type of contradiction because he is convinced, with Kant, that human knowledge, essentially, works to solve metaphysical antinomies which he considers insoluable.

des Tages und die Leidenschaft zur Nacht).[62] The law of the daylight corresponds to the attempt of reason to clarify the obscurity of existence, to discover God manifested in the world, to give meaning to life; in stringent contrast, the passion for the night is the unending temptation to supress life, to accept existence as a useless passion, to agree with the destructive work of time. The two moments seem to be antithetic, but Jaspers liked to consider them as mutually complementary, integrating man in his contradictory aspects.[63] "We find a blind happiness of the *Dasein* only when it abandons itself to confidence in transcendence. It is a sort of apprehensive happiness that is born from the consciousness of a challenge overcome and of ills possible in the future. In this abandonment we experience a painful feeling which shares simultaneously the joy of a danger overcome and the pain of a hidden future joy."[64]

Again religious terms are needed by Jaspers. He called this abandonment "faith." Faith in a possible *One,* transcendent and mysterious, and yet epitomizing human desires, hopes, and expectations.

In the final pages of his *Philosophie* Jaspers expressed doubts about all forms of polytheism. Transcendence needs *Oneness:* "My God is also the God of my enemy."[65] His enthusiasm for Giordano Bruno, one of the favorite authors of his younger days, brought him to speak of a vision of Neoplatonic unity, mystic and dynamic at the same time. The existential path of man, always difficult and often cruel, makes room for this final goal of supreme unity. The vagueness of this doctrine does not need comment; but it is relevant to stress Jaspers' conviction that material things, human events, the variety of philosophical theories are *symbols* of this universally inborn longing for the final unity. The real question is not whether Hegel's dialectics or Freud's psychoanalysis is true: "They do not convince me either through reasoning or through empirical observations. The real question is to know which *symbol* of expression is *truer* existentially and which one is farther away from the

---

[62] *Ibid.*, pp. 102–116.

[63] The student of philosophy might be confused by this loose Jasperian use of the term "contradictory." In the context of moderate realism "contradictory" is reserved only for sentences expressing opposite judgments, not for ontological reality. Not all opposed sentences express contradictions, some are only contrary. For instance, *contrary* are the two sentences: All men are happy; no man is happy. *Contradictory* are the two sentences: All men are happy; some men are not happy. Only in this last example, the first sentence denies the truth of the second and vice versa. Jaspers did not have formal training in logic and therefore his approximate use of terms should not create confusion.

[64] K. Jaspers, *Philosophie*, Vol. 3, pp. 117–127.

[65] *Ibid.*, p. 75.

truth."[66] One thing remains unquestionable for Jaspers: Existence only is the book from which to read the symbols of transcendence. "I understand transcendence only in as much as I live it in my life. If I diminish, if I extinguish myself to the point of becoming an empty consciousness lost among others, transcendence disappears for me. If I sense it and I live it, transcendence becomes a being which is the only being for me."[67]

Beware of the shallow forms of symbols which pretentiously present transcendence to you as an easy goal. They are deceitful. Among them Jaspers found liberal arts, esthetics, particularly music. Thomas Mann sounded the warning against them when he wrote that they are Trojan horses, made for the destruction of the real commitment of man; liberal arts, when separated from the philosophical meaning of existence, are instruments of superficiality, they create emptiness and presumptious exaltations which are "human, too human," to use an expression dear to Nietzsche[68] when he denounced the Wagnerian "madness of the Germans." Art, to be truthful to itself, must be a "symbol" of philosophy and must search transcendence.[69]

6. *Man, Technology, and Society*

In 1929 Jaspers wrote for the Goschen paperbacks *The Intellectual Movements of the Present.* The work was published in 1931 simultaneously with the *Philosophie* and with a minor change of the title: *Die geistige Situation der Zeit*[70] (*The Intellectual Situation of our Times*). Within two years, the volume was translated into English, Spanish, and Japanese.[71]

Die geistige Situation der Zeit is an invitation to act with conscientious responsibility. The theme is familiar to us: "Man is mind and the situation of man as man is a mental situation."[72] But the mind presents man with the insidious temptation to use abstract principles to judge a concrete situation. This temptation, once accepted, brings death to the existential man, because he loses his chance to exercise his freedom.[73]

---

[66] *Ibid.,* p. 148.

[67] *Ibid.,* p. 150.

[68] *Ibid.,* p. 120.

[69] *Ibid.,* p. 192. These Jasperian ideas about art must be seen in the historical moment in which they were written. Berthold Brecht defended with his fiction, at the same time, the thesis that life was art and expression. The artists of the club "Der Brinke" had an analogous goal, to express through painting the radical limitation and hopelessness of human existence.

[70] Jaspers, *Die Geistige Situation der Zeit,* (Berlin: de Gruyter, 1931).

[71] The English translation, as we noted previously, has the title: *Man in the Modern Age,* (London, 1933). Our quotations are taken from the edition of Doubleday Co., Anchor Books, 1957.

[72] *Ibid.,* p. 4.

[73] *Ibid.,* p. 23.

Besides, he loses his joy of living, which must remain a struggle toward transcendence. In these conditions he would cease to feel the profound inspiration that comes from creating his own morality because he would have the answers before the questions, the solution of the problem before the problem. Consciousness therefore is not static, but dynamic; its nature is wholly in its actual movement toward its own transcendence.

The evils of the present age are listed by Jaspers in a series of "absolutes" of which man has become a slave: science uses absolute formulas, philosophies patronize absolute findings, religions claim absolute divinities. Since the seventeenth century the sciences have not recognized their limited field of experimental research; their monstrous plan was to reduce the whole reality of nature and man to a technical structure. Everything was meant to be functional: but if man is part of this functionality, whose purpose is served?

Total mechanization of man equals slavery of man,[74] with the unhappy result of a utopian equality that represents the death of the individual and the birth of a new mastodonic aberration: the State. Its existence should be beneficial: "The concrete content of the state is the providing of man with opportunities for the free fulfilment of his occupational ideals in all their multiplicity — ideals which cannot be fulfilled so long as he remains a mere function of the apparatus; and the substance upon which the state works consists of human beings who, through education, have acquired the power of participating in their historical tradition."[75]

But who knows the real nature of the state, this enormous Leviathan, that establishes force and coercion as the main tools for its success? The individual accepts the state as an ineluctable necessity: Fascism and Communism are easy ways out for man who pretends to forget his own self under the cruelty of their oppression.[76]

In the end, the situation of twentieth-century man leads to a crisis: he is checkmated. For him good and evil, life and death, success and failure are meaningless. Good intentions are rooted in selfishness; the genius is always accompanied by abnormality. Yet man exists: what should he do with himself? Again, the turning point in this work is like the one which we analyzed in *Philosophie* and which is common to all existentialists from Kierkegaard to our days. We mean the awakening of man to his own dignity. The world has been desecrated. A reconsecration of the world demands man's reawakening to his transcendent destiny.

[74] *Ibid.*, pp. 33–38.
[75] *Ibid.*, p. 91.
[76] *Ibid.*, p. 96.

To be truthful, it seems difficult to find in *Man in the Modern Age* any ideas that are not contained in *Philosophie*. Perhaps one can say that *Man in the Modern Age* reveals a Jaspers more in contact than previously with the actual political world in which he is living. Jaspers seemed to see political storm clouds gathering in the skys of Europe: all the conditions were ready for Jaspers to prove to man the authenticity of his existence and his determination to reach his own transcendence.

The irrationality of these events reminded him of the necessity of faith in human destiny. Later he wrote of those trying days: "Something immutable in our origin might be upholding us, not to be changed in its meaning by any historic disaster; yet the changeable facts had to be seen and grasped anew from this immutable standpoint."[77] His "immutable standpoint" for twelve long years of persecution remained firm: man is surrounded by the mystery of transcendent vocation which is nameless because of the finitude of human thinking. Those twelve years of forced retirement were a splendid opportunity for long-due meditation: could he give a name to the transcendence to which man is called?

7. *The Encompassing*

The first attempt at a solution of this problem appeared in a series of lectures given in 1931–1932. Then Jaspers introduced the new concept of *Umgreifend*: Encompassing. It was another attempt to describe human knowledge. In fact, Encompassing is the ever changing and widening horizon of our understanding. For instance, I know my friend John through his extraordinary dedication to teaching. From there I increase my knowledge of him as a man of exceptional intellectual ability; and this quality gives me the chance to discover his love for human beings, for social justice, for human rights. Encompassing, Jaspers says, can be properly compared to a thrilling experience well-known to all mountain climbers: for them each step toward the top is a generous gift of a new and wider horizon. They experience progressively the grandeur of nature and the infinity of God. "We always live and think within an horizon. But the very fact that it is an horizon indicates something further which again surrounds the given horizon. From this situation arises the question about the Encompassing. The Encompassing is not a horizon within which every determinant mode of Being and Truth emerges for us, but rather that within which every particular horizon is enclosed as something absolutely comprehensive which is no longer

---

[77] K. Jaspers, *Philosophy and the World*, p. 266.

visible as an horizon at all."[78] So Jaspers spoke in the spring of 1935 to the students of Groningen (Holland) where he gave five lectures, published as *Vernunft und Existenz* (*Reason and Existence*). The Encompassing delineates with unequivocal precision the opposite nature of philosophy and natural science. The latter lead to a deadend: atomic physics cannot go beyond the inquiry of the atom. The opposite is true for philosophy: "One runs into the infinite unless one arbitrarily sets limits by some unquestioned purpose or contingent interest."[79] Jaspers went further and used a language which is familiar to classic philosophy when he said that empirical sciences dealt with the behavior of things but never questioned the meaning of things in themselves. Heidegger presented the same problem by quoting the famous words of Aristotle: "And indeed the question which was raised of old and is raised now and always as ever the subject of doubt is: what is Being?"[80]

Was Jaspers turning to metaphysics? The answer is unequivocally negative. Jaspers never departed from the Kantian solution of this problem. The Encompassing is for him a living proof of a human longing for metaphysics, which is tragically beyond his ken. "The Encompassing appears and disappears for us in two opposite perspectives: either as Being itself, in and through which we are — or else as the Encompassing which we ourselves are, and in which every mode of Being appears to us."[81] For Jaspers, the second perspective of this quotation is, since Kant's time, unavoidable. "Although we know or at least take into account the fact that the Encompassing which we are is in no wise Being itself, still this can be seen in critical purity only *after we have* gone to the end of the path opened up by Kant."[82] But

---

[78] K. Jaspers, *Vernunft und Existenz* (Wolters, Groningen, 1935). English trans. *Reason and Existence* by Earle (New York: Noonday Press, 1955), p. 52. This translation will be used in the following pages.

[79] *Ibid.*, p. 53.

[80] Aristotle, *Metaphysics*, 1028b.

[81] *Reason and Existence*, p. 58.

[82] *Ibid.*, p. 54, Jaspers does not conceal the uncomfortable conclusions of his reasoning. The Encompassing is. the logical limit of philosophical research. Therefore, by its own nature, it is abstract. Jaspers himself wrote: "Philosophy, wherever it is successful, consists of those unique ideas in which *logical abstractness* and the actual present become, so to speak, identical. The basic drives of living philosophy can express themselves truly only in purely *formal thought*" (*Ibid.*, pp. 49–50). Now the question: if the Encompassing is a "purely formal thought" does Jaspers' existentialism (born as a strong affirmation of concreteness against the "useless philosophy of the abstract Aristotelian essences") need the help of abstractions as a means of expression? The answer of course is evident: abstract ideas are necessary to anybody expressing anything. Jaspers' embarrassment is just this: the Encompassing, which is the idea of a logical essence, is seen as the horizon of the existent reality.

the enormous difference between Kant and Jaspers (and with him, most existentialists) is to be found in the fact that once Kant had reached the conclusion that the mind cannot have any claim on metaphysical values, he resigned himself to it as it is shown by his doctrine of schematism in the *Critique of Judgment*. This is not true for Jaspers. He officially accepted Kant's position and simultaneously began his sorrowful sequence of recriminations and complaints about the choice made. Further, Jaspers' real philosophy consists of an effort to overcome Kantian limits, as if he were eager to prove to himself that, after all, he was wrong.

In this context it is most interesting to examine the progressive analysis he made of his "Encompassing." "Encompassing" presents itself in three different ways: as *empirical existence* in the succession of actions and reactions to the material world; as *universal consciousness* interpreting Being from a point of view valid for everybody; finally, as *dialectical spirit* reporting the consciousness of eternity within time and witnessing a totality of being as the final goal of human knowing. These are three aspects of one reality: "The distinction of empirical existence [*Dasein*], consciousness as such, and spirit do not imply separable facts. Rather they represent three starting points through which we can come to feel that comprehensive Being which we are and in which all Being and everything scientifically investigable appears."[83] Jaspers acknowledged, therefore, the fact that Being itself is revealed either as *universe* or as *transcendence*. But he could not recognize the transcendence of Being without the individual man conceiving it. This conception is the *reasoning power* of the existent. "Existence only becomes clear to reason; reason only has content through the existent."[84] Jaspers preferred therefore the law of the daylight to the passion for the darkness, and it was no minor achievement in a world that was bracing for a confrontation of brutal forces. This Jasperian reason is above all an inexhaustible impulse to see clearly, to dissipate darkness, to establish communication with others. "To be genuinely true, truth must be communicable."[85] Truth is not there for everybody to grasp as a ready-made piece of furniture. Truth is openness to others, to different experiences, to the practical needs of the *Dasein*, to the exigencies of universality, to

It is only honest to add that Jaspers is not alone in this game of condemning formal logic by using it. All existentialists and all those philosophers who deny the unquestionable bond of mutual correspondence between reality and the mind must accept the same fate: if they use logical terms, at least implicitly, these terms are considered valid. Yet, the purpose in using them is to demonstrate that they are invalid.

[83] *Ibid.*, p. 58.
[84] *Ibid.*, p. 67.
[85] *Ibid.*

spiritual convictions. Truth is more dependent on the cooperation of many than on its objective aspect which in its totality is never achieved.

Perhaps this continuous insistence on appeals and encouragements is one of the most positive aspects of Jaspers' thought. When he accepts the challenge of being constructive, he fails his purpose. His aim is a total revindication of the individual, who must affirm himself through the meaning of the Encompassing, which is neither individualized nor individualizing. Now Jaspers speaks of truth as a result of communication among many. But is it logical to speak of a truth, made up of communications, without a previous knowledge of what is objectively true? Similarly, if man is just contingent, the idea of man and of all human historical values must be contingent. Jaspers said, and his terminology is not lacking suggestiveness, that truth as communication among men reveals love for one another, and truth is mutual love. The truth of being cannot reside in the relations among beings if we want to avoid the reduction of the absolute to what is relative.

Leibniz said of his monads that they did not have windows. The existents of Jaspers run the risk of presenting themselves as windows facing windows, without anything to see and no one seeing. This is the price always paid when a philosopher fails to see that being precedes action and that truth always comes from being.

8. *Logic and Truth*

The year 1938 must have been a difficult one: Jaspers, the philosopher of communication, was sealed off completely by state censure: even writing was forbidden to him[86] But no one could prevent him from thinking and conversing with his wife and Heinrich Zimmer, the renowned orientalist. When Zimmer fled Hitler's persecution and came to the United States, his library remained with Jaspers, a precious gift during his forced seclusion. It was then that Jaspers thought out his last great work, *Philosophic Logic.* In his autobiography he wrote: "Our labor on *Philosophical Logic* was one of inner self-preservation. It was a work done in the shadows darkening all our days, not with youthful vigor as at the time of our *Psychology of World View,* nor on the confident heights of life as at the time of our *Philosophy.* Around us was the silence of seculsion in a state of having to hold out, and sudden fears."[87]

The reader must be aware by now that each work of Jaspers deals

---

[86] The last works published before the Gestapo closed in on him were: *Nietzsche, Einführung in das Verständnis seines Philosophierens* (Berlin: de Gruynter, 1936), and *Descartes und die Philosophie* (Berlin: de Gruynter, 1937).

[87] *Philosophy and the World,* p. 281.

with the same problem: man, the existent and the transcendence in front of him. But each work presents a bolder and wider "Encompassing" than the previous one. We can say that Jaspers lived paradoxically between one philosophical position which seemed obsolete and insufficient to him and another philosophy which was still to come; therefore, he did not have any choice but to continue to search for the true philosophy.

The inspirational theme of *Philosophical Logic* had been discussed in *Reason and Existence*. Now it comes back with greater lucidity and depth, and it can be reduced to the fundamental problem of all existential philosophies. They care about the existent, singular, personal, contingent situation: the description is different for different existentialists but the problem is the same. Yet this concern for the existent must take the form of abstract ideas: if I say that the truth of man consists in his own individual existence, I refer necessarily to all possible human existences. Philosophically speaking, I use universal concepts in the formulations of all problems, including those aiming to prove false the universality of human knowledge. Jaspers understood that and he set out "to view the abstraction of basic knowledge as the pure concretion that will last no matter what."[88] His "solution" is more an act of good intention than a real solution, and it can be reduced to the following program: "I have to accept the universality of my knowledge, but I will not resign myself to remain inside of it. I will not be a hopeless collection of sterile abstractions. I will go out because the *truth of my thinking is in the movement of my thought.* Logical abstract formulas do not hold the monopoly of truth, they do not hold any truth; but they are and they must be used as vehicles to the truth which is always and only existential and therefore particular and individual."

The expression "movement of thought," it seems to us, is ambiguous. If we understand it as "movement different from my thought but captured by my thinking" (for instance, the succession of events), then truth consists in the intellectual comprehension of these events. If "movement of thought" is understood as "thought itself moving and progressing," as an effort to understand something, then this something continues through its vicissitudes and changes and our thinking is progressive because of the new data which we discover and which we attribute to the same thing. Thinking is unthinkable without an object thought. Existentialism, in our case Jaspers' existentialism, which claims to be a philosophy and therefore a logical sequence of ideas, resents the laws of logic; in fact, it establishes an alienation between logic and being, as if no agreement were possible between them. The

[88] *Ibid.*, p. 281.

conclusion, we repeat once more, is a total "Scheitern," checkmate, with the consequent "anxiety" situation.

But let's examine the general design of *Philosophical Logic*.[89] It was meant to be of four volumes: the first one on the meaning of truth and its various manifestations at the different horizons of being; the second, on the categories of thought; the third, on the dialectical methods of research; the fourth, on the structure of scientific knowledge and philosophic systems.

Only the first volume *Von der Wahrheit* (*About Truth*) was published after the war in 1947. With the aging of the author, it remains doubtful whether the other volumes will ever be published.

Truth is not possible without communication. Communication is a work for reason, not for the intellect. The intellect requires scientific precison, but truth is infinitely more. Truth demands communication with being; truth therefore implies a movement in which we are open to infinite horizons in the effort to give a name to all things, to establish relations with them, to be familiar with them and to love them.

Only our reason can achieve this goal, because reason means progress, faith, and love. "We cannot understand the mystery of being directly; therefore, we never hold a truth with a final possession; we live a temporal existence (*in Zeitdasein*): truth for us is only a way."[90]

Reason does not repudiate the work of the intellect, which moves by steps with unilateral attention to one facet of being, thus establishing the variety of sciences. They can be considered as different steps through which reason goes in its ascent toward the understanding of all forms of being. The intellect therefore is dominated by the fixation of the system; on the other hand, reason, as a magnetic force, conquers all delays and strives for a goal superior to scientific knowledge. In a word, reason is the patient unending force which aims at the unity of an absolute transcendence.

Jaspers at this point clarified his thought with a comparison which is most useful to our purpose. He said that *Philosophical Logic*, in its task of tracing the arduous path of human reason toward transcendence, can be compared to the Aristotelian *Philosophia Prima* (*Metaphysics*), but with one fundamental difference. Aristotle spoke of an ontology, which, according to Jaspers, was closed in itself, without open horizons.

---

[89] K. Jaspers, *Philosophische Logik,* Erster Band: *Von der Wahrheit* (Munchen: Piper, 1947). Only a few pages of the last section have been translated into English: *Die Objektivität als Chiffer* (pp. 1002–1054) under the title *Truth and Symbol* (New York: Wayne Publishers, 1959), and *Vollendingder Wahrheit in Urspringlichen Anschauungen: ein Beispeil: das Tragische Wissen* (pp. 915–960), translated under the title: *Tragedy is Not Enough* (Boston: Beacon Press, 1952).

[90] K. Jaspers, *Von der Wahrheit*, p. 1.

The new Jasperian logic used a new term, "periontology," to stress the thrust of reason toward the grasping of being rather than the Aristotelian discussions of being as if reason had already grasped it.

Here is how Jaspers himself explained symmetrically the discrepancies between Ontology and Periontology:[91]

ONTOLOGY	PERIONTOLOGY
The Absolute is indefinable. His indefinability is overcome through the analysis of *the meanings of the essence of created things.*	The Absolute is indefinable. His indefinability is overcome through reason reaching progressively larger *encompassing* horizons, beyond the limits established by the *objectifications* of scientific knowledge.
From the Absolute *derives* each existent.	The "Encompassing" is inconceivable as a source explaining our existence. Our only first is the *Dasein,* ourselves, present and striving with love and communication (i.e., with reason) toward the Absolute. Philosophy illuminates our longing for the Absolute.

The opposite epistemological ground of these two positions is of Kantian origin, and Jaspers never questioned Kant's conclusion. According to the philosopher of Königsberg, "No being of which we have knowledge is being as such." The ambiguity here lies in the confusion between being and necessary being. *Kant did not see that each being of which we have knowledge is being.* This statement is basic for all philosophical discussion: the distinction between necessary and contingent being comes in a second time. If we approach the epistemological problem, as Kant and Jaspers did, with the prejudice that our knowledge, to be valid, must reach immediately both the contingent and the necessary being, then we declare that human knowing is a bankrupt operation. In this case a rational approach is impossible, and the solution to all human problems will be rooted in irrationality.

Jaspers was no exception to this rule. Once he established the failure of the mind to understand what is real, he postulated a philosophy which he accepted as true because he could not explain it. Thus, as a host of philosophical mystics (Plotinus, Bruno, Schelling, etc.) did before him, he announced that our existence is an unending effort to

---

[91] *Ibid.,* p. 160.

reach the originating One, because we all feel the attraction of the infinite. Reason therefore does not explain the neoplatonic conclusions of Jaspers; on the contrary, neoplatonic immanentism is a natural conclusion because reason does not explain it.

Reason shows that paradox, contradiction and vicious circles are the qualifications of the existent. Logic is rational because it discovers the irrationality of existence. Therefore I communicate with others more on what I do not know than on what I know about the mystery of being. We are all united, bound together as shipwrecked persons, in the presence of Being, mysterious, inscrutable as an infinite ocean.

Thus I know myself and my existential destiny. When finally I reach the awareness that the infinity of the universe cannot be within my reach, then by losing the infinite, I find my existential self and paradoxically, I feel the Oneness of all things. Then only one language is allowed, the most eloquent of all — silence.

Now we might understand the reason that allows Jaspers to state that "thought is meditation (*Mitteilung*) for unity": "*Mitteilung* is the instrument in time to reach the One. We transcend the divisions of our thought not by avoiding them, but by taking them lumped together. There is such a thing as a thought illuminated by Being (*seinsdurchglithes*), that is, a thought that by neglecting the consideration of the object thought of or the thinking subject, manifests being itself."[92]

Jaspers cannot be more specific in this difficult matter; if he were, he would speak of an ontology. But he continues, page after page, to postulate an absolute unity of which human thought reveals the necessity without being able to give logical reasons for it.

Thought is language and therefore communicates; things are the words of being and the huge fracture in being that prevents our complete understanding of it is like an open space we have to cross to reach perfect comprehension.[93] The English representatives of logical positivism considered language as an assembly line of tools to be named with strange new words; Jaspers refused to agree with them. To his mind, they petrified the movement of our thought, reducing it to mechanical utensils. They missed the question completely. In daily life as well as in scientific and political activities, illusions and utopias have their way with reality: truth is mistreated in a succession of ideologies which dazzle everybody's eyes for a short time with the novelties of their suggestive ideas. Their nature is to be partial and unilateral: they do not serve the truth, which is total and universal.

Falsehood (*Taushung*) is precisely a partial truth, made possible

[92] *Ibid.*, pp. 246–249.
[93] *Ibid.*, p. 395 ff.

by the fracture of being, by the variety of Encompassings. But a partial truth cannot be ignored; on the contrary, it must be lived with the consciousness of all other truths, in the communication and finally in the shock of the checkmate: all partial truths create a vacuum in which, mystically and intuitively, appears the ineluctability of the One Truth. It is a progressive movement of penetration operating on the ground of experienced insufficiency of all human experiences. The unity of Truth is reached only in the *Durchbruch* (breakthrough): "What is absolute finds its way through what is relative."[94] I will not regard history as providential or casual, I will be neither dogmatic nor skeptic, because I know that reality is not in front of me already defined as good or evil. What I know is that reality continues to become in the movement of my thought.

In the *Durchbruch,* truth assumes one of two forms: either it is *exception* or *authority;* both of them seem conquests of the multiplicity of individual views and realistic acceptances of the historical process of the existence; they are forces necessary for human living. Exception stimulates discussion and progress; authority offers a concrete ground for experimentation for freedom.

An existential view demands historical authority, Jaspers thought, but he excluded Christian revelation as an historical authority. "An experience similar to Paul's experience on the road to Damascus (*ein Damaskus-Erlebnis*) can easily break a man and make a fanatic out of him; a conversion is always tied down to the danger of losing the existential perspective of life."[95]

The conversion situation is labeled by Jaspers the Catholic solution[96] (*Standpunkte de Katholozität*) as opposed to the existential situation of reason (*Anspruch der Vernunft*). But he missed the point completely. For instance, he said: "It is absurd that God is man or that a man is God." You might think that this statement holds great hope. After all, we know how Jaspers came to his neoplatonic conclusions. But all hopes vanished when he added: "For a philosopher, the humanity of God is

---

[94] *Ibid.,* p. 743.

[95] *Ibid.,* p. 855. This statement is in opposition to the whole development of Jaspers' thought. He is against "conversion" because conversion is a rebellion against the authority of tradition. We might agree on that, but it is difficult to come to the conclusion with Jaspers that because "conversion" is against tradition, it is also against existence. The *Dasein* is precisely in continuous tension to overcome its previous experiences and therefore its interest is for the future, which cannot be repetitious of the past.

The same enigmatic aspects are quite relevant in the last years of Jaspers, particularly in his surprising efforts to interpret history "scientifically" rather than existentially.

[96] Jaspers' knowledge of Catholicism derived from assiduous conversations with Maria Salditt, a Catholic who assisted him in the writing of *Von Der Wahrheit.*

an absurdity leading to error." And he does not justify his statement. Actually, the reason for his strong antagonism to religious faith is a fear that revelation might destroy human freedom. It is somehow paradoxical that this man, who fought all his life for an aperture to the infinite, closed himself hermetically to the perspective of a divine source of knowledge for man. He would rather think and write of myths, love, and symbols of the Absolute always conceived as transcendence.

We have examined the main themes of the first volume of *Philosophical Logic*. Frankly, many ideas are nebulous and gray, which should not surprise us Jean Wahl, after the Second World War, spent long hours translating German works of existentialism into French. He found Jaspers' works hard to understand and he wrote to him asking for some help. Here is the answer that Jaspers sent back: "I carefully try to avoid excessive clarity in my terminology. Clarity of ideas is a process always in the state of becoming through the movement of thought, not through the definition of concepts."[97]

❄   ❄   ❄

9. *Guilt*

On April 1, 1945, the American troops brought freedom to Heidelberg. Jaspers saw himself thrown overnight into politics. He accepted political responsibility. He advised the allies, with the fervor of a man reborn to the joy of dignity and freedom, to establish a nonpolitical German government. He thought (and theoretically he was right) that democracy was the result of time and education. His advice was not followed, and he resumed his teaching at the University of Heidelberg, where, during the fall semester 1945–1946, he developed a theme of burning actuality, the atrocities perpetrated by the Nazis during the war, *Die Schuldfrage*. [98]

It is evident to us, and it appeared evident to him too, that the staggering magnitude of the Nazi genocides could not be clarified by explanations from his philosophy. Therefore, Jaspers preferred to forget his philosophical theories, and in the *Schuldfrage* he initiated an open and honest exchange of ideas with his students and with his countrymen in the effort to shed some light on a human aberration that will remain

[97] Letter written by Jaspers to J. Wahl on November 8, 1949 and reported in Wahl, *La pensée de l'existence*, p. 286.

[98] K. Jaspers, *Die Schuldfrage* (Schneider-Heidelberg, 1946). Translated into English: *The Question of German Guilt* (Dial Press, 1947; Capricorn Books edition, 1961).

forever one of the darkest of guilt-ridden crimes in the history of mankind.

The keynote is crystal clear: "Political liberty begins with the majority of individuals in a nation feeling responsible for the politics of their community."[99] This statement in its boldness and actual reference to the German situation was not accepted with enthusiasm, to say the least. But Jaspers was not looking for popular consent. Just four months after his liberation in August 1945, he seemed to play the part of the German conscience when he said: "We did not go into the streets when our Jewish friends were led away; we did not scream until we too were destroyed. . . . We are guilty of being alive. We know that before God; this humiliates us."[100] The same scourging voice, with Old Testament overtones of a prophet speaking to his people in the name of God, was making itself heard in the pages of *Die Schuldfrage:* "In the past years there were Germans who demanded martyrdom for us other Germans. . . . Thus I could hear myself rebuked from 1933 on, by friends, men and women."[101]

Without doubt, Jaspers came out of twelve years of suffering fears and persecution with a guilty conscience, as if he did not suffer enough, as if nothing short of death could have cleared an honorable German during those awful years of Hitler's madness.

Guilt is discussed in *Die Schuldfrage* from four points of view:

a) *Criminal Guilt,* perpetrated in violation of the human rights, is under the jurisdiction of human tribunals. The trials at Nurenberg were an outstanding example.

b) *Political Guilt* originates from the responsibility shared by all the citizens for political failures of the social structure to which they belong. They all stand ready to pay for a political error.

c) *Moral Guilt* concerns itself with individual consciences and with the human beings who have the right to expect help and protection and love.

d) *Metaphysical Guilt.* Jaspers becomes solemn at this point. Metaphysically we are guilty when we witness massacres and rude barbarism and we do not accept sacrifice, even the supreme sacrifice to oppose it.

And Jaspers continues: the sacrifice should be accepted even if and when we know that it will be useless because the same evil will reign after our deaths. In this supreme confrontation of values, man finds himself naked before Transcendence, since all other aspects of life are

[99] K. Jaspers, *Die Schuldfrage,* p. 121.
[100] Reprinted in *Wandlung,* Vol. 1, No. 1, 1945.
[101] K. Jaspers, *Die Schuldfrage,* p. 105.

drowned by the independent tyranny. If we decide to die, with humility and with dignity, in our death we find the transcendent meaning of our life.[102]

Jaspers faced difficult days on account of these ideas. He left Germany to accept, in 1948, a full professorship at the University of Basel.[103]

❖   ❖   ❖

Basel, the charming Swiss town, has become the center from which the philosopher of communication carries on his efforts to convince all men of the greatness of human destiny.

His thought inclined to be more practical because he felt the need for action. It is a human phenomenon, from Plato to the present, that philosophers cannot conceal a strange form of resentment, when, in their declining years, they are not consulted on the practical ways of making this world a better place to live in. They are convinced that they know the secrets for a better society. Jaspers was no exception. He lived in Switzerland, but his heart was in Germany. Radio, television, lectures have been the tools of his communication: to the present day, his intrepid voice is still heard.

On the other side, the old Jaspers could not resist the temptation to present a final synthesis of his theoretical principles. We could expect a strong restatement of faith in existential anxiety; but that was not the case. In his work, *Von Ursprung und Ziel der Geschichte*,[104] Jaspers

---

[102] It is well known that the controversial play *The Deputy* represented this Jasperian doctrine. It is also evident that we need not agree with these ideas which take in human hands values and judgments that belong only to God. Heroism and martyrdom are sublime achievements when each individual offers his own existence to defend other existences equally worthy and immortal. But if you demand that a man, high in power and responsibility, posit an action which might result in the useless sacrifice of other persons, then you do not know that human beings are sacred and inviolable in their decisions to be free; then you are guilty of an insidious form of Machiavellism because your end demands immoral means, because you expect one man to take in his hands the lives of many.

[103] In the last months at Heidelberg, Jaspers lectured on *Philosophical Faith* (the lectures were published under the title *Der Philosophische Glaube* [München: Piper, 1948]).

Nothing new can be found in this work besides what was said previously about the Jasperian faith. His faith is an act of confidence in human reason. He chose the word "faith" because it implies a commitment of the whole person in continuous communication with the human community. Jaspers considered "religious faith" as an unjustified attempt to make absolute a particular view of God and by doing so, he placed himself squarely outside the framework of religious faith. In fact, he did not understand that religious faith is an acceptance of a mystery superior to human understanding. Particularly opposite to his view was a doctrine that accepts religious faith as a gift of God to man. Since Jaspers did not reach a personal God, he called "faith" the rational striving of man toward the transcendent unknown.

[104] K. Jaspers, *Von Ursprung und Ziel der Geschichte* (München: Piper). English translation: *The Origin and Goal of History* (New Haven: Yale University Press, 1953).

presented a great design of universal history with evident attention to a systematic, almost a scientific approach to the historical phenomenon of man.

The soul of this system is the ineffable One, which Jaspers inherited as we know from his neoplatonic convictions. "The One is rather the infinitely remote point of reference, which is origin and goal at one and the same time; it is the One of transcendence. As such it cannot be, so to speak, taken captive; it cannot become the inclusive possession of an historical faith that could be enforced upon all as truth *per se*. If Universal History, as a whole, proceeds from the One to the One, it does so in such a way that everything accessible to us lies between these ultimate poles. There is a becoming of unities, an enthusiastic seeking of unity: and then, again, a passionate smashing of unities. Thus this deepest unity is elevated to an invisible religion, to the realm of spirits, the secret realm of manifestation of Being in the concord of souls."[105]

A personal God was impossible for Jaspers. Since his youth, he reserved the word "person" to physical human beings who gave him the tenderness of their love and protection and he could not break this traditional family tie and use the word *person* for an invisible entity. He was impressed, as many people are, by the geometrical precision of Spinoza's definition of substance, which assumed new and stronger dimensions when compared by Jaspers to what Kierkegaard called the "infinite qualitative distinction" between God and man. In a word, the whole tradition, from Heraclitus to Plotinus, Bruno, Spinoza, and Schelling was the only angle of historical philosophy which made sense for Jaspers. He went so far as to discover in the unity of universal history an "axial period," that is to say, the span of time in which the "Oneness" of history became evident to all mankind. This blissful human miracle took place between the years 800 B.C. and A.D. 200 when in China Lao-tze and Confucius, in India the Upanishads and Buddha, in Greece Homer and Plato, and in Palestine the Prophets enlightened the world with their wisdom.

If history is the instrument through which different and separated existences meet and become a spiritual unity, the "axial period" was the time in which simultaneously and in different places a consciousness of a universal bond was felt by the civilizations of the world: then history became conscious of itself. The signs of this climactic human event were seen when myth changed into philosophy, cosmic religion became human ethics, the world of epics and lyrics assumed existential

---

[105] Jaspers, *The Origin and Goal of History*, chap. 1.

meaning, an ineffable fate was spoken of by the heroes of Homer and Sophocles.

But history is not static: the axial period came under strong criticism in China and Greece precisely because the human unity is not stable. The times we live in are no exception to the rule: we are witnessing an astonishing triumph of man over nature together with a disquieting confusion in regard to man's knowledge of himself. Our period of time can be related to the axial period insofar as we live in an age that reminds us more of the approaching end of history, for the axial period was an exultant indication of the dawn of human history. Yet the axial period was not the beginning and similarly our civilization will not be the end of this human venture, though we are made aware every day that civilization will be destroyed and that human striving for a final solution is futile. We are making a childlike progress toward a unity which is symbolic of the eternal Oneness of Being.

What makes this work, *The Origin and Goal of History*, outstanding in the sequence of Jaspers' philosophical ideas is its nonexistential outlook on history. Jaspers seemed to forget the existent in order to speak of his destiny. No philosopher, particularly no German philosopher, has ever been satisfied with analytic research. We do not agree with Jaspers when he postulates a Spinozian unity of Being, but everybody agrees with him when he tries to find a logical synthesis for the plurality of the existences.

A series of radio conversations on social and political affairs was published in 1958 with the title *Die Atombombe und die Zukunft des Menschen.*[106] What must we do faced as we are by the possibility of a total destruction of mankind? "Our time thinks in terms of knowing how to do it," even where there is nothing to be done. We want to find salvation in a technological conquest of technology — as if human use of technology might itself be subject to technological direction. Our thinking is not wholly serious until we come to the end of our know-how. *Our age must learn that some things are beyond "doings."*[107]

The atom has created a limit-situation, a *"Grenz-situation,"* beyond which there is no hope. Let's try to avoid that "beyond"; we all are faced with a problem that does not suffer duplicity of mind, diplomatic skills, or genial intuitions: if we want to survive this time, we must be honest and authentic with ourselves. This naked honesty, which must be so complete as to make sincerity useless and suspicious, presents

---

[106] K. Jaspers, *Die Atombombe und die Zukunft des Menschen* (München: Piper, 1958). In English: *The Future of Mankind* (Chicago: The University of Chicago Press, 1961; Phoenix Edit., 1963).

[107] K. Jaspers, *op. cit.*, Eng. tr., Foreword.

us with a fact: all preventive methods of *an intellectual nature* are insufficient and lead to disaster. Politics finds its meaning in *something* of a *superpolitical nature*. Deny this norm, for the sake of argument, and you will have to use force, in our times, atomic force. Justice is always threatened by injustice, honesty by dishonesty, and reason tells you that you have a right to defend what is right.

The answer indeed cannot be found in human reasoning; it comes from a religious respect for the sacredness of the individual. Jaspers echoes the words of St. Augustine: *res sacra, homo*: man is a sacred thing. Now this sacredness requires personal sacrifice which blossoms only from an ethical life. If the majority of citizens know how to renounce their point of view and thus establish communication with their fellowmen, nationally and internationally, then political life opens up hopes for the future of mankind. "In any event, the gate to the future is sacrifice — either the sacrifice of all human existence or the sacrifice of human existential interests, offered to let mankind become truly human."[108]

We console ourselves in the thought that we belong to the free world, but we must know that "Every individual in the free world who appears unconvincing to the others, who displays the seamy side of misused freedom in lawlessness, arrogance and greed, inflicts a defeat upon freedom by his very existence. The free world can be saved only if its members prove its value."[109]

Actually what we do does not follow this ethical rule centered on sacrifice. We all are impenitent believers in reason. And we do not realize that reason gives the kiss of death to everything that comes in contact with it: reason objectifies everything and in the process it alienates us from our problems. If we are troubled, we hope in some automatic device (physical, psychoanalytic) which should free us without infringing upon our freedom. The same consideration is true at the social level: economy, strategy, military power, diplomacy, supposedly should be the miracle-workers that hold the future of human freedom. History proves however that these have already led to war. The new way of thinking originates from the consciousness of our freedom and its necessary limitations: we know that we must be engaged, that our personal engagement protects our freedom by giving freedom to others.

Jaspers offered some good examples and some of questionable value. Germany must be unified if Germans are to share the burden of the common sacrifice. But Germany should continue to be divided: it is a sacrifice for the balance of power between East and West. All nations

---

[108] *Ibid.*, p. 172.
[109] *Ibid.*, p. 110.

should agree on a limitation of power. Even the United Nations should continue to exist. Their representatives in the corridors and meeting rooms of the huge building in New York City are a splendid proof of the failure of politics based on reason. In fact, the diplomats of the United Nations know better than anyone else that they will not get anywhere: their occupation is to deceive each other with the high type good manners that seem to be a monopoly of their own. But their presence in the building of the United Nations is a perpetual warning that it is time to change; therefore, the United Nations should continue.

*   *   *

For us it is time to leave this discussion of Jaspers' philosophy. Without doubt he is a great personality among the philosophers of the twentieth century, and existentialism cannot be understood without him.

He lived what he thought. From the beginning, he discovered the importance of natural sciences and he defined their limits. He had a clear perception of the centrality of man and his freedom. He also saw the destiny of man and his transcendence, but he did not reach the person of God. Too many prejudices, of Kantian and neoplatonic origins, interfered with the conclusions Jaspers aimed at. Transcendence remained always nameless for him.

Hence his conviction that Christianity in general and Catholicism in particular were wrong. Ironically, the patrimony of Christian philosophy was Jaspers'.

Truth is communication and communication is love for mankind: this is his message. His rationalistic convictions prevented him from understanding that communication remains meaningless, to use an idea so dear to Martin Buber, if it is not rooted in our colloquy with the source of all persons: God.

Though we do not agree with many of Jaspers' conclusions, we have no small cause to rejoice when we consider that his honesty and perception have contributed much to our century.

chapter IV

The Phenomenology of
Edmund Husserl

INTRODUCTION: The Problem of Science at the End of the Nineteenth Century

At the close of the nineteenth century the positivists, who were still firmly in control of European academic culture, were forced to realize that all aspects of the existent, from astronomical phenomena to human thinking, could not be explained by the rigid laws of deterministic causality. Many thinkers, not only among the logicians and philosophers, but also among scientists, opposed this dogma of absolute determinism. Minkowski's experiments showed that time and space could no longer be conceived as objective dimensions, static, homogeneous, and unrelated to the mind of the observer. The old academic discussion about the fifth Euclidian postulate revealed the possibility of non-Euclidian geometries. Lobachevski proved that it was possible for two parallel lines meet in a process to infinity and that the sum of the three angles of a triangle could be more than 180°. Heisenberg, with his principle of indeterminacy, carried the rebellion against classical physics into the area of nuclear physics. Medical science was soon to find phenomena (hysteria is one of them) which would challenge the theory of psycho-physical determinism. And almost paradoxically, mathematics itself seemed to experience an inside rebellion which questioned the theoretical foundations of its own existence. New mathematical horizons, statistics and imaginary numbers, hinted at the possibility of new conclusions.

The first decades of the twentieth century produced several creative thinkers — Hilbert in mathematics, Einstein in physics, Planck and Bohr in microphysics, Freud in psychotherapy — who brought order to their respective fields. But each science seemed to grow autonomous, with an evident interest in immediate practical results. Science was "scientific" when it worked: but it was relatively unconcerned about its logical premises.

Without doubt, the dream of the Renaissance man never came closer to its realization: man was on the verge of becoming the king of the universe and the master of its secrets. Actually, however, man became the victim of his own genius. Instead of becoming a true sovereign, he was in danger of being a real slave to scientific research that proceeded without human goal and without theoretical unity. The confusion spread into the field of morality, where the absence of philosophy, once considered the queen of all the sciences, was agonizingly felt. The political horizon also darkened: new wars, unprecedented for their power of destruction, caught unawares men who were still staring in awe at the new discoveries and who were facing in helpless confusion the new technological revolution.

Before the catastrophes of World War I struck, the Hapsburg Empire, the principal victim of that war, produced a new man — Edmund Gustav Albrecht Husserl. His enthusiasm at first was for mathematics, the language of the new revolution. But then he decided to abandon his promising meditations on the calculus of variables. He had another project, doubtless more ambitious, on his mind: the amalgamation and reunification of all sciences and of all human undertakings under one principle of logic. To understand this powerful thinker, we must first turn to an examination of background from which he emerged.

1. FRANZ BRENTANO, BERNHARD BOLZANO, KARL STUMPF

"No one who does not love mathematics may enter this building." These words were written in prominent letters over the entrance of Plato's Academy. Plato knew that philosophy was impossible to those who did not develop the habit of contemplating essences. The mathematician must neglect the superficial aspects of reality (color, taste, odor, etc.) to concentrate on the values of numerical relations, which are ideal and imperishable. Plato, and many philosophers after him, taught that philosophical contemplation depended on the mind's ability to contemplate objective reality in the absence of tangible sense objects.

Husserl is one of the few contemporary philosophers who was first a mathematician. His presence among the philosophers is even more remarkable because he understood the scientific nature of philosophy and, with unique intuition, he held philosophy to be the foundation of all the sciences.

Husserl was born in Prossnitz, Moravia, April 8, 1859. It is useful to remember that Moravia was a province of the Austro-Hungarian Empire, whose secret of power (a real Machiavellian *instrumentum regni*) was to protect and foster a cultural scholastic tradition. The environment in which the young Husserl began his studies dealt in rigid systematic ideas and concerned itself with conservative goals. Nevertheless, the political fortunes of the Empire were in decline. The culture's mosaic-like nature (there were Czechs, Austrians, Hungarians, Italians, and others as well) became the foundation of national unrest. The claim that the emperor received his authority from God was looked upon as a relic of past times. And we need only remember that both Franz Kafka of Prague and Sigmund Freud of Vienna were subjects of the Austrian government to sample the meaning of the new ferment in the old empire.

In this environment, after preparatory work at the Leopold-städter Realgymnasium of Vienna and the Deutsche Realgymnasium of Olmütz, Husserl entered the University of Leipzig and in 1878 the Friedrich Wilhelm University of Berlin. In Berlin, after years of doubt and indecision, Husserl finally found himself. Excellent mathematicians, Kronecher and Weierstrass, were his teachers; he was fascinated by the splendor of their logical demonstrations in mathematics. And the philosophical meaning of calculus became a question that constantly haunted his mind. Now in Berlin, he realized the basic error of W. Wundt, whose lectures had attracted his attention during his sojourn in Leipzig. Wundt, the founder of the first laboratory of experimental psychology, was too subservient to the positivistic method; he was concerned about the behavior of man, but he did not question the nature of this behavior. F. Paulsen, a renowned lecturer at the University of Berlin, was asking his students to consider the first principles of all the sciences. The young Husserl thought such a consideration worthy of a life's work. He knew that periodically many great thinkers of Western civilization, from Plato to Raymond Lull, to Leibniz and Schelling, dreamed of a *mathesis universalis*. Husserl decided to join ranks with them: the problem of his vocation in life was definitely solved.

In March, 1881, Husserl was in Vienna, working on his doctoral dissertation: *Beiträge zur Theorie der Variationsreshnung*. And in Vienna he met Franz Brentano, who was more responsible than any other man for his intellectual development. Brentano (1839–1918) was a Catholic priest and a professor at the University of Würzburg. A booklet written in opposition to papal infallibility in 1869, prior to the definition of Vatican Council I, caused Brentano's difficulties with the Church. He did not comply with the defined doctrine on the infallibility, so he was defrocked. He contracted a secret marriage against the laws of the Church and the Empire. After losing his teaching assignment, he lived as a *Privatdozent*, tutoring students. It must be said that Brentano was not a Giordano Bruno: he rebelled against the discipline of the Church, but he did not rebel against the traditional philosophy. On the contrary, his teaching and his thinking present scholastic concepts with new vigor, new terminology, and new meaning in contemporary philosophy.

Brentano's goal was to analyze the act of perception. And he gladly accepted this challenge because another philosopher, W. Wundt, was trying the same analysis. About 1865 both published important books on psychology; for both the scholastic notion of "perception" was the center of attention. Perception is an act of knowledge of which we have consciousness. I do not perceive when I simply feel cold, but only when I realize that I feel cold. Perception is therefore the act of contact between the outside world and the individual, between the physical stimulus and the knowing subject. Wundt's interest was more physiological, anatomical; he intended to dissect, analyze and possibly measure the components of the act of perception. Brentano's interest was strictly philosophical. Wundt cared about related elements within the act of perception, but he forgot that the real problem was to explain the relation between the human person as knower and the outside world as known. Wundt was a psychologist, and his famous laboratory in Leipzig was the birthplace of the kind of experimental psychology Herbart and Fechner hoped for at the beginning of the nineteenth century. Brentano did not deny the importance of Wundt's work; he just reiterated that his interest was the nature of human knowledge.

Nothing is more challenging and more rewarding, albeit frustrating, than trying to understand the human act of knowing. Knowing, says Brentano, means interfering with the existence of an object without changing it, without manipulating it. The first quality of human knowledge is (as Aristotle says) to be in relation with something else, by representing it.

Living, breathing, vegetating are human phenomena, interrelated reciprocally, but they do not have to represent their own relation. The act of knowledge *contains*, somehow, the objects known. This is its enigma: what is the meaning of this "containing"? How is it (to use once again the words of Aristotle) that the knower "becomes all things," becomes involved with and identified with anything that he knows?

Brentano calls this quality of mind *intentionality*. He says, "Every act of knowledge is characterized by what the Scholastics called the intentional (or mental) existence of an object; we call it the relation to an object, the direction toward an object; we could also call it immanent objectivity."[1] For Brentano this intentional object is immanent; it is in the mind of the knower and it is the only way we are able to understand the outside world.

The question is: Do we really reach the outside world through this intentional act. Brentano, here breaking with Aristotelean-Thomistic realism, affirms that the intentional object is *more evident* and *more real* than the object itself: the intentional object is in fact completely mine, it belongs to the life of my consciousness, it cannot conceal to me aspects of itself, as the outside world can do. Moreover, according to Brentano, when I possess this intentional object, something wonderful happens to me: I have consciousness of the object thought of and I have consciousness of myself thinking of that object: the representation (of the object) and the representation of this representation reach perfect unity. Now if we call the representation of the representation "reflection" we understand what Brentano means when he says that each intellectual act is rich in many aspects: the understanding of the object and the comprehension of myself understanding the object. Aristotle had said that the plurality of intentional acts is justified by the plurality of the objects. Brentano disagrees, finding Aristotle a cold analyst of the object. Attention must be given to the knowing subject: the intentional object of the mind is not only a perception but also a reflection of the perception. If this reflection is another act different from the perception, a third act of knowledge will be required to sanction the first reflection and the mind would have to face a process *ad infinitum,* with the final result that the ideal object of the mind could never be known.

Brentano's analysis, under the evident influence of Kantian philosophy, has other aspects. The perception of the intentional object is more than an idea, as Thomas Aquinas had said; it is also a judgment, a synthesis, in the Kantian way, although the explanation given by Brentano is far different from Kant's. When I say: "The flower is red," the whole rationalistic tradition would explain this by saying that I attribute the color "red" to the flower, that I refer one representation to the other, that, in effect, I make a synthesis. Hence numberless recriminations were exchanged by philosophers relative to the question: what guarantees this synthesis, experience or the rational terms of this judgment? In Kant's language: Is this a judgment *a priori* or a judgment

---

[1] Brentano, *Psychologie,* p. 111 ff.

a posteriori? Brentano has an original solution to this problem: the validity of the judgment resides in the verb "to be," uniting the subject with the predicate. When I say "the flower is red" I mean to say "there is a red flower" or "there is redness in this flower." A judgment is not valid if it is not reducible to *existence*. This is the wealth of the intentional object of each perception: it always carries within itself the immediate evidence of the *existence*. This doctrine is carried so far as to reduce the analytical judgments (e.g., the sum of the angles of a triangle equals 180 degrees) to existential judgments. Of course Brentano does not face the problem of the universality of the analytic judgments. When he reduces them to existential judgments, he says in effect that up to now it was true that the sum of the angles of a triangle is equal to 180 degrees, but he cannot defend the universal validity of this statement.

The struggle which plagued the mind of Franz Brentano and which pinpointed the disagreement between him and his student, Husserl, centered on the relation of subject to object. Husserl accused his teacher of rationalism. In fact, it cannot be denied that Brentano defended the thesis that human knowledge is a relation between the subject and the intentional object rather than between the subject and the object. Brentano's perennial advice to his students, particularly to Husserl, was to beware of the idealists: they were the enemies of reality. But Hegelianism had permeated the German culture too deeply; the influence of idealism was present in the thought and the philosophy of its strongest adversaries. Brentano was no exception to this situation: one of his brilliant courses in Vienna showed this uneasiness which he felt when he had to trust the human mind. The course was on David Hume; its object was to discuss the impossibility of predicating any aspect of the real world with irrefutability. Husserl was shaken by those lectures and their influence will be evident in the development of his philosophy.

Another priest and philosopher, Bernhard Bolzano, must be singled out for his importance to Husserl's formative years. Of Italian parentage, Bolzano was born and lived in Prague in the first half of the nineteenth century. Husserl called him "one of the greatest logicians of all times"; the history of philosophy hardly remembers his name. In 1837 he wrote a *Wissenschaftslehre* or *Doctrine of Science*, which about seventy years later influenced the phenomenology of Husserl.

According to Bolzano, a "doctrine of science" is meant to be a logical unification of all the rules that are needed for the formulation and classification of all special sciences. In other works, Bolzano is interested in finding the first principles of all the sciences. Logic is both an art and a science: it is an art because logic tries to achieve the difficult goal of scientific precision through patient research prior to science and therefore it is fallible and filled with surprises and deceptions. But logic must also be a theoretical science because it gives norms and directives which would be illogical without a pure theoretical principle to explain them. To give an example, we know that the principle of contradiction is actually presupposed in each particular science; therefore its value is superior to all empirical sciences, it is an absolute logical principle. Bolzano shows originality and analytic strength when he discusses the nature of logic as an art. He is concerned about the fact that the process of formulating logic depends on the personal structure of the mind of each individual and on his environment. Man wants to know the truth. Bolzano restates a position well known to those familiar with classical philosophy: the discussion about the prerequisites and conditions for the knowability of truth presupposes the existence of truth. Therefore, logic as a doctrine concerned with truth does not depend on the study of the mental act; on the contrary, actual thinking would be impossible without presupposing logic.

The following steps appear acceptable to Bolzano:

1. Pure logic. The first statement to be defended by anyone who begins discussing philosophy is: an objective truth exists independent of your or my opinion. The old argument against skepticism is valid for Bolzano: those who deny the ability of the human mind to attain truth are wrong because they defend the truth of what they say.

The truth of a logical principle is not dependent on the actual thinking about this principle. The content of the statement "Spring is a beautiful season" is true before I think it. Human thought recognizes the truth. It does not create the truth. In other words, human thought is just representation, not an actual operation of the truth. The same is valid from the point of view of the object; its existence or its nonexistence does not influence the validity of a mental representation. Bolzano says that divine thought creates the mental existence of ideas; human thought just re-creates in its own way these mental perceptions, most often very inadequately. Therefore divine ideas are at the same time the source and a norm of the human ideas.

2. Once this pure logic is established, the ground is ready for a theory of knowledge. Now is the time for careful evaluation of all the elements helping and interfering with *the actual* acquisition of the truth.

3. The third step is the heuristic, the art that increases true knowledge. Special attention is given to the principles that are the basis of each science and to the method which is used in reaching those

principles. Bolzano's inquiry indicates another step for the young Husserl. The mental object is clearly separated from the act of knowing.

Husserl now saw with a clearer mind the limitations of Brentano's philosophy. Brentano's position was the target of universal criticism: his disciples did not agree with his idea that the object of human perception was to be identified with our reaction to the outside stimulus.

Karl Stumpf was a professor at the University of Halle to whom Brentano sent his pupil Husserl in 1886. Stumpf and Husserl conducted research which convinced them both of the limitations of Brentano's theories. Stumpf's especial interest was the perception of space and sound. His importance should be confined to one type of experimentation concerning the nature of sense perception. Stumpf could not accept the empirical interpretation, given by the school of associationism, that the content of each one of our perceptions has to be restricted to one element. The perception is not reduced to one color, one musical note; but to a complex of elements related among themselves and yet always distinct. A color is actually a surface with one color different from others; a musical note is the result of many notes related among themselves and with the instrument. The perception offers a totality of perceptions, not only one part — here we witness the formulation of the *Gestalt* theory: in each perception we find a *form* not only a *line* of the form. Stumpf considers the original Aristotelian doctrine of the active intellect *abstracting* the essential elements in each of perception as fundamental to his thinking. Husserl prefers to speak of intuition. We shall analyze these terms and their implications later. It will suffice for the present to notice that Stumpf, in the last period of his academic life, worked at the University of Berlin, developed with great vigor the *Gestalt theories* and almost eliminated from psychological research the empiricism of W. Wundt.

2. THE PHENOMENOLOGY OF HUSSERL

Our effort to understand the background of this important philosopher has brought us to a few conclusions:

— The goal of Husserl's intellectual endeavors is an understanding of the nature of science and the relations between scientific knowledge and philosophy.

— Brentano made one important discovery: in each act of perception there is an intentional object existing before and above the experimental data obtained through sense knowledge. Husserl accepts this doctrine as basic to his research on the nature of science.

— Bolzano made Husserl aware of another definite truth: those intentional objects are independent of both experimental knowledge and of the actual thinking of each person (as Brentano thought).

The intentional object is whatever presents itself to the mind: that is, the phenomenon (*phaínesthai:* "to appear"). Husserl, using an Hegelian term, calls phenomenology the science that deals with the understanding of the diverse nature of all these phenomena.

This description of Husserl's phenomenology, though taken almost literally from his writings, is too dry and technical. Husserl aimed for a new renascence, for a time when philosophy would celebrate its greatest triumph. After the Renaissance, beginning with Galileo, man reduced his knowledge to factual findings, to an experimental research with the result that he became a stranger, an outsider, to his own findings. For Husserl phenomenology meant, first of all, rebellion against this reduction of human knowledge to factual findings: our living, thinking, and loving are factors specifically human, always open to new inquiry and new answers. Positive science is inadequate to understand these problems. Phenomenology wants to give back to man his own "subjectivity." Phenomenology aims to reveal to man, or even better to mankind, its real human meaning. Revealing is manifesting: hence man reveals himself to himself, against the betrayal of positive science: this is phenomenology.

*   *   *

Stating in broad terms, as we just did, the goals of phenomenology is not a challenging task. But the analytic study of Husserl's thought presents many difficulties. Three must be kept in mind to avoid confusion:

1. Husserl, originally a mathematician, did not know the power of splendid images; his discussion is always arid and filled with abstractions. Since his research moves on a ground totally unexplored, he often takes the liberty of forging new words and new philosophical terms.

2. Husserl, when he reached his full professorship in Göttingen, had the clear perception of the staggering amount of work to be accomplished. He looked for help. Many bright students joined forces with him. Later, in 1914, they compiled the *Jahrbuch für Phänomenologie und phänomenologische Forschung.* This publication is simultaneously an exceptional help and a formidable hindrance to the understanding of Husserl. Often the pupils changed the teacher's doctrine.

3. Husserl always remained faithful to his main goal. Yet each phase of his life marked a new development of thought. Furthermore, when in 1938 his widow fled Germany and Nazi racism (they were of Jewish extraction), she carried with her thousands of his handwritten pages.

Father H. L. Van Breda, a Belgian, is still engaged in the formidable task of editing all this material. Each newly published work sheds new light, new aspects, and the possibility of a new interpretation of Husserl's phenomenology.

We will discuss these aspects of Husserl's phenomenology:
1. Formulating the problem.
2. Phenomenology: Is it a rebirth of transcendental ideals or a new defense of the individual?
3. The followers of Husserl.

I. *Formulating the Problem*

The theme of Husserl's doctoral dissertation was the calculus of variations. But his first philosophical writings are *Über den Begriff der Zahl* (1887) and *Philosophie der Arithmetik* (1891). The theme of these two dissertations is how the idea of calculus originates in the human mind. Outstanding mathematicians, Frege, Cantor, Dedekind, defined the mathematical number as a characteristic value capable of grouping different objects under the same mathematical value. To repeat Frege's words: "I, as a mathematician, do not concern myself about the 'how': the idea $\sqrt{1}$ or the idea of a triangle was born in me. What I want to know is in what mathematical relations is $\sqrt{1}$ or a triangle with other factors."

This sort of reasoning is insufficient for Husserl. A meaningful understanding of the nature of number requires relations (*Verbinden*) established by the mind among the various objects. For instance, I have in front of me on my table three objects: a flower, an orange, and an apple. By abstraction I neglect the individual connotations of these three objects and I reach the number 3 because *I relate* them. Each number is therefore more than experimental knowledge: it is an act of my mind connecting various objects offered to me by my experience. If these premises are accepted, I understand the real meaning of calculus. It is in fact well known that my range of representation is limited. We need symbolic numbers which logically take the place of the numbers obtained through representation. The symbolic calculus is not supported by our experimental representation, but it finds its logical explanation from the *intuitive* power of the mind. Husserl is here under the clear influence of Brentano: mathematics is the result of a psychological process; its objectivity is yet to be found.

In his second work, the *Logische Untersuchungen,* Husserl is clearly in the process of abandoning Brentano. Bolzano was the new attraction.

Furthermore Husserl was under the influence of Stumpf and above all happened to be involved with unusual violence in a debate with some exponents of symbolic logic. This new trend of thought was gaining ground by the end of the nineteenth century both in England and in Germany. Husserl made it clear, reviewing a book of Schröder, that symbolic logic was a sterile game of words, useless to scientific research and worthless to any philosophical achievement. Symbolic logic, Husserl thought, is grounded on artificial definitions of ideas, to which symbolic meanings are attributed and upon which operations of calculus are developed. True logic, according to Husserl, must begin from a careful study of the natural language from which the real meaning of existing things flows.

The atmosphere in the intellectual circles of Germany became incandescent. A. Voigt, a student of Schröder, took upon himself the defense of his teacher. In 1894, G. Frege, perhaps annoyed by the fact that Husserl ignored him completely in his articles, entered the arena of polemic. Husserl, according to Frege, was guilty in his *Philosophie der Arithmetik,* of an infantile form of psychologism. Husserl felt the blow and recognized its legitimacy. He needed more meditation. For five years, while teaching at the University of Halle, he worked in silence, trying to solve the mystery of the nature of scientific and philosophical knowledge.

Finally, in 1900, he published the *Logische Untersuchungen.* The first volume, *Prolegomena to Pure Logic,* is a fierce criticism of both schools: psychologism and antipsychologism. He quoted at the beginning of his work the words of Goethe: "We hate nothing more than the errors which we have left behind us."

It is imperative, if we want to understand Husserl, to follow his criticism of psychologism and antipsychologism. Psychologism, we repeat paraphrasing Husserl, reduces human knowledge to a well-ordered description of each moment of the noetic process, without any recognition of the universality and objectivity of the laws of logic present in each act of knowing. Psychologism is therefore a new term for nominalism. When we know, we recognize two elements inherent in each act of knowing: (*a*) a contingent aspect of the object known, an aspect which is changeable and accidental; (*b*) an absolute aspect, which determines each object to be that object; we can call it the necessary form of the object. We can discover new aspects of the object and make our understanding of it richer and deeper, but each object is there before and independently of my various judgments. First of all, the natural sciences themselves would be impossible without this object, since it is the ontological foundation to which they must conform themselves. To quote Husserl: "There is no mediation between the realm of what is real and what is ideal."[2] Could mathematics be founded on repetition of numbers?

Second, psychology itself must respect the laws of logic. Husserl knew the fundamental objection which lay behind the reason advanced by psychologism for its own existence. Psychologists argued: Logic itself, the classical logic, presupposes the laws of logic and then claims to have discovered them. Husserl answered: The vicious circle does not exist, Logic does not proceed *from* logical laws, but it proceeds *according to* logical laws. Evidence is not a personal feeling granted to some acts of knowledge. Evidence is the experience of truth. Evidence is seeing that a judgment is true because it is based on a real set of laws which cannot be doubted, because they are the beginning of human thinking.

E. Lotze and P. Natorp, the school of Baden and the school of Marburg, represent antipsychologism. Actually all these people were followers of Kant. They said that universal and necessary laws do exist in each act of knowledge, but they do not belong to the objective content of each act of knowledge. On the contrary, they continue, these laws are regulative norms which make knowing possible for the mind. Husserl seemed to show unusual patience when he tried to convince the representatives of this school that they were defending a new form of psychologism. In fact, for them the validity of the act of knowing depended on the mind rather than on the object known. Husserl declared: "We are not concerned about terms, we do not care about verbal symbolism. . . . We want to reach the real world, as it is." The *Logische Untersuchungen* took on a signal importance in Husserl's life. In it he directed all his power against the nominalism which, under different names, had been infiltrating all philosophical speculation from the time of Locke and Hume. Nominalism reduced logical laws to empirical generalizations or to vague psychological formulas. Husserl meant to go back to classical philosophy. A name can never be reduced to the act of understanding. A name has a meaning that originates from an object signified by it. A name has an objective value that gives dignity to the whole process of human understanding.

II. *Subjectivism or Subjectivity?*

The *Logische Untersuchungen* may come to rank as a classic for the future students of philosophy. Husserl's most important theses are developed in this work: a profound analysis of the empirical datum,

[2] Husserl, *Logische Untersuchungen*, I, 699.

the discovery of the objective essence, the meaning of intuition, and the conclusive doctrine on intentionality.

Husserl was an original philosopher. His main goal was not to discuss the existence of God, the existence of the universe and the human person or the relations between God and the universe and the human person. All these problems, traditional in the history of philosophy, are absorbed by another one: the meaning of consciousness. Consciousness as such is intentionality. It always overcomes itself and by doing so gives a *meaning* to all things of which it is conscious.

Natorp posed the following objection to Husserl: if consciousness and the outside world as well are ultimately always in becoming, without the possibility of reaching completion, it should be said that both the universe and consciousness are aspects of one phenomenal reality. That is to say, an idealistic vision of the world is the final goal of philosophy. Husserl understood the importance of this objection, and in each of his writings the effort to escape idealistic conclusions is evident.

It is of some importance, therefore, to reconstruct several moments of Husserl's painful involvement with the Hegelian idealism he roundly rejected:

In the winter semester of 1906–1907, and later up to 1910, Husserl lectured on the "interior consciousness [meaning] of time." Heidegger published these lectures in 1928.[3] What is time for a phenomenologist, who is not interested in the so-called "objective time" as scientific astronomy considers it? Time, phenomenologically, is something perceived and meaningful because it is the expression of the order of all the phenomena lived by the consciousness.

Time, understood phenomenologically, is an intuition of many successive elements. The sound of music is a clear example. Each musical note is not perceived singularly, but in connection with all the notes. The following note is in reference to the previous one and it prepares for the successive one. This continuity is a spontaneous remembering (*Erinnerung*); each moment is rich with all the previous moments. Moreover, each moment has a meaning. Therefore, knowledge is for us the recognition of all objects as they appear in time.

Husserl came reluctantly to the final conclusion that if time is the product of intuition and if intuition is an action performed by the human consciousness, it follows that time is conditioned by consciousness itself. At this point we have the right to ask Husserl: What is the real meaning of transcendental consciousness? Is it a re-edition of Fichte's transcendental ego?

---

[3] *Jahrbuch für Philosophie und phänomenologishe Forschung*, pp. 367–496.

These are his answers: Transcendental consciousness is not the transcendental ego of Fichte, since "the transcentental ego of which Fichte speaks is not different from Fichte the man." Consciousness cannot be identified with the Kantian *a priori* that makes experience possible, or with the Cartesian *ego cogito* that divides man from his own experiences. If man (the real man, each one of us as human, as flesh and bone) enters into a moment of meditation, his own self suspends all judgments with what Husserl calls a "vow of poverty," and he discovers intentionally the universe and the meaning of truth, he discovers consciousness.

Therefore consciousness is not what the idealists thought it to be, that is, truth metaphysically conceived in its becoming, nor is it a transcendental being. *Consciousness is the meaning of all my actions as related to the actions of each human being.* My actions are not transcendental because they belong to an immanent or transcendental metaphysical reality; but they are transcendental, as are all actions of all human beings, because they have a meaning which is not just mine, since it is a meaning for all mankind. *Consciousness, therefore, is my belonging with intelligence and action to the history and the progress of human society.* Husserl is seen here simultaneously as a master of method and a searcher of truth. Perhaps it would be more appropriate to say that Husserl identified the method of research with the truth to be searched, though he was not the first in the history of philosophy to make such an attempt.

Any attempt to label Husserl's philosophy with one of the traditional names (realism, idealism, subjectivism) may well be self-defeating. The influence of Kant, of Hegel, and of his teachers Brentano and Bolzano is evident. But for the sake of clarity — now that we know that Husserl's philosophy, though parallel to Idealism, cannot be labeled "transcendental subjectivism" — we will call it "transcendental subjectivity."

We are now in the climactic phase of Husserl's thought, the battles against nominalism and psychologism are things of the past. Husserl has reached the conviction that an absolute science called philosophy is possible. It is true that this "absolute" is lurking through the years as a constant shadow of transcendental idealism. But we must repeat that the real Husserl, the man who devoted his whole existence to understanding this problem, rejected Fichte and Hegel.

He was interested in man, he was concerned about man because man seemed to be a victim of industralized science. Contemporary scientific prosperity absorbed and destroyed human dignity. He must rediscover, just as the great minds of the past did, the meaning of man. This meaning cannot be a product of empirical experimentation. Living, thinking, loving cannot be examined through laboratory experiences. They are phenomena that ask answers specifically human because they are, like humanity itself, phenomena always in process. Each human being hides within himself a humanity still to be born. It will be born if man wants it to be born and aims to be what as yet he is not. This revelation of man to himself is the new science of Husserl: each man is necessary to establish this science and to make it apparent (*phenomenon*) to the whole of humanity.

Philosophy is the science which discovers the "historical process of revelations of the universal consciousness which is inborn in humanity." This philosophy is transcendental because it deals with the consciousness of all mankind, but it is not a new brand of idealism because it is grounded on the action of each human being (subjectivity). Husserl has a term, perhaps the most repeated term in his writings, for this transcendental life of man. It is *Lebenswelt*, "the world of life." *Lebenswelt* has a past, a present, and a future (*telos*). *Lebenswelt* is intentionality because its life is becoming, is consciousness of time, is realization of truth, or, what is the same, is revelation (phenomenology).

The modern era has witnessed an almost fatal assault on the transcendental consciousness. It all began with Galileo, whose goal was to create a science of nature mathematically perfect, exhaustive of all the secrets that nature holds. Unconsciously, Galileo aimed at the destruction of the *Lebenswelt*. He aimed at the loss of intentionality when he tried to defend a pure abstract nature, a fetish in the eye of phenomenology. Rationalism from Descartes to Berkeley discovered the inadequacies of Galileo's mathematical approach, and Hume declared its complete bankruptcy. Those were the premises which brought philosophy inescapably to the *Critique of Reason*, to idealism and to phenomenology. "This revolution, the greatest of all revolutions, must be understood as the attempt to change scientific objectivity, modern and medieval, into a transcendental subjectivism."[4]

Empirical sciences are useful if they recognize the necessity of going beyond themselves to the discovery of what is essential. Philosophy is the rigorous science of essences. This mention of essences, a term familiar to everybody who knows about Plato, Aristotle, and Thomas Aquinas, might engender confusion. Plato spoke of a world of essences existing "above" the material world. Aristotle and Thomas Aquinas discovered the essence, through a process of abstraction, in each individual substance. Where are the essences Husserl spoke about? This question, as formulated, is for Husserl a clear sign of misunderstanding the meaning of philosophy. Husserl thought that essences are not

---

[4] Husserl, *Crisis of European Sciences*, p. 97.

ontological beings, static, objective, unchangeable. That would amount to going back to the pre-Galileo times when philosophers spoke of objects which the mind was ready to perceive. As we have said, the laborious process of its liberation from Galileo to the present has brought philosophy to its highest meaning, that is, to phenomenology. The essence of phenomenological philosophy is not *something* understood or factual, totally finished and realized. On the contrary, the essence is what is seen and "intentionalized" and lived as eternal and permanent by man's consciousness. Now the temptation, old as human thinking, is always present in our minds for pinning down the essentials to individually existing essences, to God, soul, man. Husserl answers that that means going back to the Middle Ages, ignoring the process of moving from the object to the subject. Husserl was adamant in rejecting any identification with idealism, but he also considered himself insulted when his philosophy was called by some uninformed critics a new brand of Platonism.

Phenomenology is precisely the opposite. *Phenomenology is the grasping of the essence which is such because man's consciousness intentionally makes it an essence, an ideal for which the whole life of a man is lived and to which his life is dedicated in work and in hope of fulfillment.* A phenomenological analysis consists in reaching these essences in the secret privacy of one's consciousness. "In this way," Husserl wrote in *Philosophy as a Rigorous Science,* "we become aware of a new science whose vast potential is yet unknown to our fellow citizens. This science belongs to human consciousness without being a psychology because it is a phenomenology [manifestation] of human consciousness and as such is opposed to a 'natural' science of consciousness."[5]

"Natural" here means the given, closed and factualized sciences, like chemistry or physics, which do not try to understand the essential forms of truth, which do not seek an ideal that gives meaning to human existence.

It might be hinted, with respect to Husserl, that his persistent reluctance to allow our minds to rest on any physical or metaphysical object makes phenomenology very hard to understand. Husserl offers an explanation for this difficulty. The mind likes to rest on visible objects. Nevertheless, each man in each judgment he makes is measuring the value of particular objects. Each man, in other words, takes essences into account. Philosophy is not possible if we do not begin with visualized objects, but philosophy does not stop at visualization. Philosophy reaches the essence intentionally seen by consciousness

[5] Husserl, *Philosophy as a Rigorous Science,* 1910.

through a complete experience (*Erlebnis*) or, what amounts to the same thing, through a complete living.

Freeing ourselves from the technical and laboratory-like frame of mind is called by Husserl *epoché*, a Greek word that means suspension. His theory was developed in the important work *Ideas for a Pure Phenomenology*.[6] The "phenomenological reduction" or *epoché* is based on the intentional power of the mind to shift direction from the physical reality to imaginative thinking, from remembering to reflection. Using this power, Husserl proposed to change our approach to understanding. We must try, if we want to reach the level of philosophy, *to suspend* our judgment on the reality or unreality of the world, on the value of empirical sciences, on everything that constitutes our way of thinking. This disengagement does not nullify the world, it just places it, so to speak, within brackets; it suspends any intentional responsibility of judgment on the existence of the world. The result is evident. From this complete suspension a residue remains beyond all doubts and abstractions; this residue is our own consciousness of all things with all their meanings. This consciousness is the condition of all knowing activities and therefore it is an intuition of essences as they are.

The whole universe, placed in this way between brackets, appears (*phenomenon*) to us perceived and thought and willed in the unifying current of our consciousness. Thus we reach philosophical knowledge because transcendent beings (that is to say, all beings which are external to us) do not present themselves in an infinite variety of changing perspective. Now, seen through the *epoché*, they reveal to us their clearly defined and unchangeable meaning. Perceived by our own consciousness, the content of each being is valued for what it is, for its essence: for instance, remembering is remembering, intuition is intuition, imagination is imagination.

Phenomenological reduction prescinds also from the fact that my consciousness is mine and yours is yours. There is a unity of consciousness or a transcendental consciousness. In fact, since it is necessary to have a consciousness if there are phenomena (otherwise phenomena would not exist, because they would not appear to anybody), in the same way a *unity of consciousness* is necessary if phenomena are to be understood as objects. Without this, unity of consciousness would not exist; different consciousnesses would be responsible for different phenomena, and we could not speak of objects.

Husserl had to acknowledge at this point the validity of Natorp's objection that phenomenology is very close to Fichte's subjectivism.

---

[6] The first volume of *Ideen* was published in 1913 in the *Jahrbuch*. The second and the third volumes were published posthumously in 1952.

We know with what zeal of conviction Husserl spoke of the dignity of the individual, of the world of life; nevertheless, Husserl could not accept the metaphysics of being, of each individual being. This metaphysical approach was obsolete for Husserl, a remnant from the days before the great revolution of the subject against the object.

Therefore Husserl was caught between the intransigent rules of transcendental consciousness and the need of saving the individuality of man. If we listen to his often announced convictions, we must speak as we have of a transcendental subjectivity. How can we ignore his dedication to the task of saving man from the snares of the technological age? But if we follow the logical development of Husserl's thought, we must recognize the fact that Husserl did not question the premises of idealism, but tried to save the individual freedom of man within the framework of the philosophy of immanence. For instance, even the spatial-temporal being studied by physics and chemistry "is a being which consciousness in its own experiences (*Erfahrungen*) posits, and is in principle intuitable and determinable only as the element common to the motivated appearance-manifolds, *but over and beyond this*, is just nothing at all."[7]

In the third part of the *Ideen* Husserl examines some fundamental problems of phenomenology. The phenomenological method requires, besides the intuition of the essence, the reflection on the intuition. This reflection is not a mysterious activity (just as the intuition of the essence was not mysterious). Reflection is the result of a patient work of observation of data which are compared and clarified. Imagination might be helpful here, just as it is helpful to the architect who presents geometrical figures and the physicist who presents new structures for the understanding of the atom. Phenomenology, both as intuition of the essence and as a reflection on the intuition, does not aim to deduce. A deductive method belongs to certain sciences, to mathematics for example, but is completely irrelevant for other sciences. Take botany for instance: the lack of mathematical precision is not a defect in the classification of plants. Therefore, each object has its own correspondent science. The first volume of the *Ideen* presents other noteworthy themes. We spoke of the strict connection between time and consciousness. This doctrine is now developed to the point where consciousness is called "a temporal scheme filled with meanings [essences]."

In each act of consciousness the *Ideen* stresses a distinction between the subjective aspect (noetic) and the objective aspect (noematic). *Noesis* is the quality of the act (intuition, remembering, reflection, volition); *noema* is the intentional content (what is perceived, remem-

_____
[7] *Ideen*, Vol. 1, par. 19, p. 76.

bered). Another quality of each act of consciousness is that of "positing" (its *thetic quality*). Husserl used these terms to stress a correlation between the noetic aspect (belief) and the noematic aspect (the essence to be perceived). "Every consciousness is either actually or potentially thetic."[8] That is to say that the logical aspect of consciousness is not something added but is the nature of consciousness itself. The medieval philosophers, from altogether different points of view of course, would have spoken of the real being rational. Husserl thinks that consciousness is real, and he tries to salvage within it an aspect of objectivity.

The *Ideen* represents without doubt the crucial point of the whole development of phenomenology. On one hand, Husserl insists on the fact that phenomenology does not mean to formulate judgments on the meaning of being; therefore, the *epoché* is used as a method of reduction. On the other hand, he speaks of "every formal-logical law that may be transformed into an equivalent formal-ontological law."[9] That is to say, phenomenology is ready to become a metaphysics. Isn't there a very close affinity with the transcendental identification of being and the finite and human consciousness? This is the language of idealism.

Husserl was aware of this conclusion. It is interesting to notice that he refused to publish the second and third volumes of the *Ideen*. Actually, he could not become more deeply involved with idealistic structures before attempting a solution, or at least a clearer vision of the huge problem of the intersubjectivity. The problem is not new for post-Hegelian philosophy, and it can be reduced to this: consciousness knows many subjects. As far as they are known, do they lose their entity as subjects and become just objects or do they continue to be subjects? We deal, in other words, with the plurality of human consciousnesses or with the fact that consciousness seems to claim a subject (a being) to whom consciousness belongs (as an activity). It is this confrontation which we keep referring to when we say that being precedes action or that action justifies the existence of being. In other words, is metaphysics prior to logic or should logic be identified with metaphysics?

Husserl tackled this problem head-on in his *Cartesian Meditations*. These are four lectures given to the students of the University of London in the spring of 1922 and then re-edited into four seminars for the students of the Sorbonne in 1929. In the first meditation, Husserl acknowledged that the Cartesian "cogito" was the necessary background for the phenomenological reduction. But, Husserl says, Descartes stopped in the middle of the road: (*a*) Descartes said that the *cogito* reveals

---

[8] *Ibid.*, par. 117.
[9] *Ibid.*, par. 148.

a *res* or a substance, a thinking substance. Therefore Descartes did not understand that the function the *cogito* is to reveal a condition or a premise necessary to all substances. (*b*) Descartes used the *cogito* as an axiomatic foundation to a system built with mathematical precision rather than for an open field for research on the meaning of reality. The formula *Ego cogito* is incomplete. It should be *Ego cogito cogitata*. These *cogitata* are responsible for the "objective" meaning of all essences present in the consciousness and which are fully revealed to the consciousness by the *epoché* as the field of research and philosophical progress. Husserl clearly stated in the final chapter of his *Ideen* that only the essence, *not the existence,* of each being is subordinated to and dependent on consciousness. But he added immediately that consciousness (and therefore philosophy) cannot be concerned about an outside world existing independently from the transcendental consciousness. Therefore, the distinction he made between essence and existence becomes irrelevant. To him the essence is *everything* which can be rationally known and knowable, so the existence is absorbed by the essence. That is to say, the essence is the only element exhausting and energizing the fullness of rationality. The phenomenologist has no choice but must think that any existence outside the consciousness is absurd and unthinkable. In fact it would be the existence of nothing, because content and meaning and ontic quality are contained and justified only within the consciousness. To hold any other position is to cease to be a phenomenologist. The Fourth Meditation comes to the categorical conclusion that "the problem of the existence of the universe is an absurd problem."[10]

Husserl faces the difficult situation of having a pure consciousness of pure content. Thomas Aquinas, still in his twenties, wrote his little work *De Ente et Essentia.* In it he pointed out that the only realistic way to consider essence is in its actual reference to existence. The very word *essence* is derived from *esse,* which means to exist. Essence means the way in which a thing exists and through which it operates. "Now what Husserl is attempting to do," says James Mullaney in his sketchy but penetrating notes on contemporary philosophy,[11] is to cut essence off from *esse;* to consider essence absolutely and in itself, apart from its reference to existence, which reference is its whole being. But the mind of man — and we have no experience of any other kind of mind — cannot long hold essence before itself in an absolute manner, independent of both actual and mental existence. When any man, including

---

[10] Husserl, *Cartesian Meditations,* p. 70.

[11] J. V. Mullaney, *A History of Contemporary Philosophy* (mimeographed), Manhattan College, New York, 1960.

Husserl, attempts to cut off essence from its defining relationship to *esse* in order to study essence in itself, he regularly makes the same unconscious error of reading into essence what belongs only to the mental existence of essence. We *must* see essence relative to existence; then we are seeing it relative to mental existence. There is neither harm nor danger in this, provided we know what is going on.

The danger is — and Husserl illustrates it — that we attribute to essence itself what is true merely of the mental existence of the essence, namely, that it is a datum of consciousness, an idea. It seems safe to state this generalization: essentialism, or the study of the essence arbitrarily cut off from actual existence, necessarily becomes idealism, the study of essence as an idea existing mentally. A great structure of imposing nonsense may be built up to disguise this degeneration of the study of essence-in-itself into essence-in-the-mind, that is, the study of ideas which is idealism. But disguises soon wear thin. And when they do, the extraordinarily simple facts reassert themselves. And the fact in this case is — a wry and unhappy fact — that Husserl, who started out to rid philosophy of psychologism, relativism, subjectivism and idealism, by his precise manner of adopting "realism" — the study of essences only — wound up, many years later, defending the very position, idealism, which it had been his purpose to defeat.

Christian philosophy through the centuries and with a great variety of methods accepted (and accepts in agreement with Husserl) the fact that intelligibility is intrinsic in each aspect of being; but it is necessary for all philosophers who acknowledge the primacy of metaphysics to hold that the activity of the human mind is limited. Therefore, one of their main tasks is to search the source from which springs that most wondrous aspect of reality, its intelligibility, which no human mind has succeeded in doing.

Husserl, too subservient to the idealistic dogma, restricting himself to the mind of the individual, believed that it was the only source for the manifestation of the essence. Consequently he made the same human mind absolute and transcendental. Now in the *Cartesian Meditations* he had to face the growing criticism that held him responsible for an unnatural solipsistic system of philosophy. Hence his attempt to open his transcendental consciousness to the autonomy of many knowing subjects. Without doubt Husserl knew that he was the last of those (from the Stoics to Plotinus, Spinoza and Hegel) who had to face the Herculean job of saving the individual man after having drowned him in the ocean of immanentism.

In the case of phenomenology the labor was more than Herculean: Husserl was aware that the plurality of subjects had to be found in the world — that world which he reduced to consciousness. Why should we doubt the real existence of a house and not doubt the existence of the persons dwelling in the same house? In the *Fifth Meditation* Husserl comes close to a formal capitulation. He speaks of a form of knowing specifically proper to each individual. This curious type of knowledge is called by Husserl *empathy (Einfürlung)*. It consists in the effect of comparing the transcendental consciousness conditioning the meaning of each being with my own individual consciousness tied to my physical body. Because of the presence of my body I should be able to perceive the otherness of my existence and therefore to accept the existence of other human subjects. A question is in order for Husserl at this point: how can phenomenology justify the *existence* of my body as a condition for the otherness of my consciousness, which itself is different from the transcendental consciousness? Husserl himself was utterly dissatisfied with such artificial conclusions. He was a long way from the dream of philosophy as a rigorous science.

In the preface to the English translation of his *Ideen* (written in 1931 and therefore after the publication of the *Cartesian Meditations*) Husserl wrote, with admirable honesty, that the problem of plurality of subjects "must by all means be thought out" (p. 12).

✿   ✿   ✿

Husserl's last years were troubled by the problem of the plurality of subjects and the evident immanentistic overtones of his philosophy. The goal of his life-long research had been to defend man and his dignity and to prove Hegelian idealism wrong. At the end of his life, the same two problems remained unresolved. Once again in the history of philosophy, the final aim of the philosopher did not coincide with the development of his ideas. Human thinking depends on the premises from which it starts rather than on the philosopher responsible for its development.

But Husserl did not waste the last years of his life in useless recriminations. *Formal und Tranzendental Logik* was written by Husserl nine years before he died in 1938. It is a work of vast vision. Experience is understood as an intellectual elaboration of the meanings of essences. Husserl insists, again with idealistic terminology, that consciousness *constitutes* the meaning of the essences. A being which is given by the experience is the same being which consciousness *constitutes*. Preceding philosophies, Husserl continues, were deficient and partial because they intended to elaborate rational schemes taken from experiences. Phenomenology is a perfect philosophy because it seeks and finds the *logos* within the experience itself. Hegel once said that his system was the last word in philosophy. Croce also claimed that privilege. Now Husserl sees his philosophy as the last possible form of human wisdom. If the power of the human mind is the final criterion for understanding reality, each philosopher should claim such a privilege. But if being is infinite (Dante spoke of the "infinite ocean of being") then each philosopher contributes to its better understanding without ever exhausting the task of philosophizing. Husserl, to be sure, claimed that he discovered the true path of philosophy, but he also admitted that progress on that path will have to continue as long as mankind exists. Philosophy therefore does not consist in reaching goals, but in continuously striving toward a better understanding of the meaning of the essence.

This same theme is developed in *Krisis der europäischen Wissenschaften*, published partially in 1936.[12] European culture is in crisis because the natural sciences do not know the object of their research. They reduce reality to "nature" mathematically formulated. Galileo was responsible for the beginning of this inert understanding of nature. After him mankind rebelled, guided by extraordinary leaders: Descartes, Hume, Kant, Hegel, Marx and finally Husserl. Phenomenology eliminates the conflict between man and nature. Furthermore, phenomenology discovers in history, in the communion of experiences of all knowing subjects, a progressive and infinite attempt toward the total rationalization of the universe into the transcendental consciousness, that is to say, into the Absolute.

III. *Husserl's Followers*

Husserl died in 1938. His manuscripts, saved by his widow from the fury of the Nazis and brought to Louvain, are still undergoing investigation by dozens of scholars. The influence of Husserl on our contemporary civilization is enormous. The phenomenological method has penetrated not only philosophy but also all the other fields of research from sociology to theology.

Among Husserl's disciples, perhaps only L. Landgreke and E. Fink have continued the idealistic developments of phenomenology. Others had abandoned Husserl to develop their only personal philosophy. Martin Heidegger is the most outstanding among them. Max Scheler and Nicholas Hartmann, of course, are greatly indebted to Husserl. Many followers of Husserl are more faithful to his phenomenological *method* than to his metaphysical involvements. Lipps, Simmel, von Hildebrand, and Conrad Martius are especially noteworthy.

---

[12] The complete work was published in 1963 by the Archives of Louvain.

In France, Sartre studied the phenomenology of Husserl to develop his own disturbed form of existentialism. M. Merleau-Ponty became interested by way of the phenomenological method in the problem of the individual, in rejecting the transcendentalism of Fichte, and in understanding the situation of each human being.

In Italy, E. Paci is responsible for a lively renaissance of phenomenological discussions. But Paci does not understand the metaphysical problem, and he speaks with a Latin enthusiasm that often obscures the actual problem. The more serious S. V. Roveghi has found interest in comparing the Husserl doctrine on intentionality with the scholastic concept explained by Thomas Aquinas. Edith Stein, a Jewish convert to Catholicism, who died at the hands of the Nazis and who was for many years an assistant to Husserl, found a similar affinity between Husserl and Aquinas.

In the U.S.A., Peirce's philosophy prepared the atmosphere for an intelligent acceptance of Husserl, and M. Farber was the founder of a school of phenomenology in the United States. A philosophical magazine still keeps alive the spirit of Husserl in this country.

In 1906, in a notebook of personal reflections,[13] Husserl wrote: "My personality will never be complete. It is denied to my person to experience the unity of the *Weltanschauung*, the unity of a culture freely developed, the unity of a vision of the world, organic, beautiful, natural. It is very painful to sacrifice the joy of an harmonious unity, of a freedom which offers the natural comfort of beauty, but I must resign myself. . . . My duty is to live for my goal and I must find my value and my interior security by searching a solution to the problem. . . ."

Thirty years later, after a lifetime spent in search of the meaning of phenomenology, Husserl wrote in the *Krisis der europäischen Wissenschaften*:[14] "Philosophy as science, as a rigorous serious science, apodictically rigorous: the dream is ended." These words were meant to describe the general situation of philosophy, but it is also fair to think that Husserl, at the end of his life, sensed that the dream of a universal phenomenology was fading away. We pointed out the reasons for Husserl's failure: he meant to reach a universal phenomenology without recognizing the reality of the existent which makes revelation (phenomenon) of being possible; hence his almost reluctant idealism and his inability to solve the problem of intersubjectivity.

He once complained that "he had the misfortune to be in love with philosophy."[15] Philosophy paid him back with a fame that he did not

---

[13] This diary is quoted in the footnote, p. 126 of the French translation of the *Philosophie als strenge Wissenschaft*.

[14] III, 9, p. 79.

[15] Introduction to the first volume of the English translation of the *Ideen*.

seek but which will remain. Throughout his own life of intellectual research and laborious understanding of the meaning of philosophy, Husserl gave luminous evidence of his absolute honesty. To be and to be respected as an honest person is no irrelevant achievement in the present condition of the world.

chapter V

Martin Heidegger

INTRODUCTION

Perhaps the most outstanding philosopher of the existentialist movement in contemporary thought, and without doubt the most mysterious, is Martin Heidegger. For the past fifty years he has commanded the attention of all those interested in philosophy. An unending series of volumes has been written about him and his work. For instance, by 1955 about 877 publications dealt with Martin Heidegger. A few years later a new bibliographical study was required to keep up with the volume of research into his thought.[1] His sixtieth and seventieth birthdays, in 1949 and 1959, were celebrated by *Festschriften*, a sort of Heideggerian encyclopedia[2] put together by admirers who belonged to all walks of the academic world: philosophers, theologians, psychotherapists, and others.

Martin Heidegger now lives in retirement in a village of the Black Forest. He has accepted the messages of Kierkegaard, Nietzsche, and Husserl and, after personal and unique assimilation, transmitted them to us in a powerful and sweeping philosophy. His presence is felt throughout the world, in Europe, in America, in Asia. Whether we are for him or against him, we cannot afford to be without him. Yet of Heidegger the man, outside of his work, we know almost nothing. Or, perhaps, we should say that we know enough to want to know more. But Heidegger is silent about his personal life. Although existentialists of all persuasions have made a point to live the doctrine they preach — what better way to be existential? — Heidegger does not betray in his works, which in a way resemble the impersonal "Summas" of the

---

[1] Cf. G. Schneeberger, *Ergänzungen zu einem Heidegger's Bibliographie.*
[2] M. *Heidegger zum 60 Geburtstag, 1950;* M. *Heidegger zum 70 Geburtstag, 1960.*

Middle Ages, any personal involvement. It is reported that he once began a graduate course on Aristotle with these words: "Aristotle was born, worked, and died," and then plunged into an analysis of Aristotle's thought without another word on the person on the Stagirite.

Heidegger's personal life is wrapped in enigma. For instance, what caused him, at twenty-one years of age, in 1910, to abandon the Society of Jesus and to begin a new life which not only ignored the possibility of religious vocation but even called into question the very existence of the Christian faith which he had inherited from his religious family background?

Other puzzles are raised by Heidegger's relationship with Nazism. What were his thoughts in 1933 when he accepted from the Nazis the presidency of Freiburg University? Why did he resign this post after only one year in office? Again, how are we to regard his relations with his mentor Husserl? On the whole these were on a cordial and personal level. But could Heidegger, when he abandoned Husserl's phenomenology, be accused of treason toward his teacher, somewhat as Aristotle has been accused of betraying Plato? Did Heidegger borrow his "original" philosophy from the closed seminars which Husserl restricted to his chosen assistants, or was the rebellious pupil the occasion for his teacher to change the direction of his phenomenological thought, leading it from an idealistic basis to a more existential approach?

The enigmatic character of Heidegger's life and thought is one of the reasons for the great interest in his person and philosophy. In the following pages we shall try to discuss some of the more significant aspects of Heidegger's contribution to contemporary philosophy, both through his person and his thought. We shall treat, in turn, the following topics: (1) Heidegger's development to *Sein und Zeit;* (2) the meaning of Heidegger's major work; (3) realism and the existentialism of Heidegger; and (4) Heidegger's thought after *Sein und Zeit.*

1. HEIDEGGER'S DEVELOPMENT TO *SEIN UND ZEIT*

I. *From Aristotle to Husserl*

Martin Heidegger was born in Messkirch, Baden, in 1889. He was the firstborn son of the sacristan of the Catholic cathedral of St. Martin. In 1905, the Jesuits accepted him in the Bertholdgymasium of Freiburg in Brisgau. To this town Heidegger remained faithful all his active life. Speaking to a group of persons from his own town in 1955, he quoted P. S. Hebel: "We are like plants, which, willingly or unwillingly, must grow from their own roots to blossom in the air and to bear fruit." A concrete, well defined situation is necessary for an authentic human reflection: the anonymity and excessive mobility characteristic of a modern megapolis are, for Heidegger, atrocious devices of dissipation.

In 1909, Heidegger took courses for one full semester in theology. It was an important semester, as is shown by the fact that in 1953 Heidegger broke his silence to say that "Without this theological beginning I would never have entered the path of philosophy. But the beginning always looks toward the future."[3] The explanation of this important confession is found in the method of hermeneutics (interpretation and explanation) used by theology. A theologian accepts the sacred word revealed by God and then tries to explain it, to make it clear and organized, to make it a *living* revelation of God. A philosopher, for Heidegger, must use the same method of hermeneutics, and this forces him to go beyond the traditional structures of artificial nature which are imposed upon reality in order to go directly to the revelation of existence. We must agree with Heidegger that a higher definition of philosophy cannot be found. But we must also emphasize the fact that theology is given its tool by God: the sacred word of revelation. On the contrary, the philosopher is in need of finding his tools, his words, his principles which, to be philosophical, ought to originate from reflection. If Heidegger seeks the revelation of existence without these philosophical tools, any word is equally valid and all he accomplishes is a factual description of reality. If he accepts the reflective character of philosophy, traditional philosophies must represent a variety of attempts at organizing reality reflectively.

We cannot agree with many critics who identify Heidegger from the beginning of his philosophical work in 1910 with the phenomenological school of Husserl. Heidegger's mentor for his doctoral dissertation (1913) was A. Schneider, a Catholic philosopher. Heidegger's first publications (an article in 1912 on "The Problem of Reality in Modern Philosophy," and a review [1914] of a volume written by Sentroul on *Kant and Aristotle*) move with secure familiarity within the framework of the Greek and medieval metaphysical tradition. In them the target of his arguments is the sterile discussion of the problem of knowledge in modern philosophy. From Locke to Hume the assumption was the same: a hostile separation between subject and object, between thinking and being, and consequently an artificial parallelism between them which was taken for granted from the beginning, thus presup-

---

[3] M. Heidegger, "Aus einem Gespräch von der Sprache." This is a dialogue with Fezuka of the University of Tokyo, published in the collection *Unterwegs zur Sprache* (Neske Pfulligen, 1953), p. 96.

posing what was meant to be the goal of their investigations.

Kierkegaard, Nietzsche, and Dilthey, who later inspired Heidegger with vigorous themes, do not appear in this first period. The pre-Socratics, in particular Heraclitus, play an important role; we may also say that during this period Heidegger's enthusiasm for Aristotle and the scholastics gradually began to wane. When did the formal transition take place? It is difficult to establish a date: our only certainty is that Heidegger underwent a possible crisis and definitely abandoned the classical philosophy inherited from the Jesuits at some point between 1915, the year of his *Habilitationschrift*, and 1927 when *Sein und Zeit* was published.

Heidegger's *Habilitationschrift* on Duns Scotus[4] is unmistakably of Aristotelian persuasions. Yet his famous openness to new formulations of problems is evident also. The study, which is dedicated to Heinrich Rickert and in which Husserl's influence is noted, is intended as an attack against the dominant historicism of the time. The main idea which Heidegger expresses in this study is that progress in philosophy is based on new answers given to the same problems, the perennial problems of human existence. For instance, in the Middle Ages, man faced the philosophical problem with an absolute confidence in his tools of investigation. Modern man doubted the validity of the same tools. Kant concluded that his categories of the mind were universally valid for scientific knowledge, but he held that these categories sprung from the mind, not objective reality, and cannot afford us insight into the inner being of things. Husserl himself, with the magic of his *epoché*, neglected any concern about the correspondence of the phenomenon to reality, but he would not neglect the various *forms* under which phenomena were represented.

Heidegger came to this conclusion: the Medievals, Kant, and Husserl work from different backgrounds and with a variety of different tools on the same philosophical problem. This could not be otherwise, because, as long as man continues to be man, the philosophical problem will continue to be the same. Although Husserl's phenomenology seemed to be a revolutionary approach, it was not. Husserl felt the necessity of a thorough "house cleaning" of all forms of subjectivism (or psychologism as he called it). Heidegger is in definite agreement with this, but Husserl's "pure logic" was in danger of being completely empty if its "forms" were not given a metaphysical content. In a famous note Heidegger suggests that Husserl's philosophy needs an openness that is *Weltanschaulich* in character, that is, an openness toward the world.[5]

---

[4] *Die Kategorien und Bedeutungslehre des Scotus* (Tübingen: Mohr, 1916).
[5] *Die Kategorien . . .* , p. 14 n.

Heidegger's dissertation on Scotus was a declaration of the perennial thirst of man for a better understanding of existence. His major concern at this time can be best seen, perhaps, in a saying Heidegger borrowed from Hölderlin: "Beyond everything, we are always looking for the absolute yet we always find relative things."[6]

With this study of *Duns Scotus* we are brought to the five years of World War I, the most enigmatic in Heidegger's life. We do not know precisely what happened; we do know that after these five years Heidegger was no longer in the tradition of classical philosophy; he was reading Nietzsche, evidently interested in personal destiny, and he found himself enthusiastically involved in the phenomenological school of Husserl. The war did not change his life much; toward the end, we find him in military uniform in an outpost close to Verdun. His health seemed to be the obstacle that kept him from active service. Some of his critics doubted his good faith and noted his passion for mountain climbing and outdoor sport, activities requiring robust health.

From the last years of the war, Heidegger worked with Husserl; he was his assistant at the university and finally he adhered without hesitation to the phenomenological movement. He must have felt, after all, that the sterile neo-Kantianism prevailing at Marburg and the immobility of neoscholasticism were insufficient for a society which had to begin again from the ruins of a national disaster. Husserl offered hope for a renewal: his philosophy was rooted in the tradition of a sound "intentionality" of human knowledge and it expanded into new horizons, which Heidegger presented to the students to whom he was assigned. He commented to them on Husserl's *Logische Untersuchungen* (*Logical Researches*).

Husserl was pleased with Heidegger's choice of a text, for he considered it a good introduction to phenomenology. But he could not suspect that Heidegger's intention was to investigate phenomenologically new dimensions of being, specifically, history and time.[7] These topics were open to many questions: Rickert and Dilthey, we know, offered an historicistic interpretation that did not, in Heidegger's opinion, do justice to the individual man. In addition, Heidegger was interested in knowing the scientist's conception of time. Could it be, Heidegger was asking, that time is something more than just a condition for human knowledge; that it molds the very structure of man? This question was about to become the main theme of his philosophy. Meanwhile, providentially, an invitation came from Marburg to join the faculty of that

[6] In German, the alliteration of the two words, *Unbedingte* (absolute) and *Ding* (thing) expresses more forcefully the mutual relation of the two concepts.

[7] Husserl held a series of lectures on time, which Heidegger edited in 1928. Cf. our chapter on Husserl.

university. Heidegger accepted: it was an opportunity to meet new people and new ideas.

II. *Martin Heidegger and Nicolai Hartmann*

Nicolai Hartmann is a significant figure in contemporary philosophy and, along with Whitehead and Maritain, a pioneer in twentieth-century metaphysics. As head of the department of philosophy at Marburg, he hired Martin Heidegger in 1923 for a full-time teaching job. From the second half of the nineteenth century Marburg had been famous for its neo-Kantian school, which produced well-known philosophers: H. Cohen, P. Natorp, and later E. Cassirer. Hartmann, however, could not accept the reduction of being to the logical categories of the *Critique of Pure Reason.* Aristotle, whose thought Hartmann knew well, prevented him from blindly accepting Kantian criticism. In addition, Husserl's investigations on the meaning of intentionality in the act of knowing convinced him that knowledge is meaningful only if it is knowledge of something, i.e., of being. Here there was common ground between Hartmann and Heidegger, and the influence of the former on the latter made their philosophies interdependent in their structure and in their intelligibility. In opposition to almost all modern philosophical trends, Hartmann agreed with Aristotle and Thomas Aquinas on the ontological nature of *all* philosophical problems. Being is before knowing: this is the fundamental characteristic of Hartmann's and Heidegger's positions. Hartmann, however, took another step, which Aristotle and Thomas Aquinas would have been reluctant to take. Hartmann says: being is so absolutely *the first,* that a final investigation of it transcends human powers. Our mind always runs into insurmountable obstacles: for instance, we cannot overcome the contradictions between freedom and determinism, immanence and transcendence. Specifically, the problem of God's existence is insoluble: the mind cannot take a position on it. And if it does, we fall into the same traps which enmeshed classical metaphysics; we build up closed systems, crowded with subtle distinctions, abstruse deductive abstractions and nominalistic values the futility of which we ourselves cannot deny.

For Hartmann metaphysics is a tissue of questions which cannot be answered logically. Thus Hartmann, who started with a solid act of confidence in being qua being (*Seiendes als Seiendes*) concludes by announcing that the same being, as far as we are concerned, is irrational. Metaphysics is impossible and its place must be taken by ontology, the science that focuses on "intelligible questions," the "intelligible aspects" of being, which by nature must be historical, becoming, ever changing.

We are tempted to label his ontology a form of phenomenology or a new edition of historicism, but Hartmann resented such labels, concerned as he was with the undeniable primacy of being, which makes knowledge possible. A second proof for the existence of "being in itself," expelling all doubts which might remain as residues of the analysis of the transcendent nature of the act of knowing, comes from the sense of reality unanimously accepted by the consensus of human communities. Hartmann is here evidently under the influence of Dilthey and Scheller. For them and for him we all experience emotionally transcendent acts (desiring, hoping, willing, acting) which have a meaning insofar as they are based on a "towardness" to being, a drive toward the real.

These few hints, taken almost exclusively from Hartmann's important *Grundzüge einer Metaphysik der Erkenntnis (Principles of a Metaphysics of Knowledge)* (1921), are sufficient for our purpose. They bring home the fact that Hartmann's ontology and Heidegger's new horizons have a more than casual affinity. Hartmann understandably saw in the newcomer from Freiburg a competitor. Students were flocking around him, because he was eloquent and because his lectures were animated by new ideas. "The path of Heidegger," Hartmann admitted, "is not without some sort of fascination." Both closed ranks and fought an identical battle: Heidegger spoke of the "openness toward being"; Hartmann defended the attempt of his ontology to rescue new meanings from the irrationality of universal being.

Hartmann and Heidegger fail to see that the things of the world, out of their contingency and dependence, demand an absolute Being and therefore the existence of a metaphysics as the supreme science of rationality.

Hartmann, however, by failing to recognize the real contingency of the things of the world, ends up confused and embarrassed. In one of his works for a comprehensive ontology, *Möglichkeit und Wirklichkeit (Actuality and Possibility,* 1938),[8] he obeyed the principle he laid down and established what is real and what is possible on the same level of existence. If we believe that everything we encounter in the world (the stars in their celestial orbits, history in its fatal conclusions, human acts in the necessity of their motivations) is self-sufficient, evidently the necessary and the possible are the same. Heidegger sensed this difficulty. His philosophy considered time as the only factor of differentiation between beings, and ultimately, for

---

[8] His comprehensive Ontology was in three parts: (*a*) *Zur Grundlegung der Ontologie (Foundations of Ontology);* (*b*) *Möglichkeit und Wirklichkeit (Actuality and Possibility);* (*c*) *Der Aufbau der realen Welt (The Structure of the Real World).*

Heidegger, time structures the very existence of man. But Hartmann did not find any way out; for him the possible is really possible (*realmöglich*) and any differentiation between possibility and reality became a question of words. The consequences for morality are even more embarrassing: if the determined alone is possible, where do we find room for choice? Hartmann in his *Ethik*, in contrast with his premises and under the evident influence of Kant's reasoning, founded moral behavior on the necessity of spiritual freedom. If human freedom cannot be explained logically, it must be postulated against logic. Thus, for him freedom is a courageous rebellion against the universal determinism of existence, of civilization, of heredity and environment. Liberty consists in the liberation of man; it does exist because conscience testifies to its existence with the satisfaction for the good we do and the remorse for the evil. This strange categorical imperative, evidently having little in common with the Kantian imperative, pushes Hartmann to a final rejection of God, who cannot be accepted, because His presence, as a fundamental norm of morality, would destroy, by determining it, the free action of man.[9]

Heidegger followed respectfully the philosophical ventures of his senior colleague with whom he shared the same persuasion of the absolute primacy of being upon knowledge, but he refused to accept the catastrophic conclusions of Hartmann's *Ethics*.

One point must be stressed strongly here: *Heidegger never denied the existence of God*. He agreed that the problem of His existence is beyond philosophical discussion. He became progressively inclined toward a solution based on an impersonal being, indeed quite obscure, conditioning the existence of the universe. Tragically, he lost the Christian faith of his family and his youth, but he refused to declare, with Nietzsche, that God was dead, because he did not know and he could not know. Therefore, to the humanistic and yet unjustified *Ethics* of Hartmann, Heidegger, disillusioned by the ruins of World War I and influenced by the destructive fatalism of Nietzsche, opposed a morality of resignation. Man, as *Sein und Zeit* presents him, is in the world without asking to be there; the only decent thing he can do is to accept his destiny with resigned dignity.

III. *The Background of* Sein und Zeit

The University of Marburg offered another opportunity to Heidegger,

---

[9] The well informed student of philosophy should not find great difficulties in discovering in Hartmann's ideas the profound scission of being (*res cogitans — res extensa*), a neoplatonic heritage of the Renaissance especially prominent in the dualism of Descartes.

for it was, from 1921, the school where Rudolf Bultmann lectured in theology and another theologian, the Swiss Karl Barth, frequently used to visit.

Bultmann and Barth led a new movement in theology. Against the "liberals" Harnack, Ritschl, and Gunkel, who advocated Christianity as an ideological and cultural phenomenon, they presented Christ as man's Savior and as the author of an historical revelation which could not be reduced to human wisdom because it was essentially divine and factually above the development of any man-made civilization.

While Bultmann and Barth were manifestly influenced by Heidegger, from a different angle Heidegger's developing ideas were evidently molded by his conversations with these two prominent leaders of Protestantism.

Bultmann and Barth came from their pastoral experience to the classroom with an identical conviction of the personal character of the encounter between man and God. But they differed in explaining it. Barth's fundamental thesis was Kierkegaard's qualitative difference between God and man. God is; man is not. Hence man's crisis. He must say "yes" to this simple fact that his being in the world is pure nothingness: *nicht Inhalt.* Under this condition, God takes over in His own most magnificent way: in fact, only God speaks of God and He actually spoke through His revelation, which is a carefully worked out plan of salvation history. Heidegger was not ready to accept these ideas; but he was ready to accept from the author of the *Commentary on the Epistle to the Romans* the doctrine of an infinite, unbridgeable distance between being as such and the individual existing things of the world. This idea became the backbone of his whole philosophy, particularly of *Sein und Zeit.*

Bultmann was more at ease with philosophical concepts than was Barth. Like Heidegger, he derived from Husserl's phenomenology a distaste for Aristotelian ideas. The Stagirite, according to them, was responsible for a Western frame of thought rooted on rationalizations which were universally accepted as true, whereas they crumbled as fantastic myths under an honest criticism. Faith itself, this authentic gift of God upon which Christianity is based, risked suffocation by the mythical superstructure of Aristotelianism. The task of the theologian therefore is to demythologize Christianity and to stop conceiving something which does not belong to the world as a human event. Heidegger projected this thought into philosophical dimensions. Again he could not say anything about God, but he knew that man has been surrounded for too many centuries by mythical conceptions. *Sein und Zeit* can be properly described as an original work of the demythologization of man. In addition to these considerations, Heidegger's experience with Barth and Bultmann had another result. In them he saw a renewed effort to reach an answer to the meaning of human existence. What should he, Heidegger, do? He was in need of an answer to the question of the meaning of man: the pressure was unbearable: after the rejection of Aristotle, the failure of Hartmann, the negative answers of the theologians, the readings of Kierkegaard and Nietzsche and the decline of the West under the irrational blows inflicted by the war, the eternal question remained: what is man?

We must, however, be careful not to present a disturbed, sleepless Heidegger roaming the University campus and asking people: What is man? From his seminary days to the present, Heidegger's Christian heritage has been evident. It can be called a joyful and sound certainty that there is openness in man; in other words, that knowledge is possible, that things are reachable, that Locke and Hume and all the moderns misunderstood the problem of knowledge and formulated it as a pseudo-problem. Add to this openness the Kierkegaardian theme that man is limited, that human finitude, that is to say, time, is a condition for the manifestation of the existence of all beings, and you have the mainstream of thoughts developed in *Sein und Zeit*. Man therefore is both privileged and sacrificed; he is open to the experience of dread and nothing, and this experience gives man the chance to find light, possibility, and *meaning*.

Heidegger's *Sein und Zeit* held that thinking itself is possible only because man, essentially opened to time, outdistances himself by creating a vacuum in which the things of the world reveal themselves. Time is therefore thinking, or what is the same, the essential condition for the revelation of all existing things.

These introductory pages should help us understand the major work which we are about to study. But the hard truth of the enigmatic life of Heidegger does not dispense us from a brief discussion of another aspect of his activity, i.e., his political involvement.

IV. *Heidegger's Political Activity*

From 1930 to 1935 Heidegger published almost nothing. Those five years witnessed a political activity which is one of the puzzles of his life and the coveted target of his opponents. The facts are well known: Heidegger has been a loner all his life. He must have suffered tremendously from the humiliating peace treaties of Versailles. His *being for death* in *Sein und Zeit* must be understood within its philosophical frame, but the tone of his description betrays the German postwar tragedy. We know of his love for his peasant origin; he liked to wear Swabian clothes, to live in the solitude of his mountains, to go skiing on the slopes dear to his youth. The Weimar Republic, unfortunately, was the antithesis of all these values Heidegger stood for. It was, theoretically speaking, almost a perfect pattern of democratic wisdom, born of the city bourgeoisie and shaded with rationalistic and socialistic tendencies.

When the occasion came, in 1929, to be noticed and admired Heidegger welcomed it. Was it the desire for power that Tacitus discovered in every human heart, or just the little glory which the meek Virgil noticed in his own behavior in the presence of his admirers? We do not know; but we do know that Heidegger went a long way along the path of Nazism. In 1933 he accepted from the Nazis the presidency of Freiburg University and became a card-carrying Nazi. His pronouncements on behalf of the Fürher were too numerous for a man of his stature. The enigma grows out of proportion if we mention the pretailored theories, mingled with platitudes and contradictions, that Heidegger, by nature so withdrawn and circumspect, wrote in *Die Selbstbehauptung der deutschen Universität*[10] in 1933. Up to then — Heidegger said — university training was aimless, without relation to the concreteness of the political situation, bound to an anonymous scientific progress. Hitlerism brought national stature to the university and consciousness of the destiny of the race to its students. Knowledge cannot be acquired simply as a tool for a profession, but the profession must be a tool for the knowledge of the destiny of the nation. The ideals of an atemporal eternal goal have disappeared; their place is taken by the nation that strives for self-determination, for freedom. Unbelievably, Heidegger identified freedom with a race's conquest of other races. The Jews for him were enemies of mankind because they sought the exploitation of a divided bourgeoisie society. The list of topics is too painful to be continued, but in the same year (1933), Heidegger may possibly have changed his mind. In a declaration, published with other professors, we read this paragraph, which hints at the fatal necessity of accepting the new situation as a sacrifice of the mind, analogous to the human existence described in *Sein und Zeit,* as an anxious exposition to nothingness: "We are sure of an uncompromisingly simple inquiry into the essence of being. . . . This inquiry by a rational science has its innermost motivation in the original courage to grow or to perish in the encounter with being. . . . For us inquiry is not the ideal idiosyncratic insistence upon equivocation at any price. For us inquiry means: expos-

---

[10] Breslau, Verlag Kirn, 1933.

ing oneself to the loftiness of things and their laws; it means not to lock out the terror or the confusion of darkness."[11]

In the following year, 1934, Heidegger resigned the office of the presidency, apparently to dedicate his time to teaching; in 1935 he declined an invitation to be president of Berlin University and wrote bitter words against false interpretations of social nationalism offered by men "fishing in the troubled waters of 'values.'" Heidegger perhaps was afraid of his political involvement, and he turned his attention to his studies, to Nietzsche and, during the war, to the fragments of the pre-Socratics. After the war, he was forced to retirement to the Black Forest where he continued to write and to publish.

Never did he try to defend himself. Only in 1959, in a final note to his *Unterwegs zur Sprache*, did he react with bitterness to the accusation that he suppressed in the 1942 edition of *Sein und Zeit* the dedication to Husserl because of the Jewish parentage of the founder of phenomenology.[12]

As was natural, many critics came to the defense of Heidegger. They spoke of the political errors of Plato as an outstanding example of dichotomy between thought and action frequent in philosophers. Sartre was among the most convinced defenders of Heidegger. In his *Critique de la raison dialectique* he claimed the necessity of a division between doctrine and the man responsible for it, contradicting the main assumption of his philosophy. Others spoke of an almost inborn naiveté of philosophers for practical decisions.[13]

It seems that there is a great confusion. Some critics spent time, particularly in the United States, to collect "proofs" beyond doubt of Heidegger's political errors. They showed a keen ability for libelous compendiums. Proofs are useless because Heidegger himself cannot deny his political affiliation to Nazism. In the same perspective, kind feelings for the political naivité of the great philosopher are irrelevant. A philosopher more than anyone else is engaged to understand the meaning of good and evil, of honest and dishonest: his thinking prepares future civilizations and he must be ready to answer for his ideas.

The unfortunate political experiences of Heidegger are a warning to everyone whose interest is learning. Persons are condemned in courts

---

[11] *The Worlds of Existentialism: A Critical Reader.* Eng. tr., Morris Freedmann (New York: Random House), p. 53.

[12] "To counteract repeated and malicious accusations," Heidegger noted that the fourth edition of *Sein und Zeit* (1935), was dedicated to Husserl. In the fifth edition Heidegger gave in to the pressure of the editor, omitted the dedication to Husserl, but retained the warm expression of gratitude to Husserl on page 38.

[13] Cf. W. Barrett, *Philosophy of the Twentieth Century* (New York: Random House, 1963), p. 163.

through indictments; but their ideas must be judged by the soundness or the weakness of their principles. And principles, we all know, are by nature before and above personal behavior.

2. *SEIN UND ZEIT*

We now begin to discuss Heidegger's major work, *Sein und Zeit* (*Being and Time*).[14] A striking difference between this work and those written later by Heidegger must be noted from the outset. His later works show little concern for methodological precision and great enthusiasm for inspirational themes. They might even leave the impression of a disorderly and whimsical Heidegger.

Nothing could be further from the truth. Heidegger was not a Nietzsche. Later he spent his energies in lively polemics against traditional methods and terminologies, but at the time of his writing *Sein und Zeit*, Heidegger was seriously engaged in finding *his own method and his own philosophical terms*.

I. *The Problem*

The problem of *Sein und Zeit* is the problem of existence.[15] Of all the problems, this is typically the "problem of man," because man alone, among all existing beings, is able to formulate the question: What is existence? We can say that just as classical metaphysics holds that the essence of God is His own existence Martin Heidegger says that the essence of man consists in positing the problem of existence. From this perspective, Heidegger was Aristotelian because he aimed to face again (*Wiederholen*) the problem which Aristotle considered of central importance when he wrote in his *Metaphysics:*

"For manifestly you have long been aware of what you mean when you used the expression 'being.' We, however, who used to think we understood it have now become perplexed."[16]

---

[14] Martin Heidegger, *Sein und Zeit* (*Jahrbuch für Philosophie und phänomenologische Forschung*), VIII. Halle: Niemeyer, 1927. English translation: *Being and Time*, by J. Macquarrie and E. Robinson (London: SCM Press; and New York: Harper and Row, 1962).

[15] The term "existence" is used with the traditional meaning of classical metaphysics. It is an inquiry into beings as beings. St. Thomas used it to speak in the same sense when he used with the other Scholastics the formula: *ens in quantum est ens*, or, *ens qua tale*. Heidegger uses the same scholastic term when he speaks of *Sein überhaupt:* being as such.

Often in this chapter the term "existent" will be used. By it is meant each individual thing, for example, a house, a dog, a man, etc. Metaphysics deals with the fundamental quality, "Existence," which makes it possible for every individual thing to be an existent.

[16] Aristotle, *Metaphysics*, B4, 1001 a 21.

Ultimately, what is the purpose of a philosopher? It is to understand the meaning of the verb "to be," the most universal and the most puzzling of all verbs. We say: "It *is* true; it *is* false; our land *is* beautiful." When we say: "the sun shines," or, "the child runs," the verb *to be* is implied (the sun *is* shining; the child *is* running), but it is not always there. One single word of exclamation, "help" for instance, implies the verb to be: "I *am* in danger," etc.

Each meaning refers to *something*, therefore to a *being*.

We saw that the young Heidegger spent a long time studying fundamental meanings: the meaning of reality, of history, the doctrine of meanings in Duns Scotus. Now he becomes aware that a distinction is possible among the meanings of each existing thing only if we refer to and if we know what is existence in general, which is shared by all existents. Could we go back to the medieval question and say that existence is a *genus* shared by all the individual beings? Heidegger evidently denies this conclusion and he uses arguments well known to Aristotle and Thomas Aquinas: if existence is predicated as a genus of all existing beings, in what does their specific difference consist? Existence is superior to all genera because any differentiations in things exist themselves.

Sein und Zeit, at this point, assumes defiant tones challenging all empiricists and pragmatists. The latter assert that metaphysics is useless. They agree that everybody knows the meaning of existence (since everybody uses it in the process of thinking), and that it is at any rate useless to question the meaning of existence because it is undefinable and beyond comprehension.

Heidegger's rebellion against such platitudes takes proportions of classical majesty. It is true that a preliminary understanding of the meaning of existence is shared by all human beings (otherwise how could they express themselves?); it is also true that definitions are not everything in philosophy (and what could define existence, if nothing is more comprehensive?); but if man does not inquire into the meaning of existence, all the other meanings of each existent must remain obscure and doubtful and man's knowledge is vain and deceitful. Heidegger resumed the studies of his younger years (particularly of the meaning of history) to analyze the crisis regarding the foundations of natural science. In our day, each science is in the process of an ever renewing awareness of its own meaning, of the meaning of its own presupposed foundations. This is not the first time this crisis has arisen, Heidegger says, but it is most interesting to assist at this new renaissance of interest on the part of the scientists in the ontological meaning of their research. After all, what is the sense of searching the meaning of space and time, life, psyche, and society, if the meaning of existence, shared by all of them, continues to be obscure and confused?

Therefore Heidegger comes to a logical conclusion: *there is an ontological priority of the meaning of existence*. The "Ontological" (*ontologisch*) is, for Heidegger, the study of existence which is not confined to a particular aspect; or, perhaps better, the ontological is the perspective under which we examine the meaning of the existence predicated of each existing being. The "ontic" (*ontisch*), on the other hand, is the study of *an* existing being in its particular relation with other beings. For instance, I study the *ontic meaning* of space if I am concerned with its physical dimensions, its continuity, etc. Kant faced the *ontological* meaning of space when he tried to probe its universal function as a means for understanding what exists within space.

The question of the meaning of existence has also "an ontic primacy." That is, each particular (ontic) problem cannot be discussed without a reference, frequently implicit and taken for granted, to existence. This is true because among all existents one alone — man — singles himself out. It is he who brings intellectual comprehensibility to the existents he knows by applying to them the original notion of being (or existence) that makes knowing possible.

Heidegger does not use the word "man," but the term *Dasein*, (*da-sein:* "being-there"). ". . . This entity which each of us is himself and which includes inquiring as one of the possibilities of its Being, we shall denote by the term '*Dasein.*'"[17] *Dasein* has the connotation of *hic et nunc;* the medievals used this terminology to denote the concrete situation of each existent. But the *Dasein* of Heidegger, man, is *hic et nunc* in an original and particular way because in him is the possibility of consciousness, revealing the *hic et nunc* of each existent. The *Da* of *Dasein* (the fact that we are always in a definite situation which we need to open up to the future) is a constitutive element of *Dasein;* it is not therefore a negligible contingent aspect. This is the main reason why Heidegger used *Dasein,* not "man" to designate the object of his inquiry. In fact "man" in common language connotes an existent complete in himself, situated in a given environment but capable of living everywhere. The term *Dasein* was used by Hegel and Jaspers, but with a different meaning. For them, basically, *Dasein* meant an empirical individual; for Heidegger *Dasein* means the *hic et nunc* of an individual or, even better, it means that which is responsible for this *hic et nunc* and not others belonging to this individual man. "*Dasein* is an entity which does not occur among other entities. Rather it is

---

[17] *Sein und Zeit,* 7; Eng. tr., p. 27.

ontically distinguished by the fact that in its very Being, that Being is an *issue* for it."[18]

Now we might be in a better position to understand what we called a moment ago the "ontic primacy of the meaning of existence." The problem of existence has an ontological primacy, we all agree, since metaphysics is the foundation of all sciences. But this is possible because *Dasein,* by reason of its ontic existence, opens up the question about the meaning of existence itself, ontologically understood. "Dasein is ontically distinctive in that it *is* ontological."[19]

---

[18] *Ibid.,* p. 12; Eng. tr., p. 32.

[19] *Ibid.,* p. 12; Eng. tr., p. 32. It is clear that *Sein und Zeit,* from the first pages, is an original work of a philosopher who was not satisfied with traditional schemes. Its originality seems to emphasize two aspects of importance for the future development of Heidegger's thought.

1. We read in *Sein und Zeit,* p. 6, that the existence of one individual being cannot be the existence of another being. *"The being of entities is not an entity."* The sentence, as many others in Heidegger's works, is filled with cryptic meanings. But from the context we are reasonably sure that he was not concerned with the problem of essences, of natures. If I ask *what* a tree is, I cannot answer that "that being is another being"; that is, that the essence of a tree is different from a particular tree growing in the forest. The essence of beings cannot be different from them. Nor was he concerned about existences; obviously one existing tree cannot be another tree. Heidegger considers classical doctrine (Avicenna, Thomas Aquinas), about essences and existences obsolete and inadequate.

Heidegger wants to know what it is that makes it possible for each being to exist in the world, to assert its presence, both as an individual being that exists open to others and yet always remaining itself. Heidegger insists in telling us that each existent is "open, comprehensible in his individuality": how is this possible if "the being of entities is not an entity," that is to say, if each being is only itself and not something else?

The problem, of course, is not new in the history of philosophy and, as it is ambiguously presented by Heidegger, it raises a host of questions. Does he mean to discuss the fact that each being is distinct from the others and undivided in itself? Then he speaks of the unity of beings, which means that each being is only itself. Yet what is it that allows us to designate all trees by the common word "tree"? They must have something in common. Thomas Aquinas in *De ente et essentia* faced this problem and called existence the element actualizing the form to the perfection of its being. Substance, existence, act of being are not separate entities somehow entering a being, but only necessary metaphysical structures of *one* being. We discover in Heidegger the same distaste for the internal structure of being that brought numberless problems to Descartes and the rationalists. If being is a conglomeration of opaque Parmenedean individual existents, how do we explain knowledge and communication?

On the other hand, if Heidegger means to discuss the fact that each existent in the world cannot explain its appearance in the world, then Heidegger is questioning the meaning of the Absolute Being, which must be capable of sharing his own being with others in such a way that they genuinely are "others" distinct from himself. This initial ambiguity runs through the pages of *Sein und Zeit:* it must be kept in mind to avoid confusion.

2. Heidegger acknowledges many meanings of being, but he fails to recognize the primary one. This fundamental error is due to an unwarranted methodological decision at the outset of *Sein und Zeit.*

The task that Heidegger expects to undertake in his philosophical work is the discovery of the meaning of *Dasein,* buried as it is by the distractions of daily life. His program is the discussion in detail of the meaning of *Dasein.* In brief, Heidegger aims to start a new *fundamental ontology of man.*

II. *The Meaning of* Dasein

In its entirety *Sein und Zeit* should have comprised two parts. The first was meant to be divided into three sections: (*a*) a preliminary analysis of *Dasein,* (*b*) time as the unifying category of *Dasein,* (*c*) time as the horizon of the problem of being. The second part in the intention of the author was supposed to deal with the exposition of the *new ontology,* after the traditional ontologies were demonstrated as inadequate and wrong. Heidegger had in mind Aristotle, Descartes, and Kant as the main targets of his criticism.

In effect, only the first two sections of the first part have been published. Thus, *Sein und Zeit* is an existential analysis of *Dasein,* a preparatory study to the problem of being, with short digressions on the meaning of time as related to *Dasein.*

We must stress the word "analysis," because Heidegger's intention is to describe the results of his observations related to *Dasein.* Therefore it is "existential," not "essential" analysis; it is existential because the fundamental traits of *Dasein* experimentally gathered are never static and necessary: on the contrary, they consist in *"possible* ways and orientations" which we choose to give to our existence. To make this concept clear, we must follow Heidegger in the

---

He agreed with Thomistic philosophy that research into the metaphysical meaning of being as being (existence as existence) is arbitrary and useless if it does not start off from the analysis of a given particular existent. But then, arbitrarily we think, he decides that the human *Dasein* should be this particular existent object of his research. The reasons he gives for this choice are attractive: *Dasein* is open to the understanding of reality; it posits the problem of being and therefore the possibility of an answer; it has an implicit formulation of the problem which is present in every man: the philosopher must make it explicit.

We do not object to his choice, if the human *Dasein* is selected because it is *one* of the existents; but if it is selected because it is man, then the choice is an unacceptable source of confusion. Heidegger is critical of Aristotle because he focused his inquiry on the physical substance or "the utensils" (*Zuhanden, Vorhanden:* anything which is closed in itself for a specific usage). But Heidegger goes to the opposite extreme. He makes man the pattern for explaining physical things, and he provokes a dangerous confusion between knower and known: which one of the two should reveal the truth of existence? The dilemma between the "subjective" and "objective" aspects of reality is evident; and it is also evident that Heidegger made the choice, rationalistic and Kantian in nature, by which the truth of the object must be found in the knowing subject.

effort to understand his philosophical vocabulary, an attempt often difficult but necessary for grasping his philosophy. There is a difference between what is *existential* and *existentiell*. *Existential* makes *Dasein* what it is.[20] *Existentiell* is an aspect or an activity (of *Dasein*) which is made possible by *Dasein's* being structurally what it is. To be in the world is *existential*, to exercise an activity is *existentiell* because it presupposes, but it does not interfere with, the existence of *Dasein*.

We mentioned *to be in the world* (*in der Welt-sein*); it is the most basic characteristic of *Dasein;* it means to be localized in a situation, surrounded by other existents, in a sphere of meanings which gives to *Dasein* the opportunity of understanding them.

Nothing new, you might be tempted to comment; this doctrine is as old as Aristotle's description of his *individuum*. But Heidegger adds: there is something new. The "being in the world" of *Dasein* is not an accidental qualification, the way Aristotle catalogued it; it is the most profound root of *Dasein*, that is, what makes it open to the world is a desire to transcend itself. *Dasein* transcends itself by relating itself toward other beings; it transcends present things by relating them to future things, and transcends particular entities to see them organized in the whole universe. The universe is not created by *Dasein*, but it is inconceivable without *Dasein*, just as knowledge is inconceivable without a knower. Nor does the universe create *Dasein*, but *Dasein* is inconceivable without the universe, just as the knower is inconceivable without anything to know.

Descartes, Heidegger continues, failed miserably in his philosophical effort because he spoke of *res cogitans* and *res extensa* as two autonomous, self-sufficient entities: he continued to develop the radical misconception that is responsible for the failure of the whole Western philosophical thought, grounded, as it was, on unrelated entities.

In his later works Heidegger excepted the pre-Socratics, particularly Heraclitus, from this judgment of the history of philosophy. He found an affinity between their mythical symbols and his own thinking. Also the Christian *mundus* of St. John, St. Paul, and St. Augustine was found by Heidegger (in *Das Wesen des Grundes*, 1929) as a community of spirits, though divided in its physical perspectives.

Of course, Heidegger does not deny that the goal of all philosophers is a systematic vision of the universe; after all, with what else could philosophy be concerned? What Heidegger accuses other philosophers of is their failure to understand the original primacy of the human

---

[20] If *Existential* denotes the fundamental qualities that make the *Da-sein* what it is, we are reminded by the traditional *moderate realism* that essence is what makes everything what it is. Can anybody, including Heidegger, speak of anything without presupposing that it is what it is?

Dasein's relation to other beings. We will see that, if we make an exception of some aspects of the pragmatic movement, no philosopher can be compared to Heidegger. For him relation comes *before* and is constitutive of each existent, which *is after* and *because* of its relations: *Dasein is* because it *is in the world:* its metaphysical structure is *being in the world.*

III. *The "Worldishness"*[21] *of* Dasein

In the universe each being refers to all the others; this reference is evidently an action of the human *Dasein* which gives meaning to the situations, actions and interactions of everything. The "worldishness" of all existing beings is therefore the basic condition for their comprehension and, to some extent, it could be compared to the Kantian *a priori* if we make one important distinction: the *a priori* forms of Kant are conditions established by the subject, whereas Heidegger's worldishness is originally in the universe. Perhaps the pre-Socratic conception that each being belongs to its own space and time, to which it tends to return when separated, might help us understand Heidegger's idea of worldishness.

Dasein acknowledges the presence of all existents in a first moment as utensils (*Zuhanden*) and as natural things (*Vorhanden*). "To be in the world" is, therefore, ultimately to recognize the spatiality of the world. But let us be alert enough to avoid the traditional diatribes about space (Newton, Leibniz, Kant, Einstein). Heidegger prefers to say that space is in the world rather than say that the world is in space; nor can it be said that the human *Dasein* "produces" space. These traditional approaches are meaningless if, with Heidegger, you agree that the only thing we can do is to recognize that *Dasein* reveals, discovers the spatiality of the world by accepting its own situation and its own projections: situation and projection are two points of reference, simultaneous and different; in other words, they are spatial elements. The question becomes even more interesting: *Dasein* makes space possible and at the same time it is made possible by space. It is the same as saying that *Dasein* is open, disclosed (*erschlossen*): its luminous overture is dimensionally related to all beings; therefore, it is spatial. But, we must insist, *Dasein* does not "create" (this is a forbidden word for Heidegger) space, nor does it create the world. This is true even

---

[21] We translate *Weltlichkeit* as "worldishness" rather than "worldliness" (according to the suggestion of M. King, *Heidegger's Philosophy*, p. 36, [New York: Macmillan, 1964]), to emphasize the philosophical meaning of "world-forming" intended by Heidegger rather than "belonging to the manners of the world" conveyed by the English "worldliness."

though without *Dasein*, space and the world would not exist. *Dasein* is the first to be involved with and conditioned by the space and the world. This fundamental limitation of *Dasein*, this existential situation, is well expressed by the German language that uses the impersonal pronoun *man* for the common, standardized behavior of *Dasein*. English has similar usage when we say, "it is said; it is done; it is thought." Here we mean to speak of the common habitual behavior characteristic of *Dasein*.

Is this an original characteristic of man or does it connote some kind of "fall"? It could be both, since *Dasein* is open to all possibilities by its own ontological nature. But, at any rate, it does represent a fall (*Verfallen*) in respect to other more *authentic* possibilities.

Authentic and *unauthentic* are important words for Heidegger's *Dasein*: they mean success and failure and, what is important, they introduce values of a moral nature which Heidegger's ontological premises excluded as belonging to the traditional philosophy. We will discuss further this aspect of his thought.

Within the horizon of the worldishness of *Dasein*, Heidegger discovers three more basic structures: *Befindlichkeit*, *Verstehen*, and *Rede*.

Befindlichkeit (state of being present) is the fundamental feeling that one has of himself. Through this feeling *Dasein* feels its own presence. (We say: I feel great; I feel miserable.) Besides, *Befindlichkeit* is the ground for all the other sentiments. Thus, man accepts through his feeling the fact that he is engaged with his living; he is thrown (*Geworfenheit*: thrownness) into the stream of existence and he must swim to keep his head above the water of events. Living is fighting, with victories and defeats. No wonder that Heidegger uses his phenomenological training to analyze with minute details and with evident satisfaction various emotional situations. He speaks of emotional moods (*Stimmung*), of emotional inclinations (*Gestimmtsein*), and he stresses with particular emphasis the meaning of dread (*Angst*), fundamental in the life of *Dasein*.

The concept of *Dread* is well introduced by its partner — with which it shares its painful consequences in the life of man — fear (*Furcht*). We fear something which we encounter or might encounter in the world: a thing, a situation, another *Dasein*. Fear originates from a partial knowledge that we have of this thing, a situation or another *Dasein*; they present us with hostile obscurity and suspense: they are *imminent*; they might spare us or they might strike out at us. Fear is preoccupation with the uncertainty and imminence of a threat, and yet fear demands tension, deeper engagement with life. If you give up in the presence of fear, you give up living; you are dead.

Dread is different from fear. When I am under the pressure of dread, I cannot speak of a thing, a situation, or another *Dasein*. Dread is totally undetermined: it is inevitably present, it is oppressing and anonymous, invisible; it shakes the fibers of my heart; it changes my dreams into nightmares; it makes me lose contact with friends, with reality, with life. Between fear and dread I discover the same difference that exists between disgust for something and nausea. If I analyze myself, in a moment of tranquillity of mind, I make a truly dreadful discovery: dread is not just a sickness of the mind and the body; dread is identical with *my being in the world*. I do not have any choice: if I am human, if I am open to other beings, I have one destiny: to live in dread, in a state of anguish which makes me hurry to work to forget myself, to alienate myself from myself. Indeed, dread is an *authentic* possibility of man.

Another basic structure of *Dasein* is comprehension (*Verstehen*). *Dasein* is not thrown into its existential situation as a stone, but as a possibility (*Seinkönnen*). Comprehension illuminates *Dasein's* possibilities in relation to the possibilities of the meaning of all the other existents. They are first seen as instruments, and then they are seen by *Dasein* in their structural unity and thus they *become* nature. But Heidegger knows that "nature" is a word with unmistakable Aristotelian meaning and therefore he carefully explains that nature signifies "alternatives," "projects" for *Dasein*. If man is not a completely finished man (as Aristotle thought) but an existent whose being is engaged, the contact of man with nature assumes the meaning of discovering the possibilities of this new situation. Comprehension is the act of this discovery; by its nature it is under a beam of light that enriches man and it is recognized as meaningful by him.

The third step of this mutual cooperation of *Dasein* with the world comes from a cooperation of fundamental sentiment (*Befindlichkeit*) and comprehension (*Verstehen*), with the mechanism of expression: speech (*Rede*). The situation, revealed as *fact*, understood in its *possibilities*, becomes *word*.

Heidegger cares little whether the expression of *Dasein* becomes sound or sign: silence is often more eloquent than words. Expression is the crossroad of human experience: convergent and divergent elements make it dynamic and interesting; listening and communicating, accepting and refusing, joys and sorrows belong to this human phenomenon that links humans to humans and all mankind to the universe.

Heidegger reaches out with secure hand to uncover the indigent poverty of the theories of language developed by the continental and British schools of logical positivism. At most, they have stopped to discuss only one facet of human expression. They seemed to center their attention on the proposition as the essence of expression: thus grammar becomes logic, a logic of dead entities, of *Vorhanden*. Heidegger considers them frustrated Aristotelians, because they care about the definition of things, as if they had a meaning without relation to *Dasein*. Worse than that, their frustration is rooted in their empiricist conviction than the exterior aspects of something are its essence, and they do not realize that their main trouble is an intellectual superficiality that forces them to play with words, pretending an involvement with philosophy that they do not have.

IV. *The Existentiality of* Dasein

The student of Heidegger knows that his main temptation is to look back and represent in synthesis the ideas previously discussed. Jaspers often indulged in this temptation.

At this point of *Sein und Zeit,* Heidegger does precisely that. The material is represented under one heading: existentiality. It could be considered a pause to gather energies for a fresh start.

Existentiality (from the Latin *ex-sistens:* being outside) is a good term for stressing the *openness,* the *towardness* of *Dasein*. Through its fundamental sentiment and its comprehension, *Dasein* knows its "facticity" (*Factizität*),[22] that is to say, the involvement of things with *Dasein* which makes them things, and the involvement of *Dasein* with things, which makes *Dasein* to be *Dasein*.

And up to this point, we are, with Heidegger, repetitious. But now comes the question: How can *Dasein* become authentic and avoid being unauthentic? The danger of falling down (*Verfallensein*), of shallow living, of routine life is present for every man. The phenomenology of this "everydayness" given by Heidegger is most interesting: speech, separated from comprehension and sentiments, becomes *idle gossip* (*Gerede*); comprehension becomes *superficial curiosity* for the unusual (*Neugier*); the crystal clear consciousness of a situation becomes ambiguity (*Zweideutigkeit*).

Heidegger does not hesitate to show his concern for the frightening possibility that the human *Dasein* might be trapped by shallow, boring "everydayness." Man must react and find his authentic self, his human vocation to spiritual goals. We are now reaching the most interesting Heidegger, the man who lived with the Jesuits and aimed to become one of them, the man with a soul religiously Calvinistic, tempered to a rigid interpretation of life as obligation.

---

[22] *Facticity* is a new English word commonly used in discussions of contemporary philosophy.

Dasein (what we said about it should have brought this point home) *cares;* it cares about itself and about everything around itself. Heidegger had heard from the Jesuits that *God cares* so much that Christ died for those who were the center of His interest. Now *Sein und Zeit* aims to be just a phenomenological description of man, and phenomenology does not say anything about God because His place is taken by man. Therefore Heidegger makes his supreme effort and presents *Dasein* as a source of care, taking from Christian thought the most precious secret that Christ revealed about God and attributing it to man. The task is not easy. The Jesuits used to speak of a "spiritual retreat" to discover with powerful impact the fact that God cares. Heidegger has the same idea: to prove that the essence of *Dasein* is care, we must proceed by steps, by meditation. And Heidegger suggests that the topics of this meditation should be some of those that St. Ignatius proposed in his fundamental work of Christian asceticism: the meaning of death, of conscience, of guilt, and of resolution.

Heidegger cannot carry his parallelism with Ignatius of Loyola further. Heidegger has chosen to talk about care, goals, and obligations. But he cannot talk about God because he does not have anything to say about Him, not even that He exists.

But let us follow, by steps, this strange round of the godless "spiritual retreat" of *Dasein*. The goal, we must keep in mind, is to reach the evidence that *Dasein* is *care* (*Sorge*).

First meditation: Man must die. Death is an enormously strange factor for *Dasein*. As long as it does not come, death cannot be experienced. Once it has come, it is too late to hope for any understanding, since the *Da* (here) of *Dasein* is removed. Death is therefore not to be considered as the end of a stream of experiences nor the fulfillment of an obligation. Rather meditation on death is for *Dasein* a powerful stimulus to reach its complete meaning before death arrives. This existential and authentic structure of *Dasein* is called by Heidegger "being toward death" (*Sein-zum-Tode*). *Dasein* has the presence of death streaming in its veins as the most certain of its possibilities, as the last possibility, that of the last *im*possibility. In other words, death is not added to *Dasein*, but *Dasein* finds it in the fundamental sentiment and understanding of itself. This possibility of the last impossibility is so present that each *Dasein* reacts in a different way. Perhaps dread is the most common reaction. But often we escape the anticipation of death, through distraction and work. Death itself, which is always and only *my* death and the death of *my* world, is interpreted as a natural homogenous phenomenon. People die (*man stirbt*), we say, as if we were not included. We also reach the exaggeration of glorifying one's death as heroic or saintly, and we do not think that death is the final end of man. If we want authenticity or, what is the same, if we care to know that *Dasein cares*, our death must be kept always in front of us, we must learn how to anticipate its possibility, we must run forward in thought toward it. We must defeat death by accepting it. The "running forward in thought" reveals to *Dasein* that it is lost in "itself" and brings it face to face with the potentiality of being itself. Here *Dasein* is unaided by the care of others, but is itself in passionate actual freedom — toward death (*Freiheit zum Tode*) — being certain of it and dreading it, yet being independent of the illusions of the "one like many."

Second meditation: Man is guided by his conscience. In the Christian perspective, conscience is for man the sounding board of the will of God. For Heidegger conscience is a calling, a manifestation of an intention which cannot use words to make itself heard, a silent and pressing invitation. These are suggestive expressions, but they are not too clear. Who is inviting whom? Heidegger says, with some embarrass- ment, that *Dasein* invites itself to be itself against the dissipating temptations of the world. It is a sort of self-introspection. But we sense that Heidegger is short of ideas in discussing this topic. As a matter of fact, rather than telling us what the meaning of his "conscience" is, he indulges in long perorations against the traditional Christian concept of conscience. Christians say — he insists — that conscience is the voice of God, yet they do not understand that the root of misconception has to be found in the Western mania of presupposing a natural thing (substance) beyond each natural phenomenon. Natural things (*Vor- handen*) are unthinkable without the *Dasein* that makes them natural. Therefore, the Christian conception of conscience is begging the ques- tion and is trapped in a vicious circle.

Heidegger should not speak of vicious circles when he talks of Christian ideas, unless he aims to throw back to Christianity that same argument which must be used against himself. His frame of mind is thoroughly Christian (death, conscience, guilt). His effort consists in framing these ideas in a new system with a gigantic inversion of values that is reminiscent of Hegel's arbitrary reasoning when, in his philosophy of nature, he tries to reduce scientific research to his own dialectical principles.

In the case of Heidegger, why should one accept as evident his basic assumption that *Dasein* is openness to the world without *anything which does the opening*? We are just humans and therefore we recognize our human limitations when we insist on saying that a vicious circle is patently evident at the very beginning of Heidegger's philosophical venture, which postulates an action without anyone doing it.

Third meditation: The sinner is a slave of his sin. *Dasein* is conscious of the limitations springing from its origin. It is always in debt, the debt for existence; therefore it carries a guilt (*Schuld*), because it was thrown into being when it did *not* do anything to deserve it since it was not existing.

If *Dasein* was thrown into existence, the logical question is: who is the thrower? But this is a forbidden question for Heidegger, who aims to destroy the traditional logic of the West. We must be satisfied with the fact that we were born, that from the beginning we were marked by this "original sin." Therefore Luther and Calvin understood better than other Christians, in particular better than the Catholic Church, that man *essentially* is negative rather than positive. The consciousness of this negativity makes man realize the formidable task of his existence: he must redeem himself, submerged as he is in a situation of desperate heroism. Therefore he must *care*, because he knows his nothingness that wants to be.

Fourth meditation: Resolution (*Entschlossenheit*). A spiritual retreat without sound resolutions is an exercise in futility. The Christians resolve to *do* something which brings them closer to God. Heidegger's *Dasein* does not have any goal to reach since it is the epicenter of all goals. But it must become aware of its own openness or of its own most *authentic possibilities*. Originally *Dasein* discovered itself as essentially open to the world (*Erschlossenheit*); now by the resolution reached through meditation and introspection *Dasein* discovers that it is *aware* of its own openness (*Entschlossenheit*). Its actions have new meaning because they are not the result of a *Dasein* which is just there. Heidegger hates the "traditional" distinction between "theoretical and practical," between "logical and ethical." We saw that "comprehension" meant "project" and now we see that "resolution" means "understanding." But the question remains: his stubborn insistence on the distinction between "authentic" and "unauthentic" calls necessarily for a moral evaluation. The affinity with the autonomous morality of the Kantian categorical imperative is evident.

In one sentence, Heidegger offers us in his *Dasein* a secular substitute for the God of the Christian, with Christian attributes and virtues. First of all is the *caring* for all existing beings. Caring for others requires *being with* (*Mitsein*) them. *Dasein*, because of its care, is by its nature concerned with other *Daseins*. But his preoccupation is not expressed, as it was for Husserl, in "empathy" (literally: feeling oneself into another). Empathy presupposes a monotonous analogy of one *Dasein* with the others. Heidegger prefers to speak of "solicitude" or "charity," stealing words and concepts from the Christian interpretation of human togetherness. "Solicitude" and "charity" are general words; but through them *Dasein*, unique in its structure and its openness to its projects, expresses itself in a way most personal and individual. Heidegger goes so far in his humanization of the God of the Christians as to describe *Dasein's* care for others as provident and prevident, with a considerate regard and forbearance for their needs and failures. This conception emphasizes the last and most important structure of *Dasein*.

V. *The Temporality of* Dasein

The technical coldness of the terms used by Heidegger should not be an obstacle to grasp the profoundly human interest of his philosophy. He envisions man as charity and love, since this is primarily the meaning of *Dasein* as *care*. Now the question arises: Should the human *Dasein* care only about success, that is to say, about authenticity? The authentic *Dasein*, we know, is being in the world, being toward death, being conscience and sin and resolution; in a word, *care*. But the unauthentic *Dasein* does not have less right to existence. It means failure, unawareness of the world, frightened subjection to death, dissipation of conscience, almost self-vilification to the level of inert nature. The inquiry into the nature of man is not, therefore, finished: we must find a more comprehensive structure of *Dasein*, a structure that does not exclude any of its infinite possibilities. The solution traditionally offered to this problem sounds unacceptable to Heidegger. The Greeks and the Romans spoke of an "Ego," which during the Middle Ages became the even more disconcerting nature, "the soul." Ego and soul were immutable substances, unifying all human activities. Heidegger repeats, with a dignified patience, that these two standardized notions are patterned according to the inanimate things found in nature (*Vorhanden*). They cannot offer any other possibility besides being inertly what they are: how can they be the center and the reason of philosophy, of a set of knowledge which aims to find out, to grow and to organize? It is true that *Dasein* relies on an *immutable* logic (that logic, for instance, that allowed Heidegger to expound his ideas in *Sein und Zeit*), but logic is only *one possibility* springing from *Dasein*, a possibility which is codependent on *Da-sein* and its being in the world and never separable from the world.

These considerations leave only one possibility open: *Dasein* is time. This sentence cannot be understood in a loose sense, e.g., that *Dasein* is in time. It must be taken literally: *Dasein is* time. Heidegger reaches here the height of his originality and he must be understood correctly.

Time, we all agree, is a projection into the future. *Dasein*, in its structural nature of active realization as *care*, comprehension, etc., finds meaning as a being always anticipating its own being. We care not about the present and the past, which are already and therefore can in no way be modified, but we care for a better future. This projection into the future implies, paradoxically, the past understood as *Dasein* already thrown into the world, as *facticity* already situated and ready to face the future. Heidegger notices with satisfaction that the Greeks understood this unity of the past with the future when they defined the essence (the foundation of the possibility of a being) as *tò tí ēn einai* (*quod quid erat esse*): "that something which was a being."

The present results from the unbreakable bond of the past (necessity) with the future (possibility). We may be able to understand better now the meaning of *Dasein* as care: *Dasein* is a three-dimensional projection (notice, we do not say: being with three dimensions). *Dasein* is projecting; therefore, its being consists in being outside of itself: literally *ex-sistens*.

For this reason, Heidegger called the three temporal dimensions (past, present, future), the three *extases* (three realities outside of themselves). If you want, for the sake of clarity, to consider them one by one, abstractly, comprehension tends to the future, fundamental sentiment is for the past, everydayness concerns the present. But considering the three extases abstractly amounts to depriving them of their authenticity: they are themselves to the extent that one is for the other. Thus authentic is the future that "runs ahead," anxious to fulfill the projections which our past contained; authentic is our past that confides in the existential resolution of progress: without realization of its possibilities, our past is a museum of broken items, lined up in dusty galleries, without meaning. Above all, existential resolution makes our present authentic. The authentic present is called by Heidegger the *instant* (*Augenblick*), also *fulfilled present* because it embodies a conscious synthesis of the past and the future in relation to an authentic decision that considers everything as a utensil for *Dasein*.

Take away from the present this binding temporal resolution and you will have the thing, the *individuum* of Aristotle, meaningless, aimless, incomprehensible, unauthentic. This is what happens, to a certain extent, in the scientific consideration of the universe. The utensil of *Dasein* becomes the *thing* or the *subject matter* of physics or chemistry, seen in a mathematized space-time relation, anonymous and indifferent. We said "to a certain extent" because the projecting care of *Dasein* is present in natural sciences too (otherwise how could they be intelligible?). But *Dasein* does not *care* about itself as a project;

instead it contributes to the formation (physical or chemical) of the thing as *a project*, with a regional interest and regional and partial conclusions. Heidegger therefore is not against the work of the men dedicated to empirical sciences. They are honest workers, wrapped up in their own useful findings, obtained with mathematical precision for the use of the multitude of all *Daseins*. They follow mathematics with a dedicated precision that can be compared to the instinctive precision of a swarm of bees. The trouble with them though, if it is a trouble at all, is that they are oblivious and oftentimes scornful of the totality of existence. Science is possible because it is a little partial and static consideration of the infinite transcendence of *Dasein*, which always overcomes itself in the conquest of its infinite possibilities and therefore keeps the individual things of the world at a distance from the philosopher and within reach of the empiricist and the technician.

The final part of *Sein und Zeit* attempts the final synthesis: *Dasein* is time and time is history. Do not think that Heidegger is circling the same topic with the same ideas expressed by different words. It is of the nature of the phenomenological method to remain with the same topic, but the reason for the enormous success of phenomenology in our days is to be found in the widening of the horizon that allows new meanings to be discovered at each round of the investigating process.

Dasein is time essentially and simultaneously the temporal horizon to the universe insofar as *Dasein* produces time for the universe. Of course, we must not be deceived by our own words; when we say that "*Dasein* is time" we do not mean to convey static Aristotelian notions; we mean that *Dasein*, as time, produces time for itself; temporalizes itself by an act of identification with the flowing of its existence with time. And this process offers *Dasein* the opportunity of *finding and accepting authentically its own bonds with the community and with tradition*: in other words, *Dasein* becomes conscious of its being *historical* (*Geschichtlichheit*).

The revolution that Heidegger introduces by his new conception of history is therefore to be reduced to the following statement: The life of a man is not primarily a section or a piece of the universal history; vice-versa, history depends on the authentic resolution of *Dasein* to open itself up to the world and thus become historical. The time of *Dasein* is original and authentic; the time of universal history is derivative from and conditioned by *Dasein*. Heidegger's conception of history — he claims — is existential and meaningful of life and death. The previous one is essential and meaningless to man. There are a few words, of typically Heideggerian significance, that we must, as usual, become acquainted with. From the same German root we have:

geschehen, the "happening" of individual existential events. *Schiksal* is the human destiny predetermined because death is a necessity but freely accepted by *Dasein* as a challenge to its own freedom. *Geschick* is the destiny of the community to which I belong and which is strictly bound to my own destiny, so much so that I discover it *only* when I refer in my existential resolution to my origin and to my destiny.

The historicity of *Dasein* is "being in the world." Heidegger conceded that the things of the world, inasmuch as they are related to *Dasein* as its utensils, belong to history: he calls them *Welt-geschichtlich* (world-historical): a meadow becomes a famous battlefield, a spear speaks of the ancient Etruscan *Daseins.* If the things of the world are given preponderant importance in the historical milieu, we reverse the meaning of history, we make it *unauthentic* or *historic* as Heidegger calls it in opposition to the *authentic* history which is *geschichtlich.* This bad (historic) history appears to Heidegger as a self-destroying monster: *Dasein* itself is swallowed: it becomes a thing, an object. History is, in this case, a chronological sequence of dates and places; of dead civilizations and amorphous events.

History must be *geschichtlich:* the temporality of *Dasein* is the objectivity of history and its objectivity is its vitality.

* * *

These ideas — Heidegger thinks — are so evidently true, that once they are known, they cannot be denied. As a matter of fact, if we apply the common conception of time that everyone has to these new explanations, we will come to the conclusion that no conflict is possible. How does every man behave in reference to time? We all speak of now, yesterday, tomorrow; in other words, we speak of three temporal dimensions bound together and we tend to forget that we are doing the binding. Actually we are so concerned with the present, that we consider the past as an object of less value and the future as an object still to come into being. But it takes little effort to realize that past and future are given the meaning of two *dates* by us. This temporal attitude of ours is called by Heidegger *Datenbarkeit* (datableness). Dates, commemorating past events, are testimonials of the projects which *Dasein* led to completion. By its nature, we know, *Dasein* is to be with (*Mitsein*) other *Daseins:* their mutual cooperation generates the *public or chronological time.* In nonphilosophical terms, we think that watches measure this public time: philosophically speaking we understand that man is the watch and the watchmaker. When referred to him, things cease to be utensils and acquire meaning. Thus, the everyday life reveals its functional meaning derived from *Dasein.* Every time we look at the clock to check the time, we have in mind a purpose to fulfill.

The conclusive words of *Sein und Zeit* are again a warning against Aristotle. We are Aristotelians if we accept the fall (*Verfallen*) of philosophical investigation which characterized for centuries the Western culture and which is expressed by the well-known "arbitrary" hypostatizations of being: substance, accidents, matter and form.

In this context, time is a monotonous sequence of "now," "now" flashing by as objects in space. This static philosophy is gone forever: *Dasein* has established the true perspective without which philosophizing amounts to a self-deception.

3. REALISM AND MARTIN HEIDEGGER

The foregoing analysis of *Sein und Zeit*, although brief and elementary, omitted any comment, as this would only have been confusing at the time. But it seems advisable now to add a few critical observations, as these will help lead to a more complete understanding of this major Heideggerian work.

At the beginning of *Sein und Zeit*, as we saw, Heidegger offered a strong defense of metaphysics; and on the need for metaphysics he is in complete agreement with Aristotle and St. Thomas Aquinas. Yet agreement ends here, for Heidegger's concept of metaphysics differs greatly from the classical tradition. Traditionally, metaphysics has for its object being as such, and it knows essences only as related to individual existences. Essence is as such never known directly. Only after having experienced existing things is it possible, through abstraction, to give primary attention to the essence and thus formulate a body of knowledge called metaphysics.

Heidegger's position is diametrically opposed. He speaks of being as such as the object of metaphysics, but he insists that its notion does not come to us from existing beings but is an anonymous ontological environment presupposed by individual existents. The neoplatonic themes pervading Heidegger's thought, although obscure and difficult to pinpoint, are nonetheless evident.

The consequences of this position are far reaching. If existence as such is ineffable, Heidegger must begin his philosophical investigation with something else. Heidegger chose man, *Dasein,* making his metaphysics an anthropology. In his *Vom Wesen des Grundes* (1929)[23] Heidegger reacted vigorously to the accusation of "anthropomorphism" leveled against *Sein und Zeit. Dasein,* he says, is "being in the world," "being with," "understanding," "being in order to die": how can it

---

[23] First published in the *Jahrbuch für Phänomenologische Forschung Ergänzungband,* 1929, pp. 72–110.

be labeled as "closed and anthropomorphically self-centered"? Actually the surprised tone of his question confirms the accusation. In philosophy, "center" does not mean a static position, but a unifying principle which explains the meaning of the structure of all things. Now this "unifying principle" was intended to be the topic of the second volume of *Sein und Zeit* which has never been published. The paradox lies in the fact that it could not be published because it was meant to deal with the "overcoming of metaphysics," that is to say, with what is beyond *Dasein's* experience. Here do we not have a clear example of the ineffable transcendence of neoplatonism?

It should be evident, then, that Heidegger had to start from something different from existence as such. He chose to begin with man, a fact which in itself cannot raise any objection. A philosopher has the privilege of beginning his investigation from any perspective he prefers to choose. Indeed, Heidegger analyzes with depth and originality most important phenomena. He stresses the *essential* bonds existing between *Dasein* and its "being in the world," i.e., its relation to other beings. But Heidegger insists that the understanding of *Dasein*, i.e., of man, consists *originally* in *Dasein's* relation with other existents and only reflectively, as awareness of its authentic possibility, does it acquire its own identity, individuality, and existence in the world.

Therefore we have first the relation, second the *Dasein* (man) being related. In other words, action comes first, the man responsible for this this action comes second.

We do not need to say that we utterly disagree, in the name of logic and common sense. Without entering into a lengthy discussion of Heidegger's dependence on Fichte and other idealists on this matter, we can at least establish the basic discrepancy between Heidegger and the classical metaphysics of Aristotle and Thomas Aquinas. The perennial value of these two great thinkers consists in having established an unconditional primacy of *being* to *acting*, and in particular the primacy of the individual human being to individual knowing. Heidegger considered himself a crusader against the Aristotelian doctrine of "things" and "objects," and no one denies the tremendous impact of his crusade. But honesty, particularly intellectual honesty, comes before enthusiasm. We are just human and if we aim to a human understanding of the reality that surrounds us, we must insist on *this basic fact*: Heidegger's crusade springs from a mitigation of the primacy of being to doing, and this cannot be accepted.

Perhaps now is the best occasion to address a few words to those enthusiasts who claim, with the best of intentions, that philosophy and theology, to be authentic today, *must* be exclusively existential. They bind together, with unbelievable superficiality in one condemnation, true scholasticism with the nominalistic Aristotelian aberrations and meaningless distinctions of decadent scholasticism (seventeenth and eighteenth centuries): they walk on a platform of confusion and lack of meditation. An honest analysis of their sources, almost always of Heideggerian origin, would persuade them that a philosophy or a theology *purely existential* faces epistemological difficulties of such magnitude that any proposition, of philosophical or theological nature, is subjective, arbitrary, and, therefore, worthless.[24]

Our point is fundamental for an understanding of Heidegger's philosophy. He recognizes the conditions by which something exists but neglects what makes those conditions possible. Conditions of beings are, to use his terminology, "ontological"; beings themselves are just "ontic." The consequences of this doctrine invest the whole spectrum of man; they change him, making his knowledge and his freedom, his individuality and his person subjected to a sequence of traumatic experiences.

We will try to mention some of the major implications springing from the Heideggerian concept of philosophy.

1. Heidegger, prevented by his own presuppositions from discussing the actual existence of each being, tends to resolve each thing in its own "meaning" or, in other words, its usefulness for man. Why does he neglect the "meaning" that each being has for itself, that meaning that man discovers as belonging to each thing, even if it is not primarily for the service of man?

2. Knowledge for Heidegger is always a projecting into the future the "meaning" of beings. We can understand that in the context of *Dasein* as temporality. But what is the nature of this projection into the future? Heidegger insists that this projection is only contemplative and theoretical since *Dasein* aims at its own understanding. The question is: Is it possible to speak of a projection into the future without an interest of the will for something? For instance, can we say that we

---

[24] The student of theology might object to our ideas. He knows that theology is not based on the "perishable words of human wisdom" but on the living word of God, given to us as an instrument for our salvation. And we agree. But the living word of God must be perceived by man. And it cannot be perceived if man does not have adequate instruments or if man is not there at all, because philosophy has destroyed his structure. Our contention is that Heidegger has muddled the meaning of man to such an extent that any theology springing from his premises is by nature subjective and arbitrary. The same student of theology must recognize therefore that any dialogue among theologians of different Christian faiths, which is one of the greatest events of our century, must take into account philosophical presuppositions if it is to avoid the danger of being a mere exercise of good manners and pleasant atmosphere of ecumenical encounters.

do not want to do anything with this particular tree which we might know: neither wood for burning, nor a picture frame, nor an object of scientific knowledge? What is this tree? Heidegger's answer is simply that the tree is the relation between my knowledge and the project "tree." Again, for him the essence of something known consists in its relation. A tree is a utensil (*Zuhanden*) for *Dasein,* not a being in its own right.

A logic based on experience, however, demands first the presence of something and, second, its usefulness. This is true when I think of a "project": I must intervene to establish the possibility of something which is there and its usefulness. The ancient Greeks used to choose the high point for the temple of the town because it was high, not because it was the place for the temple.

3. Heidegger's *Dasein* is a being which must be and thus become authentic. The phenomenological premises of *Sein und Zeit* made it irrelevant to question the origin of man. But even within Heidegger's frame of thought many questions remain unanswered. Man for Heidegger is "being in the world" by his own final decision. If his essence is "being in the world" we deal with an external finality whose nature is to be outside, "ex-sistens." But who is responsible for the decision to be in the world? Heidegger's answer is that the essence of man is simply to be in the world. We come to the conclusion that man finds himself when he disperses himself in the world. If "being authentic" for Heidegger means recognizing his own being, man is authentic insofar as he loses himself in the world, so that complete authenticity coincides with complete unauthenticity. And Heidegger agrees with us because his *Dasein* understands that its possibility is absolute impossibility, dread, being toward death. But he does not admit that his interpretation of man is contradictory, because he fails to see the metaphysical actuality of existence as the basic element for every being to be what it is and to do what it does.

4. Heidegger sees a close relationship between dread and being in the world, so much so that we might think that dread originates in the possibility for *Dasein* of self-alienation from the world; it results from a sort of uncanniness or loneliness between *Dasein* and the world. This interpretation is rejected by Heidegger, who uses his dialectical skill to prove that, for *Dasein,* its being estranged from the world causes its being in the world. If we were to be with the things of the world as fish are in the water, we would have no awareness of the world. We are *in* the world, but we are not the world. Our alienation from it, by offering a distance necessary for a perspective of the things of the

world, is an essential condition for a profound bond with the world.

But all Heidegger says is that man is necessary for an understanding of a human world or human history. He ignores the basic problem: Is man sufficient to himself; or, and this is the same, *can* man prescind from his relation with the world? For instance, man as philosopher is called upon to judge his relation with the world: is man capable of a contemplative activity (that activity which allowed Heidegger to write *Sein und Zeit*) which exists before the world and therefore opens the possibility of man's survival when he is no longer in contact with the world?

Heidegger's existential authenticity reveals all the weakness of an autonomous morality: it must be, but it does not have any norm by which to be; it is an authenticity in suspense.

If the authenticity of *Dasein* is difficult to assess, similar obstacles confront its unauthenticity or "dispersion in the world." We often have the impression that *Dasein's* unauthenticity originates from the past bearing witness of our shortcomings, or "radical guilt" as Heidegger calls it. On the other hand, our past is a precious criterion to establish the value of our most authentic possibilities. Heidegger speaks of the past as a means for man's authenticity, insofar as our past makes us members of our country, one in language, one in tradition and patriotism. I am myself when I know the mysterious secret of my mother tongue, when my mountains and valleys and cities give me pride of belonging to them, when the sight of the flag of my country gives me emotions that words cannot express.

It seems logical to conclude that my past belonging to my country is pregnant with meaning because I relate it to the flowing unity of my consciousness and ultimately to my essence. But Heidegger does not agree. For him my past is one with my future, and therefore my consciousness is streaming into the future without an essential "self" because my future is a project with infinite possibilities yet to be fulfilled.

In Thomistic language, we say that human essence is limited; for Heidegger, limitation itself is the essence of man. In Thomistic language, human knowledge and will are what they are; with the limitations, they operate in a positive sense, in correspondence to their own being. For Heidegger, human knowledge and will are a fluid mixture of the past, which has been, and the future, which as yet is not. Therefore Heidegger, looking back to the "facticity" of the past, cannot use any criterion for authenticity or unauthenticity. One country cannot be distinguished from another, one flag from another flag; the result is a general confusion of values, with an abnormal suspicion of everything that might be foreign to what each nation considers its own authenticity.

5. Heidegger insists on considering simultaneously two instances in which traditionally, in the context of Western philosophy, the nexus identity-difference (unity-plurality) reveals itself. By doing so he confuses them. Here we refer to the infinite unity of God in relation to the plurality of contingent things and to the unifying character of human thought.

Since the problem of God cannot, in Heidegger's opinion, be discussed philosophically, the real problem of philosophy is "What is thought?" (*Was heisst denken?*) From the very beginning of philosophy the coexistence within thought of unity and diversity has been a central problem. The Presocratics felt that knowledge is a combination of similarities and dissimilarities. More profoundly in the Aristotelian doctrine, which was accepted in its essential features by the medieval scholastics, the intellect identifies itself with the essence of what is known while at the same time it is different from what it knows precisely because it has this power of becoming all things. Heidegger quotes St. Thomas at the beginning of *Sein und Zeit: Intellectus est ejus quod natum est convenire cum omni ente* — "The intellect was born to become involved with everything." This involvement or intentional openness has many facets: thought must identify itself with the object known, which is different from intellect; the essence thought must be the same under a variety of changing circumstances; besides a complex and discontinuous cooperation of emotions, interests, impressions, the intentional unity of thought remains the same. Heidegger agrees with the phenomenologists and with all philosophers in maintaining that thought means all that and much more. Therefore he asks insistently one question to which all other problems can be reduced: *What is the secret nature of this extraordinary event which is human thinking: Was heisst denken?*[25]

Heidegger's answer followed these lines. To explain the difference and the identity of thought and object known, bound together in one structure, he reduced human thought to a temporal dimension. It is a project for the future, a project with an awareness of the conditions of the past, a project keeping in mind the conditions which reveal the meaning of the present. But what can this answer mean? How successful is Heidegger's answer?

It is unsuccessful and cannot possibly succeed because each of the projects involved in knowing (past, present, and future) presupposes thinking and therefore does not constitute it. The present, we know, is the result of the three moments; but if I cannot think by my own

---

[25] Cf. in particular Heidegger's work, *What Is Philosophy?*

nature, I cannot unify the sense of the past with my hopes for the future in the authenticity of the present. Heidegger discovered original insights into the meaning of human thinking, but he did not explain its essential unity which, undoubtedly, is *in* time (Kierkegaard's instant), but is reached by the mind, not by time.

In other words, human thought, which cares about differences and their comprehension, could not care if first of all it is not itself. This is the same as saying that it is necessary, although not sufficient, that thought belong to a being identical with itself. The main objection to Heidegger's position is simply that he makes *Dasein* become authentic and individual by means of authentic thinking. By inverting values (for he makes thinking serve as the foundation of being rather than the reverse) Heidegger runs into insurmountable contradictions.

4. MARTIN HEIDEGGER AFTER *SEIN UND ZEIT*

The Heideggerian *Wandllung*, that is to say, the critical period of Heidegger's philosophy, took place immediately after the publication of *Sein und Zeit* and coincided with his return to the University of Freiburg.

It was the climactic moment of his life. The university offered him the position left vacant by Husserl, the most renowned philosopher of the world; *Sein und Zeit* was read and discussed in the universities on all continents. Above all, Heidegger felt the reassuring confidence of a man who had gained, with hard work, his own freedom. Indeed, the message of *Sein und Zeit* was an invitation to all men to be free. But this Heideggerian freedom was not a complacent contemplation of truth shining from above. On the contrary, it was an insistent inquiry, a series of simple and honest questions on the meaning of existence, on the necessity of metaphysics.

Man, Heidegger insists, finds his freedom by asking questions, relevant questions about the meaning of being, about that existential "openness" which includes each and all meanings, which contemplates and respects as valuable all roads. Therefore, the heated discussions of his commentators, as to whether there was a continuity or a break between *Sein und Zeit* and his following works, did not make sense to Heidegger, just as it does not make sense for a person lost in the night and finally saved to question whether the path from darkness to light was the right or the wrong one. The path is not the light, nor is one path better than the other; but the joy of light would remain meaningless without the darkness left behind.

The insistent quest for more light in Heidegger's works published after *Sein und Zeit* can be analyzed under the following progressive stages:

I. An attempt, which reaches its climax with *Einführung in die Metaphysik*, is made to organize a metaphysics different in nature from the Aristotelian and closer in spirit to the Presocratics. Emphasis, in this stage, is placed on the meticulous analysis of Greek and German terms; for their original meaning, Heidegger holds, hides the secret of the generation of all existents from the two poles: man and being.

II. The two works, *Hölderlin und das Wesen der Dichtung* and *Der Ursprung des Kunstwerks*, present a new interpretation of poetry, understood as an essential factor of man and, therefore, as participating in the origin of all things.

III. The third period is characterized by Heidegger's retreat and renunciation of metaphysical investigations: *Überwindung der Metaphysik*. His bitter interpretation of Western history as an accumulation of misunderstandings of existence is set forth in *Platons Lehre von der Wahrheit* and in *Identität und Differenz*.

IV. The final stage concentrates laboriously on the possibilities of an ethic and a theology to end in a mysticism detailed in minor particulars and quite confused in its premises. The significant work of this period is *Gelassenheit*.

I. *Einführung in die Metaphysik* [*Introduction to Metaphysics*]

Three rather small but important works, published in 1929, contributed to a clarification of Heidegger's goals on the meaning of metaphysics. They are: *Kant und das Problem der Metaphysik, Was ist Metaphysik?* and *Vom Wesen des Grundes*.

Kant und das Problem der Metaphysik[26] continues the theme of *Sein und Zeit*, of which it was meant to be a section of the second part, which was never published. Its goal was the "destruction of traditional metaphysics and the discovery, from the insufficiencies of the past, of new themes and new orientations."

Heidegger claimed that Kant's *Critique of Pure Reason* was a funda-

---

[26] *Kant and the Problem of Metaphysics*, English translation by James S. Churchill (Bloomington: Indiana University Press, 1962).

mental *ontology* of the type of *Sein und Zeit*.[27] Both works, according to Heidegger, considered ontology not just as a branch derived from metaphysics, but, on the contrary, as the *necessary condition* that made metaphysics possible. Kant and Heidegger both regard the metaphysical investigation of being from the human horizon, one essentially *in time:* ontology therefore comes before metaphysics and conditions it. The result is a circular structure: the comprehension of man prepares for the comprehension of existence in general, and this in turn gives meaning to the understanding of man as one of the existents. "Ontic knowledge can be adequate to the essent [to "objects"] only if the essent is already manifest beforehand as essent, that is, *if the constitution* of its being is known."[28] There is, therefore, a preontological being whose existence is presupposed by the human act of knowing. Thus the unifying activity of the intellect, which is ordered to the comprehension of existence, and the receptivity of the human senses are two aspects of the same situation of finite man. Man's task is "to receive the essent [objects], that is, offer it the possibility of giving notice of itself."[29] Sense knowledge and intellectual knowledge, which Kant had conceived as two operations mutually interdependent, become for Heidegger two elements of the same "turning toward . . . which lets something become an object."[30] This openness toward existence to give meaning to each object is, as we know, *Dasein* itself, or rather the transcendence, the "going beyond," of *Dasein.*

The impact of *Kant und das Problem der Metaphysik* consists in Heidegger's conviction that Kant himself understood "temporality" as the unifying source of sense and intellectual knowledge. Heidegger takes pains to remind us that the philosopher of Königsberg spoke in his *Critique* of the same "hidden source" of both sense and intellectual knowledge: truth is conceived as a universal intuition conditioning all knowledges, while imagination unifies in its temporal dimensions the *a priori* forms of the intellect with the raw material of the senses. What Heidegger forgets to remind us of is that he prefers to discuss the first edition of the *Critique of Pure Reason* (1770) and not the second (1776), which stresses the intellect more than the imagination as the unifying center of human knowledge. Ernst Cassirer made this point in his *Kant Studien*. He accused Heidegger of stretching Kant's ideas to serve his own personal goals. We are allowed to make another point, more per-

---

27 The reader knows that traditionally *Metaphysica generalis* was concerned with being in general, and as such it was the foundation of *Metaphysica specialis* or *Ontology* which dealt with particular individual existents.

28 *Kant and the Problem of Metaphysics*, p. 30.

29 *Ibid.*, p. 31.

30 *Ibid.*, p. 51.

tinent to our purpose: with *Kant und das Problem der Metaphysik,*
Heidegger reached a formal decision: *Dasein* was no longer just a
possible approach to the question of existence as it was in *Sein und Zeit,*
but it became a firm cornerstone of his philosophy. Therefore, only
through anthropology was the door open to metaphysics; human comprehension of being, rooted in temporality, becomes the only way to
existence and the necessary condition giving a meaning to it.[31]

This luminous openness of *Dasein* results from the cooperation of all
existing things, which are recognizable by, and only by, its activity and
which in turn are open to its action. Sartre, we will see, denied their
openness, thus maintaining the absurdity of the universe. Heidegger,
no doubt influenced by the classical doctrine of the intelligibility of all
things, holds an encounter between *Dasein* and individual existents
impossible if the latter are closed, refractory, and uncooperative.

But now we have reached a focal point in Heidegger's philosophy.
Existence in general, as a foundation of all particular things, must be
openness and manifestation but it cannot be confused with and considered an individual being in itself; otherwise it would need another
being for its own explanation, thus demanding a process *ad infinitum.*
Heidegger, who lacked a doctrine corresponding to Aristotelian abstraction, succumbs to the rationalistic temptation of conceiving being as
such, as different from individual beings. And in such a frame of thinking an old suggestive idea of heterodox mysticism finds acceptance
in his mind. *Being in general,* the source and foundation of all existing
individual beings, *is the nothingness of beings,* an abysmal and original
nothingness, simultaneously productive of all existents, creative of the
empty space in which all existents take position, a nothingness whose
nature is to nullify itself so that individual beings come into existence
without being blinded or frightened by their own origins.

These provoking assertions were made by Heidegger in a lecture at
the University of Freiburg on July 27, 1929. That lecture became famous
and was published under the title: *Was ist Metaphysik?*[32] With Socratic
techniques Heidegger asked his hearers about their personal human
situation. There were scientists in the auditorium and men of letters.
All of them, from the mathematicians to the historians, were concerned
with understanding different aspects of being. "But is it not remarkable

---

[31] One of the basic differences between the phenomenological movement and
realism depends on whether we are able to safeguard the purity of our intellectual
intuitive knowledge and its possibility of prescinding from temporal and spatial
conditions. If our intellectual activity can never free itself from time, and if further
it is declared identical with the temporal rhythm, the only conceivable being must
be evidently changing and rhythmic, necessarily dependent on human knowledge.

[32] *What is Metaphysics?* English translation by R. F. C. Hull and Alan Crick in
Existence and Being (Chicago: H. Regnery Company, 1949), pp. 353–399.

that precisely at that point where scientific man makes sure of his surest possession he should speak of something else? What is to be investigated is what-is — and nothing else; only what-is — and nothing more; simply and solely what-is — and beyond that, nothing. But what about this 'nothing'"?[33]

Logic does not help, Heidegger says; evidently any question on what "nothing" *is*, presents it as something positive and therefore contradicts itself. Nor is Heidegger satisfied with the traditional thesis that "nothing" is a grammatical substantive derived from the rational act of negation. "We assert: 'Nothing' is more original than the not and negation. If this thesis is correct, then the very possibility of negation as an act of reason, and consequently reason itself, are somehow dependent on Nothing. How, then, can reason attempt to decide this issue?"[34] The answer, of course, is no.

If reason cannot, our feelings do testify to the presence of nothing. We feel its presence surrounding us. Just as the fullness of existence is lived by us only when we experience the torturing pressure of boredom or the ineffable joy of love, in the same fashion the totality of nothing comes alive and present, often too much so. We are under the merciless blows of anxiety and dread (*Angst*). Perhaps we should not say "we," for anxiety destroys our persons, plunging them into the anonymity of nothing; for that reason it is not "you" or "I" that has that uncanny feeling, but "one."[35]

"Nothing," therefore, does not deny individual things; rather they are drawn closer by its presence. "What happens is that Nothing shows itself as essentially belonging to what-is, while this is slipping away in totality."[36] Nothing pervades the complexity of existing things, destroys (*nichtet*) itself in them. This self-destroying or *Nichtung*, as a twofold negation, is therefore the affirmation of all existing beings, just as for Hegel the synthesis was the negation of the negation of the antithesis. Only in that clear night of dread, of nothingness is what-is revealed in all its original overtness (*Offenheit*): "that it *is* and is *not* nothing."[37] It follows that the "*Nichtung* does not happen in vain: it is the profound reason that makes the existent appear to *Dasein* as 'other'; this distance guarantees freedom and consciousness to *Dasein*. . . . It is in the Being (*Sein*) of what-is that the nihilation of Nothing (*das Nichten des Nichts*) occurs."[38]

---

[33] *Ibid.*, p. 358.
[34] *Ibid.*, p. 361.
[35] *Ibid.*, p. 366.
[36] *Ibid.*, p. 368.
[37] *Ibid.*, p. 369.
[38] *Ibid.*, p. 370.

It was necessary to follow the reasoning of Heidegger's lecture of July, 1929, because of its fundamental importance in the development of his thought. The consequences are far-reaching:

a) Each individual existing being cooperates in the manifestation of existence as such, in a process comprehensive of nothing itself. Transcendence, therefore, as "being beyond" the oppressive multiplicity of individual beings, cannot be attributed to man; transcendence becomes a cosmic event, of which man is aware in his finitude and limitations. "So finite are we that we cannot, of our own resolution and will, bring ourselves originally face to face with Nothing."[39]

b) Now this human finitude is particularly clear in the oblivion and disinterest that most human beings show regarding the originality and grandeur of the ways in which each individual being manifests itself. We care about *what-is* and we are so distracted by our daily chores that we neglect to see that what-is could not be without separating itself from nothing. Only philosophers, if they are not distracted by worldly interests, have a glimpse of the depth of this problem. They understand that existence is the "nothing" of beings, not just the negation of beings, but the negation of the negation, or, and this is the same, the affirmation of beings. Hegel took the first step in this direction, but he spoke of identifying the *indeterminate* notion of existence with nothing. Heidegger insists that the *determination* of each being (that is, that action that nullifies everything else to make a being what it is) reveals the identity of existence with nothing. "Being itself is finite in essence and is only revealed in the transcendence of *Da-sein* as projected into Nothing."[40]

c) Greek philosophy brushed away the problem of nothing with a principle which Heidegger rejected as unfounded: *ex nihilo nihil fit*. Christian thought, Heidegger concedes, "gave a twist to the meaning of nothing" when it affirmed that *ex nihilo fit ens creatum*. But that is not enough. The full formula must be: *ex nihilo omne ens qua ens fit*.[41]

d) If we attempt to discover the reason compelling Heidegger to make this daring identification of existence as such with nothingness, we find revealing statements. For instance, he notes the difficulty "that if God creates 'out of nothing,' he above all must be able to relate himself to nothing. But if God is God, he cannot know Nothing, assuming that the 'Absolute' excludes from itself all nullity (*Nichtigkeit*)."[42] And we agree with Heidegger that we meet insurmountable difficulties if we try to understand how God created from nothing and

[39] *Ibid.*, p. 374.
[40] *Ibid.*, p. 366.
[41] *Ibid.*, pp. 376–377.
[42] *Ibid.*, p. 376.

how He is the reason of the differences and imperfections of created beings.

At this point Christian philosophy points to the aspect of mystery, which results from the limitation of the human mind and the infinity of the metaphysical problem. Heidegger, to the contrary, prefers to reject the mystery; he turns upside down all traditional values and he introduces the supreme confusion by identifying existence with nothing. In his own words "the very idea of 'logic' disintegrates in the vortex of more original questioning."[43]

For a philosopher of realistic convictions mystery remains safeguarded as mystery, precisely when reason is safeguarded and with reason the evidence that "being is and nothing is not." Mystery does not imply a humiliating surrender to blind ignorance; mystery demands the intellectual conviction that an absolute existent must be the origin of all beings, which he created and for whose plurality he must be responsible. Once these cornerstones are solidly established, the mind is fascinated by what Aristotle called "wonder," especially when it contemplates the relation between the finite and the infinite.

These rational motives give unperishable values to Heidegger's investigation. Read, for instance, the following memorable lines: "Only when the strangeness of what-is forces itself upon us, does it awaken and invite our wonder. Only because of wonder, that is to say, the revelation of Nothing, does the 'Why?' spring to our lips. Only because this 'Why?' is possible as such can we seek for reasons and proofs in a definite way. Only because we can ask and prove are we fated to become enquirers in this life. . . . Going beyond what-is is of the essence of *Da-sein*. But this 'going beyond' is metaphysics itself. That is why metaphysics belongs to the nature of man. It is neither a department of scholastic philosophy nor a field of chance ideas. Metaphysics is the ground-phenomenon of *Da-sein*. It is *Da-sein* itself."[44]

e) Finally, the hybrid concept of existence as such, conceived as a vague mixture of being and nothing, revealing one aspect and simultaneously concealing another, did not offer a solid consistency to Heidegger's metaphysical aspirations. Heidegger, after 1929, was forced to reject the theological mystery and to seek refuge beyond metaphysics, (*Überwindung der Metaphysik*), in the intuitive immediacy of poetry and aesthetics.

But before studying this new Heidegger, another work,[45] published in

---

[43] *Ibid.*, p. 360.
[44] *Ibid.*, pp. 378–379.
[45] *Vom Wesen des Grundes*, in *Jahrbuch für Philosophie und phënomenologische Forschung* (Ergänzungband, 1929), pp. 72–110.

1929, namely, *Vom Wesen des Grundes,* is significant in the development of Heidegger's philosophical pilgrimage.

Vom Wesen des Grundes testifies to the enormous influence of Fichte and Schelling on Heidegger, particularly in regard to the interpretation of freedom as absolute and the manifestation of the absolute in the world, by a self-denial, that is to say, the objectivization of the absolute.[46]

The Aristotelian doctrine of cause is well known. He spoke of cause of the essence and the existence, of their becoming and their finality. Leibniz unified the doctrine on causality in the principle of sufficient reason: *nihil esse sine ratione seu nullum effectum absque causa:* "nothing is without a reason or each effect requires a corresponding cause."[47] This principle is grounded on the necessity that a true reason be given for each event. That is to say — interjects Heidegger (whose displeasure with the classics of Western thought is by now well known to the reader) — Aristotle and Leibniz recognized the basic foundation of the unity of being present in each event, but they did not question its validity. In effect "true judgments by their own very nature refer to a foundation (*Grund*) upon which they agree."[48] In other words, the predicate in a judgment must have its sufficient reason in the revelation of an aspect of being as such, and it is this which establishes the cause for its agreement with the subject.

Therefore, Heidegger continues, we are open to the comprehension of being in general, and this gives meaning to each existing individual being. *Ontic knowledge* (of each individual existent sharing the nature of being as such) in Heideggerian language implies an *ontological knowledge* (of being as such present in each existent). The difference between the two is called *ontological difference.*[49]

Of course, man is the necessary instrument for the realization of this ontological difference: by linking up the universality of being as such with each individual existent he is responsible for the existence of the "world," of world's history. "All individual beings could never be revealed, if they could not find the *occasion* of being thrown into the world."[50] The occasion is given by man: he sees many possibilities, he chooses one as good or preferable to others. The possibility of a being, Heidegger calls, is the goodness of a being in the Platonic sense. The

---

[46] The student of philosophy knows this principle as the second of Fichte's "Science of Knowledge." The first is Ego or self as consciousness (thesis); the second is the non-ego, as opposed to the Ego (antithesis); the third deduces the multiplicity of non-ego (objects) from the Ego's attempt to gain a progressive consciousness of itself (synthesis).

[47] Cf. W. Leibniz, *Primae Veritates.*

[48] *Vom Wesen des Grundes,* p. 78.

[49] *Ibid.,* p. 81.

[50] *Ibid.,* p. 104.

scholastics used the same idea when they said that, from the perspective of final causality, *bonum et ens covertuntur*. Man, therefore, projects or rejects the individual existent according to its positive or negative possibilities. This projection or rejection Heidegger calls "freedom."[51] But it is most important to stress that man is not free to create his own worlds arbitrarily: Heideggerian freedom is not a human faculty, it consists in "allowing the world to act in the movement of projections and rejections."[52] Rather than freedom being in man, we ought to say that man is in freedom. Freedom, therefore, is cosmic, universal, just as Fichte conceived it, and man is the instrument of freedom.

Freedom is the very essence of things and is the true meaning of causality.

Heidegger calls freedom "the abyss of man," because man is a "far-distant being." His essence, which is so close to him, must be continually conquered, as if it were "beyond the present." The doctrine of "close-distant," often repeated in the following works, appears to be another generous effort to save metaphysics, by offering a substitute, phenomenological in nature, to the rejected classical thought. Typically, Heidegger's renunciation of the absolute Being as *causa sui*, transcendent and personal, brings him to identify the foundation of reality (understood vaguely as an indeterminate essence, separated and yet responsible for the meaning of each existent) with freedom itself. Freedom is *causa sui* and has no subject responsible for being free. The unwarranted separation between essence and existence continues to present insurmountable obstacles for Heidegger, as it did so often in the history of philosophy.

Heidegger waited for the reactions of the intellectual world, and its discontent at his new ideas was not slow in making itself heard. He answered with a series of lectures, delivered from 1930 to 1932 in Bremen, Marburg, Freiburg, and Dresden, and later published under the title *Vom Wesen der Wahrheit*.[53] With the patience of a teacher anxious to make slow learners understand, Heidegger brought up graphic examples. Take a coin, for instance; how do you know whether it is genuine or false? "Genuine coin is that real thing whose reality agrees with what we always and in advance 'really' mean by 'coin.'"[54] Truth is therefore in this "agreement": the scholastics called it *adaequatio intellectus ad rem*. But that is not all: the agreement is impossible if there is no "zone for the meeting" between the mind and the thing.

---

[51] *Ibid.*, p. 108.

[52] *Ibid.*

[53] M. Heidegger, *Vom Wesen der Wahrheit* (Frankfurt, 1949), English translation in *Existence and Being*, pp. 317–352.

[54] *Ibid.*, p. 321.

This zone is an openness, a revelation which is there in reality before the meeting, making it possible. It follows that this ontological openness is far more essential to the concept of truth than the agreement itself, which is merely a mechanical device between man and being.

The profound nature of truth is to be found in being itself, whose essence is to be free.

A basic new idea appears at this point in *Vom Wesen der Wahrheit*, which will occur frequently in the following works of Heidegger: if the structure of being as such is ontological freedom and truth, history must be a succession of *awareness and oblivion*, of being, of its fundamental aspects of existence and nothing. Thus the essence of truth, which is free revelation, is only partial if we do not consider also the oblivion of the essence (*die Verbergung*) from which the counteressence derives (*das wesentliche Gegenwesen*). This "distance-closeness" of man to reality creates the space for their encounter. It is mandatory, for the manifestation of being to man, that this vacuum exists. More than a vacuum, we should speak of a fracture, mysterious in its nature and tragic in its consequences, preventing a peaceful solution to the metaphysical and human problem.

Heidegger becomes bolder now in denouncing the futile philosophical attempts of those who do not see the tragic aspects of philosophy. *Einführung in die Metaphysik*,[55] a series of lectures held for a whole semester in 1935, places extraordinary stress on the tragic meaning of being. Heidegger looks back into the history of thought and chooses his friends and enemies.

Nietzsche, of course, is his best friend: he felt the tension between the absolute and his existence and he spoke of the will to power to fill the gap. With Nietzsche is Hölderlin. He is the poet who warned humanity to go back to the sources, to Anaximander, to Heraclitus, to Parmenides. There the tragedy between the oneness of the absolute and the multiplicity of the many was felt and lived, rather than discussed and dissected with the help of a dead logic of abstractions.

The list of Heidegger's enemies begins with Plato. After him and because of him, the whole history of the West appears to Heidegger as a sad sequence of decadence and estrangement from the true meaning of being. Heidegger's aversion to Plato is grounded on what he described as the tragic Platonic misunderstanding of existence. Plato, Heidegger argues, has seen being as an idea and has made this idea the explanation of all things, establishing a peaceful relation, logical and ethical in

---

[55] *Einführung in die Metaphysik* (Frankfurt, 1935), English translation: *An Introduction to Metaphysics*, by Ralph Manheim (New Haven: Yale University Press, 1959).

nature, between thinking and being. Thus the sense of emergency was lost, the original emergency of being and truth. Plato was a pacifist in his attempt to conceal the philosophical problem. After him Rome became the first victim: Platonic concepts were borrowed by Rome with their inadequate and misleading meanings. Christianity was dragged along in the same disaster: Heidegger does not hesitate to use Nietzsche's sweeping definition of Christianity as a "Platonism for simple people."

Heidegger thinks he has the answer to the problems obscured by the Platonic heritage of the West: Mankind will find the authentic meaning of things if it goes back to its origins, using the only two possible tools which have remained unadulterated through the centuries of Western misunderstandings: the Greek and German languages.

For Heidegger the grammatical and etymological analysis of the word "being" (Gk., *tò ón;* Ger., *Sein*) is most revealing. The infinitive form (Gk., *einai;* Ger., *sein*) is not original; the infinitive denotes a relegation of being into an empty and indeterminate stage, in accordance with the oblivion of the real meaning of being.[56]

The original root for "being" meant "to live, to emerge, to last." It comprehended two aspects: (*a*) standing-in-itself (*in-sich-stehen*) in the sense of arising (*Ent-stehen,* "standing-out-of"). This "standing-out-of" was well expressed by the Greeks when they spoke of an *éxstasis.* *Exstasis* is a word full of fascination; it reveals the mysterious emerging from nothing, it means "a process of arising, of emerging from the hidden, whereby the hidden is first made to stand,"[57] by the mediation of *Da-sein,* of man. But then the Platonic-Aristotelian-Christian tradition took over: man became "*natura*"; the dynamic emerging from the hidden was converted in a static "essence" without meaning and without life.

(*b*) Of course, this "arising from" is made possible from being's standing, from its being "permanent, enduring."[58]

This is precisely Heidegger's goal: to overrun Platonic and Aristotelian categories of being-becoming, by conceiving both of them as two original aspects of the same reality. Heraclitus and Parmenides, erroneously thought of as opposing each other, are the leaders in this new conception of philosophy. They understood that being is becoming, that

---

[56] Even more erroneous and grossly inadequate is the substitution of "existence" for "being," so often used by philosophers from the Middle Ages to our days. Heidegger holds (*ibid.,* p. 53) that the Greek form *exousia,* means "to go out, to disappear, to be nothing." The reader is aware that we do not follow Heidegger's opinion on this matter: the context in which "existence" and "being" are used tells us their meaning.

[57] *Ibid.,* p. 12.

[58] *Ibid.,* p. 52.

becoming is not an opposition to being but its original manifestation, just as the blossoming of a rose is the rose itself. They also understood that thinking (logic) and doing (ethics) are equally original with being, so that the four basic notions, of which one comprehends the other, are: being, becoming, thinking, and doing.

We think that it is important, for an understanding of Heidegger's desperate efforts to bury the Aristotelian categories, to follow his analysis of *thinking*, one of the four original manifestations of being.

Thinking is meaningful when it yields truth (*aletheía* = unveiling, unconcealment). Being must be unveiled. Therefore thinking requires (a) a relation to being, (b) a becoming manifested, (c) the preparing of an action. "Just as becoming is the appearance of being, so appearance as appearance is a becoming of being."[59] Man, therefore, in the exercise of his thinking power, cannot be a passive recipient; human comprehension, in which each existing thing receives its meaning from being, consists in the effort to understand being and to apply it to the contingent existence, which maintains the freshness of its meaning as long as the vital relation with the original being is maintained. When man grows tired in his effort to maintain this vital relation, the individual existent decays, becomes a meaningless "thing," a lost Aristotelian substance, aimless and useless, irrelevant to itself and to others.

The Greeks had a word for this dynamic tension of human knowledge. The Greek *légein* corresponds to the German *lesen:* both mean "gathering, collecting, reading," or recognition that each existent is itself (in the light of being as such), distinct from the others and yet united to them. Man is essential in this process of gathering and yet it is more accurate to say that man belongs to the process of thinking than to say that the process of thinking belongs to man. Thinking means for man to return to the purity of the first manifestation of an existent when it asserted itself in the vast multiplicity of things, as reflecting in its unique way its sharing of existence from being as such. Thinking is an attempt to maintain that original purity, often forgotten in the oblivion of the daily routine, where each particular seems to be just "a thing."

Heraclitus understood this approach, Heidegger says. His famous fragment, Number 1 in Diel's collection, reads: ". . . For everything becomes essent in accordance with this *logos*. But they (the busy men unconcerned with philosophical thinking) resemble those who have never in their experience ventured anything, although they try their hand at words and works such as I perform, separating all things according to being, and explaining how they behave. . . . From them

---

[59] *Ibid.*, p. 53.

what they actually do, when awake, is hidden; just as what they have done in sleep, is hidden from them afterward."[60]

The same theme is developed in Parmenides' fifth fragment, which is inaccurately translated, "Thinking and being, as light of the existent, and man belong to each other." "What is expressed in Parmenides' maxim is a definition of the essence of man from the essence of being itself."[61]

"Things" can be immensely overpowering if man does not force in them that openness in which each existent assumes its distinction and its place. "It is only such conflict that shows, that brings forth gods and men in their being. We do not learn who man is by learned definitions; we learn it only when man contends with the essent, striving to bring it into its being, i.e., into limit and form, that is to say, he projects something new (not yet present), when he creates original poetry, when he builds poetically."[62] Notice that poetry is mentioned here because all existents find in poetic language their first name; in the Heideggerian context, each creative action is called poetic. "The violence of poetic speech, of thinking projection, of building configuration, of the action that creates states is not a function of faculties that man has, but a taming and ordering of powers by virtue of which the assent opens up as such when man moves into it."[63]

This important period of Heideggerian speculations, undoubtedly rich with valuable insights, must be seen in the right perspective.

a) The main contribution of Heidegger's philosophy consists without doubt in his interest in the *concreteness* of existence. In his own words: "Does the designation of being as the most universal concept strike the essence of being, or is it not from the very outset such a misinterpretation that all questioning becomes hopeless?"[64]

Heidegger forgets that at least one philosopher discussed the same problem long before him. Thomas Aquinas, still an inexperienced youth of twenty years of age, in his *De ente et essentia* understood that being cannot be an indeterminate genus, though it is universal; he understood that being cannot be added to each particular thing as another being or as a superimposed existence. Thomas Aquinas saw that being for each existent is nothing other than the completion of an essence, the "act" of an essence. Therefore being does not exist indeterminately. On the contrary *it acts* from within all particular existents as the principle that makes them possible in their own individual presence.

---

[60] *Ibid.*, p. 53.
[61] *Ibid.*, p. 121.
[62] *Ibid.*, p. 121.
[63] *Ibid.*, p. 132.
[64] *Ibid.*, p. 33.

b) Being, according to the Heideggerian interpretation of Heraclitus and Parmenides, "does not let what it holds in its power dissolve into an empty freedom from opposition, but by uniting the opposites maintains the full sharpness of their tension."[65]

But Heidegger pretends to forget that the same tension had been recognized by Aristotle as a rapport between act and potency. Aristotle perceived the same problem with a sharper eye than Heidegger and the Presocratics when he maintained that it was impossible for two opposites to be identical. Act, in the Aristotelian context, is the realization of a particular form of being; potency, in itself pure possibility, receives determination from act. In other words, act is positive, and tension cannot be conceived between two contraries if it is not, as tension, positive, that is, coming from the act itself. A rapport between being and non-being exists only in virtue of what is, not of what is not. The Heideggerian presupposition which identifies being with nothing leads to the other identification of being with becoming. Both result in concealing the philosophical problem rather than providing a key to its solution. They color, from its very beginning, the whole structure of Heidegger's investigations.

c) This basic compromise makes its appearance felt in each stage of Heidegger's thought. He speaks alternatively of the contemplative aspect of being and of its dynamic goals. He urges us, on the one hand, to let being be, but he adds immediately that man must act to open a spark of light in the darkness of the universe.

These statements are not idle oscillations in Heidegger's mind; on the contrary, they are intended precisely to explain philosophical contemplation through its genesis. It is a striving for unity through a defense of multiplicity; it hopes to reach light by a sequence of shadows and lights. As Heidegger said later, he had in mind the same goal that Hegel considered essential for philosophy. The rigid logical succession of Hegelian dialectic is replaced by Heidegger with the unpredictable periodic communion of being and man.

The Christian answer to Heidegger is simple: being in its original meaning cannot be investigated if God does not enter the picture. Heidegger, resigned to the fact that God is beyond man's intellectual aims, is confident of the correctness of his vision of the universe, *which reduces God to the liaison between being as such and the existing particular essents*. He did not consider for a second that God, of whom everybody speaks, is the foundation explaining all things, which are in need of God but which are not needed by God.

With profound honesty Heidegger from the first pages of *Sein und*

---

[65] *Ibid.*, p. 121.

Zeit asked the question: Why is being predicated of all things?

Now we have his answer: The necessity of being is to be found in the necessity of its presence in all moments of human expression. Therefore being depends on language: logic, which Heidegger always considered as secondary to metaphysics, is now the key explaining metaphysics.

Once more the history of philosophy repeats itself: when God's presence is underestimated, man takes His place. Heidegger's man is a necessary instrument to the creation or rather to the naming of all things. But it must be said that Heidegger's man has a very strange task: philosophers concern themselves with decisions, with freedom and responsibility. Heidegger's man does not really decide: everything happens from his encounter with being. This is a spontaneous spark, emanating from nowhere, without an explaining cause and without a plausible motivation.

II. *Language and Metaphysics*

We have noted Heidegger's interest in the German romanticism of the early nineteenth century. This interest was philosophical in nature and was directed toward those romantics who had tried desperately to translate into poetic language the idealistic thesis of the spontaneous generation of the universe. Hölderlin, for instance, was prominent among them. For Heidegger meditation on Hölderlin's poetry was an old hobby, but in 1935 this turned into a methodic commentary; he used it in his own developing thought which had by then reached the crucial topic of the *poetic* relations between man and the whole of existence. Hölderlin's works offered an answer, and Heidegger sought to express this in a lecture given in Rome in 1935 and published a year later under the title *Hölderlin und das Wesen der Dichtung*.[66]

Johann Christian Friedrich Hölderlin (1770–1843) was, like Heidegger, a Swabian. As a student of theology at Tübingen, he met Hegel and Schelling and later knew Fichte, Schiller, and Goethe.

Hölderlin lived during a period when there was a kind of mystical exaltation in Germany. There was a passion for a political and cultural renewal. The intellectuals found shelter and respect as private tutors in wealthy families, and Hölderlin was one of these, following this life at Weimar, Frankfurt, and finally in Switzerland. But although Hegel, Goethe, and Fichte knew the sweet taste of success and admiration, Hölderlin remained poor and anonymous throughout his life. He was

[66] *Hölderlin and the Essence of Poetry*, translated by Douglas Scott in *Existence and Being*, pp. 291–316.

also made miserable by his love affair with Susette Gontard, wife of a prominent banker of Frankfurt, who used to break the monotony of her marriage by flirting with poets. In this environment Hölderlin found happiness only in his poetry. For him poetry was a faithful contemplation of the universe; it had a mission to accomplish, one of transcendent nature, because it reminded man of his origins and led him back to them, where all antitheses of nature and civilization, of science and art were fused into a synthesis that explained the human phenomenon.

For these reasons Hölderlin revered with passionate devotion the Greek poets. Before Nietzsche he discovered in them the tension between Dionysiac exaltation and Apollinian rationality. He translated them in a style which reflected simultaneously a fanatical veneration and an unsurpassed command of both German and Greek. Reading his works makes one think of him as a forerunner of Joyce and Pound. But his life was too intense. From 1802 to the end, for forty-one years, he lived in a state of nonviolent psychosis.

From these few hints one can see why Heidegger was attracted to Hölderlin. The poet was not a decadent but a passionate believer in the tremendous responsibilities of the poet, and his tragic life seemed to Heidegger a dignified protest of a man who had discovered the great secret of the meaning of life, one who was ready to wait patiently for its fulfillment.

In *Hölderlin und das Wesen der Dichtung*, man is described as the only existent who assumes a position of "intimacy" with other beings. "That which keeps things apart in opposition and thus at the same time binds them together, is called by Hölderlin 'intimacy.' The affirmation of belonging to this intimacy occurs through the creation of a world and its ascent, and likewise through the destruction of a world and its decline."[67] Hölderlin's "intimacy," therefore, corresponds to Heidegger's *logos*. "Language is man's own property. . . . Only where there is language, is there world, i.e., the perpetually altering circuit of decision and production, of action and responsibility, but also of commotion and arbitrariness, of decay and confusion."[68] Hölderlin's dictum that "we are a conversation" becomes for Heidegger "man's essence is language." For both the unity of language is basic for human communication: "where there is to be a *single* conversation, the essential word must be constantly related to the one and the same."[69] Does this mean that the permanence of being is necessary? Yes, Heidegger agrees, but being in

---

[67] *Ibid.*, pp. 297–298.
[68] *Ibid.*, pp. 299–300.
[69] *Ibid.*, p. 302.

time, that is, being known by *Dasein*, being expressed by *Dasein* is the necessarily permanent being. Therefore language is necessary for existence, which *cannot be* unless it is expressed.[70]

It follows that if we know the origin of language we come to know the origin of being. But the molders of human language are the poets, who therefore are the cofounders of being. "Because being and essence of things can never be calculated and derived from what is present, they must be freely created, laid down and given. Such a free act of giving is establishment . . . and poetry is this establishment."[71] Poetry is the formation of metaphysics, of history, of civilization. In short, poetry is what forms the universe with its meanings and ideals.

If the poet's destiny is to explain the mystery of existence, does the philosopher's task become superfluous and useless? Heidegger never answered this question satisfactorily. His philosophy progressively assumed the attitude of a commentary on poetry; it became a kind of hermeneutics of poetry. Clearly a preoccupation with language and, indeed, a concern to find the solution to philosophical problems through linguistics become overriding occupations of Heidegger in his later years.

Because of this the conference given at Freiburg in 1935 — and since often repeated — is a landmark for the student of Heidegger. It is called *Der Ursprung des Kunstwerks* and was finally published by Heidegger only in 1950, in the collection *Holzwege*. The very title of this collection of essays ("Paths in the Forest") is a clue to Heidegger's developing thought. Man is a wanderer in the forest, "where many paths run in different directions. It almost seems that one is just as good as the other. But the mountaineer and the hunter know what it means to be in the forest."[72] It means to belong to the path, to be led by it, to feel it as our only way to safety, because it is not we who lead but it is the path that moves along, revealing to us a direction and giving meaning to us wanderers.

In *Der Ursprung des Kunstwerks* the path is poetry. Heidegger reasons in the following manner. Why is it that a work of art is distinguished from all other things? Traditional esthetic theories claim that the work of art, besides being itself as everything else is, refers to other meanings, representing them allegorically and symbolically. But

---

[70] Here Heidegger compromises in a grossly contradictory way. For him the permanence of being depends on knowledge of being and conversation about being. Everyday experience tells us that the opposite is true: permanence originates from being and language is a reflection of both being and permanence. Something must exist if we are to be able to think about it and talk about it.

[71] *Hölderlin and the Essence of Poetry*, p. 305.

[72] *Holzwege* (Frankfurt: Klostermann, 1950), p. 1. The same themes are developed in another short essay written after the war, *Der Feldweg*.

then what relation exists between "the thing" (marble, sound, color) and the work of art represented by this thing? Heidegger does not make any effort to conceal his growing discontent for western philosophical solutions. These stressed three aspects of the "thing" and they did not realize that an aspect of something cannot be its totality. In this way they led to an incredible confusion, with which a self-conscious respect for sterile immobility was linked.

a) The "thing" was conceived first of all as *hypocheimenon,* that is, what lay beneath. The Latins called it *subjectum* or *substantia,* something which is underneath, invisible and supporting the appearances. This misunderstanding is so usual that the unusual (*das Ungewohnte*) and yet essential, that is, the manifestation of being, is not even considered.

b) The "thing" was seen as *aistheton,* a composite of sense values which tend to make man forget being. The *aistheton* indeed tried to take the place of being.

c) The "thing" is considered as a relation between form and matter, *hyle* and *morphe.* This is the Aristotelian conception and Heidegger regards it as the most worthy of past attempts, although it too is devastatingly erroneous in his view. The hylemorphic position attempted to explain the tension between the appearances, the accidents, and the vague and unattainable origin of those accidents within the being of the work of art. This is, Heidegger admits, a useful approach because it explains with clarity a particular section of things, namely those manufactured, made of a matter molded into a shape or form for a specific purpose.

But can we, Heidegger asks, consider all beings as utensils? A utensil is midway between a "thing" and a work of art and explains neither. Van Gogh, for instance, was fond of painting Dutch wooden shoes, but they speak of sweat and toil, of hope and life.[73] They emerge from all particular aspects and show that they are, at root, a relation binding all human worlds into a common *reliability* (*Verlässenheit*). Van Gogh, Heidegger exclaims, works the miracle of opening our minds. "In the work of art the truth of the existent is put to work. 'Put to work' means to bring up to. An existent, for instance, a pair of shoes, comes into its light through the work of art. The being of the existent comes permanently in common with its appearances. This is precisely what a work of art causes in the 'putting into work' (*das sich-ins-Werk-setzen*) of the truth of being."[74]

The traditional fixation that art "represents" or "transfigures" is be-

---

[73] *Ibid.,* p. 22.
[74] *Ibid.,* p. 26.

yond comprehension. "What should be the essence represented by a Greek temple? Who could defend the absurdity that in the frame of a temple we should find its essence?"[75] In the work of art a world becomes world (*Welt weltet*) and the "word *for the first time* becomes and remains word."[76] We emphasize "for the first time" because it appears to contain the nucleus of Heidegger's revolutionary ideas on art. For him the work of art cannot be conceived as the creation of a new world, as is the case in the making of utensils. The work of art does not transform or substitute the thing in itself: on the contrary, it gives the thing in itself, with which it becomes identifical, the opportunity to come forward and to be authentic for the first time.

Art therefore is "emerging to a meaning." It is an emerging (*aufstellen*) in proportion to the value of a being (*her-stellen*) which has been hidden and kept from manifesting itself.

At this point Heidegger draws a significant parallel between the relationship of *logos/physis* (word/nature) prominent in human thinking and that of world/earth in the area of art. Earth is the obscure origin of things, where all their distinctions are forgotten; world is light discovering distinction, direction, and proportion. Earth is the element of resistance to the world. There is a moment in which the birth of a new world is still laboring in a struggle against earth, a moment in which both world and earth are present and revealed in the unity of their opposition. In that moment *truth* is born inasmuch as things are revealed in their connection to their origin as beings which have taken a meaning in their emergence from the indefinite absoluteness of existence as such.

Truth, therefore, does not consist in mere determination (e.g., the flower is red), but in the act of determining which springs from absolute indetermination (e.g., the flower "redding" against the backdrop of green landscape). Thus Heidegger goes from an ambiguous premise to an ambiguous conclusion: "Truth is in its essence (*Wesen*) nontruth."[77] Truth is nontruth in its essence not because it can be identified with falsehood but because it is essential for truth to spring from the obscurity of indeterminateness and to maintain the memory of its origin if it aims to be itself. If this memory is not preserved, each being falls into the "usual," it becomes a "thing." Then truth is mere falsehood and deception.

Esthetics, in the Heideggerian sense, is of importance insofar as it testifies to the fact that truth *is not* itself but only *becomes* itself.

[75] *Ibid.*, p. 36.
[76] *Ibid.*
[77] *Ibid.*, p. 43.

The discussion of art opened new horizons for Heidegger. If artistic activity revealed such profound mysteries of being, why not the other basic activities of man? Heidegger drew at this point an ambitious plan: the authenticity of being must be found in the action of the state (politics); in the revelation of being as such (*das Seiendste des Seinden*) (theodicy); in the essential sacrifice (ethics); and in the philosophical questioning of the meaning of things (logic).[78]

This was a great design, but Heidegger did not have the courage to finish it. Of all the forms of being mentioned above, he probed only the artistic and the theoretical. Why did he fear to face all forms of truth? It is the topic of the following section, which Heidegger himself called *Überwindung der Metaphysik* (*The Overcoming of Metaphysics*).

III. *Die Überwindung der Metaphysik*

The fundamental reason for Heidegger's retreat from an organized discussion of all forms of truth must be found, in our opinion, in his fear of announcing the possibility of metaphysics. We face here a paradoxical situation: Heidegger started his philosophical venture with a valiant defense of the necessity of a metaphysics. Now we discover a Heidegger convinced that the revelation of being is always circumscribed by and reduced to a particular and historical world. But this amounts, for Heidegger, to a self-imposed verdict of disqualification as a metaphysician. The alternatives are clear: (*a*) complete silence, since a universal (metaphysical) discussion of being is impossible; (*b*) a presentation of a partial theory, soon to be overrun by another; (*c*) a comforting illusion that, after all, a little beam of light is given to man by which he contemplates the inevitable sequence and dispersion of all philosophical theories.

This last solution appeared to Heidegger the only possible and honest one: to observe without being involved. Truly this was a desperate situation because "theory" means "to see." Now if Heidegger chooses to see, the road of existence, though dangerous and filled with surprises, is open to him and his "seeing" cannot be kept from assuming metaphysical significance. Thus he observed that only Heraclitus and Parmenides reached the authentic problem of being.[79] Plato laid down the premises for the first misunderstanding when he spoke of a difference between true and false appearances of being. Aristotle gave struc-

---

[78] *Ibid.*, p. 50.

[79] *Platons Lehre von der Wahrheit* (1942). English translation in *Philosophy of the 20th Century*, Vol. 3, by W. Barret and H. D. Aiken (New York: Random House, 1962).

ture to the Platonic misunderstanding by organizing it into the theory of judgment which, in Heidegger's view, interprets being as a system of logical predicates. Christian philosophers widened this fracture by their theory of creation. Cartesian mechanism conceived nature as a utilitarian source of energy: technology did not spring from classical Newtonian physics (as we are often told). For Heidegger classical physics is the result of a technical conception of being. Kant and Hegel did try to reestablish the unity of the universe, that is to say, the true manifestation of being, but they thought of overcoming the distinctions of being (thinking-willing, spirit-nature, art-religion, etc.) by uniting them under one aspect of the distinction itself, and thus their answer to the problem became arbitrary.

For Heidegger the only true philosopher of our times is Nietzsche. He dared to look beyond Plato and Aristotle. He went to the origins of existence, where unity was still preserved from the oblivion imposed by man and from artificiality imposed upon reality. Nietzsche crashed the barrier between thinking and being; for him thought is will to power, or, what is the same, decisive commitment to existence, to authentic existence. Therefore, metaphysics is not associated with our ability to think: it goes beyond this, it is *Überwindung* (conquest, overcoming) *der Metaphysik*.

To understand this phase of Heidegger's philosophy, the reader must keep in mind that Heidegger, between 1936 and 1940, continued to lecture on Nietzsche's nihilism and the prospect of overcoming it without falling victim of Western metaphysics. A reflection of this intense activity is his volume *Nietzsches Wort "Gott ist tot"* published in 1950[80] and then reedited in three volumes in 1961[81] under the title *Nietzsche*.

Heidegger's Nietzsche is not the usual hero of a vitalistic vision of the universe, as most philosophers understand him. On the contrary, he is the metaphysician who does not know, but who wills the infinite possibilities of being. The doctrine of "eternal return" is the rhythm of this new metaphysics, the "superman" is the new type of philosopher. The Heideggerian Nietzsche is convinced that all the traditional values of the nineteenth century are dead. Europe kept on talking about values and gave them lofty names, "God-religion-civilization." But all Europeans knew, deep in their hearts, that all ideals were dead, from God, to democracy, to civilization. "God is not a living God if we continue our attempts to master the real without taking reality seriously

---

[80] *Nietzsches Wort "Gott ist tot,"* pp. 193–248, of *Holzwege*. Selections translated in *The Worlds of Existentialism* by M. Friedman (New York: Random House, 1964).

[81] *Nietzsche* (Neske Pfulligen, 1961), three volumes.

and questioning it, without considering whether man has ripened far enough into the nature towards which it is drawn out of Being so that he can endure this destiny because of his nature rather than with the decisive help of mere expedients. . . ."[82] Nietzsche's mission was to lead man back to reality; to tell a decadent Europe that its civilization resembled a putrid corpse which had to be removed if contamination was to be avoided. Nihilism was the new credo and Heidegger saw in it a clean start for a new and true philosophy. But once Nietzsche's outstanding contributions to philosophy have been established, Heidegger does not spare him from sharp criticism. Nietzsche's unforgivable error happened to be his very impatient, avid desire to reconstruct the values which he so ably destroyed. He forgot that the concept itself of "value" had been called into doubt. He built a new metaphysics, after he proved that metaphysics was impossible.

Heidegger is determined to avoid this pitfall. It is an interesting experience to discover in his works a progressive and ever increasing fear of metaphysical values. In *Platons Lehre von der Wahrheit* (1942) Heidegger finally gives concrete form to his fears. Western philosophy has always presented being as such as a finite existent, as something which is something. For Heidegger being as such is not "something," but it is the condition which makes "something" possible. Perhaps we should be honest with ourselves, Heidegger suggests, and recognize that no other way was open to those who defended metaphysics: Plato did not have any other choice than to admit that being is idea, just as being was energy for Aristotle, act for St. Thomas, and a confrontation of subject and object for Descartes, Locke, Berkeley, Hume, and Kant. This is the destiny of metaphysics: to reduce being to a particular existent. To René Descartes, who wrote to Picot: "The whole of philosophy is like a tree: the roots are metaphysics, the trunk is physics and the branches that issue from the trunk are all the other sciences," Heidegger (using the same metaphor), answered: "In what soil do the roots of the tree of metaphysics have their hold?"[83]

In other words, if it is the destiny of metaphysics to consider being as a particular existent, *what is the light that makes the vision of the totality of being possible?* Why does light lighten?

Evidently, Heidegger argues, this problem is presupposed by metaphysics because this light is not an existent but the condition for every existent. Heidegger's fascination for understanding human knowledge runs through the whole of his meditations and his resentment against

[82] *Nietzsches-Wort*, in Friedman, *op. cit.*, p. 236.

[83] *Was ist Metaphysik* (1949). Translated in *Philosophy of the 20th Century* under the title: "The Way Back into the Ground of Metaphysics," pp. 207–218.

traditional metaphysics is grounded precisely on his conviction that metaphysical systems are artificial obstacles between man and his knowledge of being.[84]

Heidegger makes his point with a significant reference to Christian theology. He defends the thesis that metaphysics has infiltrated religious sentiment and with disastrous consequences. The Aristotelian establishment of logic and metaphysics has been adopted by the official representatives of Christ. "Whether for better or for worse it may be decided by theologians, on the basis of their experience of what is Christian; only they should keep in mind what is written in the first Epistle of Paul the Apostle to the Corinthians: 'has not God let the wisdom of this world become foolishness?' (1 Cor. 1, 20)."[85]

Heidegger, by now well convinced of the impossibility of a Christian interpretation of existence, lectures all Christians on intellectual humility. And his words are welcomed with gratitude. Yet he must know that Christian humility invites man to accept the revealed word with reverence, to adore with boundless joy the Divine Persons responsible for their Revelation to man. But Christian humility cannot destroy the human person and his intelligence, for without them communication with God is impossible.

Heidegger refused Christian faith because it appeared to him as a "round square,"[86] and he preferred to accept a "light" previous to metaphysics and responsible for man's communication with reality. But this very light must submit to an inescapable dilemma: if this light *is*, it must be, in its own particular way, *a being;* if it *is not, nothing* does not posit any problem; therefore, it is beyond the interest of human understanding.

Intellectual humility consists in the recognition that man understands, but he does not understand everything. Heidegger, faced with the limitations of human understanding, postulates something irrational beyond human possibilities. He is not aware that his assumption amounts to a destruction of all human limitations. In fact, for him everything which is meaningful is measured by human thinking and consequently man is a necessary element to the whole universe. Again the peculiar version of Heideggerian neoplatonism asserts itself: man is never overcome by superior beings; man is always there facing the whole of existence. Being and man are related in a partnership which prevents both of them from being absolute, necessary, or independent. Man's

---

[84] *Ibid.*, p. 210.

[85] *Ibid.*

[86] Cf. p. 187 f.

task is to be the "custodian and the shepherd of all beings pasturing in the universe."

On the other hand, we must admit that this attitude of Heidegger, lost in the wilderness without a faith in God, is intensely human and humanly humble. His desire for reaching beyond conventional metaphysics sounds the note of the Augustinian restlessness for everything which is limited and contingent. Perhaps we deal here with the most profound aspect of this philosopher who knew how to represent our times with its anxious impatience for more and for better. His efforts to express the contemporary anxious desire for reaching "beyond" the contingent and the physical often persuaded him to use arguments which seem an exercise in mental gymnastics and which are simultaneously deeply human and moving. For instance, he discovered that in an ancient German document the verb "to be" (*sein*) was spelled *seyn*,[87] Could it be — Heidegger dares to question with a magnificent explosion of childlike astonishment — that the ancient writer used the "y" with the intention of crossing the word, SEIN, since Being is so overpowering in its meaning that just naming it is impossible? The neoplatonic doctrine of the ineffability of the absolute and the ancient Jewish tradition of reverence for the unmentionable name of the Lord find a new application in this Heideggerian device for expressing the inexpressible.

Thus Heidegger reaches his conclusion: Plato, Aristotle, Thomas Aquinas, and all the other metaphysicians might have done a good job for their times; they answered the need of other generations to which their partial vision of existence appeared integral and sufficient. But their vision now is inadequate and unilateral.

The true twentieth-century philosopher's destiny demands that he reach beyond metaphysics and engage in a constant dialogue with the infinity of being, which does not have existence, meaning, or purpose without man, but which is at the same time beyond the contingency of human existence.

IV. *Gelassenheit* (*Serenity*)

Every philosophical synthesis meets its greatest challenge when it is confronted by ethics and morality. Heidegger's philosophy is no exception to this principle and the extension and magnitude of the moral problems waiting for an answer are of staggering proportions.

First of all, the well-known Heideggerian convictions in regard to metaphysics constitute the main obstacle: Heidegger cannot speak of

---

[87] *Uber "Die Linie"* published in *Beitrag zur Festschrift für E. Junger* (1955). Published a second time by Klostermann (Frankfurt, 1956) — English translation: *The Question of Being,* by W. Kluback and J. T. Wilde (Twayne Publ., 1958).

a final end toward which the actions of man are directed. To be specific, man's ethical end cannot consist in the fact that he is, for Heidegger, necessary to being's "creation and preservation," for that function of men is previous to any finality.

Man forgets himself when he concentrates on being, and it is right for him to do so, but simultaneously he should not reduce being to an existent, which is particular and partial. In the same way, when man concentrates on individual existents, he is wrong because he forgets the totality of being, and it is this which really counts; yet it is his task to think about individual existents and thus to give meaning to them.

So Heidegger's man is always right and always wrong. His ever increasing exhortation to reach being beyond the contingent or at least not to reduce it to a contingent existent leaves our minds perplexed and wondering.

In 1946 Jean Beaufret wrote to Heidegger asking explanations about these moral problems. Heidegger replied with a firm position:[88] the only ethics worth considering, outside of his own, is the ethics of humanism, which placed man in the center and the goal of human behavior. But humanism is wrong, because it makes man an entity enclosed in itself. Humanism defends a closed and therefore empty morality. Man alone, taken as an absolute value, is for Heidegger a sound without a meaning, a word without significance. Sartre, says Heidegger, did not avoid this pitfall: his philosophy conceived man as an *ego cogito*, as a subject sufficient in itself and therefore closed to others. This resulted in the philosophy of absurdity.

If the moral problem is to be understood, man must see his life as an openness between himself and Being. "Only insofar as man, existing for the truth of being, belongs to being, can being itself give those directions which must become laws and rules for man."[89]

"Openness and communication" with being are the key words to Heidegger's ethics. But we cannot be too happy with such an answer. We agree with Heidegger that man projects himself into being and the resulting "world" is made of ethical or unethical values. But ethics encompasses a wider horizon, ethics projects itself into a future "world" which still does not exist or into a past "world" which demands and expects fidelity to values already sanctioned and accepted as valid.

Heidegger searched for an adequate answer for many years. At last, in 1955 he gave the answer in his own town of Messkirch in a lecture published under the promising title of *Gelassenheit*.[90] The occasion was

---

[88] Heidegger's answer to Jean Beaufret was published under the title *Brief über den Humanismus*.

[89] *Ibid.*

[90] *Gelassenheit* (Neske Pfulligen, 1959), pp. 1–28.

a commemoration of another illustrious son of Messkirch, the great musician C. Kreutzer.

Kreutzer invites us to sing and dance, yet his powerful music also invites us to think. Much thinking goes on in our days, a thinking of an economical nature. It is, Heidegger admonishes, an adulterated thinking (*das rechnend Denken*). It is preoccupied with immediate success and deprived of peace and serenity. Profit-making thought fails to reflect on the real values. The boldness of science coordinated with industry looks for comfort and pleasure beyond the neglected meaning of man. "Nobody ponders on the sad fact that our computer-minded society plots with the instruments of technology against the meaning of life and against the nature of man with consequences which will prove that the explosion of the H-bomb was a minor misfortune for mankind."[91]

Of course the successful combination of science and technology is welcomed by Heidegger. The danger lies in considering this aspect of reality as exhaustive and final, as if technical thinking did not derive from thinking itself. Heidegger's solemn advice to his fellow Germans is contained in one word: *Gelassenheit* (serenity) when confronted by technical instruments. Man must say "yes" to technical utensils, but he must say "no" to their pretense of monopolizing all the meanings of being. The openness and the serenity of man in this technical age springs from the mystery of the technical world itself. Who can reveal the reason which compelled mankind to choose, of all possible civilizations, this one put together by computers and H-bombs. Heidegger's concern for his countrymen is deeply moving: he exhorts them to be faithful to the *Bodenstandigkeit*, to the homeland. In the post Hitler period, this took on the meaning of men's "thinking essence" rather than a geographical Germany.

Now this serene fidelity (*Gelassenheit*) to the authentic destiny of man transcends all logical contraditions to establish an unbreakable encounter between man and being. In other words *Gelassenheit* is mystical in nature, superior to human discussions, real only to those who refuse to talk about it, because they are aware of it as a most intimate experience of love. In his essay *Zur Erörterung der Gelassenheit* (Discussion on the meaning of Serenity),[92] Heidegger wrote: "In this *Gelassenheit* perhaps a human endeavor is hiding which is more profound than all the actions of the world and more meaningful than all the creations of mankind."[93] *Gelassenheit* is "pure expectation," stripped and free from any particular and selfish interest. This absolute openness is possible

---

[91] *Ibid.*, p. 23.
[92] *Ibid.*, pp. 29–73.
[93] *Ibid.*, p. 35.

because Being itself is by nature an invitation to encounter, an irresistible magnet for human communication. "We are accustomed to say that we penetrate the horizon with our sight. But then this wonderful experience does not depend on us, but on the horizon itself which is open to us. *Gegnet* is the infinite openness, which encompasses everything and unites everything in such a way that all things are respected in their serenity and are sustained and maintained by the openness of being."[94] *Gegnet* is another word which Heidegger dug out of an old lexicon of Bavarian dialect. *Gegnet* resulted, Heidegger thinks, from the fusion of two words: *gegen* (against) and *eignen* (reunification). In fact, being, in its openness toward man, opposes (*gegen*) the various particular existents, and thus defends their individuality while uniting (*eignen*) them with the wholeness of its own universality.

The affinity of these suggestive ideas with the classical concept of the intelligibility of being does not need any illustration. Christian overtones are often present in Heidegger, who insists in manifesting his gratitude for the privilege of human thinking (*Denken-Danken*): "There is a sort of gratitude which is not grateful primarily for something received, but for the privilege of being able to be grateful."[95] But the fundamental, irreconcilable opposition remains. The intelligibility of all existents flows for Christian philosophy from the divine *Logos*, the unique and transcendent Intelligence unifying the meanings of all created things, visible and invisible. On the contrary, Heideggerian intelligibility of things is not rooted in God, of whom Heidegger knows nothing. Since it is evident to him that an intelligence must be responsible for the meaning of all things, he settles for human intelligence. "Evidently the essence of man is to be open to being; its openness belongs so completely to human essence that it is inconceivable without man."[96] The historicity of being necessarily follows the historicity of man, and there is here an interdependence which cannot, we think, give rise to the intelligibility of all things. In fact, *Logos* is bound to unify and explain in itself all possibilities and therefore it must be superior to all possibilities: the existence of something remains without any sense if it cannot be distinguished and differentiated from all the other possible ways in which it could exist. Heidegger returned to this idea in a lecture which he gave at Frankfurt in 1957 on the occasion of the 500th anniversary of that University.[97] The new angle of perspective

---

[94] *Ibid.*, pp. 39–42.
[95] *Ibid.*, p. 62.
[96] *Ibid.*, p. 64.
[97] *Identität und Differenz* (Neske Pfulligen), pp. 1–34. English translation: *Essays in Metaphysics*, 1957.

from which this lecture considers the same problem of the relation of being to man is the principle of identity (A-A).

The history of philosophy tells us that the principle of identity has been understood in different ways by different philosophers. Plato, Leibniz, Kant, and Hegel discovered (each of them in a different way and for different purposes) the possibility of an ontological identity in reality, not just a logical one. Identity is for them the unity of all differences, a unity by which all differences are mediated in a bond that makes a being, in its various features, equal to itself.

The crucial question, as we all know, is how far should this process of unification go? Classical philosophy attributes to the existence of something (which is the substance) the unity of all differences (accidentals). For Heidegger the unity is given by the reciprocity of Being and thought, where being is taken for "intelligibility" and thought for man. The shadow of an immanentistic vision of being grows with alarming proportions and Heidegger senses the affinity between his thinking and the Hegelian position.

But he took care to stress three major differences with Hegel:[98]

a) Hegelian philosophy posits the absolute becoming of being as a totality of all individual existents. Heidegger on the contrary, conceives all individual existents in relation to being, but differentiated from it.

b) Hegel considers the history of human thought and civilization as a continuous and progressive contribution of all men. Heidegger stresses, in each philosophical period, the long journey yet to be fulfilled into the understanding of the new opening of existence.

c) Hegel believes in an absolute synthesis of all philosophies of all times, namely his own thought. Heidegger is against this. In fact, he advises a reverse approach, which he calls Schritt-zurück, i.e., a running back through the centuries to discover data proving the oblivion to which past philosophers condemned real being. This oblivion, Heidegger repeats, is the heart of metaphysics. And then he develops a most disturbing idea: Metaphysics took upon itself the responsibility of splitting the unbreakable unity of being in two branches: on one side, ontology was meant to reconcile the presence of being in each existent; on the other, theology dealt with the loftiest of all existents, God himself. These two autonomous artificialities, in continuous need of reconciliation, gave birth to a third monstrosity — formal logic.

Hence the final Heideggerian verdict on metaphysics is this: it divided the unity of being, whereas from the beginning of intellectual thinking, the human mind always tried to give a unifying meaning to reality.

It is obvious that it is not accurate to speak about philosophy as

[98] *Ibid.*, pp. 35–75.

exclusively concerned with the unity of being. Of course everybody agrees that the task of the philosopher is to reach a higher synthesis which is not possible to the empirical scientist and to the artist. But a meaningful unification of reality remains useless if the individual plurality of the unified existents is not safeguarded.

Using a language which Heidegger considers distasteful, we cannot speak on *the metaphysical level* of the unity of differences if they remain just differences and are not components of a basic unitary element.

Even more biased and groundless seems Heidegger's accusation that classical metaphysics has never sought *logically* the explanation of the differences existing in reality. The main problem of traditional metaphysics has always been and still is the safeguarding of the unity of existence in the diversity of its manifestations and of the substantial autonomy of created things, despite their dependence on God.

Heidegger is unfair to Christian theology when he labels God the highest of the existents, as a man-made entity in contrast to the absoluteness of his "Being as such." Christian theology deals with the Supreme Being who is the foundation of himself and of all existents. But Heidegger, who resented his early Jesuit training, looks down with scorn on a God trapped by Aristotelian language into the immobility of a *causa sui*. "Man may neither pray to this God, nor may he sacrifice to him. Confronted by *Causa sui* man may neither fall to his knees nor sing and dance."[99]

And we could agree with him in his judgment of the God of the Christians, if we were not aware that the Aristotelian-Thomistic philosophy is just one effort, limited in time and space, to represent with concepts, inadequate as they are, a transcendent God.

But every Christian knows with absolute certainty that only faith allows us to recognize the identity between the *causa sui* and the living, loving God of Abraham, of Jacob, of David, of the God of Augustine and Pascal, the living God who did not disdain to be a man and to walk the streets of Galilee.

In conclusion, the gigantic effort of Martin Heidegger, with its gratuitous premises and its tortuous developments, is a new instance proving the fallacy of all philosophical speculation outside of moderate realism: Man takes the place of God, and the human mind assumes divine power.

But Heidegger's philosophy is also a warning: Christian realism cannot anymore be presented to twentieth-century man with the same concepts and categories which gave light and conviction to the man of the thirteenth century.

---

[99] *Ibid.*, p. 65.

chapter VI

The Philosophy of Jean-Paul Sartre

INTRODUCTION

The life and philosophy of Jean-Paul Sartre are outstanding in contemporary philosophy. They constitute the last act in a drama with a tragic ending. The *dramatis personae* are man and the immense and mysterious universe which surrounds him.

The philosophers of the Middle Ages used to say *esse est intelligibile*: being is the source for understanding. The idealists later offered their own reading of this dictum: being must be reduced to human thinking. They refused to grant that beyond what man actually understands there exist many possibilities for a more complete comprehension of reality — in fact, for an understanding of the real reason explaining all things and their limitations. A similar denial of the limits of the power of human thought is found today in every variety of naturalism. For naturalism defends the existence of a massive, irrational, and unthinkable being that is beyond human knowledge. While naturalism is now as widespread in the sciences and literature as it is in everyday life, the influence of Cartesian rationalism and eighteenth-century illuminism has given it a peculiar shape in modern France. One must read Jean-Paul Sartre with this in mind.

1. A VOCATION TO THE WORLD OF AESTHETICS

Many factors are responsible for the making of Sartre, the man and the philosopher. He came from Catholic and Protestant environments, yet he felt the fury of atheism in the first decades of this century in France, and the emptiness of that fury. Thirsty for knowledge, he left France for Germany where he found meaning for his life in searching

for an answer to the mystery of human existence. When the catastrophic
World War II forced itself on France, he chose the impossible life of
a guerrilla fighter, and found himself hunted as a criminal in his native
land.

In the aftermath of the war thousands of Europeans, young and old,
pondered with experiential calm the bitter words of Sartre: "Man is a
useless passion," and existentialism became the new European philosophy. But Sartre himself became a communist. He was too much of an
independent thinker, however, to respect the party line. Recently, the
aging Sartre, still possessed of a lucid and agile mind and still obsessed
by a God whose existence he stubbornly denies, wrote: "Here I am
again, the same traveler without ticket, just as I was when I was seven
years old."[1]

* * *

Sartre's father, Jean Baptiste, an officer in the navy, died a few months
before Jean-Paul was born, June 21, 1905. His widow had but one course
to follow and she returned to her family, the Schweitzers of Alsatia.
(Albert Schweitzer, who later became the apostle of the lepers in
Lambarene, Africa, was a cousin of Anne-Marie Schweitzer, Jean-Paul's
mother.) The child was the center of the family: the grandfather, the
old patriarch Charles Schweitzer, pretended to show authority and
sternness; consequently the mother was as a sister to her son: "I have
had my first experience with reality by knowing only its charming
inconsistency."[2] Indeed, Sartre's childhood was a charming inconsistency:
he was considered by the family an *enfant prodige*, and he liked it. He
felt the warmth of familial admiration for his passion for reading; he
spent hours in his grandfather's library. Books were his best friends;
they introduced him to a fascinating world of personalities and adventures; they chased away the real world that appeared to the young
Sartre crowded with shadows and dangers. "My books were my birds,
my nests, my domestic animals, my stable and my farm."[3]

He understood the fictitiousness of his situation, but he did not find
much help from his family: "I was in need of God and they gave Him
to me, but I accepted Him unaware that I was looking for Him."[4] The
truth is that his middle-class family was giving only lip service to religious practice; the naturalistic philosophy that conquered the minds
and the hearts of most Frenchmen, from the intellectuals to the

---

[1] J.-P. Sartre, *Les Mots* (Paris: Gallimard, 1964), p. 211. English translation by
Bernard Frechtman (New York: George Braziller, 1964). Sartre borrows this expression from Dostoevski's *The Brothers Karamazov*.

[2] *Ibid.*, p. 83.

[3] *Ibid.*, p. 37.

[4] *Ibid.*, p. 17.

peasants, had not spared those closest to Jean-Paul.

The young Sartre was lonely but dominated by powerful ambitions and drives. He could not waste his existence being unnoticed. He aimed to be exceptional, even eccentric, and his tools for achieving this goal were words, images, poetry. The first writings of the now aging philosopher date back to his seventh year; they are childish Alexandrine poems and exotic stories. They anticipate the lucubrations of a man who for more than thirty years thought of himself as one chosen by destiny to shape French culture. Today, old and experienced, Sartre identifies those juvenile enthusiasms with a compulsive need to substitute literary faith for religious conviction.

A professed atheist, Sartre derides and attacks all manifestations of religious values in the family, in society, and in the individual consciousness as well. As a result, he is condemned to reject any human endeavor, however successful, whenever it presumes the presence of God. Clearly this presence has haunted Sartre throughout his entire life. He is the fugitive whose restlessness might well be considered a forceful argument for the existence of a pursuing God.

His family moved to Paris, where his old grandfather was teaching French to German students. Jean-Paul studied at La Rochelle, and from 1916 at the Lycée Henri IV in Paris. In 1919 he enrolled in the Lycée Louis le Grand. Subsequently, in 1925, he entered the École Normale Supérieure, in the faculty of Belles Lettres.

The cultural atmosphere of all French universities was then under the influence of a renewed wave of idealism. (The same phenomenon existed in Italy under the influence of Croce, and in the Anglo-Saxon countries where Bradley's impact was great.) *Leon Brunschvig* (1869–1943) was Sartre's teacher. Brunschvig, a pupil of Lachelier, was considered the last representative of nineteenth-century French idealism. Brunschvig focused his teaching on one presumption that he considered axiomatic: one must have a profound aversion to metaphysics and to all doctrines about nature, essence, and substance. Spiritual substance is singled out by Brunschvig as contradictory. Spirit is an activity in continuous evolution. It is hopeless to prove the existence of spiritual substances by the deductive method because experience interferes continuously, breaks up gratuitously preestablished schemes, and stimulates a way of thinking free from metaphysical assumptions. Echoing Hegel, Brunschvig believed in history as the manifestation of the human mind. History must free mankind from all forms of prejudice and unite all men in the creation of a society guided by wisdom.[5]

[5] Cf. *Les Etapes de la philosophie mathématique*, 1912; *L'experience humain et la causalité physique*, 1922.

Sartre commented later in his life[6] that the optimism of his teacher and his Hegelian monism generated boredom among the students. They preferred to read and discuss Marx or the sharp criticism of Jean Wahl, whose *Vers le concret* challenged the gratuitous assumptions of Brunschvig. His students reacted as all students do when the teacher is weak or indecisive or unpersuasive: they turned against him and against the ideas he advocated with an emphatic defense of individual pluralism.[7] Yet Brunschvig left an indelible mark on his pupil Jean-Paul Sartre: a horror for the old static Aristotelian metaphysics, for the doctrine of essences and substances, and ultimately for the God of the Christians.

The year 1929 brought Sartre a new distinction: he was promoted, first among the candidates, to the *agrégation de philosophie*. Now by profession he became a teacher of philosophy. His teaching experience opened new horizons; he learned how to arouse the enthusiasm of his students. To reach them with the right words, to make difficult philosophical concepts understandable to them was a great challenge, and success a great reward, as every teacher knows. Le Havre was the place of his first assignment; Laon, a modest little provincial town, his second. Laon, transformed into the imaginary Bouville, offers the atmosphere and the background for his first novel, *Nausea*. Its plot develops around the historian, Roguetin, who lives temporarily in Bouville, busying himself with research work. His free time is the cause of his problem: he wanders around and notices that people are just going about their business with the unconscious resignation that habit creates. Ideals do not seem to exist in Bouville, unless monotony is one of them. One day, in the park of Bouville, Roguetin, while contemplating the roots of an old chestnut tree, experiences an intuition of sorts. The meaning of being is revealed to him. He understands that being is just there, without any justification. Being is a spasmodic, irrational thrust wholly rebellious to any rationality. The absence of finality is the heart of the matter. Humanity progresses to a goal that does not exist. Therefore existence is absurd. We must make progress, yet we do not have any motivation for this progress.

"Being is contingent. I mean to say that by definition existence *is not* a necessity. To exist means just to be there. The existent appears, associated with others, but never is the existent logically understood or defined. Some have understood this, but they have tried to overcome the contingency of reality by accepting a necessary being that is, they

---

[6] Cf. Sartre, *La critique de la raison dialectique* (Paris: Gallimard, 1960), pp. 22–24.

[7] One of Sartre's first philosophical works is the article "La Transcendence de l'Ego," published in No. vi of the journal *Recherches Philosophiques*, 1937. It is a strong defense of the individual against transcendental philosophies.

say, its own cause. But never will a necessary being explain the origins of the existent: contingency is not unreal, an apparent value that can be ignored. The contingent is the absolute, a completely gratuitous absolute. Everything is gratuitous: this garden, this town, my very self."[8]

From the time of the publication of Moravia's *La Noia* (*Boredom*) and Camus' *L'étranger* (*The Stranger*) in the 1940's, and, in our own day, Miller's *After the Fall*, Roguetin has found thousands of brothers in despair. The anxiety and frustration of this generation stands in sharp contrast to the vital optimism of Bergson and Blondel during the first decades of our century. We have to reach back to the work of Dostoevski and to *The Castle* and *The Trial* of Franz Kafka to find the predecessors of contemporary existentialism. Yet a common heritage of thought is present and working in the minds of Bergson and Sartre, otherwise so different and irreconcilable. Man for both *is not*, he *becomes. Action* comes before and generates *being*.

Strange is the mystery of human thinking. Hegel, so much talked against by both Sartre and Bergson, seems to shape the thought of each and to make of them uneasy bedfellows. From the same source have burgeoned philosophies of joy and optimism, anxiety and despair. Why? History offers the answer. A catastrophic war, soon to be followed by another more destructive and monstrous, was fought to bring to concrete realization the ideals of the philosophers of optimism. The possession of power and the supremacy of man were the ideals of both war and philosophy. The honest efforts of contemporary philosophers who seek to create a better life for mankind leave a bitter taste in the mouth of Sartre. He sympathizes neither with their efforts nor with their return to the past: their attempt to find inspiration in the Greek, the Medieval, the Romantic philosophers and in Aquinas, Hegel, and Kierkegaard is futile. To Sartre the past is a failure. The attempt to give a meaning to human existence is a farce. There is no meaning. Life is absurd.

Sartre even condemned his own early experience because he found it too optimistic and superficial: "When I was thirty years old I happened to achieve a great success indeed: I had written *Nausea* — with candid sincerity, I must say — about the unjustifiable human existence, about this saltish existence of my fellowmen. And I have *excluded* myself. *I was Roguetin.* I was the personification of my own life. And yet I have pretended to be the chosen one, the analyst of inferior human beings, a photomicroscopic camera, made of glass and iron, bent over my own liquid protoplasms."[9]

---

[6] *La Nausée* (Gallimard: Paris, 1938), p. 166. English translation, *Nausea*, by Lloyd Alexander (Norfolk, Conn.: New Directions, 1959), p. 176.

[9] Sartre, *Les mots*, pp. 209–210. (Eng. tr., pp. 251–252).

2. SARTRE AND PHENOMENOLOGY

Importance of Max Scheler in the Philosophy of Sartre

From 1929 to 1934 Sartre traveled in Greece, Egypt, and Italy. He spent 1934 in Germany at the *Institut français* in Berlin, where he came into contact with phenomenology and with the major works of Husserl and Heidegger.

Husserl left a profound impression on Sartre, who admired his Cartesian analytic method of research. But Sartre rejected Husserl's *Lebenswelt* and his enthusiasm for human history. He thought that Husserl's greatness lay in his power of analysis and in his ability to construct his philosophy from his own personal experiences. Sartre used the same method: he built a bridge between his pictures of life and his literary works and his analysis of their philosophical meaning.

In those days Heidegger's fame was limited to his *Sein und Zeit*, published in 1927. With it the *Existenz-philosophie* began to be the topic of philosophical circles, and Heidegger, along with Jaspers, was its main representative. Heidegger's concept of man as a projection of himself, developing into the three temporal *exstases*, was a main factor in the molding of Sartre's mind. According to Heidegger, man is brought by his own radical inconsistency to the heroic acceptance of human limitations. Sartre opposed this notion of Heidegger and viewed it as a repetition of Nietzsche and as a residue of German romanticism.

Max Scheler, who is often forgotten, seems to be one of the most influential men in the life and thinking of Sartre. Although Sartre did not accept Scheler's philosophy (just as he did not accept any of the previous philosophies), he found in Scheler an approach to the problem of existence that became identical with his own.

In the first decade of this century Max Scheler was an enthusiastic proselyte of Husserl. As we know, intentionality is the core of Husserl's phenomenology not only for human knowledge but also for man's affective life. Scheler here took a bold step forward. With themes familiar to Plato and St. Augustine, he reached a complete identification of the intentionality of the mind with the will's power of loving. A person reaches intuitive understanding of essences through an act of love, because understanding is not a superficial grasping of exterior elements but a living participation with the essence of the object understood. If I want to know a person, my whole self is held out toward that person. I am not satisfied with distant, cold information. I participate in his life, and I live with him the experience of his own being.

Scheler was aware that his doctrine was meaningful only when an objective order of things is the foundation of his "knowing with love." My act of knowledge is valid if there *is* something to know. If I am supposed to decide the meaning of "sweet" and "bitter," I do not have any reason to seek and direct myself toward what is sweet or bitter. The notion of "essence" had been abused and deformed on too many occasions throughout the history of philosophy. For Scheler an essence is not an empty abstraction nor a concept of the mind. Essence is the most real and concrete nucleus of each thing. Essence is *a priori*, if *a priori* means anything that exists independently of any knowing mind; and essence is material, if material means concrete (as opposed to mental) existence. In this context the title of his important work, *Formalism in Ethics and the Material Ethics of Values*[10] is indicative. For Scheler, "value" is essence itself insofar as it is worthy of being desired and possessed. "Good" is an existing thing holding a "value." "End" is the motivation that exists in each human action actively pursuing something that might or might not have the value pursued.

The careful definition of these terms was for Scheler a decisive move against the tremendous influence and confusion introduced into the world of nineteenth- and twentieth-century philosophy by Kant's *Critique of Practical Reason*. Kant was obsessed by the conviction that human action must be autonomous, that objective values or essences are unknowable. Moreover, Kant considers selfish and therefore immoral any human action performed with the intention of reaching some concrete goal ("matter") like health or peace of mind or happiness. It is well known that for Kant the norm of morality must be purely formal and the value of the human act ought to depend on the universal law: "act as though the maxim of your action were by your will to become a universal law of nature." If well understood this Kantian formalism makes man supreme arbiter of his own actions and, what is worse, of the finality of his actions. We are dealing, Scheler emphasizes, with the very cause of the crisis of contemporary life. Kant has confused the objective value with the subjective end of a human action. The end of a human act may possibly be the achievement of a value, or it might not be. The value is not affected by the action, because the value is objective.

Scheler is here in perfect communion of ideas with Plato and, without any doubt, with Husserl. But when he makes another step forward, he seems to find difficulties. He defends the thesis that neither experience nor rational thinking are capable of discovering objective values. Objectivity of values is the final result of an intuition produced by our feelings.

---

[10] Published for the first time in the *Jahrbuch* of Husserl and then in a volume in 1921 and 1927.

The value does not depend on an arbitrary choice of human feelings, but reveals itself to the heart of man. This happens in various degrees almost hierarchically: from *sense values* (pleasant versus unpleasant) to *vital values* (healthy versus sick) to *spiritual values* (beautiful and just versus ugly and false) to *religious values* (saint versus sinner). The heart understands reasons that the mind fails to understand, Scheler repeats with Pascal. Here Scheler reveals his weakness: his lofty construction has sandy foundations because of his bias against metaphysics.

In his works *Forms and Essences of Sympathy* (1923) and *The Eternal in Man* (1921), Scheler applies his theories to the meaning of man and God. Man is not a pure reason or an empirical entity. Man is an incarnation of a value (knowledge with love) in a material reality (the body). Not only is the person an individual but his own world too is individual; each person sees values individually. Persons, though individual, communicate and comprehend because each earthly value bears the character of the same maker, God. The ontic insufficiency of things and persons reveals the presence of God, the maker and the final magnet of all existing realities. Philosophers talk about the possibility of demonstrating God's existence. Scheler is prepared to say that God demonstrates His existence to man. The religious experience begins with man curious about God, but ends with God giving completion to the act of man. Human society itself is like a dangerous jungle until mutual love makes all human beings understand that God is the only source of all social levels. In the immediate aftermath of World War I, the human warmth that Scheler brought to his interpretation of human and divine love was a magnificent proof of the depth of his mind and heart.

Sartre felt the power of Scheler's convictions. Sartre's books, though aiming at a denial of all the theses so dear to Scheler, are written with the same nostalgic love, with the same intensity of affection. Unfortunately Scheler learned soon that philosophy requires cold, organized reason if it is to survive. He was the first victim of his own intuitionism. A premature death prevented Max Scheler from further meditations. But before his death, he went through a disturbing crisis that led him to accept nineteenth-century monism, the target of the whole of his previous philosophy. In *The Situation of Man in the Cosmos* (1928), he spoke of one life unfolding gradually from the higher levels, which are the weaker, to the lower ones of the inorganic world, which are the most powerful and primitive sources of energy. Again, with paradoxical pleasure man celebrates his own ephemeral autonomy from the transcendental conscience by his ability to say "no," to reject a situation (*Neinsagen können*). Sartre carefully noted this lonely hint of a pessimistic overtone in Scheler, the most brilliant and confident German thinker of his day. That trifle of pessimism was a prelude to the giant steps that Sartre would take to carry his sad gospel of despair to the modern world.

3. THE THEORY OF THE IMAGINATION

From 1935 to 1939 Sartre was a member of the faculty of philosophy at Pasteur College in Neuilly-sur-Seine. In the life of Sartre, this might be thought of as a period of restrained patient waiting. His time had not yet come. But Sartre did not sit brooding in idle discontent. A teacher is productive, and Sartre was an excellent teacher. He worked on a project which his German contacts with the world of the phenomenologists made imperative to his mind: What was the real meaning of imagination? A sense of surprise cannot be concealed when we notice that Sartre, so profoundly taken by a narcissistic admiration for his own genius, edited two volumes (the first, *L'imagination* in 1936; the second, *L'imaginaire* in 1940) on a topic so dry that it neither stirred the imagination nor excited adulation.

Perhaps some light might be shed on these two works if we think of them as Satre's attempt to understand himself. His youth, as we have seen, was a maze of ambitious projections. He had always thought of himself as a genius in the creative arts and a leader of minds in philosophy. Therefore, to investigate the imagination was to elucidate his own genius. Undoubtedly another reason for such an enterprise can be found in the widely acknowledged conclusions of German phenomenology. Husserl denied that the act of human knowing was made possible by an intermediary between the subject and the object. The question was an old one: we remember the verbose dissertations of the scholastics about the *signum quod* and *signum quo*. For Husserl the object itself, without any medium, was intentionally known by the subject.

The fact of the matter, however, is quite clear: the society in which we live surrounds us with symbols vividly representing other objects. Madison Avenue owes its fame and its millions to advertising. TV skillfully makes us identify fresh air and invigorating spring scenery with cigarettes that the government tells us may be dangerous to health. Politicians speak of new frontiers and the great society. Movies take us for a few hours into a world of fantastic unreality. Bethoven's *Ninth Symphony* is successful in giving us the shivering experience of an almost religious ecstasy. We live in a world of imagination. Consequently, for modern man, the object of Sartre's inquiry is a significant one. What, indeed, is the task of imagination in the act of human knowledge if the imagination does not belong to the act of knowing, as the phenomenologists contended? Why do we use it as frequently as we actually do?

Sartre's answer to this problem is equally clear. Contrary to the phenomenologists who deny it and to the behaviorists who identify it with mental perception, Sartre thinks that imagination, though separated from knowledge, is necessary to produce an act of human knowing. His reasoning in the matter takes the following course:

a) Imagination does not aim to create its own object. Imagination reaches out to an already existing object. I imagine my friend living far away. He is the object of my imagination. "It is wrong to think that there is a world of images and a world of objects. Each object is susceptible of being a present real object or the object of imagination, depending on the point of perspective from which it is seen."[11]

b) Imagination is a state of consciousness. It is a peculiar state of consciousness, different both from the concept and from the act of perceiving. With the concept imagination has something in common: it offers a well-defined object which is present to the mind regardless of the physical existence of the object itself. On the other hand, imagination shares with the act of perceiving the characteristics of presenting an object well defined within the framework of time and space, with all the environmental aspects of a given existing object.

c) Yet existence is not a quality required by the object of imagination. If I imagine a person, it does not matter whether the person is absent, or dead, or totally nonexistent. Often a portrait or a caricature or a vignette invites the imagination to weave a striking piece of work.

All these complexities, discovered within the mystery of imagining, give Sartre the occasion to express his distaste for positivistic attempts to probe into the mystery of human knowledge. The positivists tried to localize the functions of knowing into cerebral compartments. For them, perceiving meant to recognize the imprint of the object in the brain, and imagining was a feeble and fading use of perceiving. The problem remains, Sartre suggests, not without a hint of caustic irony. In fact, how can the positivists make a distinction between perception and imagination if perception itself is merely a copy of the thing-in-itself, which is never reached by the mind?

As far as this particular problem is concerned, Sartre speaks with the calm and wisdom of a father of the Church: knowing is the act of human consciousness that establishes an equation between the mind and an existent thing in time and space. Imagining is the act of human consciousness that establishes an equation between the mind and an

---

[11] J.-P. Sartre, "L'imaginaire," *Psychologie phénoménologique de l'imagination* (Paris, 1940), p. 34.

object that does not necessarily exist in time and space.

Why do we have imagination? Sartre tackles a problem which philosophers of old found puzzling and mysterious. Duns Scotus could not forgive Thomas Aquinas for his patent concern for essence and his neglect for the *haecceitas* of the individual. Yet Aquinas' originality of thought insists on considering the existent, more than the Aristotelian essence, as the object of human knowledge. Sartre is aware of the same difficulty. The mental concept concerns itself with the essence. But man is not happy with his conceptual knowledge. When I think of my friend Pierre, Sartre argues, who went to Berlin, I do not mummify him into a dreadful concept. I desire to have him present in my imagination, whose very life feeds on individual details. I see the features of his face; I represent to myself the suit which he wears; I imagine him sitting at a table in a sidewalk café in Berlin, drinking dark beer. My imagination is so vivid that my eyes turn to him, and I almost talk to him as if he were present. Husserl had absorbed imagination into the intentional act of knowing. Sartre gives imagination its own intentionality.

Indeed, the demand for reality, for existing living reality, this demand that is always present in Sartre's life and that makes him a restless traveler without any definite place to go, is the key to his doctrine on imagination. How else could one explain his desire for literary excellence in his youth or, later on, for leadership in his newly envisioned utopian society? "If we start from abstract thinking, we see the image to be born as an attempt of the mind to come in contact with what is present."[12]

Once the relevance of imagination in Sartre's thought is established, we must try to understand his original explanation of the "mechanics" of imagination. The phenomenological method allows Sartre to lay down two principles: (*a*) imagination takes its impetus from physical reactions, and (*b*) develops under the influence of affective motivations.

The first activity of the imagination depends on the movement of the eyes and subsequent to the movement of the eyes comes the obedience of the body. This total process can be called an awareness of the elements "space" and "time." The physical presence of my body moving in space and time gives me a primordial acquaintance with what I am and with what I can become. It places me in contact with other physical realities. It gives my mind the opportunity to project itself to other objects, ideal and imaginary, but similar to those existing in reality. In other words, it gives me the knowledge of a make-believe world where imagination finds itself at home.

---

[12] J.-P. Sartre, *op. cit.*, p. 91.

But the force behind, explaining the phenomenon of imagining, resides in the motivation, which is always an act of love or desire or hatred; in one word, an emotional sentiment.

For Sartre emotions are not solipsistic phenomena as Marcel Proust, entangled in the web of his psychological analyses, liked to believe; nor are emotions the effect of physiological malfunctioning, as William James — victim of his medical theories — tried to explain them. This great American used to say: "Take away the physiological aspects of anger and you remain with nothing!" Sartre answered: "Take away the person or the situation created by persons that make you angry and your effort to be angry will be unsuccessful."[13]

In other chapters Sartre refutes previous theories of emotion. The James-Janst theory considers human emotions as peripheral and corporeal manifestations, with the result that one emotion cannot be distinguished from the other. The Gestalt theory of Lewin and Demko has the merit of describing the transition of one emotional form to the other; but, again, consciousness is forgotten as the center and the origin of all emotional forms. Freud and Adler deserve respect for their psychoanalytic insights into the nature of emotions, but they justify a fracture between consciousness and subconsciousness: their work is incomplete.

Finally, Sartre offers his solution. The nature of emotion consists in the reaction of human consciousness to the means of success or failure that man encounters in the world. For the understanding of the future development of this thought, it is of interest to note that Sartre underlined here the fact that difficulties and obstacles do not strengthen man; they break him to the point of indifference and dejection. Thus man closes up in the shell of his own self, in the presence of tribulations, as it is evident in too many cases of mental illnesses. If we keep in mind the fact that his major work, L'être et le néant, was written at the same time (1939), we may understand Sartre's basic conception of man. Man is a sick animal, born to be a loser, with emotions that essentially are more powerful than he is. This affective motivation, which expresses for Sartre the totality of the existential aspects of man, guides consciousness in focusing its interest on detailed qualities more than on essential generalizations. Therefore he states that "joy, anxiety and melancholy are acts of consciousness."[14]

---

[13] Sartre published a brief essay on emotions in 1939. The title is Esquisse d'une théorie des émotions (Paris: Herman). In this modest work, Sartre speaks of emotions from Husserl's and Heidegger's point of view. Therefore the psychological method is attacked by Sartre as inept and unscientific. It requires an enormous collection of experiments condemned to remain useless because "man" is neglected as the center and the support of all experimentations concerning human behavior.

[14] Esquisse . . . , p. 93.

But we must take a position on this matter against Sartre, as well as against Brentano, Husserl, and Scheler. They are guided by Brentano's axiom (which constitutes a major dogma for the whole school of phenomenology) that "when I know I must also have consciousness of my knowing." The Cartesian overtones of this doctrine do not need any explanation. Rationalism did not understand the metaphysical nature of man. Rationalism confined man to one abstract characteristic, his consciousness, in which all human manifestations are supposed to find their explanation. For example, if I deny that a red rose is a thing and I reduce it to its "redness" and through this quality explain all its other qualities (above all, that the red rose is an existing thing), then I accept the same rationalistic principle that works through the whole phenomenological movement. Sartre bears the scars of these naturalistic conclusions. He cannot conceive the possibility that man is given the privilege of refusing to know, or of knowing partially with little consciousness or with no consciousness at all, as happens in our sense knowledge or on subconscious and unconscious levels. Thus he is forced to accept a final conclusion which is in open contradiction to everyday experience; that is to say, that emotional sentiments give an *objective* meaning to the things of this world. We are not surprised to learn from Sartre that Stendhal and D. H. Lawrence are outstanding examples of objective writing, though we think that objectivity was never for a moment the goal of Stendhal's and Lawrence's literary work. The first literary production of Sartre, for instance, his collection of short novellas entitled *The Wall,* is a clear instance of this theory on imagination. The style is brutal and violent. The situations described are realistic and shocking. The sequences of artistic images aim to color reality with a taste of human and physical immediacy.

The root of this Sartrean situation is always the same. He attributes to each act of knowing an immediate consciousness, a consciousness that does not reflect on the knowledge of an object taken as the basis and the reason for which knowledge becomes conscious. Sartre is always the avowed enemy of metaphysics. Consciousness for Sartre springs from consciousness alone, not from knowledge of something which is the object of consciousness. But consciousness without an object is an empty formal category. It demands its explanation from nothing, not from being; that is to say, the unconscious is expected to explain the conscious. Sartre seems to fall into the same error for which he often scored Freud.

This desperate attempt to discuss the philosophical meaning of imagination without accepting its metaphysical backbone brings Sartre to embarrassing conclusions. For instance, the maniac and the schizophrenic should be conscious of the inconsistency of their pathologicaďy obsessive imaginations. Dreams would be despoiled of their beautiful inconsistency because consciousness would reveal them as inconsistent. Sartre recognizes the seriousness of these objections. He confesses[15] that somehow consciousness becomes the victim of itself both in the case of schizophrenic obsessions and in the case of dreams. Before he denied man the possibility of unconscious actions; now he is compelled to recognize unconsciousness as an expression of consciousness itself.

In fairness to Sartre, we must take note of his doubts about this *theory of imagination* as set out in the two works which we analyze here. He admits that he could not apply a strict phenomenological method and therefore that his conclusions are only tentative and probable. But we cannot recognize a contradictory probability as probable. And we will be able to show that the same principles are accepted and defended in his major work, *L'être et le néant*.

4. BEING AND NOTHINGNESS

In September, 1939, Sartre was drafted. The enemy had violated the frontiers of France. He lived shoulder to shoulder with farmers and workers, and he learned the value of the spoken word and he understood the presence of others in all its vitality. In June, 1940, Sartre was a prisoner of the Germans, but he escaped to France in the spring of 1941 and then lived with and worked for the forces of the "Résistance." His major work, *Being and Nothingness,* which was published in 1943, was written in 1939. *L'être et le néant* (*Being and Nothingness*) is a highly technical work, written in stringent obedience to the principles which govern his whole system of thought. Indeed we deal here with a systematic philosophy unique among existential philosophies. *L'être et le néant* is not a detached impersonal work reminiscent of the medieval *Summa.* One feels the passion and the presence of the author on each page. The problems discussed and the purpose and the method of discussion are close to each individual's life and establish a new "rapprochement" of existentialism to the traditional French philosophy of life as found in Marcel, Lavelle, and Le Senne.

Of the rigid principles mentioned above, the most basic is that each existing being (*being in itself*) just is: it is atemporal, absurd, opaque, massive, uncreated, without a reason explaining its existence, without the capacity for any relation with other beings.[16] Sartre calls it "being in

---

[15] Cf. *Ibid.*, pp. 193 ff. and 21 ff.

[16] J.-P. Sartre, *L'être et le néant, Essai d'ontologie phénoménologigne* (Paris: Gallimard, 1943), p. 29 [English tr., *Being and Nothingness* (New York: Citadel Press, 1964)].

itself." This Parmenidean ontology poses a question: How in such a rigid deterministic universe could a free and knowing being like man ever exist? Sartre answers: There is in the universe another type of being, namely "being *for* itself," or human consciousness. But since we know that every thing which exists must be a "being *in* itself," it is logical to conclude that the second type of being "being *for* itself" must be non-being and therefore it must consist in nothing. Therefore man, as consciousness, is nothing.

These are the "key principles" of the philosophy of Sartre. His "Herculean labor" now is to demonstrate logically that man, living and conscious, is nothing.[17] He proceeds as follows: "being for itself," i.e., consciousness, consists in a negative presence; namely, it is a revelation of being, aspiration for being, but not actually being in itself. The nature of consciousness is, to use an expression dear to Aristotle, *pròs ti*, "toward something else." Therefore consciousness, as far as its own being is concerned, *is nothing* because it consists in going out of itself by the act of knowing and beyond itself by the act of willing. It is therefore based not only on the refusal to identify itself with other beings but also on the refusal to identify itself with itself, because its nature is not *to be*, but to overcome itself toward future possibilities. Perhaps at this point it is clear that Sartre completes a famous formula of Heidegger: "Consciousness is that being that causes the raising of the problem of being in its own being, since its own being demands the presence of a being different from itself."[18]

This *nothing* of which consciousness consists is not just a grammatical expression, it is ontologically real, born of man and contradictory to being in itself.[19] Being by which nothing comes into the world is nothing of itself.

We all know, Sartre says, that the result of our own existence as

---

[17] Actually this split between "being in itself" and "being for itself" becomes incurable because Sartre *makes* both of them *absolute* beings. No explanation is offered by Sartre. This doctrine is postulated as a first, self-evident principle. He knows that God as creator would restore the unity of the universe by giving intelligibility from the beginning to all created beings. Unhappily Sartre excludes creation, directing against this doctrine infantile sophisms. For instance, created things, according to Sartre, could not be separated from God or, if separated, would be an obstacle to God's infinity. This is equivalent to saying that if God did exist, He could only be God and He could not be consciousness because consciousness requires "another" different from itself.

[18] Sartre, *op. cit.*, p. 29.

[19] This genesis of "being for itself" or consciousness is not demonstrated by Sartre. He states the contingency of the two aspects of being "for itself and in itself." He also states the impossibility of their synthesis either into a third term (God), or in either one of the two themselves (materialistic or idealistic solution).

consciousness is dread and anxiety. "I make a date with myself for the end of this hour, this day or this month. My dread originates from the fear that I will not be there for this date; furthermore my dread comes from the fact that I do not plan to be there."[20]

Freedom is a continuous projection of new goals: we want to be engineers, poets; we want to build a house. Freedom, therefore, consists in something which as yet is not and which, once achieved, is not free anymore. Freedom is the cause and motivation of our actions, yet in itself freedom is without foundations. We try to escape from the dread caused by freedom in many childish ways. For instance, we speak of the obligations we have to keep up with the standard of living of our neighbor (as if we did not accept that standard freely), we justify our actions as the result of our previous lives (which we are free to forget), we conceive our goals as objectively valid (and we forget that these goals are given a value only by our free action that acknowledges them). This pretending is called by Sartre, sarcastically, *l'esprit de serieux* (putting on an air of seriousness): we pretend to be free from dread by using the above-mentioned pretenses. Actually we are not free; we just act knowingly in bad faith.[21]

Bad faith is an awful, self-inflicted humiliation. Is there any other way out? Sartre's answer is "no," because man is not what he is but he is what he is not. My past is not mine anymore, my future is not yet mine. I am checkmated. "Bad faith is possible only because sincerity is conscious that its goal is beyond reach."[22] The human dream is therefore to fulfill a perfect communication of one's "being-for-itself" with his "being-in-itself." That is, it means that we are to be a permanent consciousness. Again man is checkmated, because freedom aims for values which do not exist insofar as they depend on freedom itself, which cannot exist.

This gloomy atmosphere pervades the subsequent analysis that Sartre applies to all the fundamental philosophical problems: (1) time, (2) the special existence of human persons and the existence of a material world; and (3) human reactions to the cosmos.

1. *Time.* Heidegger had shown (and Sartre agrees) that time is not a casual dimension of the existent. Time is the rhythm of consciousness

---

[20] *Ibid.,* p. 73.

[21] The presence of Kierkegaard, perhaps diluted through Heidegger, is evident here. For Kierkegaard, too, dread and despair are unavoidable. The man who considers himself immune from despair represents almost a hopeless case of despair. But Kierkegaard considers despair a necessary step to salvation. The same type of reasoning is meaningless for Sartre, who does not recognize salvation.

[22] *L'être et le néant,* pp. 106–107.

inasmuch as any event is past or present only because of consciousness.[23] What is the past? "The past is the totality, an always increasing totality of being in itself, which constitutes our existence."[24] Man is, as we know, being-for-itself; yet man possesses material factors and corporeal elements which are *in* themselves, just as cosmic nature is in itself. Hence a conflict: man is primarily consciousness, i.e., being-for-itself. To retain his being-in-itself, man is bound to make a continuous effort. If I say: "I am a teacher and my determination is to remain a teacher," I accept the challenge of behaving as a teacher in continuity and against my conscious being which is in perpetual movement of fluidity. By an effort I retain "my being a teacher" against the widening tide of my consciousness. My past is therefore "that which makes me be a teacher, not a diplomat or a sailor, though I cannot do more than just recite this 'being a teacher' without ever reaching this being in itself a teacher."[25] If this value, "being a teacher," could reach a complete realization, then the human aspect of being alive as consciousness *per se* would change into an inert and obtuse being in itself. Man would not live in tension; time would be exhausted; death would have come to man. All values, therefore, which are the motivation of human actions, are inconceivable without time, just as time is inconceivable without the human mind. Furthermore, just as time cannot be exhausted, so all values cannot, by their own definition, be fulfilled. The future never becomes present; it remains a dream and as a dream slips inexorably toward the past. "How wonderful was the Republic under the Empire!"[26] said those Frenchmen who had not found in the republic what they had dreamed of!

The present is a dissipation and an alienation of man into the things of the world. This alienation causes boredom and then sudden awakening as soon as man becomes conscious of his freedom which demands new adventures. And man is in a continuous flight, from thing to thing, always haunted by the fear of being swallowed by the enormous impersonal massive being of the cosmos. Man must run from his present because he hopes to find in the future his own salvation; he hopes to find for himself a status which is simultaneously consciousness and being. Death catches up with man in his anxious search, and with death the "in-itself" celebrates its sterile victory over "for-itself." But Sartre is not the first one who had to pay for his unwarranted denial of the natures and essences of things — he is not the first who was forced to come

---

[23] Aristotle, Augustine, and Aquinas (and possibly Heraclitus himself) had acknowledged the same doctrine, though they arrived at it from altogether different premises.

[24] *L'être et le néant*, p. 159.

[25] *Ibid.*, p. 163.

[26] *Ibid.*, p. 173.

to an irresponsible nihilism, with the final result that all forms of thinking, including his own philosophy, cannot claim any existence.

To save himself and his work as a philosopher, he admits a "pure"
philosophical reflection, wholly unacceptable by his system. This reflection, against all the rules proclaimed by Sartre, is called "pure"
because it understands itself, thus saving the possibility of philosophy,
without going out of itself.

2. *The special existence of human persons and the material universe.*
Another difficult problem takes up many pages of *L'être et le néant*: the
existence of many human beings and therefore of many manifestations
of consciousness, as well as the existence of a material world in which
these consciousnesses are manifested. We agree with Sartre when he says
that little progress has been made in philosophy concerning the plurality
of consciousness. The progressive loss of the concept of the human
person is responsible for that. Since the beginning of the modern age,
when metaphysics started to be considered a relic from superstitious
times, down to the Hegelian glorification of the power of human thinking, conceived as transcendental, the main problem for most philosophers
happened to be the incommunicable individuality of man.

Sartre notices with some amount of satisfaction the embarrassment of
the positivists in discussing this problem. They admit that experimentation (their magic word for their new method in philosophy) does not
justify the existence of "other" persons. They are forced to speak of
"other" persons simply as the results of an analogy of behavior (experimentally undemonstrable) which is *before* and *above* all experience.
Therefore positivism accepts an idealistic principle, namely, that some
type of knowledge is not experiential, that is, it comes *before* experience
and is "above" and "beyond" experience. Idealism is in the same
quandary: it reduces all knowledge to the contents of consciousness.
As a result, idealism logically leads to a dilemma: either solipsism or the
acceptance of the factual existence of many consciousnesses. This, of
course, amounts to an agreement with positivistic premises.

Sartre is convinced that the best explanation for the existence of the
"other" as consciousness is to be found in Hegel's *Phenomenology of
the Mind:* Hegel speaks of the dialectical rapport between servant and
master. "The other" is the medium that makes me conscious of my own
identity. I could never be an object to myself, if "the other" did not
reflect to me the image I am for him. Thus I am consciousness to myself
and I am an object for others because they see me as an object. I am
able to represent to myself their experience and consider myself as an

object. If I am not a strong man, I will succumb to the anonymity of objectivity. I must fight and risk my life, assert myself as a person who is superior to the others. The latter will resign themselves to be servants tied to circumstances. They must recognize my superiority.

Sartre accepts this dialectical scheme, responsible though it is for the sad theory that demands diffidence and conflict as the basis of the relations existing among human beings. His remarkable development of this Hegelian doctrine focuses on the analysis of mutual surveillance exercised by each man on other men. "It is because of my being an object to others that I come to acknowledge my being a subject."[27] Sartre calls this daily experience "look." It consists in being looked upon, being observed and known. In this situation the world itself that surrounds us appears more organized by "the look" of others than by our own understanding. Paradoxically "the other" seems to be the subject and we become objects. As objects we are judged and defined. We feel pride or shame; our actions are considered bad or good depending on the "look" of others. Fear and shame, pride and resoluteness are made possible in my life because others watch my actions. Their careful eye on me provokes my resentful reaction which is the first step in my realization that I am truly a subject. According to Sartre this reciprocal objectification imposed from the outside upon a person by his fellow-man represents one of the most cruel aspects of this game of human existence.

Each one of us feels free inside. Our actions, present or past, do not constitute a menace to our freedom. The threat to our freedom comes from the outside, from the people around us whose effort is to freeze our own self in the exterior appearances of an object. Yet, my physical body, though always surpassed by my freedom, is necessary if a world is to exist. Nothing, as we saw, justifies the contingent fact that I exist, that I am here or there, under these or those circumstances. But if I exist, I must exist in one of these situations. If my freedom consists in overcoming and denying those situations, I must live under one of them. My body is "the contingent form that represents the necessity of my contingency."[28] My body is my birth, my past, my race, my social class, my nationality, my physiological structure. But my body is not I, neither is it an instrument for my freedom.[29] I am simply I, with my freedom chained by my somatic conditions. The body represents a necessary

---

[27] *Ibid.*, p. 314.

[28] *Ibid.*, p. 389.

[29] Notice how the main theme of a monolithic Parmenidean conception of being articulates the whole philosophy of Sartre. He ignores completely the Aristotelian principles of act and potency, which allowed Thomas Aquinas to speak of a substantial union between body and soul.

obstacle for my freedom to overcome. Thus the pains of sickness, the
limitations of my physical state are situations which my consciousness
accepts as instrumental for exercising my freedom. A prisoner undergoing unbearable tortures must decide for himself when the tortures are
really unbearable.

Sartre rejects the usual interpretation of the human body that
positivism has accepted from the empiricist tradition. According to the
traditional teaching of empiricists, the body is a physical object among
physical objects. This vision is useful to the anatomist or the chemist,
but the philosopher cannot agree because he cannot understand how
the body, as a physical object, is linked to the expression of freedom
and free enterprise. The philosopher cannot transfer the experimentation, performed on a corpse by means of instruments and theories, to
his own living body. For instance, the sensation I feel or the action I
perform is totally different from a sensation or an action performed by
another person. I am present with immediateness to the thing I know,
I inject myself with immediateness into the world of things with which
I come in contact. "My body always extends itself to the instrument
which it uses. My body is on the tip of the cane that helps me to stand,
my body is on the lenses of the binoculars in contemplating the stars,
my body is on the chair, in the entire home, because it is I who adapt
myself to these instruments."[30]

This marvelous analysis remains unfortunately isolated and without
a meaning for Sartre because of his lack of a constructive metaphysics.

3. *Human society.* Similarly Sartre defends a fragmentary philosophy
concerning human society. He states that Heidegger is wrong when he
asserts, in *Sein und Zeit,* the existence of a primordial sentiment of
Mitsein — "to be together in the world." Each consciousness is individual
and personal. The only consciousness of a collective "we" is a reflection
of a process of identification imposed upon us by a third person. For
instance, class consciousness is forced upon us by those who do not belong to the class. The very concept of humanity is an empty term, because it presupposes a person superior to mankind, an absolute, a God,
that God inexorably denied by Sartre, despite the necessity of His
presence so persistently felt in his writings. Therefore "the essence of
all relations among persons is not the '*Mitsein,*' but conflict."[31] This is
an evident conclusion if we think with Sartre that it is *impossible* for
us to exist as subjects related to subjects. We must conceive the other

[30] *Ibid.,* p. 389.
[31] *Ibid.,* p. 502.

as object if we are subjects, or, vice versa, we are objects if the other person is subject.[32] This thesis takes on meaning and importance when it is applied to human psychology.

Love is the impossible effort to possess the other person, not as an object, but as a free subject. But how can the beloved, if he or she is a free person, be bound and tied once forever? From Lucretius to Schopenhauer to Proust this puzzling, paradoxical nature of love has never found a solution. Sartre has the answer: the solution is impossible. On one side love is an attempt to objectivize the beloved so that his or her features, character, and past life are an object to us of perennial confidence and fidelity. On the other side, the beloved rebels against being an object without freedom and choice. The many instances of failure in love are well-known proofs of this fact.

The awareness of this contradictory nature of love explains the meaning of *seduction*. It is a revolting decision to renounce one's dignity as a subject with the intent of luring a human being into an imprudent adoration of physical values, i.e., the human body, money, etc. — the victim is helpless, the rigidity of the object overcomes freedom of the spirit. This process reaches more turbulent consequences with *sexuality*. Sexuality is a physiological disposition; furthermore, for Sartre, sexuality is an ontological phenomenon, an irresistible inclination toward others rooted in our own consciousness. In the sexual act consciousness sacrifices its freedom to an irrational desire for identification with flesh. In the sexual act consciousness is not only a longing to be flesh but also a making another person flesh alone, thereby depriving that person of his free expressions and actions. But the final frustrating irony is that consciousness cannot be flesh because sexual pleasure requires consciousness.

In Sartre's analysis the guilt complex springs from man's tragic awareness of his hopeless ineptitude at establishing a personal relation with another. Again man is checkmated. The way out presents a dilemma: either you love to be checkmated and desire the pleasure of it repeatedly — in other words, you are a victim of *vice;* or you hate it and try to destroy the unreachable other person, and in so doing you become a victim of *hatred.*

We have given some of the most significant conclusions reached by Sartre. A sad picture, indeed, deduced by his acute insight from premises which we are forced to consider erroneous. The most basic of these is

---

[32] This impossibility is again difficult to understand. Sartre wrote biographies of Baudelaire and Genet and his intention was to approach them historically as "subjects." Trying to present each of them as "a totality in his enthusiastic impetus toward being, . . . in his original relation to himself, to the other in the unity of his *inside* relations."

Sartre's misunderstanding of human nature. His prejudice against natures and essences, inherited, as we explained, from the idealism of Brunschvig, prevents him from accepting the axiomatic truth that *consciousness is an act of a substance.* The agony of Sartre's philosophy has to be reduced, after all, to the idealistic sophism that *doing is, absolutely speaking, before being* — that actions are prior to substance and do not depend on them.

Thus, if consciousness is not some kind of reality belonging to a substantial being, it is not consciousness at all; it would not belong to a given situation, it would not exist. On the other hand, if a person is responsible for the act of consciousness, we are able to explain the existence of other human beings as subjects, because we acknowledge in them the same human nature (object), but we respect them as persons (subject). If nature is denied, the existent must assume the characteristic feature proper only to natures: in our case, consciousness becomes an object.

Man cannot conceive freedom if it does not originate from being; hence we can see the rest of the contraditions of Sartre's philosophy. He forces man to be free by a continuous effort to overcome himself. He does not conceive freedom as a result of a deliberating act of the will. Rather, for Sartre, freedom precedes and conditions the act of the will. Such a freedom is not free at all, it is an absurd destiny: Sartre draws the logical conclusion: dread and despair are the lot of man.[33]

Death itself is not the answer to human life. Death is not a peaceful drifting into unconsciousness. "Christians have tried to conceive death as the final step to peace. Father R. Boisselot, in a private conversation, tried to make me believe that 'the Final Judgment' was supposed to be this step to peace. . . ."[34] Sartre does not understand this language. For him death comes to interrupt, not to fulfill, life. He confesses that he does not have an answer. The only thing he knows is that death terminates all our possibilities. But he immediately adds that man, considered previous to death, in his projection of what his being should be, is an impossibility. Man wants to be, to know, to have. Arts, sciences, work, games are some human attempts to reach the joy of possessing being. But man does not realize that his passionate desire for being brings him further and further away from being. "Every man is a passion in as much as he attempts to justify the beginning of his own existence and to constitute the self as a self-existent being (*ens causa sui*), called by religious people, God. Thus the passion of man compared to the passion of Christ is reversed, for according to Christ man hopes to lose

---

[33] *L'être et le néant*, p. 542.
[34] *Ibid.*, p. 622.

himself so that God will be born. But the idea of God is contradictory; therefore, we lose ourselves in vain. Man is a useless passion."[35]

5. *LE DIABLE ET LE BON DIEU* (THE DEVIL AND THE GOOD LORD)

In 1944 Sartre, his soul filled with disillusion, abandoned his teaching to give himself completely to literature. He prepared four novels dealing with the French Resistance against the Germans.[36] He found the theater rewarding and inspiring because dialogue represents even more dramatically than fiction the reciprocal misunderstanding of human beings and the impossibility of the human project. From *Les mouches* (*The Flies*), a classical reworking of the Greek myth of Orestes, to *Les sequestrés d'Altona* (*The Condemned of Altona*),[37] Sartre continues to be the prosecutor of all those who accept absolute values. His themes are well known: good will conceives bad faith, philanthropy is a disguised form of hatred, freedom is a compulsion to reach a nonexisting goal.

Le diable et le bon Dieu[38] is a drama of transparent philosophical meaning. It deals with a renewal of times of rebellions in the Rhineland in the sixteenth century. A sacrilegious challenge turns into a declaration of atheism. The town of Wurms is in open rebellion against its bishop. Goetz, the cruel chieftain, has seized the town with his soldiers at the orders of the bishop. Within the walls of Wurms, one single priest, Heinrich, loved by the people for his charity and understanding, stands up for his fellow priests who are threatened with death by the people. Heinrich, who has the key to a secret tunnel leading to Goetz, faces a cruel dilemma: if he gives the key to Goetz, the people of Wurms will die; if he doesn't, the priests of Wurms will die. No matter what he chooses he is guilty.

A dramatic confrontation follows in the tent of Goetz. Goetz and Heinrich measure the the depth of their own perfidiousness and both come to a conclusion: evil is inevitable. But Goetz rebels, challenges God. Although evil must be done, he will do good. His troops are ordered to abandon the seige of Wurms; he distributes his wealth to

---

[35] *Ibid.*, p. 708.

[36] Three of them have been published: *L'age de la raison* (*The Age of Reason*), *Le sursis* (*The Spoiled*), *La mort dans l'âme* (*The Death of the Soul*).

[37] In order: *Le mouches* (*The Flies*), *Les mains sales* (*Dirty Hands*), *Huis clos* (*No Exit*), *Mors sans sépulture* (*Death Without Burial*), *La putain respecteuse* (*The Respectable Prostitute*), *Le diable et le bon Dieu* (*The Devil and the Good Lord*), *Kean* (an adaptation of the anonymous work by A. Dumas) *Nekrassov*, *Les sequestrés d'Altona* (*The Condemned of Altona*).

[38] Sartre, *Le diable et le bon Dieu* (Paris: Gallimard, 1951).

the poor, and he begins a life of Franciscan poverty and love. But he cannot keep the young lady who had been his mistress for years from committing suicide, nor can he stop the people whom he has helped so generously from fratricidal slaughter. Indeed his life of Christian love and charity has yielded some interesting results! Goetz now knows better: good and evil are indistinguishable because they demand the existence of an absolute point of reference, God. And God does not exist. Goetz bursts into furious laughter when he meets Heinrich, who is eager to know about his spiritual experience. Finally there comes the famous declaration on Goetz's part of his new faith. Goetz shouts to the horrified Heinrich: "God doesn't see me, God doesn't listen to me, God doesn't know me. Do you see this empty space above our heads? It is God. Do you see this hole in the ground? It is God. God is silence. God is absence. God is solitude for man. It is I that exist. I alone have decided what is Evil. I have invented what is Good. If God exists, man is nothing. If man exists. . . . Where are you running?"[39] Heinrich runs from the blasphemies of Goetz; for him hell is better than nothing. But Goetz has lost control of himself and kills Heinrich, thus reaching the final formulation of his new philosophy: "Now the kingdom of man begins:"[40] a kingdom of murder, terror, and violence.

Sartre is a master of style; he is a professional with all the skills of the modern storyteller. Dialectical overturns of psychological situations and violent representations offer partial explanations of the enormous literary success of Sartre among the European conservative bourgeois. Paradoxically, the nihilism of Sartre is a philosophy well tailored for conservativism: for both action and progress are meaningless. The extremism of his conclusions scared Sartre himself. He wrote *L'existentialisme est un humanisme,*[41] a mild attempt to prove that man can reach serenity and meaning in his life if he frees himself from religious preoccupations, from the fear of a transcendent God. But these statements (openly contradicting the theme of *L'être et le néant* that a human society is impossible without God) are isolated and inconclusive. *L'être et le néant* with its existential conclusions remains the main philosophical message delivered by Jean-Paul Sartre to his fellowmen.

6. SARTRE AND COMMUNISM

I. *Communism: Appealing Yet Disturbing*

At the end of World War II, Sartre was the intellectual leader of

[39] *Ibid.,* p. 267.
[40] *Ibid.,* p. 282.
[41] J.-P. Sartre, *L'existentialism est un humanisme* (Paris: Nagel, 1947).

France. His works were read by millions and his plays were the rage of Parisian theaters. *Le Combat* (Camus' paper) and *Le Figaro* published, in 1945, a brilliant report from Sartre who was then in the United States,[42] where he was elected a member of the Academy of Arts and Sciences. But such fame and adulation left Sartre restless and closer to failure than success. France needed a new brand of peace, different from the selfish pacifism of the 1930's. The nation was in danger of reliving the sad experience of revolution after revolution, just as it did in the nineteenth century when despots, in humanitarian disguise, ruled.[43] Sartre resented the paralyzing impact of his own philosophy. His countrymen expected leadership from him, and he gave them abstruse lucubrations on the absurdity of existence. His desire might explain a decision otherwise hard to understand in the life of Sartre. He accepted the French Communist Party,[44] even though he could not accept the party line. "If I am asked as a writer to offer my services to the party, the answer is 'no.' Stalinism is incompatible with an honest interpretation of the literary profession."[45] Sartre was convinced that communism was in practice authoritarian, high-handed, and afraid to accept its own dialectical nature.

Moreover, Sartre was convinced that the individual in contemporary Europe needed a class pattern to reach social goals. The European bourgeoisie is dead. The proletariat is the new class, rich by reason of its vital ideology; ready to use revolution as a tool to overcome by dialectic the stagnant indifference of a capitalistic society. The tragedy is that the proletariat is imprisoned by the Communist Party. Sartre saw the need of dialogue with the party even before the death of Stalin

---

[42] One of his articles published in *Le Figaro,* February, 1945, offers brilliant comparisons between Europe and the United States of America. For Europe, according to Sartre, the basic factor is a deeply rooted individualism moving toward social ideologies. For the United States the opposite is true: a general conformism is the basic characteristic from which the individual tries to escape by reaching personal success. But is this success personal? Sartre sees it as a higher expression of a social function.

The journey through the United States offered Sartre the opportunity to stage his drama, *The Respectable Prostitute,* in the South. The theme is the lynching c' a colored man.

[43] Cf. *La Republique Française* (New York, 1945), an article reprinted in *Situa-tions III* (Paris: Gallimard, 1949), pp. 60–61.

[44] This crisis in the life of Sartre, common to many European intellectuals, is portrayed by his lifelong companion, Simone de Beauvoir, in a novel of some success, *Les Mandarins* (Paris: Gallimard, 1954). Simone de Beauvoir is also the author of *Le deuxième sexe* (*The Second Sex*) and *Morale de l'ambiguité* (*Morality of Ambiguity*). In the first of these two works she develops future perspectives for the contemporary woman in an existential society. The second volume is an attempt to derive a code of ethics from the philosophy of Sartre.

[45] Sartre, *Situations, II,* p. 280.

and the Hungarian revolt made others aware of the same need. In 1946, in a long article in his magazine *Les temps modernes*,[46] Sartre accused the hierarchy of the Communist Party of preventing a free rethinking of Marx's principles. Lack of intelligent criticism had made of Marxism an unreal abstraction that was ruthlessly and indifferently imposed on dissimilar historical and individual situations. Materialism is possible only if matter is conceived as the basic element on which a free agent is working, i.e., a dialectical project by virtue of which freedom celebrates its victory.

Marx, because of Hegel, understood materialism dialectically. Engels injected the spurious concept of matter as a substance physically defined. This concept, borrowed from positivism, responds to an hypothesis of some value for practical laboratory research, but it fails to interpret reality[47] and is against all revolutionary tenets because it considers history as a deterministic fatality.

The great task is, Sartre holds, to present these lofty philosophical ideas to the masses. Sartre accepts the challenge and develops one of his better known theories on the high mission of the man of letters.[48] Sartre's problem can be formulated as follows: What is writing? What is the purpose of writing? For whom is writing intended? The answer to these questions can be considered as the creed of the so-called *engagé* literature.

Sartre ignores the most recent linguistic theories; he ignores Heidegger's contributions and states that prose is a nature in itself, distinct from poetry, music and painting. These latter forms of art strive to create a mental image which has a meaning in itself as a re-creation in the world of art of the real cosmic world. Prose is different inasmuch as it reveals the world without recreating it aesthetically. This revelation influences the reader, it guides his actions, it creates new human moral situations. Could you mentally separate Flaubert from the French bourgeoisie? If you read the American Negro, Wright, you will find yourself in the Negro ghettos of New York or in the segregated wooden huts of the South. Therefore the writer is situated and engaged (*engagé*). In fictional writing the freedom of the author tends to awaken the freedom

---

[46] The article is also printed in *Matérialisme et révolution*, pp. 135–225 of *Situations III*.

[47] Sartre says that science is a synthesis in its goals and intentions even if its method is analytic. Science aims to unify what is known with what is still unknown. Positivism holds that analytic scientific research also explains human synthetic intentions. Cf. Sartre, *Critique de la raison dialectique*, p. 150.

[48] Sartre's ideas on this topic are contained in a series of articles published in *Les temps modernes* and later, in 1948, collected under the title *Situations II*. The volume *Situations I*, 1947, is a collection of essays on Faulkner, Nabokov, Camus, etc. *Situations III* deals with sociological problems.

of the reader with the intention of arousing interest in a particular vision of the world. It could be argued that these ideas are unfaithful to the fundamental principles of *Being and Nothingness*. There we learned that the encounter of two freedoms was doomed to certain checkmated conditions by the very nature of man. Now we learn that the writer needs a direct rapport with a homogeneous group of readers if he wants to *succeed*.

Success is a rare word in the books of Sartre. His search for readers cannot be too easy. The friars of the Middle Ages, the artists of the Renaissance, the men of letters of the eighteenth and nineteenth centuries found their own audiences, but the writer of the twentieth century is again checkmated. He comes from the tired empty climate of the bourgeoisie, one that does not have enough strength to listen or enough energy to care. On the other hand, he would like to talk to the masses who do not have enough education to understand. Again Sartre is in a quandary: Should he, through the modern mass media of communication, be the gravedigger of his own middle class or its agitator. After all, *Being and Nothingness*, as we can see here, is still valid: man is a useless passion.[49]

II. *Critique of Dialectical Reason*[50]

Postwar interest in political problems and flirtation (ambiguous and inquisitive) with Marx's theories gave Sartre a chance to join his philosophical thought to the pressing needs of our society. The enormous volume *Critique de la raison dialectique* attempts the synthesis. Actually it is the testimony of a great mind, conscious of many goals and troubled by an increasing awareness of its inability to reach them. The *Critique* begins with an article on "Existentialism and Marxism," written in 1957 for a Polish magazine. For the first time in Sartre's writings the concept of *totalization* appears as an overture to a consideration of all the aspects of an event: conditions, motives, temporal and ambiental relations.

---

[49] This tantalizing uncertainty shakes both the philosophy and the life of Sartre. Compare these two paragraphs: "We cannot rest peacefully on the lap of our social class and since it is not possible to find an easy way out, pretending to accept the stigma of belonging to a parasitic aristocracy, we must be its grave-diggers, even if we run the risk of burying ourselves" (*Situations II*, p. 276).

But Sartre confesses in the *Critique de la raison dialectique*, p. 741: "The Proletariat (very poorly understood by Marx and the Marxists) offers a fascination to the intellectuals of the petit bourgeoisie. This fascination cannot be explained by material, individualistic interests, but by the fact that the universal is the interest of every intellectual and this universal is present, at least potentially if not actually, in the working class."

[50] J.-P. Sartre, *Critique de la raison dialectique*, T. I. *Théorie des ensembles practiques* (Paris: Gallimard, 1960).

Totalization is dialectical (as Hegel and Marx have said), but if distinction is conceived as conscious opposition, a third moment is foreseen in which the opposition is overcome. For instance, the power struggle between two political parties gives rise to a reciprocal understanding opening the gates to a third party. Totalization is not a useless abstraction: each person contributes with his work, research, and studies to making of this process of totalization.[51] Therefore totalization is such only when it is actual;[52] once it is fulfilled it becomes a dead scheme like all philosophies whose goal was a static interpretation of ontological reality. Their main contribution to human civilization is, according to Sartre, intellectual sterility. They are the antidialectical forces damaging the march of the dialectic from the inside. If philosophy is totalization, interest for the universal (the influence of Brunschvig is quite evident in this moment of Sartre's philosophy), Marxism in the twentieth century is the only philosophy with rights of its own, because Marxism explains and interprets, with a universality of horizons, contemporary history.

Marx is the prophet of our times because he has modified Hegel by stressing the importance of *alienation* — the fact that the free enterprise of man alienates itself into the object of work. For instance, machines, as a result of human endeavor, act upon man and often against man. Sartre insists on reminding us that individual consciousness remains the fulcrum of human enterprises even when the alienation produced by an industrialized society seems to become preponderant. Here the momentous task of existentialism appears clear. Existentialism assumes the same ancillary functions in regard to Marxism that were performed by philosophy in regard to theology in the thirteenth century. Then philosophy prepared the theologian to accept rationally a mysterious truth which in itself transcends reason; now existentialism reminds the Marxist that individual freedom is the pedestal of all societies. Marxism organized in a party is seen as an insult to human dignity. Sartre cannot conceal his dismay. He remembers the walls of Warsaw, ugly with large signs announcing that "Tuberculosis curbs production." It is a brutal exaggeration of the alienation preached by the communist party. A quantitative value (production) is the end, a disease is the

---

[51] Heisenberg and the promoters of the new atomic physics accept the same principle.

[52] Sartre notices that the sociologists of the American school (Kurt Lewin, Kordiner, etc.) do not accept this principle. They follow the *Gestalttheorie* and conceive super-individual forms both as the results and explanations of such individual consciousness. In other words, Sartre blames their inability to understand the meaning of dialectic, subservient as they are to the Anglo-Saxon interest for the particular and the practical. One lonely exception Sartre finds is in the research conducted by Kardines on the natives of the Marquesas Islands.

agent that prevents the attainment of the end. But where is man to whom the sign wants to convey a meaning?

Philosophy, concludes Sartre, is absolutely necessary to right these wrongs. And philosophy uses a method of research made known by the sociologist Henri Lefevre.[53] It goes under the title of "regressive-progressive method." It consists in two moments: first, the various conditions of an event are sought analytically with the intention of determining its motives and the individual reasons which make it different from all the other events; then a unifying meaning is sought synthetically or progressively from the analytic research. The *Critique de la raison dialectique* aims to discover the meaning of man, in history and from history, by applying this method.

˙ Sartre, following Dilthey and Weber, restates the Kantian criticism, applying it to history, however, and not, as Kant did, to nature. With Hegel, Sartre agrees that history comprehends nature. But Sartre disagrees with Hegel when the latter says that all dialectical moments of history are determinable *a priori*. Only experience and research make historical knowledge. In this sense, we can say that Sartre, along with many other contemporary thinkers, repudiates Hegel to defend the Kantian principles. What interests Sartre are historical events: the political triumph of the French Revolution, the developments of capitalism and of the working classes in Europe and in America, and, finally, the colonial problems. These relevant events are leading to one conclusion: the individual seldom chooses to live in an organized group; rather, he adapts himself to a vegetal existence in a "human series." Men happen to find themselves in such a situation often against their own will. Nature forces them into human herds which could be described as units pulled together by outside elements of nature, expecting, ironically, to be transformed by them. Men therefore become utensils of work, pushed as they are by the economic need to change inorganic things into values for human living. This matter, manipulated and transformed by man into machines, property, etc., acquires a power of domain upon man himself. All gigantic human enterprises (from the populating of the highlands of China, to the transportation of Peruvian silver to Europe in the sixteenth century, to the use of steam in industry in the nineteenth century) have brought us to one conclusion, namely, that human work objectified in material products has struck out against humanity. Man is forced to accept consequences far beyond his intentions, he is discriminated against by the creation of social classes, he becomes the product of his own product.[54] Human freedom itself is

[53] Cf. Henri Lefevre, "Perspectives de sociologie rurale," in *Cahiers de Sociologie*, 1953.

[54] Sartre, *Critique de la raison dialectique*, p. 254.

considered a tool of production, hence exploitation and oppression. In one word, the individual reigns.

We have seen that one of the fundamental principles of Sartre's philosophy is that knowledge and civilization are by nature universal. Sartre makes a long list of the evils derived from individualism: human beings are united into a collectivity by instruments which they cannot control, for instance, by a language which is a barrier to universality, by capitalism, private ownership, by mass media such as radio and television. Prices are fixed, fashions are prearranged, competition creates an impossible atmosphere for social living. Ironically, the shortage of all these manufactured "goods" pulls the trigger for violence. My neighbor is my neighbor only because my means and his means of survival and success are the same. He might throw me out of the game and therefore I will try to eliminate him.

Sartre finds, we gather from his words, delight in this grim analysis of human society, which he identifies with Christian civilization in the West. And with an intellectual innocence which is one of the most astonishing characteristics of his mind, he turns to analyze the blessings of the new society in which the individual disappears to become absorbed by a collectivized and organized group. Here freedom is possible. The limitations imposed by the rigid laws of production, by machines and competition are changed by enthusiastic workers into powerful means for a collective freedom.[55] Now I feel identified with my neighbor because his goal is my goal and my work is his work. I obey another, not because he is another, but because his command is identical with my desire to obey. Sartre reaches conclusions that the most unschooled peasant in the French Communist Party has difficulty in accepting.

For our purpose, it must be said that these two phases of society — mechanically imposed collectivization and living, organized, free cooperation — alternate, producing a circular and endless motion. "When I am a member of a series, I do not understand the reasons that make my neighbor 'the Other.' This circular alternation accentuates all the other differences (for example, birth, organism) making men strangers one to the other. When I am a member of a living organization, I understand that 'the Other' is a practical invention, signifying us-the-identicals."[56] In the collective series the energies of the individual are dissipated, in the organized group the energies are multiplied. But the unity of the group consists in the common goal, and action is the only technique by which the common goal is achieved. If action ends, the group ends. Action

---

[55] *Ibid.*, p. 401.
[56] *Ibid.*, p. 475.

or, even better, fighting, is the soul of success. To be sure, success once obtained brings death and disintegration. Success is striving for the goal, not reaching the goal. The fear of the social disintegration produced by inertia explains a new human institution: *the oath.* An oath, rooted *in fear,* is understood to be an inside device to prevent the social group from disintegration when the outside dangers have disappeared. Sartre finds outstanding exemplifications in the French Revolution and in the Bolshevik Russian Revolution. When an oath loses its power, society is ready for political slavery; the spontaneous unity of the people is overcome by a hierarchy of usurpers and the final step is near: the tyrant takes over.

The concrete reality of history proves over and over again this circular phenomenon of free rebellion against the collective series and the ineluctable return to it. In our century we witness an interesting attempt by discredited institutions to pretend honest identification with the surging group of the masses. For example, the rules of classical economy tried to justify, on behalf of progress, rigid norms of oppression. The bourgeoisie, in the name of humanism, built social divisions close to the madness of racism. Neo-Malthusianism in France, in between the two great wars, preached birth control as a means of curbing the number of lower people threatening the existence of the privileged. But Sartre, himself, at the end of his work, does not answer the main question regarding the meaning of history. If the liberty of free people is doomed to be suffocated by future slavery, if the historical battles leave the historian uncertain and anxious, could it be that history is totalization without anyone responsible for it? Could history be a cruel joke of casual forces?

Sartre refuses to answer. He has promised to face this problem in a future volume.[57] It must be said that it is difficult to think that Sartre will find a rational foundation for history. He has denied God, he has tied man down to the work of his own hands, to social classes, to projects inadequate to the explanation of human freedom. And freedom is not free, as Sartre has said, if it is confined to the intention of human actions. Freedom has to be found in the final end of each human endeavor. Freedom comes from a free human being. If being is included as the origin of freedom, the end of human activity is also the end and death of freedom.

In 1964, Jacques Honkard, who once contributed articles to *Les temps modern,* wrote a book on Sartre with a significant title: *An Inhuman Father.* The theme of this book is easily summarized: Sartre has seduced the young people of France, by the power of his dialectic,

[57] *Ibid.,* p. 755.

into betraying their hopes and expectations. According to the author, the secret of Sartre's philter is a measured dose of a mixture compounded of Hegel, Marx, Kierkegaard, Freud. There is nothing salvific beyond this cocktail.

Actually, Sartre has become the medicine man of the contemporary world in a desperate and doomed attempt to defend human freedom. His failure is due to the unexplained premise, borrowed from nineteenth-century romanticism, that freedom as such must be absolute and unrelated to the very bonds of being. Sartre is a victim of the past, and neither the brilliance of his writings nor the acclaim of his works explains the tragic omission which allows him to think that metaphysics is dead forever.

chapter VII

Christian Existentialism in Russia and France

INTRODUCTION

All religions are by nature existential because they seek to give meaning to human existence and are consequently little interested in an explicitly scientific interpretation of the universe.[1] Indeed, the Christian religion claims unique prerogatives in solving the problem of human destiny. Christ has saved man-the-individual, who is capable of a *personal* relation with God. Of course, such a relation is not personal if it is not free, if each man is not responsible for his actions. Therefore, Christianity emphasizes the rights and duties of the individual; whereas other religions may guide the individual toward discovering the Absolute, stressing at the same time the wisdom of accepting with Stoic indifference human life as a precarious and contingent position in the great stream of being.

Christ, on the other hand, has insisted on the irreducible difference between the human person and the cosmic universe by showing himself the author of the revealed word and of a sacramental life, both powerful means to enhance a man's personal encounter with God.

For the Christian, the world presents tragic aspects only when God is absent; only before his encounter with Christ does man live a life of

---

[1] Both religion and existential philosophies aim at a common goal which may be better formulated in the following dilemma: should human existence be lived hopelessly as a gift to be dissipated before death erases the individual human existence, or should man endure this life with the consciousness that human destiny transcends his daily tribulations?

anxiety and dread. It is not a surprise, therefore, to find Christian ideas playing a decisive role in contemporary existentialism. Pascal was among the main exponents of Catholic Jansenism; Kierkegaard worked for a reformation of Lutheranism; Berdyaev aimed to formulate a "superior" Christianity. Marcel was converted to Catholicism; Barth is seeking in Kierkegaard a new approach for Lutheranism. Bultmann is sure that Heidegger's depth has given new dimensions to the Christian message. Sartre, himself, though totally atheistic, is so obsessed by Christian thought that his books resemble, line by line, an upside-down Catholicism.

This weighty presence of religious factors in contemporary philosophy can be traced to the beginning of modern times, when, almost simultaneously, the Protestant Reformation and rationalism began to develop in Europe. Luther rebelled against Rome for many doctrinal, political and personal reasons. Theologically he became convinced that human nature was corrupt through and through, that the act of faith did not integrate with good works, that faith in the suffering Christ on the cross assured salvation regardless of a person's behavior. This pessimistic interpretation of man caused many contradictions. Protestantism, in search of an authentic personal union with God, found itself severing historical and theological ties of man with God. Man found himself alone with the gigantic task of formulating a new personal philosophy and a new personal ethics.

On the other hand, rationalism had no greater success. It intended to build a new philosophy and a new society on unaided human reason. This simplex base created a host of problems. The most outstanding is the contradiction whereby modern philosophy tries to identify human values with the same power of reason that is used to denounce them as values. Since the sixteenth century, philosophy and religion have followed parallel paths: both have reached a common ground, and both have been victims of a common failure. The philosophical thrust known as rationalism seemed to have reached its zenith with Hegel, but his dialectical thought was found to be capable of all kinds of extensions and distortions. The economic liberalists of the Manchester school, for instance, sought to make Hegelian philosophy a reality of social justice, and they failed miserably. The concept of mutual egotism forced the masses to unite and filled them with hatred against the privileged and the unjust. Similarly, the secret of Protestantism was its program of religious individualism.

It is important to realize that existentialism came from the ruins of this rebellion against classical Christianity. Therefore, existentialism must confront the religion of Christ, the cornerstone and the scandal of Western civilization. Existentialism wants especially to find out whether it has a claim to acceptance by our society.

In this chapter we shall discuss (1) Russian existentialism and (2) the philosophy of Gabriel Marcel.

1. EXISTENTIAL THEMES IN RUSSIA

Nineteenth-century Russian culture was dominated by open hostility to the autonomy of reason and the philosophy of Western Europe. This feeling of hostility was present in many of the works responsible for the success of existentialism.

The Russian intellectual of the nineteenth century felt the uneasiness of a society which was about to rebel against centuries of exploitation. He resented the superiority of Western civilization; he doubted the traditions of his own Orthodox Church; he was frightened by the radical innovations of the Nihilists, a rabid rebellious group opposing the Tsars; and above all, he was aware of the absence of a system of philosophy, the main reason for his insecurity. Conversely, Western Europe, which had no interest in fragmentary Russian philosophy, was literally conquered by the works of the great Russian novelists: Chekov, Dostoevski and Tolstoi.

Leon Tolstoi became the idol of all European circles. After all, few works have a historical vision comparable to that of *War and Peace*. Yet a question comes immediately to mind: Why is Dostoevski, and not Tolstoi, the mainstay of the Western existentialists? Tolstoi is read and forgotten; Dostoevski is read and his influence becomes a preponderant factor in continental philosophy.

The question allows room for a precise answer. Tolstoi's vision, though ample and robust, leads back to the ancient neoplatonic theme. The various destinies of human beings mingle and dissolve in the stream of history. A deity overlooks the universe. Love is universal and ultimately love will conquer the presence of evil.

I. *Fyodor Dostoevski*

Fyodor Dostoevski does not agree with Tolstoi. There are no half ways with him. The balance of power in the world is not disengaged and automatic; it requires man's contribution. Either I accept the challenge of believing in God and act accordingly or everything tumbles. "If there is no God, then I am God. . . . If God exists, all is His will and from His will I cannot escape."[2]

---

[2] Words pronounced by one of the protagonists of *The Possessed*, a work meant

Fyodor Dostoevski was born in Moscow in 1821. His father was a medical doctor of some means. His mother, very religious, died young and her memory remained a constant guide for Fyodor. He won a degree in engineering at the University of Petersburg, but his vocation was literature. A major event of his life was the violent death of his father when he was killed by a servant. Fyodor became an epileptic, with a morbid tendency to link his new sickness with the disagreements he had had with his father. (Freud analyzed this aspect of Dostoevski's life in one of his first works on the Oedipus complex.) *Poor People* (1840) brought success and the acclaim of intellectuals to Dostoevski. Unfortunately, he gave his name and his enthusiasm to secret political associations. He was arrested and condemned to death. He was given the last rites of his church and was carried to the firing squad through crowds eager to witness his execution. At the last moment he was spared by the authority of the Tsar, and his sentence changed to four years of penal labor in Siberia.

Siberia brought the light of Christ to the troubled prisoner, Fyodor Dostoevski. A noblewoman, Mrs. Von Vizin, gave him a copy of the four Gospels. Fyodor spent the long hours of forced confinement meditating the teaching of Christ, and he reached the conviction that morality itself is impossible without faith in a personal God. A purely autonomous human morality cannot offer any meaning to human suffering. Ivan Karamazov, the most tumultuous personage of *The Brothers Karamazov*, rebels against this morality. In his words: "I don't want harmony from love for humanity. I don't want it. I would rather be left with unavenged suffering. I would remain with my unavenged suffering and unsatisfied indignation, *even if I were wrong*."[3]

This thesis was repudiated by Dostoevski after his encounter with Christ. He developed a new theme: life is a challenge, rooted deeply in man's soul. "The soul of man is a battlefield between God and the devil." Evil is present in the world and evil cannot be overcome either by any dialectical conception or by a moral norm or by any human ingenuity. Faith in Christ and faith in Christ alone overcomes evil. Hope in the future spiritual vision of God is the only reason making this present life understandable, and bearable. Raskolnikov, the protagonist of *Crime and Punishment*, personifies the Nietzschean superman. He decides what is moral and what is immoral; he defines justice and injustice. Why shouldn't he decide the fate of human beings? Whether they should

to demonstrate the abyss of selfishness reached by generous souls without God. Cf. F. Dostoevski, *The Possessed*, trans. by C. Garnett (New York: Dutton and Co., 1931), Vol. 11, p. 253.

[3] *The Brothers Karamozov*, translated by C. Garnett, (New York: The Modern Library, 1943), p. 301.

live or die? So he accomplishes a perfect crime; he kills without any reason other than that he wants to kill. It is a perfect crime because it is perfectly absurd. But after the crime he begins to feel the burden of his sin, the torture of his conscience, the impossibility of living with himself. And he starts his way back, a way of humility and peace revealed to him by "an inferior human being," by Sonya, the prostitute. In the presence of God, human laws and human distinctions do not count anymore. Reason itself must surrender, because such monstrous events as sickness and the pain of innocent children cannot be explained by rational considerations or by neoplatonic harmonies. Ivan Karamazov explodes with blasphemous words when he thinks of children in pain: "It is not worth the tears of that one tortured little child who beats himself on the breast with his little fist and prays in his stinking house with his unexpiated tears to 'dear kind God.' "[4]

But if God exists, why should man try to eliminate evil from the world? "Why are you so firmly, so solemnly convinced that only the normal and the positive, in short, only prosperity is of benefit to man? Perhaps suffering is just as good for him as prosperity. And man does love suffering very much sometimes. Suffering! Why? It is the sole cause of consciousness."[5] Evil is responsible for a choice placed squarely in front of man: either God and human immorality are accepted or human existence is an insoluble riddle.

Dostoevski experienced the presence of evil down to the last moments of his life. He lost a son, his first marriage was unhappy, epilepsy grew more persistent, and the passion for gambling brought poverty to his family. But he did not lose sight of eternity. *The Idiot,* one of his first works, speaks of Myshkin, the saint, who is the victim of the forces of evil. In *The Brothers Karamazov,* the last of his writings, the Christian message is announced by Alyosha, who knows the tragedy of belonging to an immoral family and who finds joy in his fight to build an existence grounded on the hope for redemption.

II. Vladimir Soloviev

Vladimir Soloviev (1853–1900) lived one generation after Dostoevski. The symptoms of imminent crisis were in the air, the voices of new ideologies resounded in the streets of Moscow. A divine power is present in each man, according to Soloviev, a power that gives meaning to human intelligence and its achievements. Soloviev did not know how to

---

[4] *The Brothers Karamazov,* p. 300.
[5] *Notes from the Underground,* translated by D. Magarsheck (New York: The Modern Library), p. 139.

write novels, but he knew how to make a penetrating and realistic analysis of Western Civilization. Soloviev discovered in Western philosophy a progressive, almost a frightening indifference to God, to the need for faith, and to respect for positive values and the individual person.

From the Cartesian dream of reducing philosophy to mathematics to the absolute dialectic of Hegel, human reason attempted to take the place of God. It was an impossible task and human reason failed as shamefully as the giants who tried to conquer Mount Olympus: Hegel prepared Feuerbach who overturned the dialectic, went to the opposite extreme, and paved the way for Marx.

Soloviev in his important work *Crisis of Western Civilization* (1874) could not hide his horror at the presumption of pure reason. He went to another extreme: following Arthur Schopenhauer and E. von Hartmann, he identified reason with an antihuman and maleficent force. Man is a concrete individual existent, a composite of thought and action, of emotions and instincts, of reason and faith. Soloviev used his own term "unitotal concrete," a convergence of all the particular functions directed by the person who is solely responsible and solely capable of initiative. The doctrine of "unitotal concrete" remained an ideal which Soloviev personally never realized. He failed to see the ways and the methods of relations between reason and faith. Ultimately he held that faith irrationally and blindly prevails on reason. He envisioned the Russian Orthodox Church as destined to lead an ecumenical movement and the fight against rationalism. Soloviev did not live to witness the fulfillment of his prophetical analysis that rationalism will beget materialism. Without doubt, he could not imagine that his country, Mother Russia, would with the October, 1917, revolution become the center of atheism. His disciples went into exile in Germany, France and Italy. One of them, Bulgakov, became a priest; Ivanov converted to Catholicism. All of them heralded a mystical sadness, a longing for the Fatherland which is common among persons forced to live in exile.

III. *Leo Shestov*

Leo Shestov[6] (1866–1938) was one of these exiles. He lived in France where he exercised a clear influence on Marcel and Camus. There is an element of radicalism in the thought of Shestov — or perhaps a natural liking for every idea, from Pascal to Nietzsche — which defies sys-

---

[6] Some of his works are: *The Idea of Goodness in Tolstoi and Nietzsche*, *The Night of Gethsemane* (on Pascal), *Philosophy of Tragedy: Dostoyevsky and Nietzsche*, *Kierkegaard and Existential Philosophy*.

tematic and rational solutions. From Nietzsche, Shestov accepted the criticism of traditional ethics, but Shestov rejected indignantly Nietzsche's morality of the superman, of the *amor fati*. Shestov thought that the task of a philosopher was to destroy philosophy, particularly speculative and ethical philosophy, for both are presumptuous attempts to reach God by reason. We must go back to the third century, to Tertullian, to find a man honestly radical and extreme as Shestov.

The corruption of man, the loss of innocence, original sin, Shestov says, are results of the first act of disobedience when Eve and Adam ate the fruit of the tree of knowledge of good and evil. The thirst for knowledge — a real *concupiscentia irrisistibilis* — makes man aware of his limits. Man, tortured by this thirst, believes that scientific knowledge is the water so much longed for. But science is *objective* and therefore it changes every object that comes within its grasp into an inert, abstract essence, petrified and incapable of life. Science possesses the touch of death; it seems to be jealous and envious of one of the most graciously divine gifts, the gifts of life and joy and friendship. Shestov presented this idea in a dramatic way: either you accept the living word of God, giver of creation and living in the heart of each believer, or you accept science which substitutes for God rational existence, that is, the divinization of the impersonal subjectivity of all mankind. Speculative philosophy is *sacrilegious* because it dares to apply scientific methods to the very existence of God. Ethics is no less sacrilegious for it attempts to kill the living word of God, which it replaces by a rational man-made law. What would this law say of the command of God to sacrifice the life of Isaac?

Shestov's positive contribution is found in a strong defense of the need of faith. Faith denies science, faith refuses evidence, faith frees man who is in danger of scientific suffocation. Kierkegaard was right when he said that faith is impossible if despair does not prepare for it, because we must stand without any human certainty, we must face the horror of being abandoned, alone, defenseless before the mystery of existence that science had tried ludicrously to mask.[7] Then we understand that faith cannot be understood, because it must be lived.

Much as it might be admired as an antidote, such an extreme attack on reason is self-destructive. Shestov fails to explain the purpose of his book, which after all must develop a sequence of logical reasoning; nor does he explain his insistence on persuading his followers in a logical manner that logic is illogical.

---

[7] Cf. Shestov, *Athens and Jerusalem*, 1938.

IV. *Nicolai Berdyaev*

Nicolai Berdyaev (1874–1948) was one of the disciples of Soloviev. France, his adopted country after expatriation from Russia, has surrounded him with respect and admiration. Berdyaev was gifted with an extraordinarily prolific mind. He founded a magazine, *The Way*, and he published many books rich with provoking ideas on the contemporary human and social scene.

Berdyaev was the son of a landowner in the province of Kiev. His mother, who came from a French Catholic family, left a decisive imprint, evident in all his writings, on the mind of young Nicolai.[8] Following a pattern of behavior common to many young people, he rebelled against his early religious education and, as a sign of self-assertion, professed atheistic Marxism. But Marxism with its homogeneous materialist platitudes was too monotonous to satisfy the brilliant mind of Berdyaev. He freed himself from Marx, but not without serving four years of his life in a penitentiary for the crime of thinking independently at a time when independent thought was considered a supreme danger by the state police. Later he escaped from the Bolshevik Revolution and, in 1922, France became his second country.

Berdyaev is essentially a religious thinker. The Protestant mysticism of Böhme is part of his intellectual structure, just as Dilthey's historicism and Dostoevski's religious drama[9] are themes nearly always present in his meditations. But Berdyaev did not disregard the philosophical aspect of human nature, and one often finds himself thinking of the personalism of Scheler and of Marcel when he tries to understand his complex personality.

With Shestov Berdyaev accepts a common point of departure: man in a state of decadence lives a false and adulterated existence. He calls it an "objectivized" spirit. The original fall was man's loss of liberty, a servitude of the subject to the object, an exteriorization. Shestov's radicalism is no solution to the problem. Absurd faith does not free man from his own exteriorization. It leaves all the problems unsolved and adds itself as an additional problem. A solution of the problem begins with a complete consciousness and appreciation of those human values (knowledge, freedom, communication, history, and religion) that lead man to accept with joy the mysterious challenge of faith.

---

[8] Cf. N. Berdyaev, *Dream and Reality, an Essay in Autobiography.*

[9] Berdyaev explains that Dostoevski is an essential element in all Russian philosophers. Cf. N. Berdyaev: *Dostoyevsky, An Interpretation* (New York: Sheed and Ward, 1934).

Berdyaev's analysis starts with epistemological overtones. "Objective knowledge" reaches the essentials of something and establishes a clear-cut distinction between the subject and the object. But the object is more than a concept reflecting an essence. The object is an *existing* essence, rich with many mysterious possibilities that are unfairly neglected by objective knowledge. This man who walks in the street with me or who rides the bus with me is, for "objective knowledge," just a composite of body and soul: a body with a certain weight, dimensions, movements and reflexes, and a soul with spiritual faculties, with tendencies and habits which objective knowledge likes to tailor scientifically into prearranged categories. Actually, if I want to do justice to this man who walks the streets or rides the bus with me, I have to supplement the objective way of knowing him with a new *existential* approach, more human and less scientific. Besides being an object defined once for all, he is for me a living being with an infinite number of mysterious possibilities existing beyond his objective qualifications. Not only my mind, but my sentiments and will, my whole being realizes the presence of this man. In brief, I have a person-to-person encounter with him; and by respecting him, I respect myself and avoid acting like a computer or a filing device.

Personalism is the proper name for Berdyaev's philosophy. "Personalist philosophy must recognize that spirit does not generalize but individualizes, that it creates, not a world of ideal values, superhuman and common, but a world of personalities with their qualitative content, that it forms personalities. The triumph of the spiritual principles means, not the subordination of man to the universe, but the revelation of the universe in personality. . . ."[10] If the soul itself is reduced by objective knowledge to a complex of objective faculties, the effort to prove the presence of the soul in man is self-defeating. The essence of man is the freedom of the spirit: "dualism exists, not between soul and body, but between spirit and nature, between freedom and necessity. Personality is the victory of the spirit over nature, of freedom over necessity."[11]

These premises bring the first conclusion: real communication among humans, a communication which is a *communion*, is possible only on the level of the spirit. I speak to another man only if I see him as another "me" who knows how to answer me, to speak to my heart, my bowels. This mutual interdependence reveals my limits and his limits, my finitude and his finitude. Hence the social nature of man postulates God. Communion among persons is possible only because each one of them is aware of his own finite existence in relation to God, the infinite

[10] Berdyaev, *Slavery and Freedom* (New York: Scribner, 1944), p. 29.
[11] *Ibid.*, p. 31.

Being. God is the "you" in each "I," the reason that makes persons understand and love each other. If the human heart is open to God, it is open to another human heart. When God is absent, there is communication but not communion among human beings. Communication, or public relations, as it is too well known, is a product of our industrialized society. Man is seen as an instrument, ranged in classes and groups: he is geared to fit a mechanized purpose in a mechanized society.[12] We belong to a society that has lost the meaning of freedom in the name of social welfare and economic security.

Without doubt, the way of the spirit is more arduous. "Personality is suffering. The struggle to achieve personality and its consolidation is a painful process. The self-realization of personality presupposes resistance, it demands a conflict with the enslaving power of the world, a refusal to conform to the world. Refusal of personality, acquiesence in dissolution in the surrounding world can lessen the suffering and man easily goes that way. Acquiesence in slavery diminishes suffering, refusal increases it. Pain in the human world is the birth of personality, it is its fight for its own nature. . . ."[13]

Reason is afraid of freedom and tends to free itself of freedom, even at the price of rejecting its own nature. True freedom (the *libertas major* of St. Augustine) consists in making the choice for being, or what is the same, for what is true and good. But this freedom is not possible if the possibility of doing evil is excluded (*libertas minor*). "Truth gives us the highest kind of freedom, but freedom is necessary for the acceptance of this truth. Truth can neither constrain, nor compel, and it cannot give freedom to man through violence."[14] If we accept the truth, we open an infinite number of possibilities, just as being is infinite. "Personality is the coming into being of the future, it consists of creative acts."[15] Therefore, a substantial freedom is productive, accepts the present to change it and make it better, always tends to the future. "Man in his creative love for God does not only invoke Him on behalf of his human needs, expecting salvation from Him: he also offers Him all the superabundance of his forces and all his fathomless liberty with absolute disinterestedness."[16]

In synthesis, the theme of the Gospel of St. John tells us: "Truth makes us free." This is developed by Berdyaev within a contemporary

---

[12] Cf. N. Berdyaev, *The Realm of the Spirit and the Realm of Caesar* (New York: Harper, 1952).

[13] N. Berdyaev, *Slavery and Freedom* (New York: Scribner's, 1935), p. 28.

[14] N. Berdyaev, *Freedom and the Spirit*, p. 29.

[15] *Slavery and Freedom*, p. 28.

[16] *Freedom and the Spirit*, p. 212. Also cf. *The Meaning of the Creative Act* (New York: Harper, 1954), *passim*.

framework so ludicrously filled with the preoccupation of saving freedom and so actually engaged in destroying it! When man refuses to understand being and hides himself with exasperation in his individual subjectivism, he begins to walk the road of slavery. The Goethian Faust, the superman of Nietzsche, Raskolnikov, and Ivan Karamazov are the victims of this monstrous mechanized society. History is the arena for the confrontation between the slavery brought about by objectivization and true *existential* freedom.[17] In history lies the attempt to discover the eternal meaning of man, not only a series of facts connected in time. Hegel pronounced his own verdict of guilty when he was forced by his own premises to consider history a closed cycle of the transcendental Idea. History has an eschatological meaning, that is, history fulfills the evolution of the universe, the victory of spirit upon nature, and therefore history implies the end of nature and the final triumph of spirit. Berdyaev envisions a human society based on the free human person, on the communion among persons, on the presence of God revealed in the community of men.

Christian religion has the power to bring about this revolution if it frees itself of the burden of rigid historical structures and of useless juridical expressions. The love of God, which is always boundless and living and universal, aims to overleap artificial boundaries. Berdyaev would like to set up a dramatic confrontation between Christians and communists. How many of those who profess Christianity in our day have reached an evident conclusion, namely, that communism, viewed historically, is a clear product of the apathy and superficiality of Christians toward the teaching of Christ? How many Christians, in their struggle against communism, make a necessary distinction between the communists who deserve love and understanding and communism's ideas, which are wrong and to be condemned? Communism holds a truth which Christians are eager to forget: economics is a condition of human existence. The concern for our own bread, Berdyaev insists, could become a selfish and narrowly materialistic preoccupation, but our concern for the bread of others is always a sign of spiritual and religious vitality. And "the others" are not just those who share our ideas. "Moral consciousness began with God's question: Cain, where is thy brother Abel? It will end with another question on the part of God: Abel, where is thy brother Cain."[18]

These are the most outstanding ideas of Berdyaev, philosopher and philanthropist, often theologian, always the artist sensitive to the meaning

[17] *The Fate of Man in the Modern World* (London: Student Christian Movement Press, 1935).

[18] Cf. N. Berdyaev, *The Destiny of Man* (New York: Harper, 1960), p. 33.

of beauty and human understanding. This sensitivity to and insistence on values that are beyond reason are responsible, perhaps, for a pessimism which detracts from the wholeness of his philosophy. We can illustrate this deep metaphysical pessimism of Berdyaev if we analyze his criticism of traditional theology.

"The religious phenomenon," he says, "has two sides. The yearning of man for God comes to light in it and the yearning of God for man. Traditional rational theology denies this yearning of God for man from the fear of introducing affective passionate life into God. For the rational concept of perfection does not admit of yearning and need in the notion of completeness; it prefers the perfection of a stone. In that case the relation between God and man ceases to be a drama of two which is capable of a resolution in a third. . . ."[19]

Berdyaev fails to see that "rational" theology accepts the limits imposed by mystery, which prevents us from explaining the life of God in human terms. But the same mystery, accepted by the act of faith, does not prevent a religious man from a personal encounter with God. This act of faith is a supreme privilege for a human being, a privilege which does not need any explanation for those who possess it and any explanation of which could not make it clearer to those who do not have it. Moreover, the act of faith makes the religious man certain that God is absolutely perfect, that He intervened in human history at the moment of the Incarnation, that He listens to the prayers of each individual, that in His infinite immutability He cares and provides for the universe He created. "Rational" theology acknowledges with humility that we will never understand, in these human conditions, the manner in which these two aspects (the infinity of God and His solicitude for man) coexist. Is it not true that one of the fundamental mysteries of faith is the divinity and humanity of Christ?

Berdyaev himself, in dealing with this topic, reveals a subtle rationalism which perhaps is the cause of the weakness of his whole philosophy. He cannot have any other concept of immutability than the physical image of the stone, and therefore he comes to the "rational" conclusion that God must be changeable. We might remark at this point that religious rationalism, from the time of gnosticism in the second century, has always rejected the axiomatic principles of logic (e.g., the principle of noncontradiction and principle of identity) as applied to natural truths and nevertheless attempted the application of the same principles to the most mysterious truths of Revelation.

The gnostics, with evident neoplatonic overtones, spoke of gradual intermediate beings between God and man. It was not difficult for the

---

[19] N. Berdyaev, *The Divine and the Human* (London: G. Bles, 1949), p. 16.

Fathers to confute them. Berdyaev, under the influence of the German mystics from Eckhardt to Böhme,[20] follows the same steps. We find visible traces of this tendency in 1935, when Berdyaev published *Freedom and the Spirit*. "Freedom does not raise us up toward nature, but toward the idea of the divine, and toward the void which is prior to being. It is rooted in non-being. Free activity is original and entirely irrational, for all rational conceptions of it involve its identification with the phenomena of nature."[21]

It is not difficult to discover in this quotation elements which belong to the best tradition of seventeenth-century rationalism. Freedom is reduced by reason to a natural phenomenon, to an object of the empirical sciences. And being itself is reduced to a natural phenomenon. Berdyaev, far from disagreeing with them, accepts these premises, and from them he proceeds to draw further conclusions and the first among them is that freedom, real freedom, does not have its roots in being. The consequences of this view in the realm of religion are even more serious than they are in the philosophy. How can man choose to do good, if he does not accept being as the foundation and the final goal of the human act? If freedom is rooted in non-being, God assumes an inferior stand and He is engaged with man in the endless job of liberating the universe. God the Creator is not the source of freedom, but He Himself is longing for a superior freedom. "Out of the Divine Nothing (the *Gottheit* or the *Ungrund*: The Trinity) God the Creator is born. The creation of the world by God the creator is a secondary act. From this point of view it may be said that freedom is not created by God: it is rooted in the *Nothing*, in the Ungrund from all eternity. Freedom is not determined by God; it is part of the nothing out of which God created the world . . . God the creator cannot be held responsible for freedom which gave rise to evil."[22]

This notion of the Trinity, it goes without saying, is diametrically opposite to the doctrine of traditional theology. The Cartesian preoccupation that conceived matter both as extension and as substance operates here with Berdyaev in his decision to find a reason explaining evil at the origins of being, as if evil were to be a metaphysical entity and not a metaphysical deficiency. Berdyaev has made meaningless the drama of evil as Dostoevski has presented it: if evil is rooted in the very essence of being, what merit or demerit do human actions deserve? Berdyaev acknowledged this difficulty when he could not avoid traces of Origenism in his conception of the Mystical Body.[23]

---

[20] *Ibid.*

[21] *Freedom and the Spirit*, p. 124.

[22] *The Destiny of Man*, p. 25.

[23] "The greatest religious and moral truth to which man must grow, is that we

Another point must be made. The Manichaean conception, though masterfully analyzed and rejected by St. Augustine, is more than a primitive nostalgia of a Middle Eastern mind prone to mysticism and inadequately exposed to mature Western thought. Manichaeism creeps in and dominates the history of human thought every time a crisis threatens to disturb the relation between reason and will. The classical example is given by Schopenhauer, Stirner, and Nietzsche, who, after Hegel's transcendentalism, postulated the reality of a negative Absolute. The same phenomenon recurs in contemporary existentialism. Those philosophers who approached God with contradictory premises have often chosen to ignore Him in a supposedly courageous act of defense of man against the unknown. Sartre is a leading exponent of this position, and Camus follows him with minor differences. Both are under the influence of the Russian existentialists, particularly of Berdyaev, who defended a contradictory idea of God.

The stimulating philosophical experience of Berdyaev's thought remains as a sign of our times, a sign rich in profound insights and profound contradictions. Berdyaev has the great merit of revealing the participation of the whole man in the act of knowledge. But he found it difficult to explain this act of knowing when he reduced it to an ineffable intuition. We must agree with him that the mind tends to objectivize and that objectification does not do justice to existing reality. But if we want to correct the mind's deviation, we must seek the remedies inside the mind itself, without condemning it. After all, we are not gods and we have to think with human instruments.

2. EXISTENTIAL THEMES IN FRENCH PHILOSOPHY: GABRIEL MARCEL

Henri Bergson's philosophy was the central force in French culture in the first decades of this century. The ideas of the intuition of l'élan vital, of the open society, were finding a sincere acceptance in a French community decidedly advanced on the road of comfortable capitalism. If a preoccupation was universally felt, this was the desire to integrate the growing welfare with the spiritual values of the French tradition. Henri Bergson accepted the task. His work was received with respect by all sorts of people: the humanists and moralists found in Bergson new expression of their old doctrines; the men of science saw in him a much needed opportunity to free their minds from the obsolete tenets

cannot save individually. My salvation presupposes the salvation of others, also the salvation of my neighbor, it presupposes universal salvation, the salvation of the whole world, the transfiguration of the world." *The Divine and the Human*, p. 201.

of positivism; Catholics, although suspicious of some Bergsonian ideas, were elated by his sharp criticism of rationalism and positivism and were openly pleased with his moral theories (for instance, the *morality of heroes* was an exaltation of the social function of canonized saints). De Broglie, the articulate pupil of Bergson, took special care to stress the affinity of the doctrines of duration and of the temporal structure of space with the most recent theories of physics, with Einstein's relativity and microphysics, for instance.

From another perspective, Bergson was accredited with a variety of signs of vital renewal. Well known is the success of the new school of painting of Paris. The novels of Marcel Proust could easily be taken as a literary translation of the philosophical theories of his distant relative, Henri Bergson. The most popular means of communication, the cinema, was used by Bergson himself to compare living duration, caught by the intuitive act, as opposed to the inert and dead "snapshots" presented by abstract reason.

The first symptoms of disenchantment with Bergson's optimism appeared in literature and in the classrooms of the French universities. The rebellious decadence of Rimbaud on the one hand and the fierce realism of Zola on the other did not sound friendly to Bergson. And both Rimbaud and Zola were forerunners of Breton, a stanch realist, and Malraux, a caustic analyst of human life. About 1930 the universities of France grew tired of Bergson. The monotony of reducing all aspects of the universe to one historical duration was bound to clash with the rights and demands of the individual and individual consciousness.

Gabriel Marcel was an eminent voice in this struggle for a cultural change. He revised critically the philosophy of his teacher, Henri Bergson, and by the end of World War I, he had reached conclusions that Berdyaev came to years later. In fact Marcel went through an early experience of meditations (published in little known works at the start of his philosophical life) that sound prophetical of the developments of French existentialism. Sartre set down the same ideas decades later with a reversed theological perspective.

The uniqueness of Gabriel Marcel consists in the fact that he did not wait for directions from Husserl, Heidegger, and Jaspers to perceive the "irreducibility of the existent," nor was he stimulated by the meditations of Kierkegaard to formulate an immediate "person-to-person" rapport between man and God. In those early days he was not aware of the "Kierkegaardian Renaissance, which was developing in Germany"[24] and it must be said that this affinity with Kierkegaard, who was still

---

[24] Cf. on this topic: Gabriel Marcel, "Regard un arrière," in *L'existentialisme Chrétien* (Paris, 1947), p. 310.

unknown to Marcel, is not surprising. One of the first philosophers to fascinate the young Marcel was Schelling, who survived Hegel by some ten years and who gathered around himself, after 1831, the forces resisting the abstract rationalism of Hegel. Kierkegaard lived in the same environment, and in 1842 he heard Schelling's Berlin lectures.

Gabriel Marcel was born in Paris in 1889. His father, a man of prominence and responsibility during the Third Republic, was an administrator of the famous National Library and later was elected ambassador to Stockholm, where he took his family to live. It was fashionable in those days for successful people to read Taine, Spencer, and Renan, and to avoid any contact with the Church and with God. Gabriel Marcel's father was no exception to this general rule. Gabriel's mother was a Jewish convert to Catholicism. She died when Gabriel was four years old and — an experience common to many existential philosophers — Gabriel continued to feel her presence, convinced that she could not have died "completely," and that something of her had to survive, invisible and intangible, yet more important than her visible aspects.[25] After a sojourn in Sweden he returned to France, ready to face the rigid training of the Lycée. He was eighteen years old when he wrote his first dissertation: *Metaphysical Ideas of Coleridge and Their Relation to the Philosophy of Schelling*.

The idealism assimilated and adapted by the practical minds of the English-speaking philosophers was then and continued to be one of the main factors of Marcel's thought. F. H. Bradley and Josiah Royce, above all, exercised a decisive influence on Marcel. They claimed that abstract scientific knowledge needed to be completed by a superior kind of knowledge, namely that of intuition. The young Marcel, a student of Bergson, could not disregard as purely coincidental these basic concerns of the French and Anglo-Saxon philosophers.

For Francis H. Bradley (1846–1924), it is fundamental to recognize, as he does in his work *Appearance and Reality* (1893), that a logical knowledge of finite objects leads to contradictions. In fact, logical knowledge focuses on external appearances and superficial relations among things without knowing, or by just presupposing, the real object. Similarly, if we have a clear idea, we must relate it to the other ideas circumscribing and defining it. Therefore, the identity of an idea depends on the diversity of many ideas. The deadlock is overcome by an immediate intuition which goes beyond reasoning. Intuition alone overcomes logical antinomies and culminates in the multiform and harmonious unity of the Absolute.

[25] Cf. G. Marcel, *The Influence of Psychic Phenomena on My Philosophy* (London: Society for Psychical Research, 1956).

Josiah Royce (1855–1916), an American philosopher, took a position close to that of Bradley. Royce does not acknowledge any philosophical value in the logical operations of our reasoning, save its utility in the contingent happenings of everyday life. But each idea has a purpose, which reveals a meaning, a hidden metaphysical meaning, giving light and reasons for the existence of the universe.

Marcel discovered interesting analogies between these Anglo-Saxon idealists and Bergson. One aspect kept them apart. Bergson, eager to reach the synthesis of a universal *élan vital*, had not paid much attention to the individual. Bradley and Royce liked to speak of the Absolute, but their interest and concern was with the individual. After all, in their countries pragmatism was a way of life, and they were reminded every day of the precious values of individual liberty. Marcel found in Bradley and Royce a problem that other philosophers found formulated in Kierkegaard: if the Absolute is responsible for the existence of the individual, how can the individual be free and autonomous in regard to the Absolute?

Bradley does not seem to add much to the Hegelian doctrine on this problem. For Hegel and for Bradley the concrete experience of the individual is essential to the life of the Absolute, which asserts itself through the activities and peculiarities of each person. Royce fought Hegel's pantheism with greater spirit. His thoughts and doubts, failures and successes in this struggle are important factors in Marcel's intellectual molding. As we saw, each idea contains for Royce the *will to reach an end*. So far, we are in the pure tradition of American thinking. But Royce adds that each idea, and therefore each practical finality, is tied to all finalities with an interdependence that pulls them together for the realization of a universal will, infinite and omnicomprehensive. This illation, far from the practical American mind, raises again the shadow of pantheism. Marcel was anxious to find an answer and he questioned Royce on many counts. First, Royce, the young Marcel was arguing, confused the two terms *idea* and *end*. Ideas are of course susceptible of a logical order in a system. They also guide and enlighten the will. But how can the will be free and aim to an end if it cannot divorce itself from the idea, from a given order of finalities? How can the will be free if it is not free of doing evil? Second, Royce thought that all individual human wills were comprehended in the divine will. Is God then simply the result of adding together all human acts, good and evil? Third, the individual without God is nothing, according to Royce. But how can Royce, by stressing the primary task of God, keep man from being destroyed? These are some of the problems which Marcel brought into his teaching when, in 1912, he started his career as a professor.[26] But his main occupation during long hours of solitude was to meditate on the mystery of God and the radical conclusions of idealism.

Marcel was too weak to be drafted by the army during World War I, so he tried to be useful to his country by serving in the Red Cross. Those days remained memorable: Gabriel Marcel went from house to house bringing to wives and children the news that their husbands and fathers had died in war. He used the kindest expressions and the most human of techniques in his work of mercy, but inside he felt the turmoil of rebellion against the anonymous authority of society organized against the rights of the human person. This interior struggle found an outlet: he wrote dramas and plays. The first one, *La grâce* (1914), was followed by a long series of others. The theme of all is the same: the human person is threatened by a society disfigured by mechanical gadgets, by standardized norms of behavior, by abstract conventional schemes. The crisis is unavoidable. The solution of the crisis is to be found in the mystery of individual existence, accepted as a being "irreducible" to any logical category, present to himself and longing for a colloquy with God.[27] Marcel preferred the dynamic exchange of ideas on the stage to the arid philosopical dissertation. "I am convinced that it is in drama and through drama that metaphysical thought thoroughly grasps and defines itself *in concreto.*"[28]

As early as 1925 Marcel's dramas began developing answers to the questions raised by Bradley and Royce. They had conceived God as a philosophical expression of an absolute synthesis. They were wrong. God is not a synthesis; He is a person. The Absolute is not a compendium of all contingent realities. The Absolute is a person, wholly mysterious in the depth of His richness; and because I am a person, I can talk to Him, I invoke Him, I do not reduce Him to a philosophical problem. Man doesn't live to organize logical systems; he lives to work out his own salvation. Philosophical systems are human devices for

---

[26] Marcel taught philosophy first at the Lycée of Vendôme, then in Paris during World War I. From 1919 to 1922 he went from Sens to Condorcet to Montpellier. Before leaving the teaching profession, Marcel, who was married in 1929, accepted the difficult task of directing the translation of foreign authors for the publisher Plon. After World War II, Marcel was famous. He received many honorary degrees, all over the world, from Japan to South America and Canada. He continues to write articles on music and drama for *Les nouvelles littéraires.*

[27] Other significant dramas by Gabriel Marcel are: *Le coeur des autres* (1920), *Un homme de Dieu* (1922), *La chapelle ardente* (1925), *Le monde-cassé* (1933), published with an article on *Position et approches concrètes du mystère ontologique, Le chemin de crête,* and *Le fanal* followed by *Le sign de la Croire* (1938–1948) and *Rome n'est plus dans Rome* (1951).

[28] G. Marcel, "On the Ontological Mystery," Chap. 1 of *The Philosophy of Existence* (New York: Philosophical Library, 1949).

the suffocation of hope, the virtue that is at the very foundation of human existence. Bradley and Royce went a long way because they understood the uselessness of the speculative reason in approaching the Absolute, but they conceived the Absolute by using schemes and ideas that were borrowed ironically from rationalistic sources.

An article written by Marcel in 1925, for the *Revue de métaphysique et de la morale*, entitled "Existence et objectivité" is commonly considered one of the first works of contemporary European existentialism.[29] In it the meaning of existential philosophy is discussed in opposition to the philosophy of objectivation. In relation to the existence of God, who cannot be reduced to a conceptual object, Marcel develops his reflections on existence. For Marcel, a philosophy that is severed from the concrete life of the individual is no philosophy at all. And he practiced what he preached. In 1927, when he published his *Journal* with its decisive religious *engagement*, Léon Brunschvig and other acolytes of the "official" French culture were scandalized. François Mauriac and Paul Claudel, the torchbearers of Catholicism in France, wrote Marcel an open letter with the famous words: "Come, Marcel, why are you not one of us?"[30] It was a prophetic call: Marcel was received into the Church on March 23, 1929.

The *Journal métaphysique*,[31] in the beginning, was far from a success. Louis Lavelle and René Le Senne were among its first admirers.[32] World War II, with its atrocities and absurdities, gathered a larger number of readers who were anxious to find some answers and consolation in the dialogues and the soliloquies of Marcel. His writings always took the form of a diary, of a collection of fragmentary thoughts that reminded the reader of Pascal's *Pensées* or of the last works of Nietzsche. He never changed his mind about the impossibility of a systematic philosophy, either idealistic or realistic, reaching the Absolute or any other existent. Marcel thinks that a systematic philosophy aims to define an *object* and to resolve the *problem* of its comprehension. Now *object*, the Latin *ob-jectum*, means something "thrown in front" of us, detached from us, seen from the outside; *problem*, from the Greek *pròs bállo*,

---

[29] In 1925 Marcel had not as yet come into contact with Kierkegaard and the German existentialists were not known. Heidegger published his *Sein und Zeit* in 1927; Jaspers was in the process of crossing from psychiatry to philosophy.

[30] Cf. R. Troisfontaines, *Existentialism and Christian Thought* (London: Black, 1950), p. 17.

[31] G. Marcel, *Journal métaphysique* (Paris: Gallimard, 1927). English translation: *Metaphysical Journal* (London: Rockliff, 1952; and Chicago: H. Regnery, 1952).

[32] Another magazine *Recherches philosophiques* (published with the collaboration of A. Koyré, J. Wahl and later J. P. Sartre and Gabriel himself) was the official voice of French and German existentialism.

means again something thrown in front of us, completely independent of us, ready to be dissected. The *object of a problem* is self-sufficient. By "self-sufficient" Marcel means that the object of a problem possesses qualities which are made manifest through proper techniques. Confronted with this object, the subject, man, does not count. "To think an object . . . is to think that for which I do not matter."[33] I do not matter because I become a thinking machine, a tool working in the assembly line organized to put out "the system." Sciences, in their assault on nature, use precisely rational schemes, and the more a science is depersonalized the more valid is its acquired knowledge. Dialectical sciences do not escape the same fate: they divide and combine subject and object in an endless game that excludes understanding the existent concretely. Western philosophy has tried for centuries to achieve the impossible: to reach the concrete existent with a monotonously long effort of abstractions. Either the concreteness of the existent is caught from the beginning or it is lost forever.

"To postulate the meta-problematical is to postulate the primacy of being over knowledge (not of being as *asserted,* but of being as *asserting itself*); it is to recognize that knowledge is, as it were, environed by being, that it is interior to it in a certain sense. From this standpoint, contrary to what epistemology seeks vainly to establish, there exists well and truly a mystery of cognition: knowledge is contingent on a participation in being for which no epistemology can account because it continually presupposes it."[34] God is not a problem because I will never be able to consider God as an object; He is always present to me as a Thou.[35] "What is preoccupying me this morning is how to understand how God can surpass me infinitely without becoming a *he* or *it* for me . . . ," wrote Marcel on December 18, 1918, and then he continued: "In reality the being I love has not gotten the qualities for me; I grasp him as a whole, that is why he is refractory to predication. . . . Nothing is more false than to identify the Thou with a bounded and

---

[33] G. Marcel, *Metaphysical Journal,* English trans., p. 229.

[34] Marcel, "On the Ontological Mystery," in *The Philosophy of Existence.* We know that this work dates to 1933. It is of interest to notice, as we shall see, that precisely in the same year a theorem was presented and rigorously brought by Kurt Gödel to conclusions that proved the fallacy of many hopes nourished by the representatives of formal logic. The theorems of Gödel, as interpreted by Ridune, demonstrated that each mathematical system containing elementary arithmetic contains also elements which mathematics cannot prove true. Therefore, any absolute conclusion is wrong and mathematical truths remain by nature incomplete.

[35] Also cf. one of the last works of Marcel: *The Mystery of Being* (Chicago: H. Regnery, 1960), Vol. II, p. 256; "Insofar as a presence, as such, lies beyond the grasp of any possible prehension, one might say that it also in some sense lies beyond the grasp of any possible comprehensions. A presence can, in the last analysis, only be invoked or evoked."

circumscribed content. Participation in divine life can only be grasped as participation in an infinite."[36]

Traditionally, evil has been discussed as a problem and Marcel says that evil cannot be a theoretical problem, because it belongs to man, to the actions of man and to his freedom. "In reflecting upon evil, I tend, almost inevitably, to regard it as a disorder which I view from outside and of which I seek to discover the causes or the secret aims. . . . But evil which is only stated or observed is no longer evil which is suffered: in fact, it ceases to be evil. In reality, I can only grasp it as evil in the measure in which *it touches me* — that is to say, in the measure in which I am involved, as one is involved in a law-suit. Being involved is the fundamental fact; I cannot leave it out of account except by an unjustifiable fiction, for in doing so, I proceed as though I were God, and a God who is an outlooker at that."[37]

Gabriel Marcel brings religion into the heart of philosophy. A philosopher is a man who does not throw around problems, he lives mysteries. And when Marcel speaks of mystery, he does not mean a revealed truth, superior to our intelligence, but he speaks of what is completely certain and personal in us, he speaks of a profound self, so much our own and so evident and so real that no formula is apt to express it. Now we understand the reason which allows Marcel to call his Journal "metaphysical." It is the same reason that works at the origin of this new philosophy of "Existentialism," that is to say, the supreme effort to find an "immediate" way to reach the existent being, outside of and without logical and dialectical mediations.

Marcel was in agreement with classical Platonism, with the modern Spinoza-type Platonism, and with contemporary philosophers, Berdyaev among them,[38] in accepting progressive degrees of knowing:

1. An immediate sense experience links man with the outside world without any disturbance from consciousness;

2. A first reflection, objective in nature, makes man aware of the subject-object relationship with the natural result that problems are formulated;

3. A second reflection goes beyond rational distinctions and links man with the universe in a creative way. Marcel conceives this reflection as a reversed Cartesian *Cogito:* I cannot say, "I think therefore I am," but rather, I think only to the extent that I live my existence and I experience my power of thinking.

This inside knowledge (indeed, this is intellectual knowledge at its

---

[36] *Metaphysical Journal*, p. 157.
[37] *Philosophy of Existence*, p. 243.
[38] Cf. N. Berdyaev, *The Destiny of Man*, p. 39.

highest level) is for Marcel and for many contemporary philosophers the only real philosophical activity. Marcel analyzed many facets of such a profound knowledge and — as it is bound to happen to all humans who try an almost superhuman task — he resented the conditions imposed on him because he was a man, conditions which forced him to express with concepts and logical ideas a sequence of thoughts aimed at condemning concepts and ideas.

The *Journal,* particularly the notes of 1914, discussed the mysterious relation of incarnation existing between an individual and his physical body. The mechanistic theory that considers a human body as a thing among physical things is dismissed by Marcel as irrelevant: things are owned, but I do not own my body; I *am* also my body. At the other extreme, idealism has incurred the endless difficulty, common to all forms of immanentism: it reduced the body to an expression of the Idea and therefore no explanation is offered, on the existential level, of the relation between one body and another. The truth is, Marcel is convinced, that the problem of the body or of a relation between one body and another is a pseudo-problem. We all feel that the body is an instrument used by us to express our soul and to reach goals for which we are longing. Furthermore the body is an *absolute* instrument of man; if we deprive the body of its functional instrumentality, it ceases to belong to philosophy and it falls back to the level of a physical organism. The body reveals to us our limits, it delineates them, it functions obediently to overcome them, to bring about progress, to establish liaisons with other existents. The body with its finitude helps us to recognize the necessity of the infinite, of the Absolute. The body is there to claim the necessity of God.

The outstanding feature of Marcel's works is this intellectual compulsion to find God at the summit of all the avenues tried by man. And God is so evident that to attempt to prove His existence with abstract processes amounts almost to a profane desecration of His divinity. "If a man has experienced the presence of God, not only has he no need for proofs, he may even go so far as to consider the idea of a demonstration as a slur on what is for him a sacred evidence. Now from the point of view of a philosophy of existence, it is this sort of testimony which is the central and irreducible datum."[39] Hegel held the same conviction that the Absolute is before all demonstrations because it is the evident principle through which all demonstrations are possible. But Marcel's Absolute is a transcendent God, a God who is a person, to whom man speaks in his prayers and invocations, from whom man expects the gifts of faith and grace.

---

[39] G. Marcel, *The Mystery of Being,* Vol. 1, p. 198.

The existent needs participation in the life of others, and first of all in the life of God. If I neglect *communion* with others, I neglect myself; if I want to be present, I must be present to someone; my intellectual life is futile if my thought is not transferred into communion with others. My freedom, which is mortified and often destroyed by the monotonous daily contact with machines and computers, finds joy and fulfillment in sharing my existence with others. Loneliness is the sin of an industrialized society. Kant, betrayed by his Teutonic adoration for the precision of his logical categories, came to realize, too late, how bitter was the price paid for his rationalism. He was forced to defend an *autonomous* freedom, and he condemned man to be alone with himself. Kant's tragedy is, for Marcel, the tragedy of the contemporary man. Our neighbor sees another neighbor as a *he*, that is to say, as a stranger walking the same street and bound to him by a mutual agreement to a cold politeness that is protected by the legal understanding that they must respect each other and that the police are ready on the corner to enforce this pact of peaceful nonaggression. This is the cold war that destroys freedom and fosters suspicion and hatred. My neighbor must cease to be a *"he"* to me, he must become a *"you."* Only when I find a *"you"* in each human being, can I accept him and love him as a free being who helps me to find my own freedom. "For me, the being I love is a *third person* in the least possible degree. Moreover, that being discovers me to myself, since the efficacy of his or her presence is such that I am less and less him for myself — my interior defences fall at the same time as the barriers that separate me from somebody else."[40]

We are here in a position diametrically opposed to the classical liberalism that conceived human freedom as a mutual limitation, a gentleman's agreement of coexistence. For Marcel, our liberties do not limit each other, on the contrary they create new relations of closeness to ourselves and to God.[41] In fact, God is the *Thou* par excellence and the reason for all human relations. To think God is to establish us in direct line of conversation with Him: "To pray is actively to refuse to think God as order, it is to think Him as really God, as pure *Thou*."[42] Faith is therefore an overcoming of the boundaries of rational knowledge in an engagement with God to whom we assert that we are ourselves, that is to say, that we are free and available and ready to obey. Faith is not

---

[40] Marcel, *Metaphysical Journal*, p. 148, Note of August 23, 1918.

[41] "If I treat another person as a *you*, I treat him and apprehend him *qua* freedom. I apprehend him *qua* freedom because he is also freedom and not only nature. What is more, I help him, in a sense, to be freed. I collaborate with his freedom. The formula sounds paradoxical and self-contradictory, but love is always proving it true. . . ." *Being and Having* (Boston: Beacon Press, 1951), p. 106.

[42] *Metaphysical Journal*, p. 160. Note of December 18, 1918.

ignorance but it is a well-calculated step to overcome and integrate the limitations of our knowledge.

It is clear that all the aspects of Marcel's philosophy are moments of the same theme: man lives in the twentieth century under the constant menace of a scientific progress that threatens to bring disaster: that threatens to obscure our need for an awareness of ourselves, of other persons, and of God. Under this threat we are concerned with *having* and we neglect *being*.[43] We develop the mentality of possession; we want to possess our body, money; we store scientific knowledge; we own our past and we attempt to control our present. This is the philosophy of isolation and self-imprisonment, a philosophy of mathematical precision and mathematical coldness, of clear and distinct ideas. "If we begin, like Descartes, by assuming that my essence is self-conscious, there is no longer a way out."[44] The Cartesian "cogito" represents with pretended honesty the acceptance of ourselves as witnesses to our own existence, thus excluding all overtures and understanding with others. Being communicates, having separates and gives rise to conflicts. When I possess something with greedy satisfaction, I exclude others. I grow concerned to defend my possession and I become a stranger to my own being because I identify my own being with my own having. Isn't this the common persuasion of the contemporary man? Don't we all judge persons by the yardstick of power and money and material wealth? Marcel does not hesitate to see the nature of the original sin and of all sins in this obstinate denial of man's own being. Suicide is a good example: a person takes his own life as if he were *to own* it.

The refreshing *Du refus à l'invocation*, written by Marcel in 1960, traces the path of fidelity *to being*. Faith, hope and charity, before theological virtues, are for Marcel the genuine characteristics of every effective human engagement. Every human being who lives his life in passive retirement condemns himself to the inertness of dead nature and he does not know that he lays the foundations for his own anxiety and despair. Human life, to be free, must seek engagement, it must be lived with faith, which is the opposite of inaction. Faith is fidelity to an engagement freely accepted and always renewed. The nature of faith itself demands dynamic progress because fidelity to being is an always renewed act, not a passive state. Such a fidelity is not condemned to recognize just what we are; it constitutes and constructs our future being. This being of ours, which is so mysterious and so far away from being objective, is rooted in an ever new and undefinable freedom of

---

[43] *Being and Having* (Boston: Beacon Press, 1951).
[44] *Ibid.*, p. 104.

the spirit.[45] Faith is engagement: being with all its mysteries is my challenge, which consists in feeling the presence of the transcendent God. He is the one who demands my fidelity. In Him my hope finds its reasons. Hope gives me strength to overcome the opposition between my will and the objective interests of worldly distractions.[46] Thus, God is for man the real reason for the great confrontation between the interior searching of the soul and the rationalizing reflection of logic. Marcel speaks of grace as a help to our own interior experience; this grace ultimately must prevail on the logic of reflection and help to resolve all problems in an intelligible manner.

Marcel is the leader of a good number of philosophers who thought, after the War, that freedom and faith and God were the issues of this century. Some critics see in Marcel another Barth or Jaspers. But Marcel is against, or at least outside, the Kierkegaardian dictum of "anxiety and despair," regarded as the *conditio sine qua non* for the conquest of God. Marcel likes to think of his philosophical research as a "Christian Socratic." Thus, for Marcel, man is a naturally free and finite being who finds himself and his God in a free and open meditation. Without doubt the times are ripe for this kind of philosophy. Marcel found himself, almost against his will, an international medium of communication for millions of human beings. He has gained the honor and admiration of the free world.[47] But he expressed disappointment in one of his last works, *Les hommes contre l'humain* (1951),[48] at "the suffocating sadness of the contemporary world." In it each human being seems to be an instrument, each relationship is made to serve a function. War is evil, but the root of evil is the fracturing of the secular friendship between man and the universe. Everybody is anxiously concerned about security; very few perceived the truth that security is a vain deception if there are no persons to secure. Persons are no more persons if they lose

---

[45] It seems that Marcel is not opposed to the definition as such but to the definition that claims to reduce being to the defined. Cf. for example, the following passage in *The Mystery of Being*, Vol. 1, p. 89. ". . . It is not certain that there is any real opposition between the personal and the suprapersonal. I should be more inclined to admit that the personal is authentically itself only by reason of whatever is in it that smashes the frame in which it is always in danger of allowing itself to be imprisoned as *ego* pure and simple. In any case, I shall be able to open a credit only to what presents itself to me as incapable of being reduced to the condition which is that of *things*. The distinguishing mark of things lies, in fact, in being unable ever to provide me with anything which can be made to resemble an answer. . . ."

[46] *Homo Viator* (Paris, 1944), p. 90.

[47] In 1949 Marcel received the Award of Literature of the French Academy. After the death of Bréhier, he was elected to the membership of the Academy of Moral and Political Sciences.

[48] Translated into English — *Man Against Mass Society* (Chicago: H. Regnery, 1952).

the joy of creativity, the splendor of love, the enchantment of wonder for beauty.

In the same year, 1951, Marcel published *The Mystery of Being*,[49] an attempt at systematization of his ideas. If system relies on the adoption of a method of demonstration, against which Marcel has always shown a warm dislike, this last work cannot be considered systematic. Speaking of Kierkegaard and Pascal, Marcel says: "From the point of view I have adopted, anguish is not and cannot be the last word. I should be so bold as to say, on the contrary, that the last word must be with love and joy; and this I say from my innermost heart. If we want to satisfy ourselves of the truth of this, we must emphasize the intelligible aspects of faith. . . ."[50]

Marcel is against any system and even denies the possibility of a system in philosophy. He knows the limitations of human reasoning, but he does not recognize that, in the present human condition, to deny any value to human reason amounts to compromising all values in man. Marcel once compared his positions with Sartre's.[51] According to Sartre, Marcel insists, we choose with our actions our values too; we are our own gods with our own world and morality. Marcel strongly disagrees: values are values to man because they are above and imposed on man. Without absolute values, that is to say, without recognition of the absoluteness of existing reality, man is a hopeless case of self-deception. Marcel has a good case against Sartre. But the reader might have a good case against Marcel. In fact, Sartre's pretenses must be defeated by reason because reason tends to organize ideas. Marcel, we must submit, is against organized thought; his own success consists in a magnificent and perhaps superhuman effort to overcome any system of ideas.

The theologian too looks with some hesitation at Marcel's thought. Marcel proclaims himself a Christian, but it is hard to delineate Marcel's thought about Christ's redemption of man. The never ending temptation to consider man capable of reaching goals that are divine, because given only by God's liberality, runs too often through Marcel's writings. For instance, the theological virtues are explained primarily as philosophical. Sin is an error of logic. Faith is not a humble acceptance of the word

[49] G. Marcel, *The Mystery of Being*. The work is in two volumes with the titles of *Faith and Reality* and *Reflection and Mystery*. They are compilations of lectures given at the University of Aberdeen for the Gifford Lectures in the years 1949–1950.

[50] G. Marcel, *The Mystery of Being*, Vol. 1, p. 197.

[51] Cf. G. Marcel, *Existence and Human Freedom*, published separately in 1946 and reproduced later in *The Philosophy of Existence*. Marcel admires Sartre in his genuinely literary productions, but he does not seem to discover philosophical ideas in Sartre's existentialism.

of God, but an act of confidence in the possibility of being. In general, the transition from the natural to the supernatural, from freedom without grace to freedom with grace is more of a human endeavor than a divine gift. The Christian believer is reminded by each page of Marcel's works that the author is a philosopher who happens to be a Christian more than a Christian who writes philosophy. But it must be said, with gratitude to Marcel, that no Christian reader can approach this great man without leaving him with profound impressions about the mystery and the privilege of belonging to the flock of Christ.

chapter VIII

Existentialism and Literature

Traditionally, literature is a reflection of philosophical ideas. This is true also for a great portion of existential literature. But there are exceptions. We have spoken of Dostoevski who used literature to establish a philosophy. With his work of fantasy and intuition be prepared for the birth of a new ideology and he stimulated profound meditation on new aspects of the human situation.

After World War I, novelists, at least the most alert among them, ceased to be followers. They refused to organize plots perfectly tailored to the whim of the large public; they were not interested in creating suspense and thrills. Novelists spoke of the human condition as it was; they developed philosophical themes and, ironically, against their own hope, they met success. Success came because the "professional" philosophers were looked at by many with disbelief and suspicion. After all, wasn't philosophy, Hegelian philosophy in particular, responsible for a strange work of persuasion, claiming that the climax of civilization was war and victory?

Husserl himself, a rigid defender of philosophy as a "rigorous science," favored attempts to make new relations between philosophy and literature. In fact, the phenomenological method underscores the description of phenomena as the basic step for clarifying the essence. Another not irrelevant consideration comes from the widespread influence of linguistic philosophies. They disregarded the traditional meaning of the word as a purely mechanical instrument of communication. The word for them is pregnant with poetical meaning, with a vital and existential significance. They profess, with Croce and Heidegger, that the spoken word is tied to the poetic intuition and that the origins of poetic intuition are found in the same consciousness from which logical reasoning proceeds.

1. FRANZ KAFKA

Franz Kafka is one of those men of letters whom the student of philosophy cannot ignore. He lived in the first three decades of this century. As a young boy, Kafka was a member of a German-speaking Jewish minority of Prague. He admired and feared his father and developed an unnatural sensibility, the sources of his anxiety and solitude.[1] As a young man, he had some friends, particularly Max Brod, and he also found some joy in the love, often tormented and anxious, of a young woman by the name of Milena. Another companion, tuberculosis, filled the few years left to Franz Kafka: he went from hospital to hospital in sorrow and loneliness.

Kafka chose symbolic figures of surprising and often absurd natures for many of his novellas, some of which were published posthumously. In the *Metamorphosis* a peaceful and normal clerk woke up one morning changed into a huge cockroach. His problem from that fateful morning onward became monumental: how could he live a normal life under these conditions? Kafka was extremely skillful in such absurd situations. (Only Gogol, in his masterful *The Nose,* and, in ancient times, Lucianus, have applied the popular fable to psychological situations with similar vividness and effectiveness.) Isn't the normal life of human society equally strange and absurd? Humans live lives, Kafka thinks, truly comparable to those of huge insects.

Kafka has left two major works of fiction, *The Trial* and *The Castle.* They are classical analyses of the hopeless state of man without faith. In *The Trial,* Joseph K. happens to find himself in court, accused of a crime which neither he nor the judge nor the jury can succeed in identifying. The lawyers for the defense and for the prosecution are a sad sight: they defend with passion and rhetorical fervor a thesis which is not clear in their minds. Actually, more than a defense, it is a heated gesticulation and a confused argumentation. The verdict is equally puzzling to the defendant. Joseph K. feels that he must have been condemned, but he is searching painfully and unsuccessfully to remember the verdict, which insists on remaining in the twilight of his subconscious. So he is freed and he starts again his usual existence, boring as ever. The end comes and is equally senseless. Two gentlemen visit with him. They take him to a deserted place and they slay him.

In *The Castle* we again find Mr. K. He has been promoted supervisor of the Castle and he means to do a good job, but his efforts to find

---

[1] Cf. *The Diaries of Franz Kafka, 1914–1923,* ed. M. Brod (New York: Schocken Books, 1949).

his way to the Castle prove unsuccessful. He is not easily discouraged; he knows now that the villagers do not want to talk. He tries to gain friends, to talk persuasively with the women, to reach the villagers in their strange psychological world of isolation. K. just wants to understand, but he has no success. The novel ends in suspension.

If *The Trial* and *The Castle* are compared, a definite change is noticeable. In *The Castle* man does not face an ineluctable condemnation: he just does not understand; he is motivated by a sincere moral effect to be constructive and useful but finds himself surrounded by an icy universal indifference. Yet man must continue to try. The enigma of *The Castle* is not insoluble: perhaps one day, when least expected, man will open the Castle, perhaps. . . .

Critics frequently ask: "What is behind the symbols used by Kafka?" His own personal life? the unhappy destiny of his race? the social conditions of a working class exploited by the privileged? The answer, confirmed recently by a great number of Kafkan publications, is quite different; the problem profoundly felt and suffered by Kafka — and certainly the center of his intense life — focused on the theological and religious aspect of human existence.[2] His work is filled with obstinate contradictions and luminous explanations. Only a literary symbol could use them both and join them together with a philosophical meaning. "The only really difficult and insoluble problems are those which we cannot formulate, because they have the difficulties of life itself as their content."[3]

If a philosopher offers contradictory solutions, he announces his failure as a philosopher, who, by definition, presumes to reason to noncontradictory conclusions. If a poet accepts contradictions, he is heralded as an inspired voice warning that a challenge lies ahead. The pitfall of the poet is an invitation to meditate; Kafka chose to be a writer, but his literary output betrayed his real philosophical soul. The "metaphysical atmosphere" of Kafka's beliefs rests on two contradictory assertions: (a) God is present in each event of human existence, but (b) God is absent from the universe.

The presence of God to man is axiomatic for Kafka. He noted with satisfaction "that in German the word *sein* signifies both to be, and to belong to him."[4] We are contingent and therefore we need the Absolute. "Man cannot live without an enduring trust in something indestructible in itself. Yet while doing that he may all his life be unaware of that

---

[2] Cf. F. Kafka, "Reflections on Sin, Pain, Hope and the True Way," in *The Great Wall of China: Stories and Reflections* (New York: Schocken Books, 1946).

[3] *Conversations with Kafka, Notes and Reminiscences* by G. Janouch (New York: 2. A. Praeger, 1953), p. 76.

[4] F. Kafka, "Reflections on Sin, Pain, Hope and the True Way," *op. cit.*, p. 264.

indestructible thing and of his trust in it. One of the possible ways in which this permanent unawareness may be expressed is to have faith in a personal God."[5]

Other texts are even more radical. He dared to announce that *believing is being*. "Believing means liberating the indestructible element in oneself, or more accurately, being. . . ."[6] We must understand Kafka's mind. He doesn't speak of God justifying the existence of all mankind in a vague and abstract way. He speaks of each individual created by God with a personal mission to accomplish and a personal vocation to fulfill. "We see every human being living *his* life (or dying *his* death). This achievement would not be possible without an inner justification: no human being can live an unjustified life. . . ."[7] Kafka emphatically denies that this justification of man comes from the cosmic universe. He can afford to say so because he is an artist and is not concerned with a patent contradiction in his thinking. In fact, he has just said that the universe, being contingent, demands the existence of God and therefore bears the imprint of its creator. Kafka is convinced that the world is the source of distraction, that it begets vague abstractions, deadly and obnoxious to our own personal problems. He goes so far as to say that the universe is the source of evil and that the physical world is relevant only because we believe in it. Evil, therefore, springs from our distorted frame of mind. To the eyes of the strong valiant man, the physical world, death itself, and the necessities of life are meaningless. Only the spiritual world counts if we accept it with blind faith. But if we try, as experience tragically testifies, to see rationally the vestige of God, we are wrong. How can we establish a relation between time and eternity? or between our responsibilities and God's? Consciousness is evil, and an evil that never ceases to try the impossible task of taking over God's role in our spiritual life. Salvation is faith, so luminous and shining that reason is totally blinded.

Kafka had moments of complete abandonment to God, but they did not last too long, and were followed by trying experiences of spiritual emptiness and torturing doubts. This spiritual rhythm from pure faith to pure reason assumed in Kafka the extreme pattern of a vicious circle. When the presence of God became so obsessive the world lost all its meaning. But was it possible at all in those circumstances to listen to God and to understand Him? The Word of God must assume some human form of expression if we want to listen to Him, since we live on earth and understand only earthly words. The

[5] *Ibid.*, p. 266.

[6] F. Kafka, "Dearest Father," in *Stories and Other Writings* (New York: Schocken Books, 1954), p. 78.

[7] *Ibid.*, p. 100.

mind instinctively turns to the pages of Ecclesiastes and to the Book of Job. A profound pessimism reveals an identical situation of sorrow between Kafka's destiny and the tragedy of his race. Heaven is stranger to earth because earth is stained with innocent blood.

The Christian attitude comes to accept a mediation of this intransigent position. For a Christian the Word became flesh so that He could be understood. Is it possible that the Jews were wrong when they refused to recognize the Messiah? Kafka's reaction is filled with resentment: "Perhaps they [the Jews] really did not recognize Him. But what a cruel God it is who makes it possible for His creatures not to recognize Him. After all, a father always makes himself known to his children, when they cannot think or speak properly."[8] For Kafka God is so blinding in the splendor of His majesty that He must free man from his own freedom. Calvin would have agreed with Kafka. For both, the only attitude possible in a world without God is to wait: "He who seeks does not find, but he who does not seek will be found."[9] The restless man, the man who is impatient, is always entangled with sin. Impatience is the root of sin because it is an urge to reach the material world, the only thing that gives man the feeling of grasping something tangible. The supervisor of the Castle, let us not forget, did not use violence to reach the Castle. Of course, sometimes the waiting becomes unbearable and Kafka again finds refuge in the humility of confident prayer and adoration. Among the cruel uncertainties of this modern world, when so heavy a darkness surrounds all human beings, one value remains squarely unshakable to the believer: suffering. "Suffering is the positive element in this world, indeed it is the only link between this world and the positive. . . ."[10] With suffering, life with joy is possible. "'I have said yes to everything. In that way suffering becomes an enchantment, and death — it is only an ingredient in the sweetness of life.'"[11]

Kafka used to repeat with ill-concealed vainglory that he refused to depend on any tradition. The fact is that an affinity with Christian mysticism, with the patience of Job, often with the "perfect joy" of St. Francis runs constantly through his work. In addition, Kafka accepts, perhaps unwillingly, in heroic resignation of the fact that we humans are limited, a doctrine that flows as a direct heritage from romanticism to contemporary existentialism. We must elaborate on this idea.

Romanticism stressed the limiting aspects of human life. Christian

[8] F. Kafka, *Conversations with Kafka, Notes and Reminiscences*, G. Janouch, *op. cit.*, p. 76.

[9] F. Kafka, "Dearest Father," *op. cit.*, p. 80.

[10] *Ibid.*, p. 90.

[11] *Conversations with Kafka, Notes and Reminiscences* by G. Janough, *op. cit.*, p. 100.

philosophy stresses man as limited. The first acts on dialectical principles. The second acts on the metaphysical concept that man is a limited being. Suffering for a Christian generates joy (though the privation of something good is always a source of pain) because he acknowledges that giving up a relative good does not compromise the enjoyment of other goods more valuable and often eternal. The Christian sees his suffering as a necessary element in the larger plan of a provident God. The romantic philosopher accepts his suffering as a senseless force of an anonymous system aimed at the destruction of individuality. There can be no doubt that Kafka is romantic rather than Christian in the analysis of human suffering. Ultimately there can be no doubt that Kafka bore tragically in his life the wound inflicted by his disregard for a sound metaphysics, for it is always in being and not in the privation of being that man finds joy and a meaning for his existence.

*   *   *

Historical reasons hold the key explanation to the pessimism of many men of letters and philosophers in the first quarter of this century. Wars and violence were effects of deep disquieting causes on the social and political level. Literature reacted through paradoxes and pessimism.

The philosophies current in those days were inadequate to face society and to change it. For instance, the French philosophy of life was basically unconcerned with the problems of the lonely individual; its strangely morbid attempt to reach the Absolute by means of exotic experience of a doubtful aesthetic nature did not supply this philosophy an answer to the ever increasing anxiety of man.

2. RAINER MARIA RILKE AND MICHAEL UNAMUNO

Rainer Maria Rilke, the delicate poet from Bohemia, almost contemporary with Franz Kafka, could be considered the interpreter to the world of anonymous protests. The themes of his lyrics were existential,[12] displaying a sincere anxiety for human contingency, and showing that the mystery of life remains though we try to pretend that we have solved it, at least partially, by thinking out philosophies and building societies. For Rilke love is a passionate attempt to overcome our contingency; our consciousness is related to time through pains and anxiety.[13]

Michael Unamuno (1866–1936) spoke with a strong voice, often more as a prophet than a man of letters on behalf of Latin Europe, in protest and condemnation of the achievements of reason. He meant to be a

---

[12] Cf. in particular *The Golden Book* and *Duinos Elegies*.
[13] R. M. Rilke, *Letter to a Young Poet* (New York: Norton and Co., 1954).

religious man, and he set himself against the sterility of science. The impetuous character of his ideas can be explained by the influence of Søren Kierkegaard, from whom he borrowed the confidence in and the enthusiasm for all human expressions which are outside or against the rational deductive process. For Unamuno the answer to man's problem rests in faith. Faith must be total, blind, identified with life, divorced from reason. *Don Quixote* is Unamuno's ideal. He feels called to preach a crusade to liberate Don Quixote from the tomb, for he is the hero of all human darings, the knight of all human faiths. We must free him from the *hedalgos* of reason, who are seizing him with the pretentious ambitions of their "whys" and their "whens." Don Quixote has become the laughingstock of barbers, curates, bachelors, dukes, and loafers of all sorts. Why don't they understand that he is the example to all of us, because he teaches us to fight, not to reach victory? Victory is the end of fighting; therefore, victory is death and desolation.

Unamuno's *The Tragic Meaning of Life* is a merciless attack on the pretenses of human reason, the "dirty human reason," as he calls it after Kierkegaard. Reason is guilty because it has declared war on life. Between reason and life reigns a perfect irreducible antithesis. "It doesn't matter from what angle you look at it. Reason is always against our desire for immortality . . . reason is against life, it tends to inflict death. . . . What is living is absolutely unstable, individual, unintelligible. Logic tends to reduce everything to identity, to genuses. . . . The mind seeks what is dead because affected by impotency to perceive what is alive. . . . Science is a cemetery of dead ideas. . . . How can reason reveal life? It is a tragic war, this war of reason against life."[14] If we object to Unamuno that his dogmatic stand against reason is absurd, he welcomes our objection with enthusiasm. For him life is true and living and filled with ideals because it is absurd. Man tries to organize his life by projecting logical systems, by discussing the possibility of immortality: He does not understand that he must live this life with faith in his own living: life has the reason for living in itself.

This intransigent imperative of faith for itself against the prudent conclusions of reason leaves Unamuno with a heavy burden of unanswered questions. Faith without reason does not suggest any reason why man should have faith. In this predicament the man of faith and the agnostic are equally justified in being what they are, because faith and agnosticism would be two equally gratuitous and humanly ridiculous situations. The same religious fervor convinced Unamuno that life is conclusively faith and that action is responsible for a sorrowful sequence of human aberrations, including the last war and the madness

---

[14] M. Unamuno, *The Tragic Meaning of Life*, Chap. 3.

of the Nietzschean superman. This philosophy of Unamuno is often known as "humanistic pragmatism." His Latin temperament, his enthusiasm for humanistic values, brought him to the American philosophy of pragmatism and its interest in the manipulation of those physical values that are useful for the creation of the dream of the great affluent society.

During the second quarter of the century, after World War I, the literary world was laboring under the pressure of total crisis. We cannot think of any man of letters who was not engaged in searching out new ideas for a new philosophy. Literature underwent the same process of soul-searching that made the times of the Renaissance and of the eighteenth-century Enlightenment famous. The problem was identical for the philosopher and the novelist: the urgency to renew the ideals and the goals of human living.

From the 1920's to the 1940's, Europe was invaded by the writings of American philosophers and authors who were bound together with their European colleagues in a desperate effort to avert the catastrophe that was on the horizon. They foresaw it, they sounded the alarm, but their anxious warnings were hardly noticed by their respective peoples, comfortably somnolent and living pleasantly in peaceful mediocre communities. But the warning signs of disaster were present: Stalin's brutality had changed Russia into a huge concentration camp; Germany and Italy schooled their youths to the necessity of killing in order to build; Spain was stained with torrents of native blood; England was hysterically trying to save a past of conquest and colonialism. At the moment of crisis, Europe began to learn from America, famous until then only for its mumbling cowboys and sensational kidnappings. The pages of Hemingway, of Dos Passos, and of Faulkner made Europeans ponder individual freedom and the privilege of agreeing to disagree. The style of American writers became a major element of analysis and meditation. The Americans wrote matter-of-factly and gave pragmatic descriptions of human emotions; they showed a love for research; and they had a confident expectation that new findings would help do away with a situation filled with metaphysical stagnation and uncertainty.

The European crisis originated in an enormous confusion about the meaning of human freedom, which the myth of romanticism could no longer explain. Reaction assumed nihilistic overtones in the books of André Malraux, a precursor of some existential currents. The same reaction saw a return to the obsolete theme of nineteenth-century vitalism in the pages of André Gide.

The case of André Gide presents some noteworthy aspects. He could not imagine, perhaps for reasons deeply rooted in French pride, that the "philosophy of life," or vitalism, was living feebly through its last moments. The glory of France was history. Gide rejected the idea that vitalism was responsible for the decadent moral standards in Europe, for its scornful neglect of individuals. Let us remember, as an eloquent example, the last chapter written by André Gide in *Les caves du Vatican*.[15] Lafcadius, the protagonist, is obsessed by the fact that he is living without any choice but to accept the life given him. Besides he is exposed to an infinite number of possibilities. One of them, most deadly, attracts his mind: he should be the "creator" of his own morality and he should establish his own code of ethics. In a moment which Gide considered climactic of his whole creation, Lafcadius announces his choice: "Whatever might be, let it be. That's the only way I can explain Creation."[16] Now he is free with a perfect freedom. He catches the train on which he finds an old passenger, completely unknown to him, and he kills him. His freedom of creation has reached his fulfillment, a perfect crime because perfectly irrational.

We cannot pretend that Gide was completely original. Lafcadius is a poor, steamed-out copy of Dostoevski's Raskolnikov in *Crime and Punishment*. Both tried the perfect crime: neither sought money from their victim, but each did seek the other's death to prove that he himself was alive. Under the circumstances, it is hard to forgive André Gide the unpardonable obtuseness that prevented him from understanding what Dostoevki understood. Lafcadius killed because he considered himself God. Man wants to be a creator, but if he is without God, he creates evil only. Gide believed that the philosophy of vitalism was the answer to the torturing problems of the twentieth century. But vitalism destroys human and divine transcendence and deifies man. Gide failed to understand that new situations could reject old solutions.

The new situation claimed millions of victims in World War II. Definitely, the rights of man, of each single man, were violated. Existentialism, more than ever, had the right to rise in defense of man. And existentialism rose. It permeated all structures of human thinking. It was particularly welcomed by Christian philosophers. We spoke of G. Marcel, N. Berdyaev, K. Barth and others. It is completely justifiable to say that Husserl and Heidegger reveal clear signs of Thomistic ideas in their work.

French Catholicism responded with success to the Christian literary renaissance in the twentieth century. Paul Claudel and François Mauriac are names known to everybody. In France even the professional unbelievers cannot ignore the Catholic movement in art and philosophy.

---

[15] A. Gide, *Les Caves du Vatican* (Paris: Gallimard, 1922).
[16] *Ibid.*, p. 200.

But now it is time to analyze the person and the work of Albert Camus because his influence in contemporary existentialism seems to supercede even Sartre's influence. His position runs very close to the themes of Christian thinking, though he tried desperately to resist faith in God.

3. ALBERT CAMUS

Of all twentieth-century writers, the one who perhaps has probed the meaning of man most deeply and viewed the human condition with the greatest perception is *Albert Camus* (1913–1960).

Camus developed only one theme: the absurdity of existence, and against this absurdity he fought with the passion and the vigor of a giant.

The absurdity of human existence was a theme Camus inherited from the works of Nietzsche, Gide, and Kafka. Later it became his own lived experience. For instance, we shall see that the pain and death of children and infants presented for Camus the axiomatic evidence that human existence cannot make sense. But this theme is likewise the constant complaint of Ivan Karamazov in Dostoevski. Camus seemed to depend more on Ivan Karamazov than on his own experience when he spoke with burning rebellion of children's suffering.

Camus was born into a family of indigent farm workers in Algiers. The first months of World War I brought to the family immense sorrow: his father was killed in Europe. Albert grew up among privations. But joy and laughter were not absent from his infancy. Camus himself wrote: "I was born poor under a joyful sky, in a surrounding of nature that befriends you and ignores hostility. I did not start off therefore with interior lacerations but with plenitude of joy."[17] Algiers, his great love, offered to the young Camus a Mediterranean climate full of light and sun. Outdoor life, a precious experience of friends of different races and colors bound together by an identical way of life. Camus thought that only the poor are given the privilege of understanding the deep meaning of friendship and honesty. Later the enchantment of his youth disappeared and he came to grips, as we all do, with the results of his mature thinking: he saw the complexities of human nature, he recognized the inconsistencies of his youthful ideas, he faced the brutal laws of economic need, he ran through the depressing experiences of a marriage broken off after a few months, and finally he came to know that breathing itself was not to be taken for granted. A serious case of tuberculosis threatened his life.

---

[17] A. Camus, *Actuelles, Chroniques, 1944–48* (Paris: Gallimard, 1950), p. 285 (trans. by author).

In May 1935 Camus wrote in his diary: "What I want to say is this: it is possible to look back — without any romantic sentimentalism — with real nostalgia to a lost poverty. A certain amount of years lived in poverty are sufficient to create an atmosphere of profound sensibility."[18]

Camus was deeply influenced by his indigent youth. A human ideal, so lofty and magnificent, allowed Camus an everlasting appreciation for the purest of human values, the purity of the mind and its intentions. Although Hegelian dialectic viewed this "going back" of the mind to bygone days as something morbid, existentialism rejects this stringent Hegelian law and finds delight in "going back," in reconstructing the past and, in so doing, rebelling against any law imposing limits to the freedom of man. Jean Gremier, a Catholic professor faithful to the French school of spiritualism, taught philosophy in Algiers. Camus followed him with scrupulous attention and soon came to a logical conclusion: consciousness is the beginning of philosophy. Consciousness gives to man dignity and despair. Because man comes to understand the sublimity of his ideals and the inadequate means in his hands to reach those ideals, suffering and frustrations are natural to human existence.

Camus is here an innocent victim of an equivocation which is the common heritage of contemporary thought. He agrees with Descartes that *consciousness* and not *being* is the primary object of human knowledge. Hence consciousness, which is meant to unite us intentionally with being, remains an obstacle between us as knowing subjects and the object to be known. The inability to reach the object generates suffering as a profound human frustration and pessimism.

Another element must be kept in mind, if we are to understand Camus. He spent many of his formative years in Algiers doing research on neoplatonic philosophy.[19] From Plotinus he learned that ideas are impossible without images. Therefore philosophy is empty without literature. "The only way of thinking is through imagination. If you wish to be a philosopher, write fictions."[20]

The conclusion is evident: man is endowed with consciousness. Consciousness gives back to man suffering and failure. Therefore, human existence is absurd. Yet it does exist. Therefore, the philosopher must disguise himself as a man of letters to tell all humans that the most tragic of all occupations is philosophy. A true philosopher uses artistic expressions to prove that reason is of all human activities the most inhuman. All this is combined with the basic confidence that Camus

---

[18] A. Camus, *Carnets,* May, 1935–Fevrier, 1942 (Paris: Gallimard, 1962), p. 15.
[19] The title of Camus' dissertation at the end of his graduate work in 1936 was *Neoplatonism and Christian Thought.*
[20] A. Camus, *Carnets,* May, 1935–Fevrier, 1942, *op. cit.,* p. 23.

had in the "fulness of being." His infancy was a symbol of this confidence; the Greek and Roman civilizations, rapt in the contemplation of the classical ideal of beauty, were, for Camus, another example of this confidence in life. Happiness and consciousness are indeed real values for Camus. Their reality contributes to make absurdity more absurd, because they cannot be reached. Sisyphus is man, every existing man.

We venture to say that many readers of Camus' books must wonder about the meaning of the word "absurd." In fact, "absurd" means to think that being in itself is contradictory. If that is the premise, nothing could exist, because being would deny itself in the same moment in which it begins to be. But something does exist; therefore, being must be intrinsically noncontradictory. What is contradictory, *absurd,* is man's relation to being. Man's mind seeks understanding but the world man lives in cannot be understood; therefore, man's life is *absurd.* Camus denied, without reason, that another being, different from man, could solve man's problem. Essentially, Camus' philosophy is yearning for God because only God would make it logical. But Camus was without God. He considered religious faith something utterly gratuitous. And he preferred, on the level of human attitudes, to remain gratuitously without God. He felt that the greatest act of courage for twentieth-century man was to accept the world with its contradictions and to act against them. To be constructive, to be dynamic, to accept happiness as the supreme motivation of our life, when we know that happiness is impossible: this was the challenge of life and Camus was ready for it. Nietzsche spoke of the superman eager to face the ineluctable. Camus was not too far distant from the same goal. Camus' aspiration and passion, though, were more positive and more human. His ideal man was thirsty for reality, ready to share his existence with others, a sort of a lay saint aiming at an aimless gratuitous integrity. This type of sanctity was more heroic for Camus than Christian sanctity because it was tormented by the categorical imperative of doing, by the insatiable exigence of asserting being without expecting a reward, and with the evidence that hope for a final success was hopeless.

He practiced what he preached. The young Camus sought manual jobs during his graduate studies. He worked as a salesman, a clerk, and an auto repairman. His first marriage ended in divorce after two years in 1934. In the same year, he thought that Communism was an open avenue to the challenge of a better society and he became a member of the party at the time when Spain was the theatre of a bloody war. In Algiers, he founded a *Théâtre du Travail,* and his first work *La*

Révolte des Asturies[21] was censured by the authorities. Then tuberculosis became the main concern of Camus. He traveled, with little money, in search of warm climates in lands dear to his heart and his artistic dreams. He went to France and Italy and, because he could not resist the desire of visiting the grave of Kafka, to Prague.[22] In 1937 he broke his ties with Communism. Stalin, who was seeking political friends in France against Hitler, imposed on the French Reds a moratorium of party activities. Camus rejected this with revulsion as a Machiavellian act of dishonesty.

Camus was a man of rigid principles: compromise was for him a low form of immorality. Free from Marxist dogmas, he tried again to form a theatrical group named *Le Théâtre de l'Equipe*, and from 1937 to 1939 the plays of Malraux, Gide, and Ben Jonson were staged with some comfort to Camus' unceasing desire for action. In 1938 Pia Pascal arrived in Algiers. She had a mind for organizing oppositions. Her newspaper *Algier Republicain*, which changed its title to *Soir-Republicain*, was often the target of the official government's censure. Pia Pascal accepted the articles of Camus. He acquired confidence in himself; and his articles on the misery of the people of Kabilis[23] brought his name into the official circle of famous writers.

Meanwhile the great war broke out in Europe. Camus was against it, because his whole life was a dedication to construction, not destruction. He had evidence that no reason was available for his confidence in life, but he had greater evidence that the German will to build by destroying was enormously monstrous and inhuman. The slaughter of Europeans was the beginning of a new ferment in Camus' spiritual meditation. Could the absence of values and the consequent human madness be an indictment against his basic conviction of the absurdity of being? The question was too important to be disregarded. In the *Lettres à un ami Allemand*,[24] published in a later year, an answer, though hesitant and insecure, began to take shape. Camus addressed in those letters an anonymous German youth. He spoke to him with sympathy. He acknowledged that the whole world was overcome by a frightening indifference and skepticism, making almost impossible a choice between the madness of Hitler and the will to resist him. But, Camus continued, man must be decent to himself and to others. If he

---

[21] *La Révolte des Asturies*, Essai de Creation collective (Algiers: Charlot, 1936). It is a drama on the revolt of the miners of Oviedo, in 1934.

[22] In *Carnets* Camus speaks of his visit to the Hebrew cemetery of Prague.

[23] A. Camus, *Misère de la Kabilie*, articles published in *Algier-Republicain* in 1938 and later edited in *Actuelles III, Chronique Aleènienne* (Paris: Gallimard, 1939–1958).

[24] A. Camus, *Lettres à un ami Allemand* (Paris: Gallimard, 1945).

wants to be decent, man must choose *those values which should be possible,* though the terrible daily experience makes it clear that everybody is filled with scorn and disbelief for moral principles. The real Camus is always faithful to himself; the nature of man consists in a tendency to be good and to do good. The inability of the mind to justify this positiveness of man's nature is the main reason that does not allow any other choice.

He volunteered for the draft, but he did so with sentiments of "contempt, courage and deep imperturbability."[25] Above all contempt. No other approach was possible. Man was seeking to solve the absurdity of life by using the absurdity of the war. From contempt came indifference and passive acceptance. War was for Camus a logical expression of human nature. "If it is true that absurdity must be consumed to the end, then war is necessary. Human experience cannot have an intrinsic value. Therefore all human events are sources of some form of education."[26] But one condition is again unquestionable: Camus must be where everybody is, among men, above all among those who are exposed to suffering and death. The draft board refused him. "This boy is too ill — exclaimed the recruiting officer — But I am twenty-six years old. I know what I want from my life."[27] Although Camus was denied the military uniform, no one could prevent him from fighting in civilian clothes. He went to Paris with Pia Pascal; there he used ideas and a daily paper, *Paris-Soir,* to fight the Germans. When the supreme humiliation of a total German invasion hit the French people, he fled to Algiers, soon to return to German-occupied France with an eminently dangerous assignment — the organization of the underground forces and the publication of a clandestine paper that kept alive the pride and hope of the French patriots. Those were decisive days for the philosopher of the absurd and the indifferent! Could he further waste time with Byzantine oscillations between good and evil? France, oppression, German brutality, thousands of innocent civilians sacrificed by the Huns of Hitler. Those were the facts. No time and no need for philosophical meditations.

The rhythm of historic events could not allow the interest of anyone to be focused on literary productions. But two works of Camus, *L'étranger* and *Le mythe de Sisyphe,* written in 1940, and published by Gallimard respectively in 1942 and 1943, with a delay suggested by Malraux, are among the classics of existentialism.

L'étranger is the story of man. A story written with sympathy for

[25] A. Camus, *Carnets,* May, 1935–Fevrier, 1942, *op. cit.,* p. 168.
[26] *Ibid.,* p. 172.
[27] *Ibid.,* p. 176.

man by a man whose life was yearning for sympathy and understanding. Man is a stranger on earth, which refuses to befriend him. Man knows only one thing: he is condemned to death. With this certainty, man, who is without hope, seeks subterfuge, which make him forget friendship, thrills, joys. Those who make too much out of these transient pleasures are the fools of the world; they are bound to be tortured victims of despair. Wisdom consists in a tacit indifference, in a pleasant acceptance of the daily routine.

The stranger is Mersault, a clerk in Algiers. We meet him the first time at the funeral of his mother; then we follow him day by day. His life is usual; he is not a leader. He lives with preponderant stress on the vegetative aspects of his existence. He seems to be detached from extraordinary emotions, though little things acquire great values to him. But he is not Roquentin, for one day the strange sequence of ordinary events (for instance, the casual meeting with a tenant in his own building, a walk with friends, a squabble with some Arabs) brings about the great moment of his life: he kills an Arab on the beach. Actually he had no real reason: perhaps self defense, or the obsessive heat of the African sun, or some other motive. Who knows? It just happened.

The reaction of society is quick and inexorable. Mersault is condemned to die. He is dangerous as a killer, but he is lethally obnoxious on account of his supreme indifference. "The prosecuting attorney began to speak of my soul. He said that he bent over me, gentlemen of the jury, without finding anything. He was saying that I did not have the smallest trace of a soul, nothing human in me. No one of the moral principles that protect the heart of men was accessible to me."[28] These are the words of the condemned man. He must die, not because he killed, but because no witness can say that he wept at his mother's funeral, because he did not observe any mourning period, because he did not suffer. He was denied the benefit of human emotions. The judge and the jury are scared; they are in danger of their lives because he is still alive.

Mersault finally wakes up. The imminence of death does not agree with his usual torpor. Mathematically he measures the short span of his life. He begins to feel, to experience emotions. He begins to hope: perhaps God exists; the Church has the last sacraments for him.

Life! What a strange phenomenon! He almost fell into the common trap: human hope! After this last temptation (hope is a temptation for Camus!) Mersault regains his composure: there is only one truth — death. No hope for man, just rebellion. A calm, conscious, secret rebellion that Camus considers a "conditio sine qua non" to enjoy, moment

[28] A. Camus, *L'étranger, op. cit.*, p. 79.

by moment, the peace of the streaming sensations, the sound of voices and the instantaneous dancing of colors and images.

The philosophical meaning of this fiction is evident. The book exercised an enormous influence on the youth of France and of the world. The style was a major factor for the success; Camus wrote in first person, with a "staccato" style, often brutal, yet sometimes rich with burning passion and human feelings. Sartre observed that "the expression was neat, without platitudes, finished in its meaning."[29] Camus skillfully used an American technique of writing what approached the description of great human passions and emotional turmoils with the cool, pragmatic, and matter-of-fact mind of a well-trained observer.

But strangely enough, Camus is more successful in his philosophical essays. In them, he is immediate and personal. He does not build systems, he does not defend ideas, he just talks with extreme candor and honesty to the reader. In Le mythe de Sisyphe he talks of himself, of the historical moment in which he lived. From the first pages Camus details a preponderant question: Why should man live? Is suicide wrong?

"Suicide is a result of the absurdity of living." "Self inflicted death presupposes the recognition, at least an instinctive recognition, of the derisive meaning of the habit of living. It presupposes the absence of any profound reason for living, the senseless fact that this daily agitation and pain is useless."[30] Suicide is the result of absurdity, and absurdity is the result of the absence of God. Camus reversed the scholastic proof of the existence of God: from an emotional and gratuitous denial of God he came to the logical conclusion of the absurdity of his existence.

The tragedy of Camus is the same tragedy of modern philosophers from Descartes on: the loss of metaphysics and the consequent result that the mind is regarded as incapable of knowing anything that is not material. Matter cannot explain itself. Hence the philosopher has one lonely task: to count the reasons for his unhappiness. Camus was prolific in finding these reasons. Man, Camus thinks, repeats his actions with mechanical monotony, particularly in an industrialized society. Time, without finality, is a sequence of meaningless actions. Death is inexorable. The universe is against man. But absurdity awakens consciousness, and "consciousness" is an important word for Camus. We might add that "consciousness" is an important word for any philosopher who seeks with honesty to understand man. Camus began his philosophical meditation with this act of honesty in relation to his own consciousness. Will he be successful in cutting the Gordian knot of the absurdity of being? Will he be able to reach God?

---

[29] Sartre, Explication de L'étranger, Situations I, op. cit., p. 11.
[30] Camus, Le mythe de Sisyphe, p. 92.

These are the questions that are hidden and evident in each page written by Camus. But let us continue the analysis of his thought and possibly find an answer.

Consciousness reveals the enormous distance and the irreparable fracture existing between the universe and man. "Beneath each beauty lies something inhuman. These hills, the sweetness of the sky, these *capricious* designs of trees suddenly lose their meaning of illusions, which we have attributed to them, and they fade away as a lost paradise. The primitive hostility of the universe climbs through the millenia toward us. Suddenly we do not understand the universe anymore, because through the centuries we have understood of it only the signs and ideas which previously we had given to it. But now we realize how artificial those signs are and how misleading those ideas can be. The universe escapes us because it is becoming again itself."[31]

The tragedy of man is clear: rationality demands understanding, the universe imposes brutal irrationality and rejection of logic. "The irrational, the human longing for knowledge, the absurd that results from their confrontation: those are the dramatis personae."[32] Is suicide the answer? Camus denies this. Suicide forced upon man because the universe is absurd means destruction of the consciousness that discovered the absurd, when it is the only factor superior and unchallenged by absurdity.

Camus has won! He has reached the conclusion that his own existence, as person, is sacred. The basic optimism of his sunny Algiers and his innate love for life have caused the miracle. The human person, not just the thinking machine of Descartes, is ontologically good: Camus has reached a conclusion of metaphysical importance. It is a first step.

Faithfulness to human existence, though, means the rejection of suicide coupled with a naive, all-solving faith in a Supreme Being. A consoling hope in God destroys, according to Camus, the irrationality of the universe and plunges human consciousness into oblivion and extinction. The absurdity of the world must be ever present to man in an everlasting state of mutual tension and enmity. Thus man reaches his freedom. He rejects rules and patterns. He knows the absurdity of his life and he rebels with passion and confusion and perhaps with contempt. With this frame of mind, Camus celebrates the wisdom of all the Don Giovannis of the world, of the dynamic businessmen, and of the conquerors. Sisyphus is his hero. Alone, he is determined to push the huge stone up to the top of the mountain. He sees it tumbling down to the valley. Camus says that he must be happy at the noise of that

---

[31] *Ibid.*
[32] *Ibid.*, p. 45.

falling stone, because he knows that he will go down again, and again he will start his labor and again he will enjoy his unending perseverance. The deities of Mount Olympus stare down on that little man, with the amazement of amused spectators. Could it be that they are just envious, in their idle boring dullness of inoperability?

After the liberation of Paris, Camus went back to his great love, the theater. *Le malentendu* went to the stage in 1944. The perennial thesis of the absurdity of life is once again the theme of the play. Jan had left home twenty years before for the big city, where he found wealth and the love of a wife and children. Now he wants to come back to his place of birth in the countryside of Moravia. The old mother is still living with his sister, Martha; they own a lonely inn, miles away from other people. Nobody recognizes him, and he loves to keep his anonymity. But at night he feels his solitude while waiting for his wife. "That is it. In any hotel room, all evening hours are difficult for a lonely man. Meanwhile, here in the living flesh of my body the old wound does not heal. I know the name of that wound, it is the fear of eternal solitude, the fear that never an answer will come."[33] The answer comes. His mother and sister slay him in his sleep. When the wife comes, Martha fulfills her cruel sadistic pleasure by explaining her own theories. Jan did not die accidentally. He died according to a preestablished plan. A plan so universal and comprehensive that it doesn't allow any human being to recognize his country on this earth.

Caligula was acted on the stage the following year. Almost imperceptibly, a gleam of light is shed in this play, revealing Camus' struggle to conquer the absurd. Caligula has gone almost insane. His wife Drusilla has died. Why such an absurdity? Caligula is the emperor. He reacts with senseless destruction and slaughter. Then he seeks peace of mind in a revealing conversation with Scipio: "Perhaps I'm wrong. I do not come to any conclusion. Perhaps my freedom is not good."

Finally in 1950 *Les justes*[34] was ready for the stage. It is a cornerstone in Camus' anxious searching. The place is Moscow during the social agitations of 1905. Sergy, the Grand Duke, is the target of a group of conspirators led by Stepan, an extremist ready to use all means against the tyrant. His ethics are Machiavellian: violence now, understanding later. One of his men is Kalyayev. He will throw the bomb. But when the carriage of the Duke is ready for the attack, Kalyayev notices that two small nephews of Sergy are in the carriage. He hesitates and changes his mind. "I love all those who live in my own town. I am fighting for them, I am ready to die for them. Why should I strike

---

[33] A. Camus, *Le malentendu, suivi de Caligula* (Paris: Gallimard).
[34] A. Camus, *Les justes* (Paris: Gallimard, 1950).

down my own brothers? I am not the one who will increase a living injustice for the sake of a dead justice." Camus has found a positive element, a rule, a responsibility of man for man. Now, of course, the question is: Where does this rule and this responsibility stem from? Camus seemed to fear that question. Man should ignore it. He cannot be simultaneously Sisyphus and God. Man is just Sisyphus. Then let him work without asking questions and receiving answers, lest he risk being a man.

La peste,[35] a major novel, dealt with this problem with that honesty and earnestness we had occasion to mention before and which is Camus' greatest asset. Man's dedication to man must be unconditioned, absolute, and without expectation of results: that is Camus' commandment. The people of Oran come to grips with a monstrous problem: a lethal epidemic that threatens everybody. They were living the somnolent life of a colorless amoral indifference. Now the pestilence sounds the alarm. They acquire consciousness of the disease and of themselves. Tarrot, Rambert, Rieux have different experiences, deal with different people, but they all come to the conclusion that their peace of mind, their very hope for survival depends on their dedication to minimize evil in the world. They cannot save the sick and the dying, but they can care for them. Saving is not human, caring is human. God up there, if he exists, should save. But he doesn't save. Why shouldn't man rebel against him? "Is it possible to reach holiness, without God? This is the only real problem that I can think of in our days."[36]

We do not have to add that Camus never came to deny the existence of God. If God did not exist, the metaphysical "revolt" of Camus' personages would be a revolt against "nothing." They are themselves, because they have a God whom they think cruel. Rieux, one of the protagonists in The Plague, muses to himself: "Since the order of the world is shaped by death, it might be better for us and for God if we refuse to believe in Him and if we fight against death with all our energies, without bothering to raise our eyes to the heavens, where He sits in idle silence."[37] Camus discussed this stubborn revolt of man against God in L'homme révolté.[38] A splendid doubt, developed with articulate destiny through the pages of this work, can be formulated in a few words: Is it possible to love and to reach holiness without God?

Camus is obsessed by the problem of evil. His familiarity with neoplatonism, with St. Augustine and with Pascal is not sufficient to

[35] A. Camus, La peste, Chronique (Paris: Gallimard, 1947). Eng. tr., The Plague.
[36] Ibid., p. 279.
[37] Ibid., p. 118.
[38] A. Camus, L'homme révolté (Paris: Gallimard, 1951). Eng. tr., The Rebel.

offer him a reason for understanding evil. His tenacious resolution to understand life completely was too persistent and yet too inhuman. At least Saint Augustine lived in a world of values that gave life meaning. But in this century, with millions of innocent human beings slaughtered, displaced, and exploited, evil is not so simply accepted because a standard of values has disappeared. Now Camus is frightened, and with Camus all mankind, because evil was presented as the result of human reason and wisdom. Killing and torturing were justified in the name of ideologies and civilization.

Human ideas produced assassins: in Russia, in Spain, in Germany, almost everywhere. Man cannot afford to live individually; it would amount to dying individually. Man must unite to fight the absurdity of life and yet must live it.

Now *Le mythe de Sisyphe* reveals its inadequacies. "The sentiment of the absurdity of being, if it is taken as a code of action, makes killing at least indifferent and therefore possible."[39] "The error of our times is to think that we are able to establish and formulate rules of action that stem from a desperate emotion, whose dialectical rule, insofar as it is an emotion, is to be overcome."[40]

It is a decisive moment for Camus: in *Le mythe de Sisyphe* he had overcome suicide. Now another victory: man sees the *absurdity* of life. But he could not see it without being himself. We revolt against absurdity and by doing so we assert one undeniable value: *our own human life*, understood as a patrimony "equally enjoyed by each human being."[41]

This is an outstanding example of the philosophical method and achievement of existential research. When it is honest and constructive it starts with phenomenological descriptions, it progressively recognizes the insufficiency of the phenomenon, and it comes, as Camus did, to sound metaphysical conclusions. Now that Camus knows that *human life* is a positive absolute value, he uses his strength of mind against the general trend of most contemporary thought. "It is important to notice that if being antecedes action, all forms of historicism prevalent with Hegel and after him are to be rejected. In fact these philosophies recognize the values, when values are achieved, only as results of actions. Our analysis of human revolt [against the absurdity of being] leads us to think that there is a human nature, as the Greeks spoke of it, against all the postulates of contemporary philosophy."[42] The identity of the first words of this quotation (being antecedes action) with those of Scholastic origin (*agere sequitur esse*) is one way of measuring the

[39] *Ibid.*, p. 15.
[40] *Ibid.*, p. 21.
[41] *Ibid.*, p. 17.
[42] *Ibid.*, p. 28.

depth of the new metaphysical position of Camus. He exposed himself to the sardonic criticism of the "professional" philosophers, whose major intellectual achievement was to fall in line with Sartre and with the fashionable contempt against metaphysics. They never understood it, perhaps. They knew themselves so well that they never tried to understand it. We cannot conceal a profound sense of gratitude to Camus for this ontological achievement. But death stopped the promising process. On the other hand in metaphysics one step only is not sufficient, or the first step itself comes to nought. This is the puzzling aspect of philosophy itself: the slow process of research does not make sense and does not yield results until the whole philosophical structure is defined.

The painful experience of Camus was rewarded with one value, solidly discovered. But one value alone unrelated to other values and to the Absolute created confusion and hesitation. If a moral code must be chosen, it is mandatory to establish a hierarchy of values as they share different degrees of existence and therefore different importance for man who seeks to reach them. *L'homme révolté* does not recognize this. Camus asked: "Is it possible to find a norm of morality outside of the sacred values of the Absolute?"[43] That is to say: is it possible to find the Absolute in the relative? He did not arrive to an answer. Historically Camus is convinced, as we all are, that the first actual and total rebellion of man against God came in modern times. It was a metaphysical revolt still uncertain and hidden with the "Libertins" of the fifteenth and sixteenth centuries.

Descartes broke it open. Voltaire, De Salle, and the Jacobins popularized it. The French Revolution and the Marxist revolution muddled it. Revolt and revolution are terms which cannot be used interchangably. Revolution aims to establish its own metaphysics and to be identified with an absolute order denying God and establishing the absoluteness of man. Thus the Jacobins spoke of abstract moral norms. Romanticism theorized an aesthetic of individualism. Hegel spoke of the state-morality and the communists prophesied a new city of man to take the place of the city of God. Camus condemned all these efforts of man's own deification. "If man wants to become God, he claims the right of life and death on all the other men."[44]

Man for Camus is a rebel but not a revolutionary. God for Camus cannot be considered part of the game of human life and yet man is blasphemous if he takes the place of God. Rebellion is the destiny of man, yet rebellion has a limit, it cannot become a revolution. God is there, he should be called in as the decisive factor, yet man cannot call

---

[43] *Ibid.*, p. 35.
[44] *Ibid.*, p. 302.

upon God. This is the position of Camus. Metaphysics is necessary, but metaphysics is impossible. What next? Camus answered: Next is a moderate rebellion, aiming at human solidarity as the highest goal permitted to human beings. In *L'homme révolté* we read the following words: "Dialogue on the level of man to man demands less sacrifice than the gospel preached by despotic and absolute regimes in a form of a monologue announced from the top of a lonely mountain. On the stage as in the real life that type of monologue preceeds death. Every rebel (considered under this aspect that makes him stand firm against the oppressor) fights for life, takes upon himself the struggle against servitude, falsehood, and terror and affirms that these three afflictions are the cause of silence among men, that they force them to be strangers one to the other, preventing them from discovering themselves."[45]

In the absence of an absolute morality, Camus liked to suggest a "way of thinking closer to the wildness of the Mediterranean sea than to the foggy wintry seas of the North." This vague suggestion leaves unsolved the problem of morality. Human solidarity is not an absolute norm of ethics. If man accepts this relative value as an absolute, any kind of crimes (killing persons affected by contagious diseases) would be justified. In fact no limits could be established to human behavior, and violence could be accepted, as Hitler accepted it, as an instrument for freedom.

Camus here is the spokesman for this civilization of ours. He deserves sympathy as we all do, and we recognize our sickness as he did. Hölderlin's words from his *Empedocles' Death*, words of complete dedication to the earth and to human suffering, were used by Camus as an introductory note to his *L'homme révolté*.

But an emotion (the sentiment of absurdity) cannot be healed by another emotion, though noble and magnanimous, as sympathy for human suffering may be. Camus himself registered his conviction when he wrote after the war that "not the language of the heart but merely that of clear thinking is what we need today."[46]

If emotions succeed emotions, we have another disturbing reaction, superbly personified by the judge, Clamence, in the last creation of Camus, *La chute*.[47] It is a work of six chapters only. The judge, Clamence, has retired beneath the dullness of Holland's gray sky. He now enjoys the retirement of a healthy, educated, cultured man in his sixties. He tries to convince, with the artful skill acquired in so many years of familiarity with the law, a mysterious friend that we all are

---

[45] *Ibid.*, p. 274.

[46] A. Camus, *Liberation*, a Liberation pamphlet (New York, 1961), p. 12.

[47] A. Camus, *La chute* (Paris: Gallimard, 1957). Eng. tr., *The Fall*.

guilty on this planet and that those who do not feel guilty are the despots and the tyrants. Clamence represents the dissolution of the upper middle class of "respectable" people. They appear to everybody as the custodians of civic traditions with a puritanical love for decency and morality when they are in public and with the most revolting compulsion for immorality in the secret of their consciences and private behavior.

One fateful evening Clamence neglected out of pure love of self-comfort to help a distressed young lady who took her own life. Ever since then, Clamence has been hearing, on occasion, a sarcastic resounding laughter over his shoulder. He becomes upset. He tries to evade it, to acquire again his self-assurance and confidence, but he fails. He abandons his profession and hides in Holland, loitering in taverns and walking the lonely paths of the canals stagnant with putrid water. He meets people occasionally on the streets and stops them, each one of them, to unload his burden of guilt. Perhaps, he thinks, they will tell him of their own guilt too. He might help. Clamence is a diabolic creation. His life is a hybrid mixture of guilt, fear, hope, and pity. Was he meant by Camus to be a living admonition to all of us? The question cannot be answered with absolute certainty.

In the same year, 1957, Camus was awarded the Nobel prize for literature, and he gave his well known lecture on the essence of art to the students of the University of Uppsala.[48] That lecture became the reason for so much hope and expectation. Art was then for Camus a witness to freedom, not just an objective revelation of absurdity as it had been previously. The artist chooses wonderous moments from reality. They are eloquent means of conversation with other men. That passionate conversation with men Camus did not continue. In the first months of 1960, when he was driving back to his home in Paris during the night, his car went out of control and literally folded around a tree. Albert Camus was dead. Had he lived, we like to think that his encounter with God through his meditations and search would have been unavoidable.

---

[48] A. Camus, *Discours de Suede* (Paris: Gallimard, 1957).

Index

Abstraction, xxiv, 99 *n*, 102, 177
Absurd, the, in Camus, 273; in Sartre, 206
Aesthetic sphere of life, in Kierkegaard, 9 ff
Aesthetics, and Sartre, 203 ff
Alienation, in Marx, 32
Amor Fati, in Nietzsche, 46
Analytic principle, xxii ff
Anaximander, and Heidegger, 183
Anxiety, in Sartre, 218
Apollo, in Nietzsche, 37 ff
Aristotle, dialectic, 30
Art, for Heidegger, 191 f; theory of, in Sartre, 228 f
Atomic Age, 111
Authenticity, 172; for Heidegger, 158

Bakunin, 23
Barth, K., against "liberal" theology, 147
Bauer, Bruno, on Christ, 26
Beaufret, Jean, 198
Becoming, in Sartre, 207
Being, contingent, in Sartre, 206 f; in and for itself, 217; see also *Dasein*
Benda, Julien, 65 ff
Berdyaev, Nicolai, 242 ff; communication as communion, 243 f; freedom, 244; gnosticism, 246 f; on God, 247; personalism, 243 f; pessimism, 246; rationalism, 246
Bergson, Henri, 48, 248 f; optimism, 207; and Sartre, 207
Berkeley, 128
Bismarck, and the *Kulturkampf,* 50
Blondel, 207
Böhme, influence on Berdyaev, 242
Bohr, 115

Bolzano, Bernhard, 123; doctrine of science, 119 ff; influence on Husserl, 119 f; and intentionality, 121
Bradley, F. H., idealism in America, 205; and Marcel, 250 f
Brentano, Franz, 116 ff; influence on Husserl, 119; and intentionality, 118; and mathematics, 123; and perception, 121; and Sartre, 214
Bruno, Giordano, and Jaspers, 83
Brunschvig, and Aristotelian metaphysics, 206; influence on Sartre, 205 f; and Marcel, 253
Buber, Martin, and Dilthey, 57
Bultmann, R., and theology, 147
Burckhardt, 149

Camus, Albert, 271 ff; the absurd, 273; absurdity, 279; consciousness, 277 f; emotion, 283; evil, 280; God, 273; influences on, 272 ff; man, 282; metaphysics, 282; morality, 282; *The Myth of Sisyphus,* 277; realism, 281; responsibility, 280; sanctity, 273, 280; *The Stranger,* 276
Cantor, 123
Care, in Heidegger, 161 f
Cassirer, E., on Kant and Heidegger, 176
Causality, principle of, xxi ff
Charity, in Marcel, 258
Chekov, L., 237
Christ, in Kierkegaard, 17 ff
Circularity of history, in Nietzsche, 42
Claudel, Paul, 270; and Marcel, 253
Collins, James, on Nietzsche's "fieristic monism," 44
Communication and communion in Berdyaev, 243

Communion, in Berdyaev, 243 f; in Marcel, 257
Communism, 97; of Marx, 32 ff
Comte, Auguste, and historicism, 57
"Conflict" in Sartre, 222
Consciousness, in Camus, 277 f; and *Dasein*, 86 f; in Husserl, 126; in Sartre, 217
Contemporary philosophy, characteristics of, xv ff; historical background, xvi ff
Creation, and Heidegger, 179
Croce, Benedetto, 48; idealism in Italy, 205; philosophy and literature, 262

Dasein, authenticity, 158, 172; and caring, 161; and conscience, 162; and consciousness, 86; and death, 161; dread, 158; existentiality, 160 f; fear, 159; in Jaspers, 86 ff; meaning for Heidegger, 153; openness, 160; and resolution, 163; and sin, 163; and temporality, 164 ff; worldishness of, 157 ff
Death, in Heidegger, 161; in Sartre, 224
De Broglie, Louis, physics and causality, xxiii
Dedekind, 123
Descartes, 128, 272; and Husserl, 127
D'Holbach, materialism of, 30
Dilthey, Wilhelm, *Erlebnis*, 54; historicism, 53 ff; influence on Berdyaev, 242; influence on Heidegger, 57; influence on Jaspers, 55, 57; and Kant, 53, 56
Dionysus, Nietzsche on, 37 ff
Don Quixote, and Unamuno, 268
Dos Passos, 269
Dostoevski, Fyodor, 207, 237 ff
Dread, for Heidegger, 158; in Jaspers, 81 f; in Kierkegaard, 12; in Sartre, 218
Dreyfus Affair, 66
Durkheim, Emile, and historicism, 57

Einstein, 115
Emotion, in Sartre, 214 f
Encompassing, the, in Jaspers, 98 ff
Engels, Friedrich, and Marx, 22; on Marx's method and point of departure, 24
Epoché, Husserlian, 120
Erlebnis, in Dilthey, 54 f
Essence, in Husserl, 128 ff
Ethics, in Heidegger, 198 f; in Kierkegaard, 11 f
Existence, 151 n; illumination of, for Jaspers, 88 f
Existent, 151 n
Existential, 155

Existentialism, and religion, 235, 236
Existentiality, for Heidegger, 160 ff

Facticity, in Heidegger, 165
Faith, and Jaspers, 95; in Jaspers, 84, 107; in Kierkegaard, 12 ff; in Marcel, 258; in Shestov, 241; in Unamuno, 268
Farber, Martin, and Husserl, 137
Fascism, 97
Faulkner, 269
Fear, for Heidegger, 159
Feuerbach, Ludwig, 21, 240; humanism, 28; and Marx, 28 f; notion of man, 31
Fichte, and Husserl, 126; influence on Heidegger, 169, 181
Fink, E., disciple of Husserl, 136
Freedom to death, 162; in Berdyaev, 244; in Heidegger, 182; in Jaspers, 90 ff; in Sartre, 218
Frege, 123 f
Freud, Sigmund, 115, 116; and Dostoevski, 238

Galileo, 128
Gestalt theory, 121
Gide, André, 269 f
Gilson, E., on knowledge of God, xxv
Gnosticism, in Berdyaev, 246
God, in Berdyaev, 247; in Camus, 273, 277, 280; in Heidegger, 187 ff, 200; in Jaspers, 110; in Kafka's novels, 264 ff; in Nietzsche, 43 f
God and man, in Kierkegaard, 14 ff, 17
Goethe, optimism, 38
Gogol, 263
Grenz-Situation, and Jaspers, 111
Guilt, in Jaspers, 107 f

Harnack, and liberal Protestant theology, 147
Hartmann, Nicolai, 136; on metaphysics, xix
Hegel, G. F. W., 240; on Absolute as Spirit, 25; and Camus, 272; and Heidegger, 201; historicism, 49; influence on contemporary philosophy, xvii f; influence on Marx, 33; and Kierkegaard, 13; and Marx, 24; and Nietzsche, 37; notion of dialectic, 31; and Sartre, 220 f
Heidegger, Martin, 136; on art, 191 f; being and nothingness, 177 f; and care, 161; and creation, 179 f; on *Dasein*, 153 ff; on death, 161; and Descartes, 156; and Dilthey, 57; and empiricism,

152; estimate of Nietzsche, 194; ethics, 198 f; existence of God, 146; existential openness, 174 ff; existentiality, 160 ff; *Existenz-philosophie,* and Sartre, 208; facticity, 165; freedom, 182; *Gegnet,* 200; German language and philosophy, 184; the *geschichtlich* and the *historisch,* 167; on God, 187 f; Greek language and philosophy, 184; and Hartmann, 144 ff; and Hegel, 201; and Hitlerism, 148 ff; and Hölderlin, 183; and Husserl, 143; importance of poetry, 190 f; intimacy, 189; introduction to metaphysics, 175 ff; judgment of Sartre, 198; life, 139 ff; and metaphysics, xix f, 151, 168; his *Mitsein* and Sartre's "conflict," 222; philosophy and poetry, 262; and realism, 168 ff; relation to Aristotle, 141 f; resolution, 163; and Scotus, 142 f; and *Sein und Zeit,* 151 ff; serenity, 197 ff; and sin, 163; space, 157; temporality, 164 ff; and theology, 141; on "things," 186, 191; on thinking, 173 ff; time, 143; time and Sartre, 218 f; and transcendence, 179; on truth, 192; and U.S.A. political critics, 150; view of ancient Greek philosophers, 183

Heisenberg, Werner, 114; indeterminacy, xxiii

Hemingway, 269

Heraclitus, importance for Heidegger, 183 ff

Hess, Moses, influence on Marx, 21, 27

Hilbert, 115

Hildebrand, von, 136

"Historical courses," in Spengler, 61

Historicism, 48 ff, 57

Hobbes, Thomas, *homo homini lupus,* 27

Hölderlin, influence on Heidegger, 183, 188 ff

Honkard, Jacques, *An Inhuman Father* (Sartre), 233

Hope, in Marcel, 258

Huizinga, Johan, and historicism, 51 f

Humanism, ethics of, 198

Hume, David, on causality, xxi f

Husserl, Edmund, 48; consciousness, 126 f; differed from Brentano, 119; and Descartes, 127; on empirical sciences, 128; *epoché,* 130; on essences, 128 ff; and Fichte, 126; and Heidegger, 143 f; intersubjectivity, 132; intuition, 131; life, 116 ff; on *Lebenswelt,* 128; and metaphysics, 131; notion of philosophy, 128; phenomenological reduction, 130; phenomenology of, 122 ff; and phenomenology, 129; philosophy of mathematics, 123 f; on psychologism, 124 f; reflection, 131; on subjectivity, 125 ff; time, 126; transcendentalism, 132; transcendental subjectivity, 127

Imagination, in Sartre, 211 ff

Intentionality, 118 f

Intersubjectivity, in Husserl, 132

Intimacy, in Heidegger, 189

Intuition, in Husserl, 131

Irony, in Kierkegaard, 10

James, William, 48

Jaspers, Karl, and Christianity, 74; communication, 88 f; and *Dasein,* 86 ff; and Dilthey, 55, 57; empirical sciences, 81, 87; the encompassing, 98 ff; existential consciousness, 81; faith, 84, 95, 107; formative years, 69 ff; freedom, 90 ff; and God, 110; *Grenz-situationen,* 81, 92 f; and *guilt,* 107 f; on historicity of man, 89 f; the *historisch* and the *geschichtlich,* 98; idea of University, 72 n; illumination of existence, 88 f; and Kant, 69, 100; and Kierkegaard, 69; Kierkegaard and Nietzsche, 50; on man, 96 ff; and Mayer, Ernst, 73; mechanization, 97; and metaphysics, 82, 93 ff; need for a Worldview, 78 ff; and Neoplatonism, 110; and Nietzsche, 69; and the One, 95; ontology, 104; periontology, 104; and psychopathology, 76 f; reason, 103; on society, 96 f; and Spinoza, 74; transcendence, 83 f; truth, 71, 73, 80, 101 ff; and Weber, 60, 69; *Weltanschauung,* 78 ff

Kafka, Franz, 116, 263 ff; *The Castle, The Trial,* 207; God, 264 ff

Kant, on causality, xxii ff; and Dilthey, 53, 56; influence on contemporary philosophy, xvi f; influence on Jaspers, 69; and intentionality, 118; and Jaspers, 100; and Marcel, 257; optimism, 38; and possibility, 8; and Scheler, 209; and Windelband, 58

Kierkegaard, Søren, 50 ff; aesthetic sphere of existence, 9 ff; a Catholic conscience, 17; concept of irony, 10; dread, 12 f; dread and Sartre, 218 n; ethical sphere of existence, 11 f; existence of God, 17; and God's omnipotence, 16; and Hegel, 13; imitation of Christ, 18; and Jaspers, 69; life, 5 ff;

man and God, 14 ff; metaphysics, 15 f; possibility as category, 7 ff; *saltus qualitativus*, 14; scruples, 18; the sphere of faith, 12 ff; and Unamuno, 268
Kulturkampf, 50

La Mettrie, materialism of, 30
Landgreke, L., disciple of Husserl, 136
Lassale, Ferdinand, 23
Lavelle, Louis, and Marcel, 253
Lebensphilosophie, 63
Lebenswelt, in Husserl, 128
Lefevre, Henri, and Sartre, 231
Leibniz, and cause, 181
Le Senne, René, and Marcel, 253
Life, absurdity of, for Sartre, 107
Lipps, 136
Lobachevski, 114
Logical positivism, 105
Loneliness, in Marcel, 257
Lotze, E., 125

Malraux, André, 269
Man, and God, in Kierkegaard, 14 ff; historicity of, for Jaspers, 89 f; in Jaspers, 96 ff; in Nietzsche, 42 ff
Manchester school, 236
Manichaeism, in Berdyaev, 248
Marcel, Gabriel, on body, 256; and the Cartesian *Cogito*, 255; charity, 258; on communion, 257; faith, 258; on God, 254; God as *Thou*, 257; hope, 258; influences on, 249 f; on Kant, 257; life, 250 ff; loneliness, 257; problem and mystery, 254 ff; on religion, 255
Maritain, Jacques, on person, xxiv f
Martius, 136
Marx, Karl, and Berdyaev, 242; and Feuerbach, 28 f; formative years, 24 ff; and Hegel, 24; life, 20 ff; and positivism, 49; and Sartre, 228 ff; and Weber, 60
Mauriac, François, 270; and Marcel, 253
Mayer, Ernst, influence on Jaspers, 73
Mayer, Gertrude, and Jaspers, 73
Merleau-Ponty, M., and Husserl, 137
Metaphysics, xvii ff, 94 *n*, 195, 202; in Heidegger, 151, 168; and Husserl, 131; and Jaspers, 82, 93 ff; in Kierkegaard, 15; for Nietzsche, 41
Miller, Arthur, *After the Fall*, 207
Minkowski, 114
Mommsen, 49
Montaigne, and Nietzsche, 39
Moravia, *La Noia*, 207

Natrop, P., 125
Neoplatonism, and Jaspers, 110
Niebuhr, 49
Nietzsche, Friedrich, 50 ff; *amor fati*, 46; attack on Plato, 43; attack on Strauss, 39; and the birth of tragedy, 37 ff; and Christ, 43 f; and the circularity of history, 41; Dionysus and Apollo, 37 ff; fieristic monism, 44; on God, 43 f; and Hegel, 37; influence on Heidegger, 183; influence on Jaspers, 69; life, 36 ff; man and history, 42 ff; and metaphysics, 41; morality, 41; overman (superman), 45 ff; and Shestov, 241; and the Wagners, 37; Zarathustra, 40 ff
Nihilists, 237
Nissl, and Jaspers, 75
Nothingness, in Heidegger, 177 ff
Number, nature of, 123

Ontology, 176; in Jaspers, 104
"Openness," existential, 174; in Heidegger, 200
Ortega y Gasset, José, human freedom, 63 f
Overman, of Nietzsche, 45 ff

Paci, E., and Husserl, 137
Parmenides, and Heidegger, 183 ff
Peirce, C. S., 137
Periontology, in Jaspers, 104
Person, in Sartre, 220 ff
Personalism, of Berdyaev, 243 f
Pessimism, 267; of Berdyaev, 246
Phenomenology, 121 ff; and Sartre, 208 ff; meaning of, 129
Planck, Max, 115
Plato, and Heidegger, 183
Platonic *daimon*, 10
Platonism, and Marcel, 255
Plotinus, and Camus, 272; and Jaspers, 83
Poetry, importance of, for Heidegger, 190 f
Positivism, 48; characteristics of, xvii f
Possibility, in Kierkegaard, 7 ff
Protestantism, spirit of, 236
Proust, Marcel, and Bergson, 249
Psychologism, 124 f
Psychopathology, and Jaspers, 76 f

Ranke, brain histologist, and Jaspers, 75
Rationalism, 236; in Berdyaev, 246
Realism, 95 *n*, 177 *n*; and Heidegger, 168 ff; and mystery, 180
Reason, in Jaspers, 103

Renan, 250
Rickert, Henry, 79; and "School of Values," 59
Rilke, Rainer Maria, 267
Ritschl, and Nietzsche, 37
Rovighi, S. V., and Husserl, 137
Royce, Josiah, and Marcel, 251 f
Ruge, Arnold, on society, 26
Russian existentialism, 237 ff

Sanctity, in Camus, 273
Sartre, Jean-Paul, absurdity of life, 207; aesthetics, vocation to, 203 ff; after World War II, 226 f; anxiety, 218; and Baudelaire, biography of, 223 n; on becoming, 207; "being for itself," 217; "being in itself," 217; and Bergson, 207; and Brentano, 214; and Brunschvig, 205 f; and communism, 204, 226 ff; communism, the contribution of Marx, Engels, Hegel to, 228 ff, passim; conflict, not Mitsein, 222; consciousness, criticism of his theory of, 224; consciousness, as nothing, 217; consciousness, source of, 215; and contingent being, 206 f; Critique de la raison dialectique, 228; and death, criticism of his theory of, 224; and death, disagreement with Boisselot on, 224; Le diable et le bon Dieu (The Devil and the Good Lord), 225 f; dread, 218; dread, and Kierkegaard, 218 n; early writings, 205; education of, 206, 208; emotion, and Adler, 214; emotion, 214 f; and engagé literature, 228; L'être et le néant (Being and Nothingness), 216 ff; L'existentialisme est un humanisme (Existentialism is a Humanism), 226; family, 204 f; freedom, 218, 234; freedom, criticism of his theory of, 224; freedom, man's checkmated, 218; freedom, threat to, 221; free enterprise and alienation, 230; and Genet, biography of, 233 n; hatred, 223; and Heidegger's Sein und Zeit, 208; and Hegel, 207; and Hegel's Phenomenology, 220 f; and history, an unanswered question, 233; and Honkard, 233; human body, 221 f; human nature, misunderstanding of, 224; human society, 222 ff; and Husserl, 137, 208; L'imaginaire, 211; L'imagination, 211; on the imagination, 211 ff; inherent contradiction in his system, 219 f; and D. H. Lawrence, 215; and

Lefevre, 231; life and works, 203 ff; Les mouches (The Flies), 225; Les sequestres d'Altona (The Condemned of Altona), 225; love, 223; man as sick animal, 214; and Marx, 228 ff; metaphysics, enemy of, 215; and Mitsein, criticism of Heidegger's, 222; naturalism, 203; Nausea, 206, 207; Nausea and the absurd, 206; past as failure, 207; person, objectification of, 221; person, in the universe, 220 ff; and phenomenology, 208 ff; presence of God, 205; and relation of Heidegger to Nietzsche, 208; as Roguetin, 207; and Scheler, 208 ff; seduction, 223; sexuality, 223; and sociology, 230 n; and Stalin, 227; and Stendhal, 215; theory of art, 228 f; theory of emotion, criticized, 215; time, 218 ff; time and Heidegger, 218 f; totalization, 229; The Wall, 215; and World War II, 216
Scheler, Max, 136; disciple of Husserl, 208; The Eternal in Man, 210; Formalism in Ethics and the Material Ethics of Values, 209; Forms and Essences of Sympathy, 210; on God and man, 210; influence on Sartre, 208 ff; and Kant, 209; and nineteenth-century monism, 210; objectivity and intuition, 209 f; and pessimism, 210 f; philosophy of, 208 ff; and Plato and Augustine, 208; The Situation of Man in the Cosmos, 210; understanding and love, 208 f
Schelling, influence on Heidegger, 181; influence on Marcel, 250; and Jaspers, 83
Schleiermacher, 13
Schopenhauer, influence on Nietzsche, 38
Sciences, empirical, in Husserl, 128
Serenity, in Heidegger, 197 ff
Shestov, Leo, 240 f
Simmel, G., 136; and Dilthey, 56 n
Sin, in Heidegger, 163
Society, for Jaspers, 96 f
Soloviev, Vladimir, 239 f
Space, in Heidegger, 157
Spencer, H., 250; historicism, 57
Spengler, Oswald, philosophy of history, 61 ff
Spinoza, influence on Jaspers, 74, 83
Stein, Edith, and Husserl, 137
Stirner, Max, influence on Marx, 27
Strauss, David, and Nietzsche, 39; on Gospels, 21, 26

Stumpf, Karl, 124; influence on Husserl, 121; on perception, 121
Subjectivity, 125 ff
Superman, *see* Overman

Taine, 250
Temporality of *Dasein*, in Heidegger, 164 ff
Theology, 170 *n*, 195, 202; in Berdyaev, 246; and Heidegger, 141; in Marcel, 260
"Things," in Heidegger, 186, 191
Thomas Aquinas, St., 154 *n*, 155 *n*; on being, xx; on essence and existence, 133; and intentionality, 118
Time, in Heidegger, 143; in Husserl, 126; in Sartre, 218 ff
Tolstoi, Leon, 237
Tonquedec, J. de, misunderstood Kierkegaard, 15
Transcendence, for Heidegger, 179; in Jaspers, 83 f
Transcendentalism, in Husserl, 132

Truth, in Heidegger, 192; in Jaspers, 71, 80, 101 f

Unamuno, Michael, 267 ff

Value, philosophy of, 58 ff
Van Breda, editor of Husserl's works, 123
Vitalism, 48

Wagner, and Nietzsche, 37, 40
Wahl, Jean, 206
Weber, Max, historicism of, 59 ff; influence on Jaspers, 60, 69; and Marx, 60
Weltanschauung, 53
Windelband, Wilhelm, and Kant, 58; and the "School of Values," 58 ff
Wonder, 180
Wundt, 117; positivism, 116

Young Hegelians, 21, 25